THE ROUTLEDGE HANDBOOK TO ACCOUNTABILITY AND WELFARE STATE REFORMS IN EUROPE

There is growing concern that welfare states are inefficient, unsustainable and lack popular support. New Public Management reforms affected the balance between managerial and political accountability and disrupted administrative, legal, professional and social accountability, causing confusion as to whom public organizations are really accountable.

The Routledge Handbook to Accountability and Welfare State Reforms in Europe assesses multi-dimensional accountability relations in depth, addressing the dynamic between accountability and reforms. Analyzing how welfare state reforms oriented towards agencification, managerialism and marketization affected existing relationships in services traditionally provided by public institutions, the theoretically informed, empirical chapters provide specific examples of their effect on accountability. Expert contributors explore the relationship between accountability and performance and the impact of reforms on political, administrative, managerial, legal, professional and social accountability. The role of specific actors, such as the media and citizens, on the accountability process addressing issues of blame avoidance, reputation and autonomous agencies is discussed.

Comparative chapters across time, countries, administrative levels and policy areas are included, along with discussions linking accountability with concepts such as legitimacy, democracy, coordination and performance. This handbook will be an essential reference tool to those studying European politics and public policy.

Tom Christensen is a Professor in the Department of Political Science at the University of Oslo, Norway.

Per Lægreid is a Professor in the Department of Administration and Organization Theory at the University of Bergen, Norway.

'This book not only provides the most up-to-date map of tensions between logics of consequences and appropriateness of contemporary welfare states. It also discusses ways to cope with its paradoxes, contradictions and trade-offs. This publication is a perfect GPS for all those that navigate within and between responsibility and accountability of our welfare states.'

Geert Bouckaert, President of the International Institute of Administrative Sciences, and Professor at the KU Leuven Public Governance Institute, Belgium

'The welfare state has been central in legitimating contemporary governments, and accountability has been, and remains, a fundamental democratic concern. But both of these factors in contemporary political life continue to evolve. This handbook examines the intersection of these two factors, and the manner in which they continue to evolve. This is important reading for any student of contemporary governance.'

B. Guy Peters, University of Pittsburgh, USA

'We live in an age of administrative and policy reforms. But we often do not understand their effects very well. This outstanding set of essays by leading scholars in the field delves deeply into the complex world of welfare state policy reforms and changing accountability mechanisms. Anyone interested in these topics will find this collection an invaluable, indeed an essential, source of insights and ideas.'

Joel D. Aberbach, University of California, Los Angeles, USA

'A very rich volume that combines a sophisticated approach of accountability with detailed analyses of welfare state reform. It brings together Europe's best scholars on accountability and welfare state reform and provides a concise analysis of contemporary welfare state reform and its effects on accountability relations.'

Mark Bovens, Utrecht University, the Netherlands

THE ROUTLEDGE HANDBOOK TO ACCOUNTABILITY AND WELFARE STATE REFORMS IN EUROPE

Edited by
Tom Christensen and Per Lægreid

LONDON AND NEW YORK

First published 2017
by Routledge
2 Park Square, Milton Park, Abingdon, Oxon OX14 4RN

and by Routledge
711 Third Avenue, New York, NY 10017

Routledge is an imprint of the Taylor & Francis Group, an informa business

© 2017 selection and editorial matter, Tom Christensen and Per Lægreid; individual chapters, the contributors

The right of the editors to be identified as the authors of the editorial material, and of the authors for their individual chapters, has been asserted in accordance with sections 77 and 78 of the Copyright, Designs and Patents Act 1988.

All rights reserved. No part of this book may be reprinted or reproduced or utilised in any form or by any electronic, mechanical, or other means, now known or hereafter invented, including photocopying and recording, or in any information storage or retrieval system, without permission in writing from the publishers.

Trademark notice: Product or corporate names may be trademarks or registered trademarks, and are used only for identification and explanation without intent to infringe.

British Library Cataloguing in Publication Data
A catalogue record for this book is available from the British Library

Library of Congress Cataloging in Publication Data
Names: Christensen, Tom, 1949– editor. | Lægreid, Per, editor.
Title: The Routledge handbook to accountability and welfare state reforms in Europe / edited by Tom Christensen and Per Lægreid.
Other titles: Handbook to accountability and welfare state reforms in Europe
Description: New York, NY : Routledge, 2016. | Includes bibliographical references and index.
Identifiers: LCCN 2016022797| ISBN 9781472470591 (hardback) | ISBN 9781315612713 (ebook)
Subjects: LCSH: Public welfare administration – European Union countries. | Welfare state – European Union countries. | Government accountability – European Union countries.
Classification: LCC HV238 .R68 2016 | DDC 361.6/8094 – dc23
LC record available at https://lccn.loc.gov/2016022797

ISBN: 978-1-472-47059-1 (hbk)
ISBN: 978-1-315-61271-3 (ebk)

Typeset in Bembo and Stone Sans
by Florence Production Ltd, Stoodleigh, Devon, UK

CONTENTS

List of figures   *viii*
List of tables   *ix*
Notes on contributors   *x*
Preface   *xii*

1 Introduction: accountability and welfare state reforms   1
   Tom Christensen and Per Lægreid

PART I
Theoretical and conceptual issues   **13**

2 Democratic order, autonomy and accountability   15
   Johan P. Olsen

3 Accountability, performance and legitimacy in the welfare state: if accountability is the answer, what was the question?   31
   Werner Jann

4 Combining agency and stewardship: welfare reforms and accountability   45
   Thomas Schillemans

PART II
Accountability in welfare state areas   **59**

5 Hybrid welfare administrative systems and changing accountability relations: comparing the development of the Danish and Norwegian systems   61
   Tom Christensen, Flemming Larsen and Karsten Vrangbæk

6 Public sector reform and accountability dynamics: the changing welfare administration in Norway and Germany   75
   Bastian Jantz

7 The welfare state in flux: individual responsibility and changing accountability relations in social services   90
   Piret Tõnurist and Wouter De Tavernier

8 Dimensions of accountability in healthcare   105
   Karsten Vrangbæk and Haldor Byrkjeflot

9 Accountability through performance management? Hospital performance management schemes in Denmark, Germany and England   119
   Karsten Vrangbæk, Tanja Klenk, John Appleby and Sarah Gregory

10 Accountability, legitimacy and immigration control: the inclusion of social actors in asylum regulation in Norway, Denmark and Germany   133
    Tord Skogedal Lindén, Ina Radtke and Karsten Vrangbæk

11 Welfare reforms, accountability and performance   146
    Per Lægreid and Kristin Rubecksen

PART III
Accountability in unsettled situations   **163**

12 Accountability, transparency and societal security   165
    Tom Christensen and Martin Lodge

13 Accountability under inquiry: inquiry committees after internal security crises   180
    Julia Fleischer

14 Accountability relations in unsettled situations: administrative reforms and crises   194
    Tom Christensen and Per Lægreid

15 Accountability in times of austerity: democratic and constitutional gains but learning loss?   208
    Hanne Foss Hansen and Mads Bøge Kristiansen

16 Regulatory reform, accountability and blame in public service delivery: the public transport crisis in Berlin   223
    Tobias Bach and Kai Wegrich

PART IV
Accountability, administrative reforms and multilevel governance   **237**

17 Principles meet practicalities: challenges of accountability reform in the British civil service   239
Thomas Elston

18 Multiple accountabilities in public–private partnerships (PPPs): how to unravel the accountability paradox?   255
Tom Willems and Wouter Van Dooren

19 Digital era governance reform and accountability: the case of Denmark   267
Niels Ejersbo and Carsten Greve

20 The dynamics of the EU accountability landscape: moving to an ever-denser union   280
Anchrit Wille

Index   *294*

FIGURES

6.1	Accountability approaches	77
7.1	Transition in accountability, causal model	92
17.1	UK agency population, 1988–2010	246
17.2	Distribution of policymaking responsibilities between justice ministries and agencies, 1993–2011	247
19.1	Path to digital government in Denmark	273

TABLES

4.1	Two modes of governance and accountability	52
6.1	Comparing the dynamics of accountability	87
7.1	Overview of results by case	97
8.1	Dimensions of accountability in healthcare	112
9.1	The learning perspective: improving organizational effectiveness	122
9.2	The steering and control perspective: improving organizational efficiency	123
9.3	The legitimacy perspective: enhancing trust and public support	123
11.1	Administrative reforms in labor/employment and hospital administration in Norway, Denmark and Germany	152
11.2	Types of accountability (percent)	155
11.3	Summary of multivariate regression analysis (beta coefficients, linear regression)	155
11.4	'Thinking about your policy area over the last five years, how would you rate the way public administration has performed on the following dimensions?' (percent)	156
11.5	Summary of multivariate regression analysis (beta coefficients, linear regression)	157
12.1	Task-related characteristics in intelligence, food safety and flood defense	168
12.2	Forms of specialization and coordination	169
12.3	Expectations related to accountability, trust and transparency	171
12.4	Number of societal security organizations	172
12.5	Sectoral characteristics of accountability and transparency provisions in societal security	175
12.6	Overview of similarities and differences	176
13.1	Ad hoc accountability forums set up in the aftermath of the two crises	183
13.2	Key executive ad hoc accountability forums in Norway and Germany	185
14.1	Accountability changes – reform, crisis and interpretations	202
15.1	Analytical framework for assessing accountability	211
15.2	Effects of the new regime as seen from the three perspectives on accountability	219
16.1	Blind spots of accountability and control in two ideal-type institutional models	227
17.1	Implementing accountable management doctrine through agencification reforms	243
20.1	The accountability matrix: accountability forums in relation to executive actors	285
20.2	The EU accountability standards (based on mission statements of institutions)	286
20.3	The development of accountability practices in the EU (index)	287
20.4	An evolving multilevel accountability network	289

CONTRIBUTORS

Appleby, John. Professor, Chief Economist, The King's Fund, UK.

Bach, Tobias. Associate Professor, University of Oslo, Norway.

Byrkjeflot, Haldor. Professor, University of Oslo, Norway.

Christensen, Tom. Professor, University of Oslo, Norway.

Van Dooren, Wouter. Associate Professor, University of Antwerp, Belgium.

Ejersbo, Niels. Senior researcher, KORA, Danish Institute for Local and Regional Government Research, Denmark.

Elston, Thomas. Postdoctoral Research Fellow, University of Oxford, UK.

Fleischer, Julia. Associate Professor, University of Bergen, Norway.

Gregory, Sarah. Dr, Researcher in Health Policy, The King's Fund, UK.

Greve, Carsten. Professor, Copenhagen Business School, Denmark.

Hansen, Hanne Foss. Professor, University of Copenhagen, Denmark.

Jann, Werner. Senior Professor, Potsdam University, Germany.

Jantz, Bastian. Research Fellow, University of Potsdam, Germany.

Klenk, Tanja. Professor, University of Kassel, Germany.

Kristiansen, Mads Bøge. Post doc., University of Copenhagen, Denmark.

Larsen, Fleming. Professor, Aalborg University, Denmark.

Lindén, Tord Skogedal. Senior Researcher, Stein Rokkan Centre for Social Studies, Uni Research, Norway.

Lodge, Martin. Professor, London School of Economics, UK.

Lægreid, Per. Professor, University of Bergen, Norway.

Olsen, Johan P. Professor Emeritus, University of Oslo, Norway.

Contributors

Radtke, Ina. Research Fellow, University Potsdam, Germany.

Rubecksen, Kristin. Senior Researcher, Stein Rokkan Centre for Social Studies, Uni Research, Norway.

Schillemans, Thomas. Associate Professor, Utrecht University, the Netherlands.

De Tavernier, Wouter. PhD Fellow, Aalborg University, Denmark.

Tõnurist, Piret. Junior Research Fellow, Tallinn University of Technology, Estonia.

Vrangbæk, Karsten. Professor, University of Copenhagen, Denmark.

Wegrich, Kai. Professor, Hertie School of Governance, Berlin, Germany.

Wille, Anchrit. Associate Professor, University of Leiden, the Netherlands.

Willems, Tom. Postdoctoral Researcher, University of Antwerp, Belgium.

PREFACE

This companion provides a comprehensive, state-of-the-art review of current research in the field of welfare state reforms and accountability in Europe. Aimed primarily at a readership with a special interest in contemporary welfare state reforms, the book offers a refreshing and up-to-date analysis of key issues of the relationships between reforms and different accountability dimensions.

The collection offers readers an international perspective on the important welfare sector reforms and their relationship to accountability that has occurred in a number of European countries over the past 20 years. It comprises a general introduction and 19 chapters divided into four thematic sections. The introduction clarifies the ambiguous and multidimensional accountability concept and discusses how to understand and assess accountability, as well as the links between accountability, reform and performance. Part I addresses conceptual and theoretical issues focusing on democratic order, autonomy and accountability in unsettled situations, on performance and legitimacy in the welfare state as well as on institutional theory, stewardship theory and agency approaches.

Part II examines accountability relations in core welfare state areas such as labour and welfare administration, healthcare and immigration, comparing countries such as Denmark, Norway, Germany and the United Kingdom. Part III addresses accountability relations in unsettled situations by addressing societal security and crisis, as well as comprehensive reforms. Part IV examines accountability relations, administrative reforms and multilevel governance. Accountability reforms in the British civil service and multiple accountabilities in public-private partnerships, as well as digital era governance reform and accountability and the dynamics of the accountability landscape in the EU, are studied.

The book contains chapters by 29 researchers from Belgium, Estonia, Denmark, Germany, the Netherlands, Norway, Germany and the United Kingdom. Four of the chapters address conceptual and theoretical issues and 16 are theoretically informed empirical analyses of different accountability relations related to welfare state reforms in European countries. Eight of them are comparative chapters addressing two or more countries.

The book is the result of an international professional network that has developed over the past 10 years. Most of the chapters in this book are the outcome of the International Political Science Association's Permanent Study Group on 'Structure and Organization of Government' (SOG) conference on 'Accountability and Welfare State Reforms' in Bergen, 19–20 February

Preface

2015. Many authors in the book are furthermore part of a large comparative European project focusing on how contemporary reforms in core welfare state areas in Norway, Germany and Denmark are affecting different accountability relationships ('Reforming the Welfare State: Democracy, Management and Accountability'), funded by the Norwegian Research Council. A main focus is on accountability to whom and how the trade-offs between political, administrative, managerial, legal, professional and social accountability are changing in the areas of hospital management, welfare administration and immigration.

There are a number of individuals and organizations to whom we owe our thanks. An acknowledgement goes to our networks of colleagues and friends who share an interest in welfare state reforms and accountability relations. Without their enthusiastic responses to our invitation to contribute to this volume, it would never have been finished. We are also grateful to the Norwegian Research Council that funded the research project that contributes to a major part of the chapters. A special thanks to our international partners, Professor Werner Jann, Potsdam University, Professor Karsten Vrangbæk, Copenhagen University, and Associate Professor Paola Mattei, Oxford University.

Thanks are also due to our publisher, especially Rob Sorsby, who has been very instrumental in launching this book project. We also thank the Uni Research Rokkan Centre that has managed the research project, and especially Simon Neby, who has been the project manager. Thanks also to the Department of Administration and Organization Theory, University of Bergen, for valuable administrative support, and a special thanks to Ulrikke Schill for excellent technical assistance in supervising the preparation of the manuscript. We also express our gratitude to our home departments, the Department of Political Science, University of Oslo, and the Department of Administration and Organization Theory, University of Bergen.

Tom Christensen and Per Lægreid
Bergen/Oslo

1
INTRODUCTION
Accountability and welfare state reforms

Tom Christensen and Per Lægreid

Introduction

For many years, there has been a growing concern that welfare states do not achieve their objectives, are inefficient and not sustainable in financial terms, and lack popular support. A series of reforms has been introduced to address these challenges, many of them following some kind of New Public Management-inspired reform trajectory (Pollitt and Bouckaert 2011). This entailed granting more autonomy to welfare agencies, transferring responsibilities to public managers or introducing of market instruments and competition with private providers. Traditional service delivery by public organizations in clearly defined hierarchical settings has been challenged. Both NPM reforms oriented towards agencification, managerialism and marketization, as well as more recent so-called 'whole-of-government' or post-NPM reforms, seeking to improve cooperation and collaboration across policy sectors and levels, have challenged the traditional welfare state and made it more complex (Christensen and Lægreid 2007; Flinders 2014).

The underlying idea behind many welfare state reforms, often ideologically driven, was to enhance accountability and at the same time performance and legitimacy of welfare arrangements. But in practice, these reforms in many areas have created complexity, conflicts and confusion over who is accountable to whom for what and with what effects. Some claim that there is accountability overload (Halachmi 2014), while others point to accountability deficits (Mulgan 2014a). One aim of this book is, accordingly, to understand how administrative reforms in the welfare state have affected the existing accountability relationships in welfare services (Mattei 2009; Lægreid and Mattei 2013; Jann and Lægreid 2015). It tackles these questions by looking into reforms in important welfare sectors, especially labor market and health, and beyond, in different European countries.

New public reforms do not necessarily replace old reforms. In many cases, the new reforms are adding to the old reforms, in a layered way (Streeck and Thelen 2005), leading to complex and mixed relations between public sector organizations, on the one hand, and the political-executive leadership and parliament, on the other. Traditional forms of vertical accountability are combined with new forms of horizontal or diagonal accountability (Bovens 2007; Schillemans 2008), for example to regulatory bodies and audit offices, as well as to stakeholders, through media and to the public in general.

Accountability challenges are typical for 'wicked' problems such as social cohesion, unemployment, poverty, public health and immigration (Byrkjeflot et al. 2014). They represent transboundary issues that are highly complex, contested and ambiguous; transcending organizations, policy sectors, administrative levels and time frames. These issues become even more salient when governments are faced with budgetary scarcity, Europeanization and globalization. One objective of the book is to analyze the accountability of emerging coordination practices, and to assess their value in countering public sector fragmentation, as a result of NPM-inspired reforms, and loss of legitimacy.

The book revolves around the dynamics between administrative (re)organization, performance, accountability and legitimacy in modern welfare states. Recent welfare state reforms have aimed at the establishment of managerial accountability and semi-independent, 'non-majoritarian' agencies, paying less attention to the issue of how to maintain and develop mechanisms for political accountability and legitimacy. New Public Management reforms, as well as post-NPM reform initiatives, have affected the balance between managerial and political accountability across welfare sectors and countries, but also other accountability relations, such as administrative, legal, professional and social accountability, are affected (Byrkjeflot et al. 2014; Askim et al. 2015). This has created confusion over to whom public organizations and their leaders are accountable. To what extent has it been possible to combine the various modes of accountability? How, why, for what and to whom are leaders in public organizations in the various welfare services held accountable? The focus is on changes in formal as well as actual accountability relations. The challenges of multiple accountability relations and the relationship between accountability and input legitimacy, as well as output legitimacy, will be focused.

This volume contains chapters assessing how specific examples of welfare state reforms affect formal and actual accountability, as well as the relationship between accountability and performance. Moreover, the chapters discuss the impact of recent reforms in the welfare state on political, administrative, managerial, legal, professional and social accountability. Finally, the book also discusses the role of specific actors in the accountability process – such as the media and citizens/customers. Accountability, blame avoidance, reputation and autonomous agencies will be addressed. Comparative chapters are included, as well as chapters that link the discussion about accountability with other concepts such as legitimacy, democracy, coordination and performance.

Most of the chapters in this book are the outcome of the International Political Science Association's Permanent Study Group on 'Structure and Organization of Government' conference on 'Accountability and Welfare State Reforms' in Bergen, 19–20 February 2015. Many authors in the book are furthermore part of a large comparative European project focusing on how contemporary reforms in core welfare state areas in Norway, Germany and Denmark are affecting different accountability relationships ('Reforming the Welfare State: Democracy, Management and Accountability'). A main focus is on accountability to whom and how the trade-offs between political, administrative, managerial, legal, professional and social accountability are changing in the areas of hospital management, welfare administration and immigration.

Conceptual clarification

Accountability is an ambiguous, contested and multidimensional concept. One can distinguish between accountability as a virtue or as a mechanism (Bovens 2010). Accountability as a virtue understands accountability as an ideal, goal or a normative standard for behavior. It focuses on the performance of actors and to what degree they are being or acting accountable. Accountability is an outcome or a dependent variable, often seen as a synonym for good governance or 'corporate social responsibility'.

Introduction

Accountability as a mechanism sees accountability more as a mean and an independent variable. It is the more passive relationship of being held accountable. It is a mechanism to secure proper behavior and the focus is more on formal arrangements and practices, as well as on instruments to foster good governance. A core question is if the mechanism works. Accountability as a virtue or as a mechanism is closely related. There is no virtue without a mechanism and no mechanisms without standards, and standards tend to be constructed in the process. In this book, the focus is more on accountability as a mechanism than as a virtue.

The well-known definition of the concept of accountability as a mechanism looks at accountability as: 'A relationship between an actor and a forum, in which the actor has an obligation to explain and justify his or her conduct, the forum can pose questions and pass judgment, and the actor may face consequences' (Bovens 2007: 452). Thus, the relationship between the actor and the different forums is seen as evolving in three steps that together constitute accountability: information, discussion and consequences/sanctions (Brandsma and Schillemans 2013; Jantz et al. 2015a).

A comprehensive analysis of accountability relations requires an assessment of who is accountable to whom, for what and why, through which procedures, what kind of arguments and justifications are provided, and what kind of sanctions are available. Bovens (2007) differentiates between the question of accountability 'to whom' with respect to the nature of the forum (political, legal, administrative/managerial, professional, social) and accountability 'for what' (finances, processes, performance). But these distinctions can be somewhat confusing since political accountability is also concerned with legal and professional matters (Jann and Lægreid 2015). If administrators do not follow the law or accepted practice, politicians will be blamed. Legal accountability is again not only a concern of courts or tribunals, but also of political and administrative actors. Different kinds of information concerning legality and fairness are part of political accountability, and this is also true for concerns about results and performance, that is managerial accountability. Questions of managerialism, legality and professionalism can thus be seen both as accountability for what (what kind of information?) or accountability to whom (what kind of forum?). All these dimensions are thus highly interwoven (Jantz and Jann 2013).

The traditional *forums* are, following Bovens (2007):

- political accountability towards elected politicians, either between the cabinet and parliament or between political and administrative leaders in government;
- administrative (or bureaucratic) accountability between superior and subordinate leaders and units, related to ministries, agencies, or divisions/departments;
- legal accountability towards courts and tribunals, or as internal aspects of administrative activities;
- professional accountability, related to peers and internal professional competence, or professional associations; and finally
- social accountability towards external users/clients/customers, stakeholders or interest groups, including public reporting, as well as citizens, stakeholder panels/boards and media.

Different from this is the *content* of the obligation, that is accountability for what, what kind of information is offered and what kind of questions are asked? Here, one can distinguish between:

- finances – are resources used appropriately and sparingly?
- procedure – are procedures and decisions correct and fair?
- performance – are results achieved, and are activities efficient and effective?

Finances are about 'input' criteria, while procedure is 'throughput' criteria. The last 'output' criterion has become more prominent lately, and is labeled variously as *managerial accountability* through contracts, management by objectives or results, performance measurement and so on (Bouckaert and Halligan 2008; Askim et al. 2015). These criteria can be combined with different fora, that is political accountability is usually concerned with all three criteria, as is administrative accountability, and even financial accountability through audit institutions has changed, since they have gradually become more interested in performance and evaluation (Jann and Lægreid 2015). The same holds true for social and professional accountability.

Third, one can address the problem of the many hands (Thompson 1980) or the question of who is accountable. Here, the focus is on the actors, which might be individuals or organizations, or more generally 'the system'.

Finally, one can distinguish between the nature of the obligation, that is in which direction does accountability work, vertical (political, administrative, managerial, legal), diagonal (audit offices, ombudsmen, supervisory bodies) and horizontal (social, professional) forms of accountability based again on the content of the obligation and the nature of the forum. While vertical accountability relations tend to be mandatory and formal and can result in sanctions, horizontal accountability relations are more voluntary, informal and indirect, and the consequences might be softer. The diagonal accountability forums are in-between and often operate in the shadow of hierarchy, as in the case of the audit institutions (Jantz et al. 2015b), ombudsmen, regulatory surveillance, oversight and supervisory bodies, anticorruption commissions and human rights commissions. There are no direct sanctions, but consequences can be severe (Schillemans 2008).

Especially, the concept of *managerial accountability* has created some confusion, and the relationship between administrative and managerial accountability has been ambiguous (Askim, Christensen and Lægreid 2015). Traditional bureaucratic accountability in the welfare state implied that the bureaucrats were supposed to be accountable for compliance with rules and regulations and for following the appropriate processes and procedures. Contemporary welfare state reforms have tried to transform the bureaucrats into managers that are held accountable for their performance on given objectives. It is this substantive content of what managerial accountability entails that generates concerns about its implications for democratic government (Day and Klein 1987; Mattei 2009).

Even more confusing is the use of the concept of *market accountability*. The NPM reforms have introduced incentives, competition, markets or market-like instruments such as pricing of services, choice for users and contract arrangements in welfare services. This has led to new forms of managerial information. But it does not really add a new forum. Accountability involves giving account, but one might question whether the market requires providers to account to customers or users (Mulgan 2014b). It might, however, influence and change traditional fora, especially political and social.

Understanding accountability

Accountability may be seen to be related to how we formally organize the state, both relating citizens to government and internally in government. Institutions, leaders and other actors enact their accountability in relations to formal structures that both enable and restrain action (March and Olsen 1983). Accountability may also be seen according to more economically oriented theory as a series of principal-agent relationships (Strøm 2003). The sovereign people or citizens, who are the primary principals in a democracy, manifested through elections, transfer their sovereignty to representatives, who further transfer their authority, through laws, budgets and policies, to the government. And internally in government, the political executives transfer their authority to administrative leaders in the ministries and further down to agencies and other subordinate bodies.

Agency theory takes it as a precondition that there is a potential conflict between principal and agent, a related mistrust that may eventually be remedied by incentives, or eventually, thinking in more organizational terms, through different types of formal structures and regulation. Stewardship theory, on the other hand, sees the relationship more in a collaboration perspective, where the agent is representative of the united collectivity (Schillemans, this volume).

Accountability in settled and unsettled situations may be seen differently (Christensen and Lægreid, this volume; Olsen, this volume). It is easier to see the relevance of instrumental perspectives in settled situations, whether principal-agent or bounded rationality-based (March and Olsen 1983; Gailmard 2014). Settled situations normally have clear goals, strong means-end knowledge and clear lines of command, where who is accountable to whom and for what basically is unproblematic. Political, administrative and managerial accountability are in the forefront. Political salience is normally low, and decision-making is largely delegated to managers in semi-independent institutions such as agencies.

On the contrary, unsettled situations relate the complexity, hybridity and dynamics of accountability, leading researchers to use a supplementary institutional approach. Under multi-level, transboundary and hybrid preconditions, accountability channels are normally multiple (Bovens *et al.* 2008). Goals and means are ambiguous, meaning actors scoring low on rational calculation, participation is more shifting and authority is more disputed (Olsen 2014). Who is accountable to whom and for what is continuously evolving and changing. Who is to blame is often related to ambiguity, symbolic discourses and contested interpretations by different actors and forums (Meyer and Rowan 1977). Accountability is more internally related, based on traditional cultures and socialization into a professional ethic and public ethos, and actors and forums are supposed to behave in a more altruistic and integrative way (Selznick 1957).

Assessing accountability

Several studies of agencies argue that there is an accountability deficit emerging in the relationship between political leadership, on the one hand, including political-executive leaders and parliament, and agencies, on the other hand. Schillemans (2011: 7) says that this accountability deficit is related to what he labels the *formal impossibility of hierarchical accountability*, that is it is impossible for different actors in the democratic chain of delegation – citizens, parliament, and political and administrative executives – to hold executive agencies to account for their decisions, because they are semiautonomous. An aspect of this is increasing complexity, specialization and lack of capacity and attention in the top leadership and the fact that the tasks of agencies often are not the ones given priority by the top political-administrative leadership. He asks whether horizontal accountability measures may be seen as important compensatory tools in a democratic perspective, but concludes that this is often not the case, that is they are more adding to the hierarchical control measures without solving the underlying democratic dilemma, and that learning is often not stimulated in these processes. This is more of a problem when the formal frames and tasks of the agencies are complex and ambiguous, giving few directions for the actors.

Another point of view is that one have increasingly experienced *accountability overload* (Halachmi 2014), partly due to a problem of *many eyes*. There has developed a massive set of scrutiny and control measures in the public sector, ranging from increasing and ever-changing parliamentary oversight, through new systems of auditing and accounting, to internal governmental control instruments related to reporting and evaluating. The big question is whether this is ineffective, inefficient or destructive, a view many researchers in the field entertain, or necessary instruments in an increasingly complex and hybrid public sector. Bovens *et al.* (2008) have deduced what they call an *ideal type of accountability overload* related to public officeholders and agencies. It is characterized by four criteria for an overloaded accountability regime: extraordinary high demand on their capacity, large number of contradictory evaluation criteria, contains unrealistic and too demanding performance standards, and contains performance standards that may lead to goal displacement and subversive behavior.

Bovens *et al.* (2010) list three perspectives for why accountability is important, whether potentially resulting in accountability deficits or overload. A *democratic perspective* states simply that public accountability enables citizens and their representatives to make public officeholders answer for their activities, meaning that accountability is very important for the democratic process to work (March and Olsen 1995). A *constitutional perspective* relates to the prevention of corruption and the abuse of power, which is connected to the organization of countervailing powers (Behn 2001). A *learning perspective* focuses on accountability regimes as effective vehicles of learning and improvement for the executive branch, based on experience and feedback from performance (Aucoin and Heintzman 2000).

Accountability and reform

When NPM came along in the early 1980s, it was not only characterized by increasing emphasis on efficiency, markets, contracts and privatization, but also on structural fragmentation through increased vertical and horizontal specialization (Christensen and Lægreid 2007). NPM also introduced performance management systems that made the public results and control systems more complex, a trend that was further exaggerated by structural fragmentation (Bouckaert and Halligan 2008). NPM reforms made the accountability regimes more complex and fragmented, related to the overall new institutional economic perspective that was behind the reforms (Boston *et al.* 1996), resulting in problems of many hands and many eyes. Looking at the balance between different accountability types, NPM also brought more focus on managerial accountability relative to the other types. As a result of more user and consumer orientation, social accountability also came more to the forefront.

When post-NPM reforms started in the late 1990s, more as a supplementary reform wave than as substituting NPM, emphasis was more on increasing central capacity and increasing horizontal collaboration, or a combination of the two measures (Christensen and Lægreid 2007). This resulted in even more structural complexity and redundancy. The effects on the accountability regimes again changed the balance between different types of accountability. Political and administrative accountability got more of the upper hand, but an increasing emphasis on 'value-based' management and cultural remedies such as increasing public ethos and ethics also strengthened professional accountability.

A *task perspective* may supplement our understanding of accountability. It takes as a point of departure that requirements and constraints inherent in the tasks of public organizations influence the decision-making, regulation and control of these units (Bouckaert and Peters 2002; Pollitt 2008; Verhoest *et al.* 2010). One way to define their tasks is to look at how well defined and narrow agencies' tasks are. Well-defined tasks with few internal inconsistencies and ambiguities, as in the case of service provision, are the most suitable for performance control and managerial accountability. Tasks that tend to be more complex and ambiguous, often associated with professional autonomy, are less suitable for performance control. The same is the case if task activities are less observable or their effects are difficult to grasp (Wilson 1989). Another way to see tasks is whether tasks' consequentiality or political salience is high, as defined, for example, by whether or not they involve major financial resources (Pollitt 2003) and whether or not they receive much media attention (Epstein and Segal 2000). Thus, there are ambiguous relationships between reforms and accountability. Rather than asking whether government officials are more or less accountable after reforms, one should ask what kind of accountability the different actors perceive as appropriate (Romzek 2000) and how it varies with different tasks and reform trends.

Accountability and performance

Various NPM initiatives were based on the assumption that enhanced accountability would improve performance (Lægreid 2014). But the empirical evidence of whether performance measurement leads to better accountability is scarce (Lægreid and Verhoest 2010; Van Dooren *et al.* 2010; van de Walle and Cornelissen 2014). The relationship between accountability and performance is characterized by tensions, ambiguities and contradictions, and more responsibility for performance does not lead to more accountability for performance (Bouckaert and Halligan 2008). Behn (2001) claims that there is an *accountability dilemma* because performance audit tends to focus more on compliance than on performance. Dubnick (2005) claims that there is an *accountability paradox* in which more accountability actually diminishes organizational performance.

Thiel and Leeuw (2002) reveal a *performance paradox* implying a weak correlation between performance indicators and performance itself and performance measurement can enhance gaming (Hood 2006). Thus, there is a tension between performance and accountability, and more accountability does not necessarily produce better government and performance (Aucoin and Heintzman 2000; Bouckaert and Peters 2002). Thus, we cannot rely on the assumption that accountability improves performance.

A challenge is to determine under which circumstances different types of accountability can have an overall positive effect (Behn 2001). Agents are often held accountable for adherence to multiple and sometimes contradictory standards (Steets 2010). In such situations, accountability demands can have a paralyzing effect on organizations and produce 'multiple accountabilities disorder' (Koppell 2005). Accountability mechanisms generate costs and can hamper flexibility, innovation and entrepreneurial behavior. Pollitt (2011) examines critically the contested proposition that performance management systems will improve agency accountability to citizens and political representatives. If promises of accountability are to be fulfilled, then accountability mechanisms need to be adapted to the complex political environment in which they are expected to operate (Radin 2011). To meet the promises of accountability, cultural and contextual factors need to be taken into consideration (Chan and Rosenbloom 2010).

The individual chapters

The book is divided into four parts and contains 20 chapters by researchers from Belgium, Estonia, Denmark, Germany, the Netherlands, Germany and the United Kingdom. Four of the chapters address conceptual and theoretical issues and 16 are theoretically informed empirical analyses of different accountability relations related to welfare state reforms in European countries. Eight of them are comparative chapters addressing two or more countries.

Part I addresses theoretical and conceptual issues related to democratic accountability and welfare states. Johan P. Olsen analyzes the relationship between democratic order, autonomy and accountability (Chapter 2). He makes a distinction between accountability within an established regime with fairly stable power relations and role expectations, and accountability as (re)structuring processes in less institutionalized contexts and in transformation periods. Werner Jann addresses the relationships between accountability performance and legitimacy in the welfare state and asks, if accountability is the answer, what is the question? (Chapter 3). Thomas Schillemans argues for the relevance of a stewardship approach to accountability and agency issues in welfare reforms (Chapter 4).

Part II examines accountability in selected welfare state policy areas. Welfare administration, labor and employment is addressed by Tom Christensen, Fleming Larsen and Karsten Vrangbæk in their comparative study of hybrid welfare administrative systems under reform and changing accountability relations in Denmark and Norway (Chapter 5). This is followed up by Bastian Jantz's chapter on the reform and accountability dynamics in the changing welfare administration in Germany and Norway (Chapter 6). Piret Tõnurist and Wouter De Tavernier examine individual responsibility and changing accountability relations in social services in a comparative perspective and argue that the welfare state is in flux (Chapter 7).

The hospital field is examined in two chapters. Haldor Byrkjeflot and Karsten Vrangbæk analyze dimensions of accountability in health and ask if recent hospital reforms implied a change towards more formalized and sanctions-based accountability forms in Denmark and Norway (Chapter 8). Tanja Klenk, Karsten Vrangbæk, John Appelby and Sarah Gregory address accountability through performance management by comparing Denmark and England (Chapter 9).

Chapters 10 and 11 are comparing Denmark, Germany and Norway. In Chapter 10, Tord Linden, Ina Radke and Karsten Vrangbæk focus on immigration control and examine the inclusion of social actors in asylum regulation. In Chapter 11, Per Lægreid and Kristin Rubecksen analyze administrative reforms and accountability relations in health and labor administration by examining the perceptions of top administrative executives.

Part III focuses on accountability in unsettled situations such as comprehensive reform, major crises and internal security. Tom Christensen and Martin Lodge conduct a comparative analysis of accountability and transparency in the field of societal security by analyzing agencies in the area of intelligence, food defense and flood safety (Chapter 12). Julia Fleischer examines inquiry commissions after internal security crises in Germany and Norway and asks if there is more accountability and more blame (Chapter 13). Tom Christensen and Per Lægreid analyze accountability relations in unsettled situations by examining comprehensive reform and a major crisis in Norway (Chapter 14). Hanne Foss Hansen and Mads Bøge Kristiansen address the issue of accountability in times of austerity by analyzing the case of Denmark (Chapter 15). They ask if there is a democracy gain but a learning loss. Tobias Bach and Kai Wegrich analyze regulatory reform, accountability and blame in public service delivery by addressing the public transportation crisis in Berlin (Chapter 16).

Part IV addresses accountability, administrative reforms and multilevel governance. Thomas Elston examines challenges of accountability reforms in the British civil service and asks what happens when principles meet practice (Chapter 17). Tom Willems and Wouter Van Dooren address multiple accountabilities in public-private partnerships in Belgium and ask how to unravel the accountability paradox (Chapter 18). Niels Ejersbo and Carsten Greve analyze digital era governance reform and accountability by focusing on the case of Denmark (Chapter 19). In Chapter 20, Anchrit Wille examines the dynamics of the EU accountability landscape and argues that the EU is moving to an ever-denser union.

Conclusion

There can be no doubt that the most recent welfare state reforms aimed to establish more managerial accountability, for example through semi-independent, service delivery agencies and service centers, performance management, and more market-like arrangements, paying less attention to the issue of how to maintain and develop mechanisms for traditional political accountability (Christensen and Lægreid 2007). New Public Management reforms as well as post-NPM reform initiatives have affected the balance between managerial and political accountability across welfare sectors and countries, but obviously also other accountability relations, such as administrative, legal, professional and social accountability. Furthermore, many of these new reforms do not necessarily just replace old arrangements and reforms. In many cases, the new reforms build on old reforms, leading to even more complex and mixed relations between public sector organizations, on the one hand, and the government and parliament, on the other. Traditional forms of vertical accountability are combined with new forms of horizontal or diagonal accountability – for example, to regulatory bodies, audit offices, as well as to stakeholders, the media and to the public in general (Schillemans 2008).

This has to some extent created confusion over whom public organizations are accountable to. A core question is to what extent it has been possible to combine the various modes of accountability. Often, the relationship between different administrative reforms in the welfare state and accountability relations are rather blurred and not straightforward. How, why, to whom and for what are public organizations and officials in the various welfare services held accountable? The focus of many of the chapters in this book is therefore, first of all, on changes in formal as well as actual accountability relations (Byrkjeflot *et al.* 2014).

But we are also interested in the effects of these presumed and real changes in accountability arrangements. How have these reforms and the obviously much more complicated and sometimes confusing accountability relationships affected performance (Lægreid 2014; Christensen and Lægreid 2015)? Is there, as assumed by many reforms, any clear relationship between, for example, more managerial accountability and better performance, or do we face a reformist paradox where reforms may undermine rather than improve accountability relationships (Dubnick 2011)? And how does all this affect the legitimacy of welfare arrangements? What do we know, and what do we learn about the relationship between multiple accountability relations, performance and legitimacy? Rather than a tight coupling between administrative reforms, accountability and performance, there seems to be a rather loose coupling.

References

Askim, J., Christensen, T. and Lægreid, P. (2015) Accountability and performance management: the Norwegian hospital, welfare and immigration administrations. *International Journal of Public Administration*, 38(13): 971–82.

Aucoin, P. and Heintzman, R. (2000) The dialectics of accountability for performance in public management reform. *International Review of Administrative Science*, 66(1): 45–55.

Behn, R. (2001) *Rethinking Democratic Accountability*. Washington, DC: Brookings Institution Press.

Boston, J., Martin, J., Pallot, J. and Walsh, P. (1996) *Public Management: The New Zealand Model*. Auckland: Oxford University Press.

Bouckaert, G. and Halligan, J. (2008) *Managing Performance: International Comparisons*. London: Routledge.

Bouckaert, G. and Peters, B. G. (2002) Performance measurement and management: the Achilles heel in administrative modernization. *Public Performance and Management Review*, 25: 359–62.

Bovens, M. (2007) Analyzing and assessing accountability: a conceptual framework. *European Law Journal*, 13: 447–68.

Bovens, M. (2010) Two concepts of accountability: accountability as a virtue and as a mechanism. *West European Politics*, 33(5): 946–67.

Bovens, M., Curtin, D. and 't Hart, P. (2010) *The Real World of EU Accountability*. Oxford: Oxford University Press.

Bovens, M., Schillemans, T. and 't Hart, P. (2008) Does accountability work? An assessment tool. *Public Administration*, 86: 225–42.

Brandsma, G. J. and Schillemans, T. (2013) The accountability cube: measuring accountability. *Journal of Public Administration Research and Theory*, 23(4): 953–75.

Byrkjeflot, H., Christensen, T. and Lægreid, P. (2014) The many faces of accountability: comparing reforms in welfare, hospitals and migration. *Scandinavian Political Studies*, 37(2): 171–95.

Chan, H. S. and Rosenbloom, D. H. (2010) Four challenges to accountability in contemporary public administration: lessons from the United States and China. *Administration and Society*, 42: 11–33.

Christensen, T. and Lægreid, P. (2007) The whole of government approach to public sector reform. *Public Administration Review*, 67: 1059–66.

Christensen, T. and Lægreid, P. (2015) Performance and accountability: a theoretical discussion and an empirical assessment. *Public Organization Review*, 15(2): 207–25.

Day, P. and Klein, R. (1987) *Accountabilities: Five Public Services*. London/New York: Tavistock.

Dubnick, M. (2005) Accountability and the promise of performance: in search of the mechanisms. *Public Performance and Management Review*, 28(3): 376–417.

Dubnick, M. (2011) Move over Daniel: we need some 'accountability space'. *Administration and Society*, 43(6): 704–16.

Epstein, L. and Segal, J. A. (2000) Measuring issue salience. *American Journal of Political Science*, 44(1): 66–83.

Flinders, M. (2014) The future and relevance of accountability studies. In M. Bovens, R. E. Goodin and T. Schillemans (eds), *The Oxford Handbook of Public Accountability*. Oxford: Oxford University Press, pp. 673–82.

Gailmard, S. (2014) Accountability and principal-agent theory. In M. Bovens, R. E. Goodin and T. Schillemans (eds), *The Oxford Handbook of Public Accountability*. Oxford: Oxford University Press, pp. 90–105.

Halachmi, A. (2014) Accountability overload. In M. Bovens, R. E. Goodin and T. Schillemans (eds), *The Oxford Handbook of Public Accountability*. Oxford: Oxford University Press, pp. 560–73.

Hood, C. (2006) Gaming in Targetworld: the targets approach to managing British public services. *Public Administration Review*, 66: 515–21.

Jann, W. and Lægreid, P. (2015) Introduction. Welfare state reforms: managerial accountability and performance. *International Journal of Public Administration*, 38(13): 941–6.

Jantz, B. and Jann, W. (2013) Mapping accountability changes in labour market administrations: from concentrated to shared accountability. *International Review of Administrative Sciences*, 79(2): 227–48.

Jantz, B., Christensen, T. and Lægreid, P. (2015a) Performance management and accountability: the welfare administration reform in Norway and Germany. *International Journal of Public Administration*, 38(13): 947–59.

Jantz, B., Reichborn-Kjennerud, K. and Vrangbæk, K. (2015b) Control and autonomy: the SAIs in Norway, Denmark, and Germany as watchdogs in an NPM-era? *International Journal of Public Administration*, 38(14–15): 960–70.

Koppell, J. G. S. (2005) Pathologies of accountability: ICANN and the challenge of 'multiple accountability disorder'. *Public Administration Review*, 65(1): 94–108.

Lægreid, P. (2014) New Public Management and public accountability. In M. Bovens, R. E. Goodin and T. Schillemans (eds), *The Oxford Handbook of Public Accountability*. Oxford: Oxford University Press, pp. 324–38.

Lægreid, P. and Verhoest, K. (2010) *Governance of Public Sector Organizations: Proliferation, Autonomy and Performance*. London: Palgrave Macmillan.

Lægreid, P. and Mattei, P. (2013) Reforming the welfare state and the implications for accountability in a comparative perspective. Special issue. *International Review of Administrative Sciences*, 79(2): 193–5.

March, J. G. and Olsen, J. P. (1983) Organizing political life: what administrative reorganization tells us about government. *American Political Science Review*, 77: 281–97.

March, J. G. and Olsen, J. P. (1995) *Democratic Governance*. New York: Free Press.

Mattei, P. (2009) *Restructuring Welfare Organizations in Europe*. Basingstoke: Palgrave Macmillan.

Meyer, J. W. and Rowan, B. (1977) Institutionalized organizations: formal structure as myth and ceremony. *American Journal of Sociology*, 83(2): 340–63.

Mulgan, R. (2014a) Accountability deficit. In M. Bovens, R. E. Goodin and T. Schillemans (eds), *The Oxford Handbook of Public Accountability*. Oxford: Oxford University Press, pp. 545–59.

Mulgan, R. (2014b) *Making Open Government Work*. London: Palgrave Macmillan.

Olsen, J. P. (2014) Accountability and ambiguity. In M. Bovens, R. E. Goodin and T. Schillemans (eds), *The Oxford Handbook of Public Accountability*. Oxford: Oxford University Press, pp. 106–23.

Pollitt, C. (2003) *The Essential Public Manager*. Maidenhead: Open University Press.

Introduction

Pollitt, C. (2008) *Time, Policy, Management: Governing with the Past*. Oxford: Oxford University Press.

Pollitt, C. (2011) Performance blight and the tyranny of light? Accountability in advanced performance measurement regimes. In M. J. Dubnick and H. G. Frederickson (eds), *Accountable Governance: Problems and Promises*. New York: M. E. Sharpe, pp. 81–97.

Pollitt, C. and Bouckaert, G. (2011) *Public Management Reform* (3rd edition). Oxford: Oxford University Press.

Radin, B. (2011) Does performance management actually improve accountability? In M. J. Dubnick and H. G. Frederickson (eds), *Accountable Governance*. New York: M. E. Sharpe, pp. 98–110.

Romzek, B. (2000) Dynamics of public accountability in the era of reform. *International Review of Administrative Sciences*, 66(1): 21–44.

Schillemans, T. (2008) Accountability in the shadow of hierarchy: the horizontal accountability of agencies. *Public Organization Review*, 8(2): 179–95.

Schillemans, T. (2011) Does horizontal accountability work? Evaluating potential remedies for the accountability deficit of agencies. *Administration and Society*, 43(4): 387–416.

Selznick, P. (1957) *Leadership in Administration*. New York: Harper & Row.

Steets, J. (2010) *Accountability in Public Policy Partnerships*. London: Palgrave Macmillan.

Streeck, W. and Thelen, K. (2005) *Beyond Continuity*. Oxford: Oxford University Press.

Strøm, K. (2003) Delegation and accountability in parliamentary democracies. *European Journal of Political Research*, 37(3): 261–90.

Thiel, S. and Leeuw, F. L. (2002) The performance paradox in public sector. *Public Performance and Management Review*, 25: 267–81.

Thompson, D. F. (1980) Moral responsibility of public officials: the problem of many hands. *American Political Science Review*, 74: 905–16.

van de Walle, S. and Cornelissen, F. (2014) Performance reporting. In M. Bovens, R. E. Goodin and T. Schillemans (eds), *The Oxford Handbook of Public Accountability*. Oxford: Oxford University Press, pp. 441–55.

Van Dooren, W., Bouckaert, G. and Halligan, J. (2010) *Performance Management in the Public Sector*. London: Routledge.

Verhoest, K., Roness, P. G., Verschuere, B., Rubecksen, K. and MacCarthaigh, M. (2010) *Autonomy and Control of State Agencies: Comparing States and Agencies*. Basingstoke: Palgrave Macmillan.

Wilson, J. Q. (1989) *Bureaucracy: What Government Agencies Do and Why They Do It*. New York: Basic Books.

PART I

Theoretical and conceptual issues

2
DEMOCRATIC ORDER, AUTONOMY AND ACCOUNTABILITY[1]

Johan P. Olsen

Accountability and political order

Over the last decades, there has been an increasing demand for making governments and public officials accountable, and radical reforms have been advocated. There are, however, competing claims about what is involved in demanding, rendering, assessing and responding to accounts, what are effective accountability institutions, and how accountability regimes emerge and change. Accountability is conceived as a precondition for democratic government, but accountability overload is seen to reduce performance and erode public trust in democratic government (Borowiak 2011; Dubnick 2011; Flinders 2011; Bovens *et al.* 2014). Some have faith in anticipation, namely that those acting on behalf of others are more likely to act in accordance with the interests of the represented when they have to account for conduct and results (Pitkin 1972: 58). Nevertheless, heavy criticism suggests that neither anticipation nor other accountability mechanisms work perfectly. Understanding accountability claims and processes requires a re-examination of what democratic accountability means and implies and the roles of citizens, elected representatives and non-elected officials.[2]

The paper provides a frame for thinking about institutional aspects of accountability regimes and their cognitive, normative and power foundations. Accountability involves establishing facts and assigning causality and responsibility, formulating and applying normative standards for assessing conduct and reasons given, and building and applying capabilities for sanctioning inappropriate conduct. Accountability regimes are part of a political order, and the institution-centered approach used here assumes that accountability regimes are affected by, and affect, how responsibilities and powers are organized and exercised in an order. A distinction is made between: (a) accountability *within* an established regime with fairly stable power relations and role expectations, specifying what different actors are expected to do, and standards of good conduct; and (b) accountability as *structuring and restructuring processes* in less institutionalized contexts and in transformation periods when accountability relationships are shaped and reshaped as part of constituting and reconstituting a political community and its government.

A huge literature is concerned with whether agents comply with authoritative mandates and the effectiveness of different regimes when it comes to monitoring and controlling agents, detecting and preventing noncompliance, and achieving public purposes. It is taken for granted who can call whom to account for what, according to which normative standards, and why. Focus is on the knowledge basis and epistemic quality of accountability: How a political community makes sense of experience and figures out what has happened. How it constructs and legitimizes interpretations of truth and causal links between behavior and events; figures out whether things could have been done differently; and attributes responsibility, blame and praise.

There is less attention to accountability as structuring and restructuring processes beyond the idea that some pre-determined authority learns from experience and deliberately redesigns governmental institutions in order to improve accountability. This paper, therefore, calls attention to how democracies search for, and struggle over, what are legitimate accountability regimes and political orders. How existing arrangements are delegitimized and deinstitutionalized and new ones are legitimized and institutionalized. How political communities develop, accept and apply normative criteria for assessing behavior and results. How they figure out principles for the appropriate allocation, use and control of powers and action capabilities.

Making sense of the relations between accountability and political institutions then presents two challenges. The *first* is to analyze how accountability processes work, and with what effects, when accountability is governed by well-entrenched institutionalized routines. Focus is on effects of the institutions assumed to facilitate accountability; how they are organized and operate and their effectiveness in inducing desired conduct. The task is to discover and possibly punish noncompliance. Examples include investigations into whether public funds are spent as intended and laws are followed.

The *second* is to analyze where accountability regimes come from, how they are maintained and changed, and how accountability processes feed back into accountability regimes and political orders. Accountability is often presented in a technical-neutral language of efficiency and improved performance. But within this frame, it is also conceived as an inherent part of democratic struggle over political order and its power relations and normative basis. Ideas about what accountability arrangements are for, who is entitled to hold whom to account, and what counts as good reasons and reasoning can be challenged. Political orders, institutions and actors can gain or lose legitimacy and support.

The two frames differ in their assumptions about what is exogenous or endogenous to accountability processes and democratic politics. Yet, they are not alternatives. At issue are their scope conditions and how one approach may be more/less important in certain polities, policy sectors and time periods. The first is likely to be most helpful during normal times and in stable political orders with well-entrenched institutions. The second is more likely to be useful for understanding emerging polities, exceptional times and radical transformations.

This paper holds that studying accountability in an era of transformation requires us to relax several assumptions made by mainstream *actor-centered*, principal-agent approaches regarding political institutions, actors, decision-making and change. An *institution-centered* approach assumes that the degree of institutionalization of accountability practices is variable and changing. Complicated and dynamic lines of authority, power, responsibility and accountability have developed to accommodate multiple and inconsistent demands from an increasingly heterogeneous society with powerful special interests. In addition to hierarchical, specialized and open access structures, there is shifting trust in command, rules, bargaining, markets and price systems, as well as in citizens, elected representatives and non-elected officials. Institutions work through socialization and internalization, as well as through incentives and coercion. They affect actors' character, and not only their utility calculations. Understanding accountability makes it necessary to go beyond who makes formal decisions. Decision-making is less an individual choice and more a social process, difficult to disentangle. Decision-making implies drawing conclusions from complex streams of premises (Simon 1957: XII) and accountability requires knowledge about who has supplied the premises. Deliberate design and reform is one of a variety of change processes.

Discontent and political contestation are drivers of change. Controversies are sometimes linked to single events. At other times, there is mobilization around crises of confidence in accountability regimes or political orders. There might, for example, be ideology-based disputes over what a legitimate political order is and how to balance government's capacity to act on common problems and protect citizens' freedom from government intervention. Uncertainty about facts and causality, ambiguous and contested normative standards, and unclear power relations create a space for competing interpretations. Accountability processes provide opportunities for naming, shaming and delegitimizing, as well as for praising, justifying and legitimizing institutions and actors. The opportunities are also expanded because key concepts related to democratic accountability are problematic.

Organizing democratic accountability and autonomy

Democracy, rule by the people, is a normative principle for organizing the distribution, exercise, control and legitimization of power. Accountability is also a principle for organizing the relations between rulers and ruled and constituting a democratic political community and government. Making government and public officials accountable is a democratic achievement, and a legitimate order requires strong accountability institutions and control with officials exercising powers on behalf of the public. Another democratic principle is that to legitimately call someone to account requires that the actor has autonomy and discretion that can be used or misused. Accountability and autonomy must be commensurate (March and Olsen 1995: 152). No power without accountability. No accountability without autonomy.

A complication is that democracy, autonomy and accountability are slippery and contested concepts. They give some guidance, yet are open to competing interpretations and disputes regarding what institutions are most likely to secure accountability and what the proper role of citizens, elected representatives and non-elected officials are. For example, whereas (nearly) everyone embraces democracy as an ideal, the term has lost its meaning 'in a cacophony of competing interpretations' and there is a need to reconsider what citizens expect from each other and what it means to conduct oneself democratically (Hanson 1989: 69, 86).

There is, nevertheless, fairly broad consensus that the people are the ultimate source of power and legitimacy – in Madison's words, 'the only legitimate fountain of power' (Hamilton *et al.* 1964: 117). Citizenship is the key institution of democratic government and the people, as a collection of free and equal citizens, are entitled to hold their rulers to account. Officials are obliged to describe, explain and justify what has happened and why to an authoritative forum. However, polities called democracies differ considerably when it comes to organizational structures prescribing where powers, autonomy, responsibility and accountability are to be located. Hierarchical, specialized and open access structures include and exclude participants and issues differently and give citizens different roles (Cohen *et al.* 1972).

Hierarchical structure and citizens as voters

A hierarchical structure implies that decision-makers, issues and decision opportunities are ranked in importance, and that high-ranking actors and issues have access to high-ranking decisions. A favorite narrative portrays parliamentary government as a chain of dyadic-hierarchical relations of delegation and accountability. Voting in free, competitive elections is the core mechanism for authorizing representatives to act on behalf of the community and for holding them accountable to citizens. Citizens delegate power to a representative assembly. Elected representatives make authoritative decisions backed by coercion. Majority vote is a key principle. Accountability to the sovereign parliament is provided through a chain of top-down command and control from elected representatives to government, ministerial hierarchies and public administration.

For example, principal-agent approaches to parliamentary government assume who is accountable to whom and for what (Strøm 2000; Strøm et al. 2003; Gailmard 2014). Accountability is about facts and causality and compliance with orders, rules and purposes. Predetermined superiors and subordinates, principals and agents, have different preferences. There is asymmetric information and the agent is the expert. Principals formulate mandates, set normative standards, and administer incentives and coercion to induce desirable behavior by agents. Principals delegate powers to agents, monitor and make assessments of their performance. They have the capability to sanction, discipline and correct misconduct. Institutions are instruments for making rational, self-regarding agents find it worthwhile to serve the interests of the principal. All actors are self-interested. There is a culture of mistrust, concerned with agents shirking and moral hazard. The political community is held together by individual utility calculations embedded in a contract. A key question is how to organize effective accountability regimes and what agent autonomy will be helpful to fulfill the principal's preferences. Institutional change is the result of structural choice by principals. The ideas that humans are not angels and therefore have to be monitored, controlled and called to account, and that the power of the state requires institutional checks and balances, where ambition counteracts ambition, have long historical roots (Hamilton et al. 1964: 122–3; Gailmard 2014: 93).

Specialized structure and citizens in multiple roles

A specialized structure implies that participants, issues and decision opportunities with specific characteristics are linked to each other. Citizens do not place all eggs in one basket (the parliament). Polities are composite orders with a complicated ecology of interconnected and overlapping rules. There is institutional specialization, with different missions, mandates, powers, and legitimacy bases. Several interdependent yet relatively autonomous, partly self-organizing, and resourceful institutions and professions are validated as the legitimate guardians of reason, truth, justice and equity (March and Olsen 1989: 170; Olsen 2009). A majority cannot claim sovereignty and ultimate authority. There are a variety of relationships between specialized agents and forums, applying different normative criteria. Citizens are voters and also direct participants in public policymaking, carriers of rights, jury members, soldiers, members of political parties and organizations, customers, and clients.

This narrative has affinity with liberal-constitutional democracy. Liberalism is 'the art of separation' (Walzer 1984) and a story about life spheres governed by different laws (Weber 1978: 123). Institutions have emerged gradually with separate origins and histories. Over time, compromises and struggles have been encoded into configurations of institutions working according to different principles and behavioral logics. Experiences with how powers have been exercised have generated shifting popular trust in the competence and integrity of institutions and actors. The reputations and legitimacy of legislatures, executives, courts, public administrations, central banks, experts, political parties, organized interests, mass media, private enterprises and markets vary across polities and change over time. The same is true for public trust in ordinary citizens and their ability to govern themselves. Autonomy can be embedded in shared beliefs, or in powerful groups in society. Political community can be based upon a calculated contract and also a shared identity and loyalty to a community of history and fate, embedded in an enduring pact and shared traditions. In some institutional spheres, actors are expected to be self-serving utility maximizers; in others, to follow institutionalized codes of conduct and act with competence, integrity and impartiality. There are several processes of change, which are not necessarily synchronized and coordinated.

An implication is that studies of the institutional foundations of autonomy and accountability have to go beyond questions of what discretion legislators grant, for example, bureaucrats (Huber and Shipan 2002). It is not enough to study the legislative act that establishes an agency. We must pay attention to how agencies are transformed after they are formally founded (Simon 1953; Laffan 2003). Democratic government and politics have been, and still are, in competition with other resources than the ballot (Schattschneider 1960) and with other identities and loyalties than national citizenship. Authority and power founded on competitive elections are not dominant. Their importance is modified by other, unevenly distributed resources and by institutionalized rights that limit public intervention. Agencies build reputations and support that make it difficult for political authorities to intervene, and giving voluntary accounts can be part of documenting expertise and protecting or enhancing their legitimacy and autonomy. Agencies can be captured by a single constituency or develop several sources of support and thereby relative independence from each of them (Carpenter 2001; Schillemans and Busuioc 2014).

Open structure and citizens as a 'sleeping bear'

An open structure allows any combination of participants, issues and decision-making opportunities. It gives access to all citizens and their concerns. There are no predetermined principals and agents. Citizens determine the rules for living together. They can at any time call any official and each other to account, and reason-giving is the foundation of political community. There can be citizens' initiatives, referenda, popular movements, direct contact with public administration, taking issues to court, and social protests that mobilize mass media and institutions with formal powers. Accountability regimes and political orders arise, are maintained and change, as a result of which participants and issues are activated at different points in time.

Whereas citizens can demand participation and representation in all institutions affecting their lives, their motivation and capabilities are, in practice, limited. The ideal of a responsible citizen participating in the collective life of the community is difficult to achieve. Citizenship – being a member of a political community – is not the dominant identity, except under special circumstances. Attention is a scarce resource. Most public issues, handled within specialized structures, never reach the attention of the public, and most citizens are most of the time unlikely to be activated. Open structures and transparency are no guarantee for equal participation. Also, leaders' attention to reforms varies over time as issues and participants arrive or disappear (March and Olsen 1983). Available access and information are not necessarily used (Pollitt 2006: 38).

This is a narrative about a rather anarchic polity. Open, undifferentiated access structures have affinity with both ideal participatory and deliberative democracy and free-exchange (market) systems. Such structures are particularly relevant in unsettled polities, polities in transformation, and situations where established institutions are set aside due to exceptional circumstances (Olsen 2014). Accountability processes are then part of a search for, and struggle over, the terms of accountability regimes and political order and how institutions and actors are to be empowered and constrained.

In Europe today, institutions of democratic government are under attack and the hegemonic role of the territorial state is challenged. Democratic orders are more or less integrated and institutionalized.[3] They have elements of hierarchical, specialized and open access structures, and understanding accountability will require comprehension of conditions for citizens' mobilization and their use of different structures. An implication is that theorizing democratic accountability requires us to differentiate between accountability as institutional routines and reconstructive processes.

Accountability as institutional routines

Within highly institutionalized regimes, accountability is routine. There, good government implies exercising authority and power in accordance with fairly stable principles, approved procedures and recognized authority. Accountability is organized by hierarchical and specialized structures, rather than open structures. Power relations and expectations of how accountability can be achieved are taken for granted. The 'sleeping bear' is sleeping most of the time. There is widespread agreement about what different institutions are for and who is accountable to whom, for what, under what circumstances, and according to which normative criteria. It is clear who should be blamed if things go wrong. Those authorized to call someone to account do so with reference to shared purposes, norms and expectations. Those with an obligation to render accounts to some legitimate authority do what they are supposed to do. Attribution of accountability is guided by clear, well-known, stable, and socially validated roles, rules, routines, procedures, doctrines, expectations and resources. Whereas in individual cases there is deliberation and bargaining regarding what accountability means and implies, accountability processes largely take place within institutional constraints and with modest controversy (Olsen 2013, 2014).

Responsibility and accountability are social constructions and conventions by which a political community affirms the preeminence of intentional human control over history. There are repertoires of socially constructed and validated accounts and responses to accounts, influenced by what is intelligible and appropriate in specific political-cultural contexts. Favored stories are embedded in ideologies and traditions (March and Olsen 1995: 155, 161). Activities are recorded in routinized reports, but there is little perceived need to explain and justify what is done. Routinized accounts focus on deviances from shared rules and expectations. Actors are evaluated in terms of whether they perform the duties of their roles with dedication, integrity, and conformity to proper procedure and purposes. Attention is upon how effectively an institutional accountability regime governs behavior and achieves desired performance and outcomes.

In highly institutionalized (hierarchical or specialized) contexts, it is reasonable to treat authority, power, mandate, normative standards, and expectations as predetermined and exogenous. The challenge is to monitor behavior and results, make sense of facts and causality, develop performance measures and score cards, detect noncompliance and undesirable behavior, pin down responsibility, and assign blame and culpability. Key issues are how effective institutions are in detecting fraud, waste, incompetence and corruption; whether mandate and jurisdictions have been exceeded and powers usurped or misused; or whether powers have not been used to prevent undesired behavior and outcomes. Accountability is linked to improving the quality of democratic governance.

Mainstream principal-agent approaches assuming institutionalized accountability regimes capture routine situations better than unsettled, complex, conflict-ridden and dynamic contexts. They are more likely to be useful when accountability processes are concerned with single events and operational responsibility. They become problematic when system responsibility is at issue: who recruited and trained the operator, designed the system of rules and routines, monitored the operations, and so on. They are even less likely to be useful when the task is to disentangle effects of government actions upon the distribution of citizens' life chances and welfare compared to effects of economic, technological, cultural, demographic processes – situations where there are usually ideological disputes over the actual and desired role of politics and government. Often, they fit democratic rhetoric better than democratic practices.[4]

One challenge is that dissemination, assessment and sanctioning of accounts in contemporary democracies involve a multitude of institutions, organizations, networks and communities of accountability. Some specialize in providing normative standards and certificates. Some monitor and analyze performance without authority or resources to sanction misconduct. Others assess and sanction but depend on reliable information and analysis from the outside. In addition to legislative and judicial scrutiny, there are independent auditors, ombudsmen, epistemic communities, think tanks, credit-rating and standard-settings agencies, tribunals, committees of inquiry operating at arm's length from popular control, and nongovernmental watchdogs. New accountability relationships have been added to old ones, creating complex combinations of coexisting institutions (Romzek 2000; Bovens 2007; Lægreid and Verhoest 2010) and sometimes 'multiple accountability disorders' (Koppell 2005). Actors are required to provide accounts to several forums and satisfy multiple, contested and ambiguous accountability claims and stakeholders. They do so in a variety of ways and through different channels, requiring different types of information, explanations and justifications in terms of competing normative standards (Bovens *et al.* 2010). Accountability often requires pooling resources from several institutions and actors (Busuioc 2013).

One implication is that to make sense of the complexity, it has to be recognized that accountability is about more than compliance with predetermined principals and their success criteria. Accountability processes are part of a struggle over accountability regimes and the role of different institutions and actors in a political order. How, then, do accountability processes feed back into accountability regimes? How do they challenge institutionalized causal beliefs, ethical-moral standards and power relations, and possibly contribute to the reconstruction of accountability regimes and political orders?

Accountability as restructuring processes

An institution-centered approach goes beyond the assumption that accountability regimes emerge and change as a result of deliberate structural choices of predetermined principals. Attention is directed to accountability processes as part of the dynamics through which accountability regimes and political orders are constituted and reconstituted, institutionalized and deinstitutionalized (Olsen 2013, 2014). Demanding, rendering, assessing and responding to accounts are constitutive political processes. Interpretation of experience and creation of meaning; testing of causal beliefs, normative standards and power relationships; and distributing glory and blame are related to fundamental issues in political life (March and Olsen 1995; Hood 2014).

Accountability processes not only provide an opportunity for interpretation of experience and exploring how accountability may be enhanced within an existing regime. They also provide an opportunity for challenging, delegitimizing and transforming existing regimes and the codes of conduct, causal beliefs, normative standards, power relations, and identities upon which they are based. Accountability regimes can change through modifications of opportunity and incentive structures and through fashioning rulers and ruled through socialization, internalization and habitualization. Identities are endogenous to accountability processes. Identification is a fundamental mechanism in group integration (March and Simon 1958), and behavioral logics, preferences and commitments are changing and variable, not fixed and universal (March and Olsen 1989).

Accountability processes include both institutionalized routines and spontaneous demands for accounts. Such processes often take place among elites within hierarchical or specialized structures. However, democracies are self-reflecting communities, reasoning and deliberating about experience; critically re-examining ends, means and power relations. Some of the key institutions of democracy are institutions of discourse, and the quality of democratic governance is measured by the quality of its discourses and what is accepted as public truth (March and Olsen 1995: 146, 174–5). Civil society and a public space for free debate provide an open structure for sense-making, will formation and structural change (Goodin 2008). Freedom of expression, legitimate opposition and a free press are institutions that help citizens and officials to construct a moral account of the good society, recognize appropriate tasks, ends, and forms of governance, and develop confidence in their mutual motivation and capability for reason and justice.

A democratic-optimistic interpretation of accountability is that communicative rationality and experience-based learning will generate mutual understanding, adaptation and improvement through exchange of reasons and arguments. Accountability is based on discretionary reasoning and argumentation (Molander *et al.* 2012). Actors are discursively accountable to one another in an open forum and they are supposed to comply with the force of the better argument (Habermas 1996). In such a world, there will be honest reporting, free flow of information and diagnoses. Mistakes and imperfections will be discovered. There will be willingness to modify rules and routines as a result of the lessons learned.

But experience-based learning involves imperfect processes and improvement is not guaranteed. Intrusive monitoring and lack of trust can reduce motivation to speak freely. Heavy blaming and punishment of mistakes (throw the rascals out, heads must roll) creates defensiveness and formalistic rule-following, rather than experimentation, learning and improvement. Deciding who to praise or blame depends not only on hard evidence and correct causal understanding. Interpretations of experience compete for acceptance on the basis of both evidence and power (March 1987, 2010). The ability to gain acceptance for a type of discourse, an interpretative community and a special vocabulary is a source and indication of power (March and Olsen 1995: 180).

The meaning and implications of accountability are challenged when accountability regimes collide or principles confront practical situations, generating cleavages. Then a polity may be turned into a conceptual battleground and institutional building site. There are debates over competing visions of political order; what principles for organizing and governing common affairs deserve the allegiance of citizens; what legitimate power relations, identities and roles are; and who deserves to be accepted as trustworthy (Olsen 2010).

Under goal ambiguity, uncertainty and unclear control, accountability processes depend also in large part on post-event processes. The style of presentation of an account and how criticism of malperformance is met can be as important for responses as the act to be accounted for. That is, accountability processes are influenced by what arguments are given for an action or outcome; whether actors humbly submit to criticism, express regret and ask for forgiveness, or excuse, justify or reframe interpretations (Dubnick 2005). Events can be interpreted as an unfortunate but unavoidable accident, an error, due to inadequate resources and skills, a result of purposeful acts, a criminal offense, or as a system failure. Behavior can be forgiven and justified, or disapproved and punished. Accountability claims can be met with talk rather than action (Brunsson 1989). For example, the 22 July tragedy in Norway, when 77 people were killed, generated strong talk about democracy, openness and community, yet slow and cautious action (Lango *et al.* 2014). Account-giving can develop into rituals, with no negative implications (Gustavsson *et al.* 2009).

An implication is that the conception of accountability as truth-finding, a neutral technique, correct reporting and compliance has to be supplemented by accountability politics – debates and struggles over what are considered appropriate accountability regimes and good government (Costa et al. 2003; Bovens *et al.* 2010; Curtin *et al.* 2010). New regimes are often related to political contestation and the rise and fall of political groups, ideologies, cleavages, institutions and orders.

Accountability in an era of political transformation

Accounts are likely to be contested in democracies. Accountability regimes are rarely fully accepted by everyone, and the people seldom speak with one voice. Accounts are constructed in encounters between contending accounts. There are competing narratives of what happened, why it happened, who/what caused it, and whether it is good; and political actors struggle to solicit support for their understandings. In a world of interdependence, chance events, and long and uncertain causal chains, with significant effects surfacing after years, the assignment of accountability can seem largely arbitrary. Still, democracies seek to interpret history in ways that justify or condemn actions and establish responsibility. They foster demands for calling someone to account, even when experience offers little guidance (March and Olsen 1995: 158, 173–7). In transformative periods, problems of assigning accountability create possibilities for political contestation, naming and shaming, as well as collective sense-making and integrating behavior.

The last decades exemplify such an era of transformation. Public sector reforms have been based upon a new understanding of political order and government and there has been an obsession with accountability (Dubnick 2011). The main trend has been interpreted as a paradigm shift from collective responsibility to individual responsibility; away from a social-democratic order emphasizing equality and arguing that aspects of health, education and social security shall not be treated as commodities for sale in markets; toward a liberal order emphasizing emancipation from overregulation, a shorter social contract and more freedom for the individual (Dahrendorf 1988). The trend has also been interpreted as a shift from a hierarchical state and Weberian bureaucracy to a managerial state giving priority to outcomes rather than compliance with rules and procedures (Saint-Martin 2000). Such changes have been part of reconsidering the role of democratic politics and government in society and relations between levels of government.

Neoliberal-inspired New Public Management reforms, introducing corporate accountability principles, have been based upon mistrust in 'big government' and 'excessive bureaucracy'. They have celebrated limited government, structural disaggregation, privatization, competitive markets, price systems, management autonomy, performance, public-private partnerships and citizens as customers. Government has been disempowered, private actors empowered. Non-majoritarian institutions have been given more autonomy. We are said to live in the age of the unelected (Vibert 2007) and conceptions of accountability have come to rely more on watchdog agencies deliberately placed outside a unitary ministerial hierarchy and at arm's length from politics and direct electoral control (Egeberg and Trondal 2011; Busuioc *et al.* 2012). 'Autonomy' has meant detachment from the political center; often hiding a transfer from political dependencies to dependencies on markets, managers, stakeholders and rating agencies (Olsen 2009). In addition, neo-constitutionalism has promoted juridification of political life and constraints on politics. Courts have been empowered, in order to guard society against arbitrary use of majority power.

Reforms have also challenged the hegemonic role of the territorial state. For centuries, conceptions of democratic accountability have developed in the context of the sovereign state. But that role has been defied by increased international interdependence and European integration. There has been a perceived need to develop new ways of thinking about global accountability, explore new mechanisms securing accountability and popular control beyond the state, and limit abuse of power in world politics (Grant and Keohane 2005). Europe is in search of political order (Olsen 2007) and a new type of order has emerged: multileveled, multicentered, hybrid, networked and fluid. There are elements of 'normalization' (Wille 2013), but distinctions between levels of government and between the public and the private realm have become less clear. Old accountability relations have been challenged and new ones have evolved. Proposals for making institutions and actors accountable have been based upon competing conceptions of the nature, purpose and desired future of the European Union. Visions have varied among those seeing the union as an intergovernmental, supranational or regulatory entity (Bovens *et al.* 2008, 2010). The EU's financial and social crises have generated a perceived need to strengthen institutions of democratic accountability and restore popular confidence in the European project. Arguably, the result has been more accountability and less democracy (Curtin *et al.* 2010; Papadopoulos 2010).

Reforms have made the loci of accountability more unclear and balancing political-administrative control and institutional and professional autonomy more difficult (Christensen and Lægreid 2006; Lægreid and Verhoest 2010; Lægreid 2014). Accountability to the EU, international human rights regimes, courts and markets has constrained accountability to domestic voters and parliaments. How can democratic accountability be safeguarded when government is embedded in networks across levels of government, institutional spheres and the public-private realms? When governance is based upon informal partnership and dialogue, more than hierarchical command and formal control relationships (Michels and Meijer 2008: 168; Klijn and Koppenjan 2014: 246)? Reforms have contributed to increased attention to the results achieved by the public sector, but functional superiority and efficiency gains have been difficult to prove (Verhoest *et al.* 2004). It has been mused on whether reinventing governance implies reinventing democracy (Pierre 2009) and there have been efforts to reassert the political center and political leadership (Dahlström *et al.* 2011).

A narrative of change in accountability regimes has, however, to be held together with a narrative of inertia and 'historical inefficiency' (March and Olsen 1989). The European state has showed considerable resilience, in spite of discontent with its ability to deal with the needs and interests of citizens. Observations of difficulties of cutting back the public sector have been supplemented by observations of how neoliberalism has survived the financial crises since 2007 (Crouch 2011). Like welfare state ideology, market ideology is embedded in strong institutions and supported by powerful actors. Theories of accountability have to take into account that the political saliency of accountability is not static, and a key question is under what conditions, and through which processes, does accountability capture public attention? There is a need to understand when accountability is politicized and who gets into the fights (Schattschneider 1960). When is the 'sleeping bear' sleeping because processes and outcomes are perceived as satisfactory? When is inactivity caused by alienation and absence of hope of making a difference?

Theorizing democratic accountability

Whereas there is a long way to go before the intricacies of accountability processes are understood, some elementary hypotheses regarding the increased felt need for holding actors to account are probably shared by most approaches. Ceteris paribus, the more autonomy and discretion actors have, the more likely there will be accountability demands. Demands will be linked to issues and policy areas regulated by broad framework laws and open mandate allowing arbitrary judgment, rather than precise institutionalized standards, rules and procedures.

Accountability claims are likely to be triggered by indications that something is wrong (e.g. real or perceived performance crises and scandals and confrontations over what constitutes proper political order and good government). Such claims are also more likely when there is reduced economic slack (Cyert and March 1963), compared to resource-rich polities and periods that allow more autonomy.

An institution-centered approach holds that theorizing democratic accountability and the growing demand for accountability requires studies of how accountability regimes change as well as how they operate. Accountability processes are part of both complying with and challenging established regimes, and the latter in particular is important in periods of institutional experimentation and transformation. Principal-agent approaches have, however, given more attention to making existing accountability regimes more efficient than to regime dynamics. As a consequence, the substance of accountability has primarily been related to facts and causality relevant for control and compliance. Power relations between principals and agents and normative standards have been taken for granted. The political order is assumed to be in equilibrium, or change is a result of structural choices of principals. An institution-centered approach attends to how accountability processes are part of the structuring of accountability regimes, power relations and normative standards. Limited feasibility of establishing unambiguously causal responsibility creates a problem for academics, but space for accountability politics.

Theorizing accountability also requires us to explore how competing approaches interpret political-democratic orders, institutions and actors, and sources of accountability problems. Principal-agent approaches to parliamentary government interpret democratic order in terms of dyadic principal-agent relations between the people, elected representatives and other officials. Contemporary democracies are, however, compound and dynamic orders with a variety of specialized mechanisms for rendering, assessing and sanctioning accounts. Responsibilities and powers are dispersed between partly autonomous levels of government, institutions of government and private groups with a power base of their own. There are competing and contested accountability claims, appeals to different audiences and normative standards, and multiple channels of accountability. Hybrid regimes with mixes of self-governance and external control are tried captured by the term 'accountable autonomy' (Fung 2001: 75); referring to a certain independence from central power, rules and oversight combined with local initiative, dialogue between officials and citizens, transparency, horizontal account-giving and learning. Understanding accountability dynamics requires us to examine how democracies cope with and legitimize accountability at different levels of government and institutional spheres while remaining a community of cooperation.

Principal-agent approaches see political orders as based on a constellation of interests and power and a calculated contract. An institution-centered approach calls attention to the possibility of authority – order founded on a belief in its legitimacy and a felt duty to follow prescribed behavior (Weber 1978: 31). An example is administration governed by public service values, due process, fairness, impartiality, honesty and democratic control; administrators who see themselves as 'stewards' of the public good, sharing goals and principles with their political principals (Schillemans 2013). Actors are governed by authority within a zone of acceptance that defines legitimate purposes, methods and powers (Simon 1957: 12). History matters, and demands for accountability will be less likely the more an institution historically has shown competence, honesty and integrity. As a corollary, the less trust there is in authorities, the more likely are demands for accountability.

Arguably, principal-agent approaches overestimate the importance of electoral mechanisms, the dichotomy between politics and administration, and the hierarchical relation between elected representatives and other officials. An institution-centered approach perceives public administration as more than technicians implementing and enforcing ends and rules determined by elected representatives. Administrators take part in defining problems and shaping policies. Citizens have direct channels to public administration, and under some conditions they trust administrators, experts and judges more than elected representatives. The quality of citizens' lives, their subjective satisfaction and the legitimacy of government depend crucially on governmental institutions that work on the basis of integrity and impartiality (Rothstein 2011). It has been claimed that if Aristotle were writing today, he would be more an administrative theorist than a political theorist (Harmon 1995: 206).

An institutionally differentiated and specialized order legitimates competing behavioral logics, and an institution-centered approach suggests that accountability regimes are least likely to be dominated by self-serving actors calculating private expected utility in societies with strong civic identity and citizenship. The stronger shared ethical-moral standards, we-feelings and solidarity a society has, the more likely that accountability will be governed by relatively autonomous institutions, and the less demand for accountability. Autonomy does not imply the right to arbitrarily exploit discretion for personal gain. It is a political trust, embedded in a mandate and general principles. Discretion is guided by an institutional identity that largely meets codes of appropriate behavior and criteria of reason and justice, as understood by the population. Citizens have their values, interests and worldviews accommodated routinely without continuous participation. They are not obsessed with possible misuse of political and administrative powers. Consequently, demands for accountability increase under conditions of normative fragmentation, confusion and contestation, where shared codes of behavior no longer guide behavior and a new order organized around another mobilizing narrative has not emerged.

Principal-agent approaches give most attention to *external* control through opportunity structures, incentives and coercion. Elections, political-administrative hierarchies and institutional checks and balances are the dominant institutional mechanisms. Accountability is achieved by selecting and removing agents with certain characteristics for/from office, hierarchical command, or reciprocal control established through vertical or horizontal separation of power. If incentives are such that the agent's expected utility of complying is greater than not complying, accountability is achieved independent of the motives of actors.

An institution-centered approach attends to how *internalized* identities and role conceptions are formed in accountability processes and elsewhere, supplementing external controls. Accountability processes might facilitate the development of identities, roles and self-restraint through communicative action. Congruence in norms, behavioral codes and expectations might develop through reciprocal discovery of normative validity through deliberation among initially conflicting parties, or through socialization and habitualization. Rather than constraining the autonomy of government and public officials, these processes affect how discretion is used. Democracies do not, however, trust a single mechanism. Actors do not act solely on predetermined personal preferences or the dictates of an institutional role. They are influenced by their interactions with others, in dialogue and struggle. Accountability politics involve interaction between external and internalized controls and because both are imperfect, it is useful to study frictions in all the mechanisms institutions work through to secure human cooperation, problem-solving and accountability (Olsen 2013: 460, 2014: 110).

Principal-agent approaches usually see problems of accountability as caused by agents, not principals. This is an assumption reducing their usefulness, even in routine situations, because accountability problems may be caused by 'forum drift' rather than 'agency drift' (Schillemans and Busuioc 2014). An institution-centered agenda recognizes that democratic accountability is an ideal difficult to realize. Making assumptions about citizens' participation, consent and approval calls for realism regarding citizens' motivation and capacity. There is no guarantee that citizens or their elected representatives will be motivated and capable to live up to the roles prescribed for them as principals. Democratic politics often provide vague compromises, difficult to implement and enforce, and inadequate resources.

Epilogue

Accountability as routine is fairly well understood. It is more problematic to capture democratic accountability in periods with ideological battles over political order and attempts to 'reinvent' government. Democratic *orders* and *institutions* and their distribution of powers and autonomy; democratic *actors* and their relationships and behavioral logics, attention and activity level, are not constant. They vary, and an institutional agenda explores conditions under which accountability processes attract few or many participants and issues, and the role of institutions and citizens in fashioning accountability regimes. The question is relevant not least because it is unclear whether Europe is in a transition period or has reached a new normal. It is not obvious whether the 'sleeping bear' will be sleeping in the decade to come, how angry he will be if he wakes up, and how he will relate to existing accountability institutions and their access structures.

Notes

1 This chapter is a reprint of Olsen (2015). It is reprinted with approval from the editors of *Governance*.
2 The paper is based on a keynote speech at the SOG Conference: *Accountability and welfare state reforms* in Bergen, Norway, 19–20 February 2015. Thanks to Madalina Busuioc, Morten Egeberg, Robert E. Goodin, Åse Gornitzka, James G. March, Margo Meyer, Thomas Schillemans and two anonymous reviewers for comments and help.
3 'Institution' refers to a collection of rules and organized practices, embedded in structures of meaning and resources that are relatively invariant in the face of turnover of individuals and changing external circumstances (March and Olsen 1989, 2006). Rules prescribe codes of appropriate behavior for specific roles in specific situations. Structures of meaning explain, justify and legitimate behavioral rules. Structures of resources create capabilities for acting. Resources are routinely tied to rules, empowering and constraining actors differently and making them more or less capable of acting according to codes of behavior. *Institutionalization* implies: (a) Increasing clarity and agreement about rules. Standardization and formalization of practice reduce uncertainty and conflict concerning who does what, when and how. As some ways of acting are perceived as natural and legitimate, there is less need for using incentives or coercion in order to make people follow prescribed rules. (b) Increasing consensus concerning how behavioral rules are to be explained and justified, with a common vocabulary, expectations and success criteria. There is a decreasing need to explain and justify why modes of action are appropriate. (c) The supply of resources becomes routinized. It takes less effort to obtain the resources required for acting in accordance with prescribed rules. Corollary, deinstitutionalization implies that identities, roles, authority, explanations, justifications and resources become contested. There is increasing uncertainty, disorientation and conflict. New actors are mobilized. There are demands for new explanations and justifications of existing practices. Outcomes are more uncertain, and it is necessary to use more incentives or coercion to make people follow prescribed rules.
4 'Capture' here refers to the *explanatory* power of a principal-agent approach. However, because many public sector reforms are based on principal-agent thinking, these models might be evoked in unsettled periods and in the aftermath of a crisis for criticizing behavior and events (Schillemans 2013).

References

Borowiak, C. T. (2011) *Accountability and Democracy: The Pitfalls and Promise of Popular Control*. Oxford: Oxford University Press.
Bovens, M. (2007) Analysing and assessing accountability: a conceptual framework. *European Law Journal*, 13(4): 447–68.

Bovens, M., Curtin, D. and 't Hart, P. (2010) *The Real World of EU Accountability: What Deficits?* Oxford: Oxford University Press.

Bovens, M., Goodin, R. E. and Schillemans, T. (eds) (2014) *The Oxford Handbook of Public Accountability*. Oxford: Oxford University Press.

Bovens, M., Schillemans, T. and 't Hart, P. (2008) Does public accountability work? *Public Administration*, 86: 225–42.

Brunsson, N. (1989) *The Organization of Hypocrisy*. Chichester: Wiley.

Busuioc, M. (2013) *European Agencies: Law and Practices of Accountability*. Oxford: Oxford University Press.

Busuioc, M., Groenleer, M. and Trondal, J. (2012) *The Agency Phenomenon in the European Union: Emergence, Institutionalisation and Everyday Decision-Making*. Manchester: Manchester University Press.

Carpenter, D. P. (2001) *The Forging of Bureaucratic Autonomy*. Princeton, NJ: Princeton University Press.

Christensen, T. and Lægreid, P. (eds) (2006) *Autonomy and Regulation: Coping with Agencies in the Modern State*. Cheltenham: Edward Elgar.

Cohen, M. D., March, J. G. and Olsen, J. P. (1972) A garbage can model of organizational choice. *Administrative Science Quarterly*, 17: 1–25.

Costa, O., Jabcko, N., Lequesne, C. and Magnett, P. (2003) Introduction: diffuse control mechanisms in the European Union. *Journal of European Public Policy*, 10(5): 666–76.

Crouch, C. (2011) *The Strange Non-Death of Neo-Liberalism*. Cambridge: Polity.

Curtin, D., Mair, P. and Papadopoulos, Y. (2010) Positioning accountability in European governance: an introduction. *West European Politics*, 33(5): 929–45.

Cyert, R. M. and March, J. G. (1963) *A Behavioral Theory of the Firm*. Englewood Cliffs, NJ: Prentice Hall.

Dahlström, C., Peters, B. G. and Pierre, J. (eds) (2011) *Steering from the Centre: Strengthening Political Control in Western Democracies*. Toronto: University of Toronto Press.

Dahrendorf, R. (1988) *The Modern Social Conflict: An Essay on the Politics of Liberty*. London: Weidenfeld & Nicolson.

Dubnick, M. (2005) Accountability and the promise of performance: in search of the mechanisms. *Public Performance and Management Review*, 28(3): 376–417.

Dubnick, M. (2011) Move over Daniel: we need some 'accountability space'. *Administration and Society*, 43(6): 704–16.

Egeberg, M. and Trondal, J. (2011) EU-level agencies: new executive centre formation or vehicles for national control. *Journal of European Public Policy*, 18(6): 868–87.

Flinders, M. (2011) Daring to be a Daniel: the pathology of politicized accountability in monitory democracy. *Administration and Society*, 43(5): 595–619.

Fung, A. (2001) Accountable autonomy: toward empowered deliberation in Chicago schools and policing. *Politics & Society*, 29(1): 73–103.

Gailmard, S. (2014) Accountability and principal-agent theory. In M. Bovens, R. E. Goodin and T. Schillemans (eds), *The Oxford Handbook of Public Accountability*. Oxford: Oxford University Press, pp. 90–105.

Goodin, R. E. (2008) *Innovating Democracy: Democratic Theory and Practice After the Deliberative Turn*. Oxford: Oxford University Press.

Grant, R. W. and Keohane, R. O. (2005) Accountability and abuses of power in world politics. *American Political Science Review*, 99(1): 29–43.

Gustavsson, S., Karlsson, C. and Persson, T. (eds) (2009) *The Illusion of Accountability in the European Union*. London: Routledge.

Habermas, J. (1996) *Between Facts and Norms*. Cambridge, MA: MIT Press.

Hamilton, A., Jay, J. and Madison, J. (1964) [1787] *The Federalist Papers*. New York: Pocket Books.

Hanson, R. L. (1989) Democracy. In T. Ball, J. Farr and R. L. Hanson (eds), *Political Innovation and Conceptual Change*. Cambridge: Cambridge University Press, pp. 68–89.

Harmon, M. M. (1995) *Responsibility as Paradox: A Critique of Rational Discourse on Government*. Thousand Oaks, CA: Sage.

Hood, C. (2014) Accountability and blame-avoidance. In M. Bovens, R. E. Goodin and T. Schillemans (eds), *The Oxford Handbook of Public Accountability*. Oxford: Oxford University Press, pp. 603–16.

Huber, J. and Shipan, C. (2002) *Deliberate Discretion? The Institutional Foundations of Bureaucratic Autonomy*. New York: Cambridge University Press.

Klijn, E. H. and Koppenjan, J. F. M. (2014) Accountable networks. In M. Bovens, R. E. Goodin and T. Schillemans (eds), *The Oxford Handbook of Public Accountability*. Oxford: Oxford University Press, pp. 242–57.

Koppell, G. G. S. (2005) Pathologies of accountability: ICANN and the challenge of 'multiple accountabilities disorder'. *Public Administration Review*, 65(1): 94–108.

Lægreid, P. (2014) Accountability and the New Public Management. In M. Bovens, R. E. Goodin and T. Schillemans (eds), *The Oxford Handbook of Public Accountability*. Oxford: Oxford University Press, pp. 324–38.

Lægreid, P. and Verhoest, K. (2010) *Governance of Public Sector Organizations: Proliferation, Autonomy and Performance*. London: Palgrave Macmillan.

Laffan, B. (2003) Auditing and accountability in the European Union. *Journal of European Public Policy*, 10(5): 762–77.

Lango, P., Lægreid, P. and Rykkja, L. H. (2014) Etter 22. juli. Justis- og beredskapsdepartementets ansvar for samfunnssikkerheten. In A. L. Fimreite, P. Lango, P. Lægreid and L. H. Rykkja (eds), *Organisering av samfunnssikkerhet og krisehåndtering*. 2nd ed. Oslo: Universitetsforlaget, pp. 60–76.

March, J. G. (1987) Ambiguity and accounting: the elusive link between information and decision making. *Accounting, Organizations and Society*, 12: 153–68.

March, J. G. (2010) *The Ambiguities of Experience*. Ithaca, NY: Cornell University Press.

March, J. G. and Olsen, J. P. (1983) Organizing political life: what administrative reorganization tells us about government. *American Political Science Review*, 77: 281–97.

March, J. G. and Olsen, J. P. (1989) *Rediscovering Institutions: The Organizational Basis of Politics*. New York: Free Press.

March, J. G. and Olsen, J. P. (1995) *Democratic Governance*. New York: Free Press.

March, J. G. and Olsen, J. P. (2006) Elaborating the 'New Institutionalism'. In R. A. W. Rhodes, S. Binder and B. Rockman (eds), *The Oxford Handbook of Political Institutions*. Oxford: Oxford University Press, pp. 3–20.

March, J. G. and Simon, H. A. (1958) *Organizations*. New York: Wiley.

Michels, A. and Meijer, A. (2008) Safeguarding public accountability in horizontal government. *Public Management Review*, 10(2): 165–73.

Molander, A., Grimen, H. and Eriksen, E. O. (2012) Professional discretion and accountability in the welfare state. *Journal of Applied Philosophy*, 29(3): 214–30.

Olsen, J. P. (2007) *Europe in Search of Political Order*. Oxford: Oxford University Press.

Olsen, J. P. (2009) Democratic government, institutional autonomy and the dynamics of change. *West European Politics*, 32(3): 439–65.

Olsen, J. P. (2010) *Governing Through Institution Building*. Oxford: Oxford University Press.

Olsen, J. P. (2013) The institutional basis of democratic accountability. *West European Politics*, 36(3): 447–73.

Olsen, J. P. (2014) Accountability and ambiguity. In M. Bovens, R. E. Goodin and T. Schillemans (eds), *The Oxford Handbook of Public Accountability*. Oxford: Oxford University Press, pp. 106–23.

Olsen, J. P. (2015) Democratic order, autonomy, and accountability. *Governance*, 28(4): 425–40.

Papadopoulos, Y. (2010) Accountability and multi-level governance: more accountability, less democracy? *West European Politics*, 33(5): 1030–49.

Pierre, J. (2009) Reinventing governance, reinventing democracy. *Policy & Politics*, 37: 591–609.

Pitkin, H. F. (1972) [1967] *The Concept of Representation*. Berkeley, CA: University of California Press.

Pollitt, C. (2006) Performance management in practice: a comparative study of executive agencies. *Journal of Public Administration Research and Theory*, 16: 25–44.

Romzek, B. (2000) Dynamics of public accountability in the era of reform. *International Review of Administrative Sciences*, 66(1): 21–44.

Rothstein, B. (2011) *The Quality of Government: Corruption, Social Trust and Inequality in International Perspective*. Chicago, IL: University of Chicago Press.

Saint-Martin, D. (2000) *Building the New Managerialist State*. Oxford: Oxford University Press.

Schattschneider, E. E. (1960) *The Semi-Sovereign People*. New York: Holt, Rinehart & Winston.

Schillemans, T. (2013) Moving beyond the clash of interests: on stewardship theory and the relationships between central government departments and public agencies. *Public Management Review*, 15(4): 541–62.

Schillemans, T. and Busuioc, M. (2014) Predicting public sector accountability: from agency drift to forum drift. *Journal of Public Administration Research and Theory*, 25(1): 191–215.

Simon, H. A. (1953) The birth of an organization: the Economic Cooperation Administration. *Public Administration Review*, 13: 227–36.

Simon, H. A. (1957) *Administrative Behavior* (2nd edition). New York: Free Press.

Strøm, K. (2003) Delegation and accountability in parliamentary democracies. *European Journal of Political Research*, 37(3): 261–90.

Strøm, K., Müller, W. C. and Bergman, T. (eds) (2003) *Delegation and Accountability in Parliamentary Democracies*. Oxford: Oxford University Press.

Verhoest, K., Peters, B. G., Bouckaert, G. and Verschuere, B. (2004) The study of organizational autonomy: a conceptual overview. *Public Administration and Development*, 24(2): 101–18.

Vibert, F. (2007) *The Rise of the Unelected: Democracy and the New Separation of Powers*. Cambridge: Cambridge University Press.

Walzer, M. (1984) The resources of American liberalism: liberalism and the art of separation. *Political Theory*, 12: 315–30.

Weber, M. (1970) Politics as a vocation. In H. H. Gerth and C. W. Mills (eds), *From Max Weber*. London: Routledge & Kegan Paul, pp. 7–128.

Weber, M. (1978) *Economy and Society*. G. Roth and C. Wittich (eds). Berkeley, CA: University of California Press.

Wille, A. (2013) *The Normalization of the European Commission: Politics and Bureaucracy in the EU Executive*. Oxford: Oxford University Press.

3
ACCOUNTABILITY, PERFORMANCE AND LEGITIMACY IN THE WELFARE STATE

If accountability is the answer, what was the question?

Werner Jann

Introduction

Accountability is one of the most widely discussed concepts of public administration research and teaching in the last decade. But why is this the case? Obviously, accountability is, like its counterpart transparency, a 'magic concept', and an indispensable part of the prominent and omnipresent discourse on 'good governance', as well as a significant element in debates about public sector reform (Pollitt and Hupe 2011). The same holds true for performance, which has been a magic and contested concept ever since New Public Management (NPM) entered the discourse about 'modern' processes and structures of the public sector. But the third term in the title of this paper, legitimacy, even though it is one of the basic concepts of political science and democracy and is at the heart of Max Weber's theory of bureaucracy, has been surprisingly absent from current debates about the challenges of modern public administration, and for that sake also about the future of the welfare state. In this chapter, I will argue that different concepts of legitimacy lie at the heart of most debates about accountability and performance, and that a better understanding of the relationships between accountability, performance and legitimacy can clarify some of the puzzles of contemporary research.

This chapter builds on recent research on how contemporary public sector reforms have been affecting accountability relationships in modern welfare states. A main focus in this research has been to describe, understand and explain how the balance between organizational autonomy and traditional forms of democratic accountability is changing, and how the trade-offs between political, administrative, managerial, legal, professional and social accountability are affected. What happens with political accountability as welfare states face reforms? Accountability in this kind of research is treated as a mechanism (and not as a virtue) (Bovens 2010), but still mainly as a 'dependent variable', because the aim is both to map and explain the changing nature and content of these mechanisms and their effects (Christensen and Lægreid 2001).

Empirical findings, among others, in labor market, welfare, health and migration policies have offered a wealth of information about changing mechanisms of accountability, the changing role of traditional political accountability, and about the impact of NPM and post-NPM reforms on accountability relationships (Jann and Lægreid 2015; see also contributions in this volume). But accountability, transparency and other magic concepts are not ends in themselves. The questions remain: What are they for, and why are they so popular?

My assertion is that the underlying rationality (i.e. the underlying aim or even 'causal model' of many management reforms), albeit mostly not very clearly expressed and perhaps not even well understood, was to enhance accountability and through that the performance and legitimacy of welfare arrangements. The term legitimacy was seldom used, but the background of many reforms was a growing concern that welfare states are seen as inefficient, do not achieve their objectives, are not sustainable in financial terms, and are therefore losing popular support. All kinds of New Public Management (NPM) inspired reforms were suggested and introduced, granting more autonomy to welfare agencies, transferring responsibilities to public managers, or even introducing some kind of market instruments and competition with private providers. All this so the underlying assumption would create more or 'better' accountability mechanisms, and thus better performance and in the end more support for welfare arrangements and the welfare state. This kind of reasoning was, for example, very prominent in Germany, where NPM reforms were and still are supported by many social democrats and were even proposed and supported by the trade union of the public sector (Jann 1997; Lægreid 2014).

The question is whether these assumptions hold true. In this chapter, I will use changing accountability relationships as the 'independent variable', trying to show whether and how they were supposed to and have influenced performance and legitimacy. In order to do this, I will look briefly and rather schematically into three different relationships (i.e. between accountability and performance, accountability and legitimacy, and performance and legitimacy). I am interested in legitimacy as the ultimate aim of managerial reform and accountability changes and I will try to clarify how these three 'magic concepts' interact, both normatively, theoretically and empirically.

Accountability and performance

The relationship between accountability and performance is supposed to be close. Sometimes performance, accountability and transparency are treated as nearly identical and simply axiomatic, 'a good thing in itself', a virtue (Talbot 2005; Bovens 2010), and as Barbara Romzek (2015: 28) states, 'In its simplest sense accountability is answerability for performance, which, if it is working properly, should result in a reward or a sanction' and 'to do accountability you need performance information; accountability without performance information is a hollow concept'. But for some time both the empirical and theoretical relationships have been widely discussed in the literature and are contested. Even the direction of causality is unclear, some assume accountability enhances performance, while others claim it is the other way around (for summaries, see Pollitt 2011; Lægreid 2014; Christensen and Lægreid 2015; Jantz et al. 2015).

Normatively, this relationship is at the core of the NPM agenda. NPM assumes that new forms of performance management (i.e. output and outcome measurement, contract and result steering, incentives and sanctions) between and in public organizations will enhance the performance of these organizations. Thus, new forms of managerial accountability between principles (e.g. ministers and ministries) and agents (e.g. new forms of public agencies and new types of public managers; i.e. not traditional bureaucrats and bureaucracies) would make these agencies perform better by clarifying organizational goals, diminishing problems of information asymmetries, reducing drift, shirking or whatever undesirable behaviors of agencies or bureaucrats were suspected. This is also the core agenda of principal-agent theory.

The assumed relationship works in two steps. On the one hand, it is presumed that performance reporting and management will make public organizations more accountable and responsive, both to political principles but also ultimately to clients, citizens and the general public (performance enhances accountability). By providing information not only about inputs but also about intended and achieved results (i.e. outputs and outcomes), new forms of evidence and data are generated, which improve and alter the debate between administrative actors and different forums, which are at the core of each accountability relationship (Bovens 2007: 452). At the same time, by providing new and better information, ultimately also positive or negative incentives or sanctions can become better targeted and more successful. Combined with more managerial autonomy, this will give managers and specialized, single purpose agencies clearer goals, more flexibility, more incentives and better instruments to achieve desired results (accountability enhances performance).

Both assumptions are empirically contested and the relationship between accountability and performance is characterized by tensions, ambiguities and contradictions. There is no straightforward coupling between accountability and performance (Christensen and Lægreid 2015). Even friendly observers conclude that:

> the positive effects of performance management on the steering and controlling of public sector organizations and on their performance have been overestimated ... different variants of misuse and several dysfunctional effects of performance measurement exist, for example symbolic use of PIs, negligence of qualitative aspects, misuse of data for personal interests, and so on.
>
> *(van Helden and Reichard 2013: 13)*

Most of the empirical evidence about the problematic and uncertain relationship between accountability and performance can be summarized under the broad and well-known concepts of bounded rationality, opportunistic behavior and unintended consequences.

First, performance measurement and management are confronted with problems of task complexity, contradictory goals and values, and ambiguous causality. It is very often hard to define and measure government performance, and it is even harder to establish clear causalities between management instruments, organizational behavior, and policy outputs and outcomes. At the same time, more managerial accountability may lead to accountability overload or even 'multiple accountabilities disorder' (Koppell 2005), and in the end to opportunistic behavior, to manipulating numbers (hitting the target and missing the goal), gaming, target ratcheting and other forms of opportunistic behavior (Jann and Jantz 2008). The more information is produced, the larger are the incentives to manipulate this kind of information. And finally, there is the unintended effect of what Pollitt (2011) has called the 'tyranny of light'. The more information is produced and processed, the more distrust between actors develops (Flinders 2011).

If the relationship between (managerial) accountability and performance is complex and blurred at best, the question remains: Why are both concepts so popular, and why especially has accountability become such an important concept of public sector reform? Recently, the 'why' and 'what for' of accountability have been addressed from the perspective of 'reputation management' (Busuioc and Lodge 2015). The assertion is that accountability is not about reducing informational asymmetries, reducing drift, shirking or whatever, but it is about managing and cultivating one's reputation vis-à-vis different audiences. It may be more 'path-dependent' and appropriate than consequential. It is about being seen as competent, reliable, fair, performance-oriented, etc. This way, it is possible to explain why 'those supposedly holding to account are not particularly interested in this task, while those supposed to give account do so through distorted information, and/or with motivation-depleting results' (Busuioc and Lodge 2015: 3). Accountability 'serves as a way to justify one's existence and can therefore become central to an organization's . . . sense of identity' (Busuioc and Lodge 2015: 4). In this understanding, reputation is a source of bureaucratic power, allowing organizations to 'strengthen their autonomy, build alliances, enlist political support and ultimately, help ensure their survival' (Busuioc and Lodge 2015: 5).

This definition of reputation comes very close to legitimacy (see also the distinction of technical, moral, procedural and performative competencies, which look very much like Suchman's different forms of legitimacy) (Suchman 1995). The main difference seems to be that reputation can be understood as manipulative or manipulated, it is probably not deserved, it is only about appearing to be successful, reliable, fair and so on, like in the famous quip of Groucho Marx, 'The secret of life is honesty and fair dealing. If you can fake that, you've got it made'.

But this points towards a rather narrow and manipulative concept of accountability and legitimacy. Reputation and legitimacy are seen as something that can be managed like anything else, so in the end this appears to be only a new twist of the managerial revolution, where you do not try to manage performance, but reputation. Obviously, the relationships between accountability and legitimacy are more complex, and also legitimacy is a broader concept than reputation, so in order to understand the problematic relationship between accountability and performance, we have to come to a better understanding of the concept of legitimacy.

Accountability and legitimacy

Opposite to the contested relationship between accountability and performance, the relationship between accountability and legitimacy has not been discussed in great detail (but see March and Olsen 1995: 143ff.; Moes 2009; Rothstein 2012; Olsen 2013; Moore 2014; Olsen 2015). The reason seems to be the very fundamental, complex and comprehensive nature of the legitimacy concept. There are, as mentioned, some 'practitioners' theories' assuming that more accountability will not only lead to better performance, but will also enhance the legitimacy of public decisions, policies, organizations and, in the end, the legitimacy of the modern welfare state, but these are based more on 'intuition' than on systematic theoretical or empirical evidence. Considine and Afzal (2011: 375) suppose that 'those elements of NPM that increase responsiveness, tailoring of services, and efficiency may help drive stronger attachment of citizens and élites to key state institutions'. But at the same time, they also speculate 'those that push services out to contractors who then care little for creating public value and only seek to maximize profits will have the opposite impact on legitimacy'.

In order to clarify this entangled relationship, it is helpful to systematize what is meant by legitimacy, and how different meanings possibly can be operationalized. As with most fundamental concepts in the social sciences, such as democracy, authority or autonomy, legitimacy is a contested concept. But legitimacy is also a central concept in neo-institutional theory and in the most comprehensive survey of the large and diverse literature on organizational legitimacy, the author concludes that 'many researchers employ the term legitimacy, but few define it' (Suchman 1995: 572). In order to overcome this unsatisfactory state of affairs, it makes sense to start from Suchman's broad summary definition of legitimacy as a 'generalized perception or assumption that the actions of an entity are desirable, proper, or appropriate within some socially constructed system of norms, values, beliefs, and definitions' and further distinguish legitimacy as a relationship between an actor or organization and an audience (or forum) based on self-interest (pragmatic), on normative approval (moral), or on taken for grantedness (cognitive) (Suchman 1995: 574; see also Scott 2013).

In addition, it is helpful to introduce a distinction, originally suggested by Fritz Scharpf (1970, 1999) between input and output legitimacy, and its recent extension by Vivien Schmidt towards throughput legitimacy. In this approach, the general definition and distinction of legitimacy builds on Weber (and later Easton), and relates to the extent to which (input) politics, (throughput) processes and (output) policies are acceptable to and accepted by the citizenry, such that citizens voluntarily comply with government acts and decisions, even when these go against their own interests and desires (Scharpf 1999; Schmidt 2013). Finally, it is important to remember that, again following Weber, 'legitimacy is a belief, an empirical phenomenon to be established as other socially relevant subjective phenomena, and not something to be inferred from compliant behavior nor deduced from the presence or absence of its presumable determinants' (Mayntz 2011: 138).

Unfortunately, this broad concept of legitimacy is very hard to operationalize. Concomitant concepts that are often used as proxies are 'trust', in institutions, organizations and persons, or even generalized social trust, 'confidence' in or 'satisfaction' with institutions and actors, or, as mentioned, their 'reputation' (Newton 2001; Christensen and Lægreid 2005; Van de Walle 2013; Greiling 2014). Suchman concludes his survey of the literature with the not very optimistic observation, that researchers currently possess little systematic knowledge and evidence comparing the effects of organizational activities on multiple types of legitimacy, or comparing the effects of multiple types of legitimacy on organizational outcomes. Legitimacy as a concept is not homogeneous, and the different facets of legitimacy are not always compatible (Suchman 1995: 602). This paper cannot solve the complex puzzle of empirical 'measures' for legitimacy, but in order to better understand the composite nature of legitimacy and to point towards possible future research, it makes sense to more clearly distinguish its main characteristics.

Following Scharpf (1999: 7ff.; see also Peters 2013), *input legitimacy* thus refers to the participatory quality of the democratic process leading to government policies, laws and rules as legitimized by the traditional 'majoritarian' institutions of electoral representation. It encompasses the democratic principle of 'rule by the people', meaning that political decisions are derived from the preferences of the population in a chain of accountability, linking those governing to those governed. Democratic legitimacy thus requires mechanisms or procedures to link political decisions and government policies with citizens' preferences. In modern democracies, these mechanisms are mostly reflected in representative institutions in which political decision-makers can be held accountable by the means of elections. The democratic doctrine of the German constitutional court, for example, frames this as the 'uninterrupted chain of legitimacy', from voters via elections, parliaments, governments, ministers, ministries and agencies, to policies and governmental acts. Input legitimacy, as Schmidt stresses, depends on citizens expressing demands institutionally and deliberatively through representative politics while providing support via their sense of identity and community.

But this is not the only form of legitimacy, even in modern democracies. It is accompanied by *output legitimacy* (i.e. the capacity of a government or institution to solve collective problems and to meet the expectations of the governed citizens). 'Output legitimacy requires policies to work effectively while resonating with citizens' interests, values and identity' (Schmidt 2013: 7), or, as Scharpf (1970) argues, democracy would be an 'empty ritual' if the democratic procedure was not able to produce effective outcomes (i.e. 'achieving the goals that citizens collectively care about'). Citizens expect governments to solve collective problems, or at least alleviate them. A system that is exemplarily democratic, meeting the highest participatory standards, but which cannot guarantee acceptable policies, for example levels of safety or social standards, will not be legitimate and will not be able to survive. On the other hand, a system that 'provides the goods' but does not meet at least minimum democratic standards is also not seen as sustainable. This idea of the 'good dictator' is rejected on normative-theoretical grounds, since citizen participation in public affairs is seen as a value in itself, as an indispensable part of human emancipation. It is also rejected on analytical-theoretical grounds, since only open discussions, negotiations and communicative rationality will generate mutual understanding, adaptation and improvement through exchange of reasons and arguments and, in the end, experience-based learning. A core assumption of modern democratic theory is that democracies have a unique ability to learn from experience (Olsen 2013, 2015). This may be contested by the output achievements of countries that hardly meet democratic criteria such as Singapore or China, but also there citizen reactions to policy failures appear to have some influence on governments, but without threatening the domination of the ruling party (Peters 2013: 366).

Vivien Schmidt adds to this the concept of *throughput legitimacy*. Different from the performance-oriented legitimacy of output and the participation-oriented legitimacy of input, throughput legitimacy is process-oriented, and based on the interactions – institutional and constructive – of policymaking actors:

> Throughput, in short, encompasses the myriad ways in which the policy-making processes work both institutionally and constructively to ensure the . . . accountability of those engaged in making the decisions, the transparency of the information and the inclusiveness and openness to 'civil society'. As such, it constitutes a third and distinct criterion in the normative theoretical analysis of democratic legitimacy, alongside output and input.
>
> *(Schmidt 2013: 7)*

Throughput legitimacy, in other words, demands governance processes that are characterized among others by transparency, inclusiveness, openness and fairness. More generally, one could argue that a decision, a policy or an organization possesses legitimacy if it is arrived at or if it is decided in a formal and procedurally correct and accepted fashion (see Weber's legal-rational legitimacy and Luhmann 1983).

The distinction to input and output legitimacy may not always be quite obvious, but in throughput legitimacy it is not (only) the democratic legitimacy of organizations and decisions that counts, but whether rules and expectations of legality, impartiality, financial and legal accuracy, expertise and due process have been followed. This is again closely related to the 'quality of governance' agenda, where bad throughput – consisting of oppressive, incompetent, corrupt or biased governance practices – is seen as the main reason of legitimacy deficits. Bo Rothstein has argued for some time that the ability to control corruption and respect for rule-of-law principles and impartiality are more important in explaining the perception of government's legitimacy than are democratic rights and welfare gains, and that meritocratic bureaucracy and rule of law thus have made a strong comeback (Rothstein and Teorell 2008; Rothstein 2012; Pierre and Rothstein 2013). He even argues that social trust may run from trust in the quality of government institutions responsible for the implementation of public policies to trust in 'most people'. Good public administration is thus a causal factor for high levels of public and generalized trust (Scandinavia as an example).

Procedural rationality, rule of law, fairness, impartiality, reliability and expertise are, as Johan Olsen has argued, the core ingredients of the classical concept of a Weberian bureaucracy (Olsen 2006, 2008). Bureaucrats are servants and guardians of legal and professional rules and a constitutional order, balancing three possibly competing principles, i.e. hierarchy (democracy and politicians as gatekeepers), rules (law and courts as gatekeepers) and expertise (knowledge and professions as gatekeepers). Rationality, and thus (legal-rational) legitimacy, is in this understanding an attribute of organizational structures and the procedures to reach decisions and outcomes, and not of the outcome itself. Schmidt's observation of the rising importance of 'throughput legitimacy' echoes Olsen's reflections on the 'ups and downs', and particularly the strong comeback and 'rediscovery' of bureaucracy. Bureaucracies are, as Olsen stresses, shaper and amplifier of cultural values, identities and standards of behavior, and it is exactly these values and standards that are at the core of throughput legitimacy.

Vivien Schmidt concedes that the different forms of legitimacy are sometimes difficult to disentangle, throughput has sometimes been discussed in output terms, where particular institutional or discursive processes (that is legality or fairness) are seen as preconditions for (or elements of) better output performance, and occasionally in input terms, where (again these) certain institutional processes or deliberative interactions are preconditions for (or again elements of) better input participation (Schmidt 2013: 14), but they are still helpful to understand why there are different forms of accountability, how they relate to different forms of legitimacy and how they interact.

Following from these three forms of legitimacy, we can distinguish three forms of accountability: traditional political and democratic accountability, which mainly follows chains of principal-agent relationship between citizens, politicians and bureaucrats and is concerned with the democratic chain of command; outcome- and output-oriented accountability, which is mainly interested in performance, effective policies and 'value for money' by managers and for citizens, clients and 'customers'; and throughput-oriented accountability, where formal procedures, due process, fairness, expertise and similar values are at the center of attention again.

Exactly these distinctions have been at the core of recent debates about changing accountability regimes. Empirical studies indicate that traditional democratic input legitimacy is losing ground, while non-majoritarian organizations gain legitimacy. An indicator is the rising trust in central banks, courts, ombudsmen and independent regulatory agencies (the 'age of the unelected') (Olsen 2015), while traditional democratic actors, such as parliaments, governments and especially political parties and politicians, are losing acceptance. In nearly all Western democracies, we can observe declining numbers of voters and fewer party members and declining levels of trust towards government. So the overall hypothesis is that we experience declining levels of legitimacy through traditional representative democracy, hierarchy and principal-agent accountability (Peters 2013).

The rising importance of managerial forms of accountability through NPM-oriented reforms towards performance measurement and management are part of this development. They are again closely linked to a rising belief in output legitimacy. The emphasis on the central role of managers, on performance management, and on providing services to 'customers' all tend to depoliticize the processes of governing and to emphasize the production of services rather than the democratic mechanisms for selecting policies (Peters 2013: 368). We have thus a rising suspicion towards traditional forms of democracy and, supported by the diminishing support of old-fashioned social democracy, some evidence that the traditional welfare state is losing support. NPM reforms strengthen and reinforce this belief in output legitimacy and accountability.

But the most striking development in recent years has been the proliferation of other and new forms of accountability, sometimes labeled horizontal or diagonal accountability through audit institutions, administrative and specialized courts, but also professional associations and finally citizen and client organizations, user groups and the general public (Schillemans 2008). Using the concepts of accountability theory, the overall development can be characterized as declining relevance of traditional political and administrative fora, while in most countries legal, financial, professional and social fora become more prominent. At the same time, one can argue that legality, due process, fairness and expertise gain in importance as elements of accountability (i.e. the well-known characteristics of a Weberian bureaucracy). These values never disappeared, but were traditionally supervised and enforced through the processes of political accountability. Recently, all kinds of 'diagonal' and 'horizontal' forms of accountability have been added. All in all, there can be no doubt that it is throughput legitimacy and accountability that have been gaining ground.

It is important to realize that the nature of the internal or external forum, be it political, administrative, legal, professional or social, should not be confused with the nature of the accountability criteria (i.e. politicians, bureaucrats, judges and professionals are interested in input, output and throughput criteria) (Jann and Lægreid 2015). Our empirical studies show that elements of output accountability (concerning performance and results) have become more important in deliberations, but also elements of input accountability (traditional, hierarchical and democratic chains of legitimacy) are still going strong. They have certainly not disappeared. But in all areas, there is also clear evidence that elements of throughput accountability have become evermore imperative.

Accountability does not only mean that actors are judged on their responsiveness to participatory input demands, or that they can be held responsible for the output and outcome of their decisions. Modern accountability is strongly concerned with the quality of these decisions in terms of procedure and due process, and it is in this last dimension where most of the accountability revolution of the last years can be observed, at least in the rising importance of new forums, actors and concerns. It is obvious that the performance-based legitimacy of the 'output' variety is insufficient for legitimization of political systems, that outputs and outcomes also require 'input legitimacy' through democratic participation and control, but both also require procedural throughput legitimacy (i.e. substantive values and principles guiding performance and process that make the performance valued and trusted).

Whether and how accountability does have a strong positive impact on legitimacy is hard to establish. Vivien Schmidt argues that, unlike input politics and output policies, where more of either is at least likely to increase the public's sense of democratic legitimacy, with throughput processes, more of it may have little effect on public perceptions of legitimacy, while less of it in the wake of corruption, incompetence and exclusion may bring down the whole house of cards. Violating throughput legitimacy through insufficient accountability, transparency, inclusiveness or openness can have a major negative impact on public perceptions of legitimacy.

Performance and legitimacy

But what else influences legitimacy? As we have seen, the concept of performance can be slippery and ambiguous. In its recent NPM understanding, it is only concerned with the problem-solving capacity of policies and decisions, with effectiveness, efficiency, citizen satisfaction and value for money (i.e. output and outcome accountability). But the performance of political systems and institutions can also be linked to the democratic quality of decision-making and to elements of legality, fairness, professionalism and expertise. It is thus necessary to try to better understand and conceptualize the relationship between all these forms of performance on legitimacy. In order to do this, it is again helpful to return to institutional theory.

Intuition and reasonable expectations suggest the better the performance of the welfare state and its organizations, the higher its legitimacy. But neo-institutional theory at least suggests other possibilities, especially using the concept of decoupling (Meyer and Rowan 1991). Maybe the relationship is not as close as suspected, and maybe even actors are actively engaged in loosening or obfuscating this relationship. And finally, the relationship could also work the other way: the more legitimate political-administrative systems are, the better their performance.

Suchman suggests a helpful distinction between pragmatic, normative and cognitive legitimacy that resonates with Scott's three pillars of institutional theory (Scott 2013). Pragmatic legitimacy is closely related to the logic of consequentiality (i.e. organizations are judged as legitimate if they perform as promised). Neo-institutional theory suggests that the stronger the technical environment, the greater the need for pragmatic legitimacy (Scott and Meyer 1991). Whenever outputs are somewhat easy to measure or at least to observe (Wilson 1989), organizations' legitimacy will depend on these outputs. But Suchman also suggests that:

> in a world of ambiguous causality, the surest indicator of ongoing commitment to constituent well-being is the organization's willingness to relinquish some measure of authority to the affected audience (to be co-opted, so to speak). Displaying such responsiveness is often more important (and easier) than producing immediate results.
> *(Suchman 1995, with reference to Selznick 1949; Meyer and Rowan 1991)*

This is exactly what we observe concerning the growth of different forms of 'social accountability', engaging clients, customers, user groups and the environment in accountability arrangements at the expense of traditional political accountability, and also as a substitute for difficult or contested managerial performance measurement and management.

Neo-institutional theory is even more helpful in arrangements where the institutional environment is stronger than technical considerations, and here the assumption is the stronger the institutional environment, the greater the need for normative and cognitive legitimacy. This again means that managers are more interested in manipulating symbols and rituals, because that is much easier than to influence performance or 'tangible real outcomes'. And again, this is what we observe in different forms of opportunistic management behavior (gaming and so on), and which is the basis of the new interest in 'reputation management' (Carpenter and Krause 2012).

At the same time, measures of performance may become morally proscribed (consequential legitimacy as rational myths). Public organizations create legitimacy by embracing socially accepted techniques and procedures, most significantly in the absence of clear output and outcome measures and causalities. This is again what we observe in the 'audit revolution' (Powell 1999), and which may be behind the growth of procedural or throughput legitimacy. It is very hard to measure performance and to establish clear causalities, but at least we are following all the procedural rules of performance management. Another similar way of conceptualizing these developments is 'mimetic isomorphism' (DiMaggio and Powell 1983).

Here, not only the procedures, but the structure, of public organizations become important again, most significantly the structure and characteristics of classical bureaucracies.

> Institutionally prescribed structures convey the message that an organization is acting on 'collectively valued purposes in a proper and adequate manner' ... structures, like procedures, serve as easily monitored proxies for less visible targets of evaluation, such as strategies, goals, and outcomes.
> *(Suchman 1995: 581; see also Meyer and Rowan 1991: 50)*

Throughput legitimacy is thus not only procedural, but also structural, and may therefore be a good substitute for simple input and output legitimacy.

Finally, cognitive legitimacy can also play an important role. Even though 'for things to be otherwise being literally unthinkable' is the most slippery of all concepts of legitimacy, taken-for-grantedness represents both the most subtle and the most powerful source of legitimacy. If alternatives become unthinkable, challenges become impossible, and the legitimated entity becomes unassailable by construction. So Suchman advises that at the cognitive level, 'accounts should be simple or even banal, not only explaining organizational behavior, but also making it seem natural and inevitable' (Suchman 1995: 596).

This brief inspection of neo-institutional theory's contributions towards the understanding of the sources of legitimacy can obviously only be very cursory. But it suggests that the importance of output and outcome performance for the institutional legitimacy of public sector organizations, and the public sector in general is probably more limited than usually supposed. Input and especially throughput performance may be more important, or at least easier to modify, influence and manipulate by managers and politicians, and also easier to monitor and evaluate by outside observers or 'fora'.

The relationship between legitimacy and performance may even be reversed; the more legitimate institutions are, the better they can perform their tasks. Bo Rothstein argues in this direction, but also here the evidence is not easily summarized. The obvious observation that in nearly all rankings of 'good governance' those countries that are occupying the top ranks are also scoring highest on measures of democracy and welfare may hint into this direction (Pierre and Rothstein 2013; see also Holmberg and Rothstein 2015 for a discussion of a large number of indicators and their blurred internal relationships).

In the same direction point some results from the 'sustainable governance indicators' (SGIs) of the Bertelsmann Foundation. The SGI tries to measure, with the help of both OECD data and expert assessments, the quality of the policy performance, democracy and governance capacities in all OECD and EU countries (www.sgi-network.org). Not very surprisingly, in all three categories, the Scandinavian countries, as well as Switzerland, New Zealand and Germany, reach top ranks. When we had a closer look at the relationship between the different clusters of indicators (Jann and Seyfried 2009), we found that policy performance showed the strongest relationship not with 'executive capacity' (measured with indicators such as strategic capacity, inter-ministerial coordination, evidence-based instruments and so on), but with 'executive accountability' (measured with data about citizens' participatory competence, the media, and the professional and advisory capacities of intermediary organizations). Also, the status of democracy showed a strong positive relationship with policy performance, but when looking at the indicators in more detail we found that it was particularly the 'rule of law' indicator that explained most of the correlation. All these data are somewhat questionable, as are the significance of some of the correlations, which again are obviously open to different interpretations concerning the directions of causality, but all in all these data hint clearly towards the interpretation that policy performance is strongly dependent on the legitimacy of institutions, and here again mostly on what we have called input and throughput legitimacy, and not the other way round. Strong policy performance is probably much more the consequence of, rather than the reason for, strong legitimacy.

Discussion and conclusion

This chapter started from the reflection that in the widespread discourse about accountability, the aspect of 'why accountability, and for what?' has been somewhat neglected. We know a lot about different fora, forms and foci of changing accountability relationships (Jann and Lægreid 2015), but it is somewhat unclear why the concept has reached this kind of popularity. The answer, this chapter suggests, is the 'missing link' of legitimacy. Or, to rephrase the question in the subtitle, if accountability is seen as the answer to many problems of the contemporary state, the underlying question is about legitimacy. The rising concern for accountability is both a reaction to direct challenges of traditional input and output legitimacy, and to the underlying growth of throughput legitimacy.

Performance may affect output legitimacy through more and better government performance, but this link is very ambiguous, as is the link between accountability and performance. But, on the other hand, more traditional performance criteria, such as due process, fairness, impartiality and expertise, may strongly influence throughput legitimacy. But causality in these relationships is not easily established; a stronger demand for throughput legitimacy may enhance new forms of accountability, and vice versa. So at least for the time being, we are more observing mutually reinforcing processes and coevolution rather than clear causal processes.

In the literature, changing accountability mechanisms and their consequences have usually been related to the advent of NPM-style public sector reforms and their fundamental concern with performance measurement and management, as well as with the obvious difficulties of these reforms and the ongoing move into post-NPM kinds of reforms (Christensen and Lægreid 2013). This chapter argues that the underlying assumptions of principal-agent relationships (and their expectations of opportunistic behavior, economic incentives, close monitoring and so on) play an important role in the popularity of the concept of accountability, but that they are not sufficient to understand the rise and the changing empirical characteristics of the concept. While normative and theoretical arguments, based mainly on principal-agent assumptions, point towards a close relationship or even nearly Siamese-twin concepts (i.e. the more accountability, the better performance), empirical studies observe tensions, ambiguities, contradictions and unintended consequences. There is no straightforward coupling between accountability and performance. Instead, trust and collaboration may be weakened or destroyed through intensive monitoring, and instead of cooperation, compromise and integration, suspicion, confrontation and disintegration of public organization may develop (Olsen 2014: 112). So the appearance of new forms, fora and foci of accountability cannot be explained by their close relationship to performance.

The association between accountability and legitimacy is much less well researched. This has to do with the broad and encompassing concept of legitimacy, which does not lend itself to plain forms of operationalization and management. When distinguishing three main forms of legitimacy, input, output and throughput, it becomes obvious that accountability is concerned with all three of them, though with the help of different processes, organizations and actors. Input legitimacy is at the core of traditional political and hierarchical accountability. The main concern is that democratically elected actors representing the interests of citizens and voters have a direct influence on the actions of public organizations and public managers, and through that on the output and outcome of administrative activities and policies. Output legitimacy, on the other hand, is mainly concerned with the effectiveness, efficiency and 'value for money' of government policies and activities. It is not important whether they are democratically controlled, but whether they solve collective problems and meet the expectations of the governed. This is also the main concern of modern forms of output accountability, through advanced instruments of performance measurement and management.

But the most interesting development is the growing importance of throughput legitimacy, which is mainly concerned with the legitimacy of procedures and structures of public organizations, and the values they confer. It is not mainly the participative quality of public organizations and policies nor their performance that are at the center of attention, but the quality of how these policies have been formulated and especially implemented (i.e. values of legality, due process, fairness, expertise, professionalism and so on). This again relates to the growing prominence of what has been called horizontal or diagonal accountability (i.e. accountability fora and concerns that are not part of traditional hierarchical, democratic accountability, but instead rely on courts, citizen participation, watchdog agencies, independent audit institutions, professions and so on). Also, the recent 'return' of bureaucracy and the values that bureaucratic institutions strengthen and confer belong to these developments.

New forms of accountability, both output- and throughput-oriented, do not replace or supersede established ones, such as democratic accountability, but all of them coexist and sometimes reinforce each other. We observe processes of layering but not of replacement. How strong the impact of new accountability regimes on different forms of legitimacy is, is for the time being hard to establish. We lack sufficient empirical and theoretical studies. But it is highly plausible that the rise of new forms of accountability is strongly influenced by new or renewed legitimacy demands.

Finally, the relationship between performance and legitimacy has to be better understood. Here, we observe that forms of pragmatic legitimacy, stressing direct utility for participants (i.e. outputs and outcomes), are important and are becoming more so, especially in highly technical environments. But at the same time, we know from studies based on institutional theory that processes of decoupling may occur, and normative or cognitive forms of legitimacy may be much more important than pragmatic, consequential ones, especially in highly institutionalized settings. Legitimacy is conferred by appropriate, proper and desirable procedures and structures, or is even 'taken for granted'. Citizens or clients are involved in accountability relationships, are even co-opted, conferring normative legitimacy, and proper procedures and structures are stressed. Again, this is what we have observed in changing accountability arrangements. In the end, the relationship between legitimacy and performance may even be reversed. Strong output and policy performance may be much more the consequence of than the reason for strong legitimacy.

All these observations should help us to understand the recent developments and puzzles of accountability arrangements, and should point to further, better-informed research. But we do not only need more empirical research; we also need more informed theorizing linking different forms, fora and processes of accountability with different forms of legitimacy and performance. It is rather obvious that new forms of governance (i.e. what has been labeled New Public Governance), stressing more and new kinds of actors, a more fragmented public sector, more public-private partnerships, more networks and negotiations, need new forms of legitimacy. This is what we have been observing in the last few years, with the growth first of output, and more recently with the renaissance of throughput legitimacy and the corresponding forms of accountability.

At the same time, we can also observe a comeback of bureaucracy and bureaucratic values of throughput legitimacy, accountability and 'good governance'. But this will certainly not be enough to secure the overall legitimacy of modern political orders, which are 'multi-levelled, multi-centered, hybrid, networked and fluid' (Olsen 2015). So the relationship between changing public organizations and processes, public policies, reforms and their legitimacy, the old concerns of Max Weber, should be more on the forefront of our research and theorizing than they have been in recent years. The old, fundamental questions of our discipline are never solved, but have to be tackled again and again, as the famous Gruk tells us, 'problems worthy of attack, show their worth by hitting back'.

References

Bovens, M. (2007) Analyzing and assessing accountability: a conceptual framework. *European Law Journal*, 13(4): 447–68.

Bovens, M. (2010) Two concepts of accountability: accountability as a virtue and as a mechanism. *West European Politics*, 23(5): 946–67.

Busuioc, M. and Lodge, M. (2015) The reputational basis of public accountability. In *CARR Discussion Paper 78* (May 2015). London: CARR, pp. 1–23.

Carpenter, D. P. and Krause, G. A. (2012) Reputation and public administration. *Public Administration Review*, 72(1): 26–32.

Christensen, T. and Lægreid, P. (2001) New Public Management – undermining political control? In T. Christensen and P. Lægreid (eds), *New Public Management: The Transformation of Ideas and Practice*. Aldershot: Ashgate, pp. 93–119.

Christensen, T. and Lægreid, P. (2005) Trust in government: the relative importance of service satisfaction, political factors and demography. *Public Performance and Management Review*, 28(4): 487–511.

Christensen, T. and Lægreid, P. (2013) Beyond NPM? Some developmental features. In T. Christensen and P. Lægreid (eds), *The Ashgate Research Companion to New Public Management*. Farnham: Ashgate, pp. 391–404.

Christensen, T. and Lægreid, P. (2015) Performance and accountability: a theoretical discussion and an empirical assessment. *Public Organization Review*, 15(2): 207–25.

Considine, M. and Afzal, K. A. (2011) Legitimacy. In M. Bevier (ed.), *The Sage Handbook of Governance*. Los Angeles, CA: Sage, pp. 369–85.

DiMaggio, P. J. and Powell, W. W. (1983) The iron cage revisited: institutional isomorphism and collective rationality in organizational fields. *American Sociological Review*, 48(2): 147–60.

Flinders, M. (2011) Daring to be a Daniel: the pathology of politicized accountability in monitory democracy. *Administration and Society*, 43(5): 595–619.

Greiling, D. (2014) Accountability and trust. In M. Bovens, R. E. Goodin and T. Schillemans (eds), *The Oxford Handbook of Public Accountability*. Oxford: Oxford University Press, pp. 617–31.

Holmberg, S. and Rothstein, B. (2015) Good societies need good leaders on a leash. In C. Dahlström and L. Wängnerud (eds), *Elites, Institutions and the Quality of Government*. Basingstoke: Palgrave Macmillan, pp. 13–32.

Jann, W. (1997) Public management reform in Germany: a revolution without a theory? In W. Kickert (ed.), *Public Management and Administrative Reform in Western Europe*. London: Edward Elgar, pp. 441–60.

Jann, W. and Jantz, B. (2008) A better performance of performance management? In KPMG International (ed.), *Holy Grail or Achievable Quest? International Perspectives on Public Sector Management*. KPMG International, pp. 11–25.

Jann, W. and Seyfried, M. (2009) Does executive governance matter? Executives and policy performance. In Bertelsmann Foundation (ed.), *Sustainable Governance Indicators 2009: Policy Performance and Executive Capacity in the OECD*. Gütersloh: Verlag Bertelsmann Stiftung, pp. 145–86.

Jann, W. and Lægreid, P. (2015) The reform of welfare states: management, accountability, and performance. *International Journal of Public Administration*, 38(13–14): 941–6.

Jantz, B., Christensen, T. and Lægreid, P. (2015) Performance management and accountability: the welfare administration reform in Norway and Germany. *International Journal of Public Administration*, 38(13–14): 947–59.

Koppell, J. G. S. (2005) Pathologies of accountability: ICANN and the challenge of 'multiple accountability disorder'. *Public Administration Review*, 65(1): 94–108.

Luhmann, N. (1983) *Legitimation durch Verfahren*. Frankfurt am Main: Suhrkamp.

Lægreid, P. (2014) Accountability and public management. In M. Bovens, R. E. Goodin and T. Schillemans (eds), *The Oxford Handbook of Public Accountability*. Oxford: Oxford University Press, pp. 324–38.

March, J. G. and Olsen, J. P. (1995) *Democratic Governance*. New York: Free Press.

Mayntz, R. (2011) Legality, legitimacy and compliance. In N. C. Bandelow and S. Hegelich (eds), *Pluralismus-Strategien-Entscheidungen*. Wiesbaden: VS Verlag für Sozialwissenschaften, pp. 138–49.

Meyer, J. W. and Rowan, B. (1991) Institutionalized organizations: formal structure as myth and ceremony. In W. W. Powell and P. J. DiMaggio (eds), *The New Institutionalism in Organizational Analysis*. Chicago, IL: University of Chicago Press, pp. 41–62.

Moes, J. (2009) Accountability – eine Antwort auf Legitimationsprobleme in neuen Governancestrukturen? In S. Botzem *et al.* (eds), *Governance als Prozess*. Baden-Baden: Nomos, pp. 29–54.

Moore, M. (2014) Accountability, legitimacy, and the court of public opinion. In M. Bovens, R. E. Goodin and T. Schillemans (eds), *The Oxford Handbook of Public Accountability*. Oxford: Oxford University Press, pp. 632–46.

Newton, K. (2001) Trust, social capital, civil society, and democracy. *International Political Science Review*, 22(2): 201–14.

Olsen, J. P. (2006) Maybe it's time to rediscover bureaucracy? *Journal of Public Administration Research and Theory*, 16(1): 1–24.

Olsen, J. P. (2008) The ups and downs of bureaucratic organizations. *Annual Review of Political Science*, 11 (June): 13–37.

Olsen, J. P. (2013) The institutional basis for democratic accountability. *West European Politics*, 36(3): 447–73.

Olsen, J. P. (2014) Accountability and ambiguity. In M. Bovens, R. E. Goodin and T. Schillemans (eds), *The Oxford Handbook of Public Accountability*. Oxford: Oxford University Press, pp. 106–23.

Olsen, J. P. (2015) Democratic order, autonomy, and accountability. *Governance: An International Journal of Policy, Administration, and Institutions*, 28(4): 425–40.

Peters, B. G. (2013) Responses to NPM: from input democracy to output democracy. In T. Christensen and P. Lægreid (eds), *The Ashgate Research Companion to New Public Management*. Farnham: Ashgate, pp. 361–74.

Pierre, J. and Rothstein, B. (2013) Reinventing Weber: the role of institutions in creating social trust. In T. Christensen and P. Lægreid (eds), *The Ashgate Research Companion to New Public Management*. Farnham: Ashgate, pp. 405–16.

Pollitt, C. (2011) Performance blight and the tyranny of light? Accountability in advanced performance measurement regimes. In M. J. Dubnick and H. G. Frederickson (eds), *Accountable Governance: Problems and Promises*. New York: M. E. Sharpe, pp. 81–97.

Pollitt, C. and Hupe, P. (2011) Talking about government: the role of magic concepts. *Public Management Review*, 13(5): 641–58.

Powell, M. (1999) *The Audit Society: Rituals of Verification*. Oxford: Oxford University Press.

Romzek, B. S. (2015) Living accountability: hot rhetoric, cool theory, and uneven practice. *PS: Political Science & Politics*, 48(1): 27–34.

Rothstein, B. (2012) Political legitimacy for public administration. In B. G. Peters and J. Pierre (eds), *The Sage Handbook of Public Administration*. Los Angeles, CA: Sage, pp. 407–19.

Rothstein, B. and Teorell, J. (2008) What is quality of government? A theory of impartial political institutions. *Governance*, 21(2): 165–90.

Scharpf, F. W. (1970) *Demokratietheorie zwischen Utopie und Anpassung*. Konstanz: Universitätsverlag.

Scharpf, F. W. (1999) *Governing in Europe: Effective and Democratic?* Oxford: Oxford University Press.

Schillemans, T. (2008) Accountability in the shadow of hierarchy: the horizontal accountability of agencies. *Public Organization Review*, 8(2): 179–95.

Schmidt, V. A. (2013) Democracy and legitimacy in the European Union revisited: input, output and 'throughput'. *Political Studies*, 61(1): 2–22.

Scott, W. R. (2013) *Institutions and Organizations: Ideas, Interests, and Identities*. Thousand Oakes, CA: Sage.

Scott, W. R. and Meyer, J. W. (1991) The organization of societal sectors: propositions and early evidence. In W. W. Powell and P. J. DiMaggio (eds), *The New Institutionalism in Organizational Analysis*. Chicago, IL: University of Chicago Press, pp. 108–40.

Selznick, P. (1949) *TVA and the Grass Roots*. Berkeley, CA: University of California Press.

Suchman, M. C. (1995) Managing legitimacy: strategic and institutional approaches. *The Academy of Management Review*, 20(3): 571–610.

Talbot, C. (2005) Performance management. In C. Pollitt, E. Ferlie and L. E. Lynn (eds), *The Oxford Handbook of Public Management*. Oxford: Oxford University Press, pp. 491–517.

Van de Walle, S. (2013) NPM: restoring the public trust through creating distrust? In T. Christensen and P. Lægreid (eds), *The Ashgate Research Companion to New Public Management*. Farnham: Ashgate, pp. 309–20.

van Helden, G. J. and Reichard, C. (2013) A meta-review of public sector performance management research. *Tékhne*, 11(1): 10–20.

Wilson, J. Q. (1989) *Bureaucracy: What Government Agencies Do and Why They Do It*. New York: Basic Books.

4
COMBINING AGENCY AND STEWARDSHIP
Welfare reforms and accountability

Thomas Schillemans

Introduction

The past decades have witnessed large changes in the advanced welfare states of the Western world. Some of these changes involve substantive policy changes, while in many other respects changes in the welfare state, in essence, surmount to changes in the governance regimes of welfare (Jessop 1999; Bonoli 2005). The reforms in the welfare state have modified the ways in which central governments interact with the agencies delivering welfare services and have led to changes in entitlements, rights and procedures for citizens. Where the 'old' welfare state was very much about delivering social outcomes, or sometimes even about social engineering, as Larsson *et al.* (2012) provocatively put it, the reformed welfare state has adopted a much more procedural and structural focus. Contemporary welfare state policies often center on questions pertaining to the optimal governance of welfare regimes, in which strict responsibility for socially desirable outcomes is no longer the exclusive burden of states and elected politicians (Byrkjeflot *et al.* 2014). This development is fueled by the international retrenchment of the welfare state and ensuing blame games (Pierson 1996).

In the changing landscape of the contemporary welfare state, modern governments need to find ways to steer and coordinate the diverse entities involved in the production of public services *and* to control and hold them effectively accountable (Christensen and Lægreid 2006). In this chapter, we will refer to the *combination* of these activities as 'governing' welfare agencies. Many public sector reforms in the past decades have been inspired, explicitly or implicitly, by agency theory. This has led to proposals for measurable targets, a shift from an acclaimed input to an output focus, to the de-aggregation and specialization of (welfare) agencies and to a more managerial approach in general (Pollitt and Bouckaert 2004). In studies of public sector accountability, the principal-agent framework has also been leading (Schillemans and Busuioc 2015). In response to the practical and intellectual dominance of the rational principal-agent approach, however, critics have looked for alternative paradigms of governance, including the stewardship approach (Davis *et al.* 1997), which is central in this chapter.

Theoretical approaches tend to have hegemonic ambitions and implications. They are easily applied to all cases and exclusively so. However, welfare agencies have various tasks, and some theoretical approaches will be more relevant in some cases and under some circumstances than in others. The empirical 'tests' of stewardship theory underscore this point. In a number of studies where stewardship theory was tested as a viable alternative to agency theory, various researchers had mixed fortunes with mixed results (Dicke and Ott 2002; Van Slyke 2006; Schillemans 2013). This suggests that the optimal governance regime of (welfare) agencies and services will rest on a combination of theoretical approaches, contingent on the task of the organization and its specific task environment.

This chapter develops an analytical perspective on the governance and accountability of welfare agencies that combines elements from agency theory with elements from stewardship theory. The chapter starts out with an introduction to both theoretical approaches and commences to describe the ideal typical governance regimes of welfare agencies according to these two approaches. The chapter then proceeds to analyze how the accountability of welfare agencies can be theoretically analyzed. The analysis focuses on variance between healthcare, welfare and immigration. Together, our analyses will sketch a mixed and complex picture, opening up avenues for finding the right mix of tools with which accountability can be organized appropriately in the disaggregated contemporary welfare state.

Agency theory and stewardship theory

Agency theory and stewardship theory are both *institutional* theories focusing on how behavior and choice in organizations are predicated on institutional contexts. Agency theory provides a 'flexible framework for modelling innumerable variations in institutional arrangements' in order to understand how they induce 'desirable behaviour by agents' (Gailmard 2014: 90). Stewardship theory is similarly rooted in an institutional framework and is related to other institutional approaches to accountability. Here, institutions shape the behaviors of participants and accountability mechanisms and practices may be institutionalized themselves (Olsen 2014: 109).

From this common institutional basis, both theoretical approaches develop deliberately *contrasting* ideas of relationships in government and in organizations. Agency theory is modeled on an economic perspective of the behavior of persons and organizational units, and is in essence based on the idea of a purchaser and a provider of a service (Waterman and Meier 1998: 174). Agency theory has been developed in order to open up the black box of organizations (Jensen and Meckling 1976: 306). Participants in often-dyadic relationships are assumed to be rational, self-centred utility-maximizers tied together in contractual relationships. As a consequence, agency theory rests on the inevitable, or at the very least the permanently latent, 'clash of interests' (Schillemans 2013) between principals and agents (Shapiro 2005; Gailmard 2014).

Stewardship theory, on the other hand, is very much a psychological and sociological critique of the dominant approach, aiming to offer richer assumptions of human behavior (Davis *et al.* 1997: 20). Stewardship theory focuses on situations where agents are motivated by prosocial goals, which can be embedded in organizations, in professions or in professional fields. Where agency theory starts out from conflicting interests, and seeks to find ways to mitigate those interests, stewardship theory starts out from assumptions of continuous or aligned interests between participants where stewards aim to serve the interests of their principals (Davis *et al.* 1997: 24). The 'steward essentially wants to do a good job, to be a good steward of the corporate assets' (Donaldson and Davis 1991: 51; see also Block 1993).

From their contrasting first principles, both theories construe radically different governance models for one's agents – or stewards – in the welfare state. Agency theory would define the job of governing welfare agencies as one of exercising sufficient and efficient control (White 1985). As welfare agencies, as all other agencies, are understood to be rational and self-centred, and as their relationship is spawned by information asymmetries, central governments as principals need to find ways to keep their potentially obstinate welfare agents in check. Principals have reason to be concerned about how their agents use their discretionary powers. Through the lens of agency theory, principals may fear to suffer from classical ills such as hidden action, hidden knowledge, adverse selection and moral hazard. This fear has a rational basis as agents are known to exploit the advantages they reap from superior knowledge and expertise (Posner 2002).

Stewardship theory, on the other hand, aims to gauge the conditions under which stewardship can flourish. Assuming that welfare agencies are intrinsically motivated to do a good job, stewardship theory seeks to identify and create a governance model in which they can do so optimally. Stewardship theory has accordingly been used to analyze processes, behaviors and results in organizations where it seems far-fetched and hard to assume strictly goal-oriented and selfish rational behaviors by individuals. One illustrative area of application is the family firm. In family firms, 'private' values such as trust, self-realization and improving performance are mingled with 'public' values such as making a profit and career development. For many participants in family businesses, the quality of mutual relationships, the stability of the organization over time and the interests of other, even unborn, generations may bear upon individual choices. In these settings, stewardship theory is found to be a viable alternative or complement to agency theory (Vallejo 2009). More in general, the theory is said to be principally applicable to situations where agents can be expected to be motivated by prosocial motivations.

The centrality of motivation

The most fundamental distinction between both theories lies in their conceptions of human (and organizational) motivation. Agency theory is based on economic theories, assuming largely individualist human and organizational behaviors where extrinsic motivation is the prime stimulant. Stewardship theory, on the other hand, is based on psychological and sociological analyses of human behavior and assumes that intrinsic motivation *and* collectivism suffice to explain behaviors (Van Puyvelde *et al.* 2012: 437). Stewards are agents who are motivated by some of the 'higher' values, such as personal growth, altruism and also a sense of belonging and self-realization (Davis *et al.* 1997). The ideal-typical intrinsic motivation of stewards contrasts with the extrinsic motivation assumed by agency theory.

Particularly in nonprofit and welfare settings, the relevance of collectivism – or the logic of appropriateness – and the genuine desire to serve social or societal goals are important (Kluvers and Tippett 2011: 278). These notions concur with the currently booming literature on public service motivation (Vandenabeele 2008).

Once we understand the behavior of welfare agencies in terms of intrinsic motivation, this leads to a redefinition of their relationship with central government as its principal. To begin with, it suggests that both parties will to some extent have overlapping or aligned interests (Donaldson and Davis 1991; Van Slyke 2006). This fundamentally dampens the assumed tensions between central government and its welfare agencies. The same point has been made by some authors using agency theory, who have stressed that the interests of organizations in the public sector are relatively, rather than principally, conflicting (Waterman and Meier 1998).

Furthermore, once we understand principals and agencies as contributors to the same cause, this also tweaks their relationship. Agency theory assumes a strictly hierarchical relationship, where the principal needs to find ways to guard his interests and to exert optimal control of agents. The principal also draws on an institutional power base that supports this asymmetric and hierarchical relationship. Stewardship theory, on the other hand, conceives of a much more symmetrical and less hierarchical relationship (Davis *et al.* 1997). In these settings, a low power distance, combined with a personal style of leadership and close and frequent informal contacts, is beneficial. This helps to tie both parties together and reinforces their joint commitment to the same values and cause. Conversely, once principals resort to their institutional power base and use extrinsic motivation, this also distances agencies from them. Empirical evidence suggests that increased extrinsic rewards in the public sector will drive out some of the intrinsic motivation of employees (Georgellis *et al.* 2010).

From contrast to composition

There can be no doubt that professionals and managers in the welfare sector operate on the basis of potent doses of intrinsic motivation. In addition, human capital and personal efforts are crucially important for some services, for instance in healthcare and education. However, it would be utterly naive to fully disregard the relevance and importance of self-interest and extrinsic motivations in these settings as well. Public sector managers and professionals are neither angels nor wholly altruistic stewards. It is more realistic to assume a combination of self-centered *and* prosocial, of intrinsic *and* extrinsic, motivations among persons and organizations operating in the welfare sector. This means that *both* theoretical perspectives have some relevance and this calls for a combination of approaches. The combination of theoretical approaches is possible, as the theories are so closely related. Stewardship theory is developed as a critique of basic models of agency theory and has been coined a 'limiting' case of agency theory where preferences are aligned (Caers *et al.* 2006: 42) but also as an 'addition' (Brennan and Solomon 2008), as well as the 'other end of a continuum' (Kluvers and Tippett 2011: 278; see also Schillemans 2013).

Existing empirical studies of stewardship theory in public administration settings strongly support the idea that agency and stewardship are best seen as extremes on a continuum. A number of researchers have tested stewardship theory as a viable alternative to agency theory, particularly in government agency/third-sector organization settings, but, we presume to the slight disappointment and annoyance of some of the researchers involved, the theory did not fully 'fit the bill' (Dicke 2002; see also Van Slyke 2007; Schillemans 2013).

In private sector studies using stewardship theory, board composition, board structure and organizational ownership are generally used as indicators of 'stewardship' (Van den Berghe and Levrau 2004: 463; Dulewicz and Herbert 2004). These indicators are rather blunt. They are based on specific assumptions of the behaviors of board members and they also significantly reduce the complexity of the theory to a single crude, possibly strong but nevertheless reductionist, indicator. In this chapter, we suggest a much broader operationalization. It takes the existing governance regime between government departments and welfare agencies as its point of departure. The governance of agencies is conceived of as a set of six tasks. When public tasks are delegated to agencies, government departments perform (at least) these six different tasks, both ex ante and ex post (Woods and Baranowski 2002; Schillemans 2013). Government departments need to: (1) select an agency (who is going to do the job?); (2) engage in relationship management; (3) transmit their preferences; and (4) stipulate additional due procedures in their contracts. Ex post measures include: (5) monitoring requirements; and (6) incentives (how will the agency be rewarded?). Accountability is at the core of this model, as it is a 'relational concept' (tasks 1–2), and is about legitimate expectations (tasks 3–4) and potential sanctions (tasks 5–6).

Agency theory and stewardship theory stipulate quite different ways in which these six governance tasks should be fulfilled. We discuss each of them in turn and will develop the extreme positions on the continuum between agency and stewardship, being fully aware of the subtleties and many variants of agency theory 'in the middle' (Gailmard 2014). As the objective of this chapter is to find the 'optimum' between both extremes, however, it is necessary to develop those extreme theoretical positions first.

'Governance' in six contrasting propositions

1. Selection

The crucial first analytical step refers to the 'to whom' question (Bendor *et al.* 2001). Which steward or agent is most suitable for the job, or, in words favored by agency theorists, what selection of agents does not suffer (or suffers the least) from the disadvantages of adverse selection and moral hazard? The selection process in the market serves as the ideal in agency theory. Selection is ideally competitive – there are many potential agents flaunting their stuff – and short-lived: contracts should be renewed, renegotiated and retendered after some time. Competition serves to motivate agents to provide optimal value for money and to stimulate their creativity in terms of efficiency, effectiveness and innovation. The constrained time frame serves to keep everybody on their toes and necessitates periodic re-actualization of services. The selection process, then, is also very much a game in which the conflicting interests between principal and agent are articulated, matched and ultimately aligned during negotiations.

Stewardship theory, on the other hand, would suggest a rather different type of selection process. Selection here is not about the quest for the optimal performer, but is the quest for a steward whose interests and goals are most optimally aligned, perhaps even congruent, with the specific task at hand. Principal and steward do not confront each other on the basis of conflicting interests; their goals and interests are, in essence, the same. The task of the principal is simply, although this is by no means simple at all, to find the steward with maximally consonant interests and goals.

2. Relationship management

Relationship management can be seen as one of the bonding costs associated with contracting and delegation (Jensen and Meckling 1976). In agency theory, the formal aspects of this bonding process assume center stage. As the rules of the game are highly formalized in targets, reporting requirements and retendering procedures, relationship management is organized along those same lines and formalized moments of interaction. In its most extreme form, informal contact is not necessary. Stewardship theory, on the other hand, presupposes a low power distance and social and physical nearness between principal and steward (Davis *et al.* 1997). Both parties interact on a relatively equal basis and use informal meetings to align their actions and insights to each other.

3. Preferences

Once the agent or steward – the appropriate welfare agency, in this chapter – has been selected, the principal needs to specify his or her preferences in terms of desired outputs or outcomes. As 'slack' (Shapiro 2005), 'shirking and sabotage' (Brehm and Gates 1999) are reasonable expectations of the behavior of rational and self-centered agents, it is necessary to specify one's preferences in clear-cut targets and relevant bottom lines. This is quite different for principals and stewards who in essence share the same goals and preferences. Their interaction should be characterized by a low power distance (Davis *et al.* 1997) and they should conjointly participate in the development and operationalization of relevant preferences and expectations.

4. Procedures

Following the same logic guided by the apprehension of adverse selection, principals also need to stipulate in detail what additional procedural rules agents are expected to comply with. These additional procedures relate to the allocation of inputs and internal processes and constraints. It is theoretically possible for principals not to define additional procedural requirements at all, if they don't care how targets are met or against what costs and externalities, as is done for James Bond ('a license to kill'). However, particularly in administrative settings, there are generally many additional requirements in terms of due process and legality that need to be taken into account. Agency theory would summon government departments to specify all those important additional procedural requirements up front. Stewardship theory, on the other hand, does not depart from a control-and-comply approach, but rather utilizes forms of self-management within specified boundaries. The principal will provide a few important and generically formulated procedural constraints and will further leave it to the steward to pursue his or her own course of action. The principal will expect and trust the steward to manage these him or herself, but may engage in meta-governance in the sense of inquiring about the methods and results of self-government by the welfare agency.

5. Monitoring

The agency theory perspective on monitoring could be summarized in the well-known adage: 'In God we trust; all others we audit'. It is a natural companion to the points made above: if agents have valid reasons to underperform or shirk, and when principals are troubled by hidden information and hidden action, it is only natural to demand extensive and precise monitoring information relating to the realization of stipulated preferences, as well as to relevant procedures. Direct forms of monitoring and intervention are usually quite effective but also very expensive as they require profound investments in monitoring (McCubbins *et al.* 1987: 252). Stewardship theory, on the other hand, suggests a more relaxed and hands-off strategy: as long as the steward ascertains that he or she is in control, monitoring provisions can be leaner. There is less need for active accountability, then.

6. Incentives

Assuming that agents are self-centered and rational, financial rewards are the most logical and effective incentives available. Financial incentives are easy to understand, relatively easy to administer and they speak directly to parties requiring extrinsic means of motivation in order to perform. The use of direct financial rewards such as bonuses is generally not possible in public sector settings. A potentially powerful substitute for agencies would be the accumulation and widening of their tasks. Receiving a new task – and thus more turf, resources and a higher place in the bureaucratic pecking order – could be seen as a rational and material reward for high-performance welfare agencies. In stewardship theory, on the other hand, incentives should be aligned with the higher-order values in Maslow's pyramid, such as self-realization, verbal praise and development. Assuming that a steward is intrinsically motivated to do a good job – as has also been described in the literature on professionals and public service motivation – there can be no better incentive than being empowered to realize one's goal and to receive recognition for this honorable feat.

Sum

The differences between agency and stewardship theory are closely related to the distinction made by March and Olsen (1989) between aggregative and integrative institutions. They describe that contractual relations, as advocated by agency theory, are aggregative. The behavior of agents in aggregative institutions is guided by their desire to acquire personal, often material, gains and the institutions function by aggregating individually appreciated outcomes. Integrative institutions, on the other hand, are more normatively connected and express norms of appropriateness. Participation in integrative institutions is based on shared goals, norms and understandings. There is a normative dimension here, and ideas are important, as well as forms of collective action and shared identities. Stewardship theory is clearly connected to this approach.

The binary oppositions developed above are summarized in Table 4.1 on the following page. Taken together, these six binary oppositions suggest a sort of equalizer, where government departments and welfare agencies can conjointly find the optimum mix of agency and stewardship characteristics in order to govern their relationship. The table also reveals how the six constitutive tasks are elements of the accountability relationship between governments and welfare agencies.

The theoretical oppositions serve as an analytical device that can be used to analyze and problematize accountability and governance in the welfare sector. In order to demonstrate its use, and the types of insight such an analysis might yield, we will apply this analytical device in the next paragraph in an analysis of developments in three distinctive welfare services: healthcare, welfare and immigration.

Welfare between agency and stewardship

Healthcare, welfare services and immigration belong to the most important, and most contested, services in the welfare state. In recent years, as this book aptly demonstrates, there have been many changes in the governance of these welfare services, with profound relevance for accountability. How do they rank on the axis between agency and stewardship?

When we look from a distance at these cases, it is important to note that there are some salient commonalities and differences between the three fields. What is characteristic of all three cases is their high political salience. In all Western countries, healthcare, welfare and immigration are consistently seen as some of the most precarious and important issues on the political agenda (Pierson 1996). What is more, political debates on these issues tend to be set in traditional left-right schemata. Political struggles over welfare have centered since the 1980s on the fight against the perceived 'over-demand' for healthcare services, state benefits and access for immigrants. The perceived over-demand in all of these areas has been pushed, apart from policies, by powerful exogenous factors. The ageing of the population and breakthroughs in medical technology have been important drivers for the rise in healthcare costs. Globalization in its many forms (Scharpf 2000) and shocks relating to (civil) war and economic crises, have in a similar way been important for the waves of immigration and unemployment.

In addition, and in relation, to these substantive challenges, the governance of these policy fields have witnessed profound changes. In most countries, welfare services were traditionally provided by state agencies, or at least by organizations with close ties to the state. This made it relatively easy to identify the policies and politicians responsible for welfare services and specific

Table 4.1 Two modes of governance and accountability

Dimensions of accountability	'Task'	Agency theory	Stewardship theory
Relational dimension	Selection	Selection is competitive, renewable, open. Interests are aligned as a consequence of the bidding and selection process.	Selection is based on matching interests and intrinsic motivation, often on a long-term basis.
	Relationship management	Relationships are formalized and formal meetings are most important.	There are many informal meetings where participants operate on the basis of maximal equivalence.
Standards	Preferences	Substantive preferences are articulated in predefined performance indicators.	Preferences are defined in terms of underlying values and operationalized conjointly by the two parties.
	Procedures	The principal registers in detail in what ways and within what boundary conditions a task needs to be performed.	The steward has substantial discretion in deciding how tasks are performed through self-management.
Information phase	Monitoring	The agency reports in detail to the parent department, so that it can verify exactly what has been done in practice.	The parent department entrusts the agency to ascertain that its services are of a high quality.
Sanctions phase	Incentives	Good performance is rewarded materially, with financial rewards or a widened portfolio of tasks. Low performance is sanctioned and leads to the loss of an assignment.	Good performance is rewarded with non-financial rewards, such as status, verbal praise and more autonomy. Low performance leads to the hunt for causes and ideally to learning processes.

failures. In recent transformations of welfare policies, however, responsibilities and allocations of tasks have become more complex, even if there have been ambitions to simplify.

Beyond the commonalities, there are at least two important differences between the three areas of the welfare state discussed here. The first relates to money: welfare and healthcare belong (with education) to the largest areas of social spending in welfare states. There has been tremendous pressure on all politicians and bureaucrats involved in these fields to cut the levels of spending, knowing that the welfare state is still a major source of political support (Pierson 1996). Immigration stands out in this respect. Although the number of immigrants has become a major topic for political contestation, certainly in 2015, the direct actual costs of immigration policies are much less disputed and are easily dwarfed by the levels of spending on healthcare and welfare. A second important distinction relates to the professional habitus of key operational officials. Healthcare is the domain of highly skilled and intrinsically motivated professionals (Freidson 2001). Highly skilled professionals often work on the basis of high levels of intrinsic motivation constitutive of stewardship theory. For the other two services, the picture is more mixed. To some extent, welfare, and particularly immigration, attract employees who are motivated to help others. They all work in, as Vandenabeele (2008) puts it, 'High-Publicness Organizations'. On the other hand, however, a large part of the operational work is of an administrative nature and it is performed by comparatively much lower-educated employees. This may mean that their intrinsic motivation can be less pronounced and that agency theory would be relatively more applicable.

Welfare: the classic case for agency theory?

At face value, welfare would seem to be the classical case for the application of agency theory. The financial stakes are towering, concerns about moral hazard and adverse selection are widespread, and at least in part warranted. This would logically call for the type of control-oriented governance and accountability that is the state of the art in agency theory. Analysis of important trends in welfare services by and large support this assumption, although there are some important exceptions and counter-trends.

To start with the *selection* of welfare agencies. In most countries, welfare services and benefits have traditionally been delivered by state agencies at either the national or the local level. In the past years of government reform, this has mostly remained the same. What *has* changed, however, was that many of those agencies were granted more autonomy in many countries when they were disaggregated from central government departments and reformed into quangos (Pollitt and Bouckaert 2004). This opened up the opportunity to govern these agencies with the toolkit developed by agency theory. In some countries, their mutual relations have evolved into a formal bidding process. It has been possible to develop specific policy targets and formal contracts. In some countries, forms of competitive tendering have been introduced where government agencies need to compete with other organizations for contracts. This all underscores the relevance of the agency perspective for the governance and accountability of many welfare services.

Furthermore, the welfare sector is renowned for its meticulous level of regulation. The preferences of the ministry as a principal and the procedures that need to be taken into account all concur with the traditional perspective of agency theory. And even stronger, many recent attempts to improve welfare services supposedly lead to increased levels of red tape (Considine, O'Sullivan and Nguyen 2014: 472). In conjunction with this, the level of monitoring is generally perceived to be quite high. Operations in welfare services often come with high registration and documentation demands. Special monitory capabilities have been built up. Schillemans (2007: 131) provides a telling example: the major Dutch welfare agencies were the subject of 27 reports by a specialized monitoring agency in the first eight months of 2006 only. This all suggests that the patterns of accountability in welfare services change over time.

However, the past years have also witnessed some reforms that are more in line with stewardship theory. One important example is that in some countries, such as Australia and the US, the government has actively encouraged nonprofit organizations to step up and to provide some of the welfare services. As third-sector organizations are driven by altruistic ideals and values, they are supposed – and often found – to be more innovative in their operations and to have greater commitment to their clients (Kelly 2007). Third-sector organizations are more strongly intrinsically motivated. Another example where the agency perspective does not fully hold is in incentives. Welfare organizations in most countries do not win bonuses, promotions or other material rewards when they do a good job. Most models of governance seem to assume a Weberian zeal and reliability in the welfare sector and relatively little has been made of positive rewards to stimulate those involved.

Immigration: the in-between?

The immigration case is, with a slight quip to the substantive nature of the issue, in-between things. Given the lower financial pressures on immigration and the much lower numbers of clients (even in 2015), the pressures on immigration are at least somewhat different from those in welfare. As in welfare, government services combine a selection function (who is allowed a residence permit?) with a development function (helping people to find their way into the new society). The former presupposes a distanced and unbiased role for government officials in line with agency theory, while the second presupposes a warmer and closer connection between the officials and the recipients of services, in line with stewardship theory. However, where these processes are directly linked, and potentially conflictual in welfare, it is much easier in immigration policies to keep the selection and the development function separated. All of this suggests that control can be easier and less demanding in immigration than in welfare.

Developments in the last years do show some similarities with welfare. To begin with, the immigration agencies in various countries have also been subjected to processes of disaggregation, opening up opportunities for external control, rewards and accountability from the center. What has been striking to see is that politicians have often opted to isolate the difficult decisions relating to admission to bureaucracies. This has been diagnosed as a case of blame avoidance (Christensen and Lægreid 2009). And, as in welfare, immigration policy is ruled by comprehensive and expansive sets of rules and regulations. Doing a proper job means, for immigration officials, to work according to highly detailed rules and procedures. This is also striking about this particular type of service – it is a procedural service much more than a substantive service. It is about applying the rules of access in a proper way, not about reaching specified social welfare goals. This is also at stake when we look at the preferences of principals. Even though they may be quite different substantively, the core ideas are often very similar in most Western countries. It is about regulating the streams of immigrants in a strict – if not outright *restrictive* – but fair way. In the background, the political debate focuses to a large degree on the numbers of immigrants, from which the agencies can only deduct that reducing the numbers is their real bottom line.

On the ground, however, there is generally much leeway for professionals *and* volunteers as the street-level bureaucrats in welfare. Governments demand much less monitoring information, demand much less accountability, from immigration than from welfare agencies. This means that there is operational room for a clearer stewardship approach. Professionals, employees and volunteers can use some space to help immigrants orient themselves in their new countries and to find a good way to settle in.

In immigration, thus, one can see that agency and steward theory are combined in different ways for the selection and the developmental dimensions of the policy.

Healthcare: professional organizations and stewards?

Healthcare would theoretically be the typical case for the adoption of stewardship theory. The important work in healthcare is performed by highly skilled professionals with strong intrinsic motivations. Working in healthcare is considered to be a 'call' by a notable number of healthcare professionals (Freidson 2001). Furthermore, healthcare distinguishes itself from the other two cases because the crucial service decisions are not about the application of some rule, but are medical decisions, governed by professional rules, norms and understandings. In addition, healthcare professionals operate with substantial autonomy, not only from the government, but also from the managers in their 'professional organizations' (Scott 1965). All of this suggests that stewardship theory would be the ticket to ride in the governance of healthcare.

The traditional structural setup of the sector supports this point. Government regulations used to provide for healthcare services, leaving it to professionals and healthcare organizations to decide and carve out exactly how and when these services were delivered. Furthermore, as noted, the core professionals are not politically dependent bureaucrats, and in many jurisdictions healthcare services are also delivered by private organizations. It would be hard to envisage a private immigration service but that is quite different for healthcare, also because not all forms of healthcare are incorporated in public healthcare provisions. In terms of the selection of agents, thus, and in the formulation of preferences, the case of healthcare clearly stands on the stewardship extreme of our dichotomy.

The picture, however, changes dramatically once we shift our focus to monitoring and the regulation of procedures. On this dimension, many recent trends, spawned by financial scarcity, are more in line with agency theory. Monitoring requirements have been growing, both internally and externally, and healthcare organizations are more and more expected to be cost-sensitive and to help reduce costs (Berwick *et al.* 2008). In line with this, there has grown a considerable concern and academic literature on the rising tensions between managers and professionals in healthcare (and other professions). In many countries, targets have been introduced in the healthcare sector as a means of accountability and preference transmission. And those targets typically solicit strategic responses (Bevan and Hood 2006). The healthcare sector is thus driven by steadily increasing costs, moving more towards the agency end of our continuum where it relates to (financial) accountability. This creates important tensions on the operational level, where professional decisions in line with stewardship collide with managerial control systems aligned to agency theory.

Conclusion and discussion

This chapter has developed two ideal-typical and contrasting approaches to the governance and accountability of welfare agencies. Welfare organizations are highly complex organizations, with a variety of tasks and embedded in complex value-laden settings. The appropriate governance of various aspects of their behavior, with different types of risks and also motivations, may mean that different types of accountability are necessary. The analytical perspectives developed in this chapter are helpful both for analyzing *and* improving the governance and accountability of welfare.

Our analysis in this chapter suggests that elements from both theoretical perspectives can be found in the three policy fields, both within and across those fields. There are some clear commonalities between the cases. Accountability pressures have gone up in all three fields, due to increased reporting and monitoring requirements, the specification of performance targets, and also because of a greater reliance on third parties. Contracting relationships with providers are clearly modeled on the economistic premises of agency theory. Simultaneously, however, governments also call on third-sector organizations and sometimes volunteers in welfare services, assuming that their intrinsic motivation will improve the quality of services, as suggested by stewardship theory.

The analysis also suggests that the combination of approaches can sometimes be beneficial, as potentially in the case of immigration, yet can also be a source of frustration and tension, for instance in the case of healthcare services. The application and potential integration of elements from both models seem to be dependent on a number of structural preconditions. The nature of the operational task, along with the identity of the 'operator', is a first important precondition. Agency theory is better suited for administrative and precise tasks delivered by agents who are stimulated to comply with guidelines and predetermined targets. Stewardship theory, on the other hand, is more suited for complex and professional tasks with more qualitative or ambiguous goals.

Historical legacies are a second precondition. Patterns and behaviors of accountability develop over time and become institutionalized in specific forms in specific fields (Olsen 2014). Fields may lean more towards one or other extreme of the continuum, simply for historical reasons. A third structural precondition is dimension of a task that is most politically salient. When concerns about efficiency and cutback management prevail, or, in more theoretical terms, when principals are concerned about slack and agency costs, the remedies from agency theory will quite naturally come forward. When, however, the quality and tailoring of services is crucial, stewardship theory is more suitable.

Agency and stewardship theory are both *institutional* theories (Davis et al. 1997; Gailmard 2014), explaining behaviors from institutional settings. They rest, however, on radically different assumptions of the motivations of individuals and organizations. This suggests in the end that the application of both models needs to be consistent with the 'type' of agent or steward offering a service, or more precisely the specific task at hand. The remedies from agency theory can help to cut or control excessive costs; the remedies from stewardship theory can help intrinsically motivated welfare agencies to perform optimally. This, however, should not only be a reflection of the status quo. Accountability can also help to transform the existing order (Olsen 2016). By introducing specific accountability measures, governments 'signal' to welfare agencies that they are seen as self-serving rational agents *or* intrinsically motivated stewards. This will, to some extent, transform their behaviors and they will move toward the expectations from the adopted approach. If welfare agencies are held accountable along the lines of agency theory, they will behave more and more as rational agents. This is a final consideration to be taken into account: What are the long-term effects of specific measures on the motivation, and thus behaviors, of welfare agencies?

References

Bendor, J., Glazer, A. and Hammond, T. (2001) Theories of delegation. *Annual Review of Political Science*, 4: 235–69.

Berwick, D. M., Nolan, T. W. and Whittington, J. (2008) The triple aim: care, health, and cost. *Health Affairs*, 27(3): 759–69.

Bevan, G. and Hood, C. (2006) What's measured is what matters: targets and gaming in the English public health care system. *Public Administration*, 84(3): 517–38.
Block, P. (1993) *Stewardship: Choosing Service over Self-Interest*. San Francisco, CA: Berrett-Koehler.
Bonoli, G. (2005) The politics of the new social policies: providing coverage against new social risks in mature welfare states. *Policy & Politics*, 33(3): 431–49.
Brehm, J. and Gates, S. (1999) *Working, Shirking, and Sabotage: Bureaucratic Response to a Democratic Public*. Ann Arbor, MI: University of Michigan Press.
Brennan, N. M. and Solomon, J. (2008) Corporate governance, accountability and mechanisms of accountability: an overview. *Accounting, Auditing & Accountability Journal*, 21(7): 885–906.
Byrkjeflot, H., Christensen, T. and Lægreid, P. (2014) The many faces of accountability: comparing reforms in welfare, hospitals and migration. *Scandinavian Political Studies*, 37(2). 171–95.
Caers, R., Du Bois, C., Jegers, M., De Gieter, S., Schepers, C. and Pepermans, R. (2006) Principal-agent relationships on the stewardship-agency axis. *Nonprofit Management and Leadership*, 17(1): 25–47.
Christensen, T. and Lægreid, P. (2006) *Autonomy and Regulation: Coping with Agencies in the Modern State*. Cheltenham: Edward Elgar.
Christensen, T. and Lægreid, P. (2009) Organising immigration policy: the unstable balance between political control and agency autonomy. *Policy & Politics*, 37(2): 161–77.
Considine, M., O'Sullivan, S. and Nguyen, P. (2014) New Public Management and welfare-to-work in Australia: comparing the reform agendas of the ALP and the Coalition. *Australian Journal of Political Science*, 49(3): 469–85.
Davis, J. H., Schoorman, F. D. and Donaldson, L. (1997) Toward a stewardship theory of management. *Academy of Management Review*, 22(1): 20–47.
Dicke, L. A. (2002) Ensuring accountability in human service contracting: can stewardship theory fill the bill? *The American Review of Public Administration*, 32: 455–70.
Dicke, L. A. and Ott, J. S. (2002) A test: can stewardship theory serve as a second conceptual foundation for accountability methods in contracted human service? *International Journal of Public Administration*, 25(4): 463–87.
Donaldson, L. and Davis, J. H. (1991) Stewardship theory or agency theory: CEO governance and shareholder returns. *Australian Journal of Management*, 16(1): 49–64.
Dulewicz, V. and Herbert, P. (2004) Does the composition and practice of boards of directors bear any relationship to the performance of their companies? *Corporate Governance: An International Review*, 12(3): 263–80.
Freidson, E. (2001) *Professionalism, the Third Logic: On the Practice of Knowledge*. Chicago, IL: University of Chicago Press.
Gailmard, S. (2014) Accountability and principal-agent theory. In M. Bovens, R. E. Goodin and T. Schillemans (eds), *The Oxford Handbook of Public Accountability*. Oxford: Oxford University Press, pp. 90–105.
Georgellis, Y., Iossa, E. and Tabvuma, V. (2010) Crowding out intrinsic motivation in the public sector. *Journal of Public Administration Research and Theory*, 21(3): 473–93.
Jensen, M. C. and Meckling, W. H. (1976) Theory of the firm: managerial behavior, agency costs and ownership structure. *Journal of Financial Economics*, 3(4): 305–60.
Jessop, B. (1999) The changing governance of welfare: recent trends in its primary functions, scale, and modes of coordination. *Social Policy & Administration*, 33(4): 348–59.
Kelly, J. (2007) Reforming public services in the UK: bringing in the third sector. *Public Administration*, 85: 1003–22.
Kluvers, R. and Tippett, J. (2011) An exploration of stewardship theory in a not-for-profit organization. *Accounting Forum*, 35: 275–84.
Larsson, B., Letell, M. and Thörn, H. (2012) *Transformations of the Swedish Welfare State: From Social Engineering to Governance?* London: Palgrave Macmillan.
March, J. G. and Olsen, J. P. (1989) *Rediscovering Institutions: The Organizational Basis of Politics*. New York: Free Press.
McCubbins, M. D., Noll, R. G. and Weingast, B. R. (1987) Administrative procedures as instruments of political control. *Journal of Law, Economics, and Organization*, 3(2): 243–77.
Olsen, J. P. (2014) Accountability and ambiguity. In M. Bovens, R. E. Goodin and T. Schillemans (eds), *The Oxford Handbook of Public Accountability*. Oxford: Oxford University Press, pp. 106–23.
Olsen, J. P. (2016) Democratic accountability and the terms of political order. *European Political Science Review* (forthcoming).

Pierson, P. (1996) The new politics of the welfare state. *World Politics*, 48(2): 143–79.
Pollitt, C. and Bouckaert, G. (2004) *Public Management Reform: A Comparative Analysis* (revised 2nd edition). Oxford: Oxford University Press.
Posner, P. L. (2002) Accountability challenges of third-party government. In L. M. Salamon (ed.), *The Tools of Government: A Guide to the New Governance*. Oxford: Oxford University Press, pp. 523–51.
Scharpf, F. W. (2000) *Globalization and the Welfare State: Constraints, Challenges and Opportunities*. Geneva: ISSA Paper.
Schillemans, T. (2007) *Verantwoording in de schaduw van de macht. Horizontale verantwoording bij zelfstandige uitvoeringsorganisaties*. Den Haag: Lemma.
Schillemans, T. (2013) Moving beyond the clash of interests: on stewardship theory and the relationships between central government departments and public agencies. *Public Management Review*, 15(4): 541–62.
Schillemans, T. and Busuioc, M. (2015) Predicting public sector accountability: from agency drift to forum drift. *Journal of Public Administration Research and Theory*, 25(1): 191–215.
Scott, W. R. (1965) Reactions to supervision in a heteronomous professional organization. *Administrative Science Quarterly*, 10(1): 65–81.
Shapiro, S. P. (2005) Agency theory. *Annual Review of Sociology*, 31: 263–84.
Vallejo, M. C. (2009) The effects of commitment of non-family employees of family firms from the perspective of stewardship theory. *Journal of Business Ethics*, 87(3): 379–90.
Van den Berghe, L. A. and Levrau, A. (2004) Evaluating boards of directors: what constitutes a good corporate board? *Corporate Governance: An International Review*, 12(4): 461–78.
Van Puyvelde, S., Caers, R., Du Bois, C. and Jegers, M. (2012) The governance of nonprofit organizations: integrating agency theory with stakeholder and stewardship theories. *Nonprofit and Voluntary Sector Quarterly*, 41: 431–51.
Van Slyke, D. M. (2006) Agents or stewards: using theory to understand the government–nonprofit social service contracting relationship. *Journal of Public Administration Research and Theory*, 17(2): 157–87.
Vandenabeele, W. (2008) Government calling: public service motivation as an element in selecting government as an employer of choice. *Public Administration*, 86(4): 1089–105.
Waterman, R. W. and Meier, K. J. (1998) Principal-agent models: an expansion? *Journal of Public Administration Research and Theory*, 173(2): 173–202.
White, H. C. (1985) Agency as control. In J. W. Pratt and R. J. Zeckhauser (eds), *Principals and Agents: The Structure of Business*. Boston, MA: Harvard Business School Press, pp. 187–212.
Woods, N. D. and Baranowski, M. (2002) *Autonomy and Influence in State Administrative Agencies*. Paper presented at the Annual Meeting van de Midwest Political Science Association, Chicago, April.

PART II

Accountability in welfare state areas

5

HYBRID WELFARE ADMINISTRATIVE SYSTEMS AND CHANGING ACCOUNTABILITY RELATIONS

Comparing the development of the Danish and Norwegian systems

Tom Christensen, Flemming Larsen and Karsten Vrangbæk

Introduction

Welfare administrative systems balance considerations for national political-administrative control and standardization, on the one hand, and local autonomy and self-rule, on the other. This balance differs between countries, and most countries seem to be characterized by mixed and partly hybrid welfare administrative systems rather than strong central control or dominant local autonomy.

Modern public sector reforms have increased the complexity of welfare administrative systems, which account for a considerable part of the public expenditures and are characterized by high political salience and a number of 'wicked issues' and dilemmas. When New Public Management (NPM) came along in the 1980s, overall public administration became more decentralized or delegated, based on principles from neo-institutional economic theory and management theory, leading to more structural fragmentation (Boston *et al.* 1996; Christensen and Lægreid 2001). More emphasis was also put on the use of performance management.

More recently, when post-NPM was introduced in typical NPM-countries in the late 1990s, as a result of worries about loss of political control and increasing fragmentation, the trend shifted towards re-centralization and stronger emphasis on central control, trying to 'put the system together again' (Christensen and Lægreid 2007). One can say that the dynamics between the reforms has been from decentralization/delegation to re-centralization, coordination and integration again. However, instead of post-NPM substituting NPM, it appears more adequate to characterize the change as layering and increasing hybridity (Streeck and Thelen 2005).

One of the typical developments of modern public administration, closely related to the modern reforms mentioned above, is that traditional trust-based and cultural responsibility relations between political and administrative leaders and civil servants have been substituted by a more formalized system of accountability relationships. With increasing complexity and hybridity in welfare administrative systems, the accountability relationships have also become more complex and ambiguous.

During the last decade, Denmark and Norway have developed their welfare administrative systems in somewhat different ways, choosing different balances and hybridity solutions. Denmark has strengthened and increased the role of municipalities, albeit within a gradually tighter legislative and economic steering regime, while Norway, after initially favoring decentralization, in recent years has aimed at more centralization and regionalization again. Our aim is to study the relationship between reforms and changes in the national accountability regimes within welfare administration, using accountability theory in a descriptive way. We expect both formal and actual accountability relations to have changed with the reforms. This may be part of deliberate instrumental decisions reacting to new contingencies, or it may be the result of a series of small steps and ad hoc adjustments based on accountability traditions and culture in the two countries.

Our main research questions will accordingly be:

- How have accountability relations changed during the period of reforms of the welfare administration in Denmark and Norway?
- What was the role of accountability debates/issues in the reform processes and designs?
- Can instrumental and cultural explanations, taken from organization theory, contribute to explaining differences in the development of accountability regimes in the two countries?

Theory

Accountability: types and relevance

In this section, we present the accountability concepts applied in this paper. We rely on distinctions developed by Mark Bovens and others (Bovens 2005, 2007). Political *accountability* is originally built on popular sovereignty including mainly two types: accountability to the parliament and accountability to the minister or the cabinet within the executive branch (Mulgan 2003). Political accountability is a core hierarchical feature in the chain of delegation implied by the 'primacy of politics' (Pollitt and Hupe 2011) or the 'parliamentary decision chain' (Olsen 1983). We will investigate reform related changes in the accountability relationship between political and administrative leaders in the welfare administration during the last decade. We will further investigate whether the balance between national and local accountability forums have changed.

Administrative accountability is related to an administrative actor in a hierarchy that is called to account by a superior for the performance of delegated duties, which is the internal aspect of this (Sinclair 1995), or to external scrutiny bodies (Van Dooren et al. 2010). *Managerial accountability* is a variety of this that focuses on the monitoring of output and results based on agreed performance criteria (Day and Klein 1987). This is different from administrative accountability, which is often more oriented towards process or procedures (Askim et al. 2015). We will investigate whether administrative accountability is changing in the two welfare administrations and whether NPM-related reforms lead to more focus on managerial accountability.

Legal accountability is about rule of law, fairness in treatment, justice, etc., in relation to the decision-making in the public sector. In some countries, disputes and conflicts will be solved by courts, including administrative courts, while other countries solve this in public debate and in political and administrative bodies. We will analyze whether formal or actual changes in legal accountability have been introduced in the two welfare administrations.

Professional accountability relates to the mechanism of professional peers or peer review in public administration. Different professions are constrained by professional codes of conduct and scrutinized by professional organizations or disciplinary bodies. It is a system marked by trusting the expertise, meaning the technical knowledge of experts (Romzek and Dubnick 1987; Mulgan 2000). We will explore the possible changes in professional accountability in the two countries.

Social accountability relates to the fact that public administration has many external stakeholders and feels the pressure to account through different means for its actions, for example as a result of lack of trust, often exposed in the media (Malena *et al.* 2004). Giving account to various stakeholders in society often is voluntary and has been labeled horizontal accountability (Schillemans 2008). However, relations to stakeholders may also be institutionalized with formal representation on boards or steering groups, etc. An important example in our case is the strong tradition for what can be labeled as 'administrative corporatism' in Denmark. In terms of accountability, this is related to the philosophy that decision and practices are legitimized by labor and industry organizations representing important groups in society and those traditional opponents finding compromises. This may also be labeled '*network accountability*' (Jantz *et al.* 2015). Social accountability is particularly relevant within this sector due to the high political salience and significant potential critique from important stakeholders.

Political, administrative, managerial, professional, legal and social accountability are all part of the 'accountability regime' that organizations and employees are subjected to at any given time. Reforms can change the different forms of accountability, introducing new forums and new accountability relations. Indeed, it may be a conscious part of the reform to strengthen some accountability relations and weaken others. We will consider these issues as we analyze our two case countries, and we will investigate the degree to which accountability changes have played a significant role in the reforms, and whether the resulting changes appear to be results of a conscious design. Alternatively, we can imagine that changes in accountability regimes are limited, ad hoc byproducts of the reforms, where existing traditions and cultural preferences are important for understanding how they evolve. Two perspectives from organization theory can be used to further describe these dynamics of change.

Theoretical perspectives: instrumental and cultural

Changes in welfare administration regimes can be explained from instrumental and cultural organizational perspectives (Christensen *et al.* 2007). A *structural-instrumental perspective* is based on the concept of bounded rationality (March and Simon 1958). It takes for granted that leaders are the central actors in decision-making processes and that they score relatively high on rational calculation and clear organizational thinking (Dahl and Lindblom 1953; March and Olsen 1983).

The perspective will lead us to consider whether the changes to accountability regimes in the welfare sectors in Denmark and Norway are characterized by hierarchical control *and/or* tug of wars and conflicts between actors on different levels. Furthermore, it points to the dynamic between formal structural changes and actual changes made and the effects and implications for patterns of influence. In accountability terms, this perspective is likely to emphasize vertical, formal and mandatory accountability relations such as political and administrative/managerial accountability.

A *cultural-institutional perspective* is based on the notion that public organizations gradually develop unique cultural informal features as a result of adapting to internal and external pressure through natural processes (Selznick 1957; Scott and Davis 2006). Public institutions develop in a path-dependent way, meaning that the context and norms and values that were dominant when the institution was established will determine the path taken later on (i.e. 'roots determine routes') (March 1994; Pierson 2004). When a reform comes along, cultural traditions will filter new norms and values, and the implementation of the reform may depend on the degree of compatibility between the reform and the organizational-cultural tradition (Painter and Peters 2009). If cultural compatibility is high, a reform will easily be implemented, while if it is low the reform will be rejected or implemented only partially and pragmatically (Brunsson and Olsen 1993). In accountability terms, this perspective is likely to emphasize horizontal, informal, voluntary and soft accountability relations such as professional or social accountability.

This perspective will lead us to focus on whether cultural factors influence the accountability changes in the two countries studied. Are the changes characterized by path-dependency and cultural resistance from central actors, and what is the potential relevance of this?

Main features of development and reforms in two welfare systems

On long-term development of the welfare administrative systems on different levels

The Norwegian welfare system has historically been based on a combination of universal and differentiating principles (Fimreite and Lægreid 2009). In the welfare administration, the universal part is primarily related to the pension system, such as old age pension, but also to employment and social services. The differentiating principle is partly used in all services.

All the three main welfare services have a long history in Norway, with pension and employment being centrally controlled, while social services have a local anchoring. The services have distinct and different histories (Christensen et al. 2007). Pension services can be characterized as traditionally Weberian with detailed rules and procedures. Employment services, on the other hand, display a wider degree of discretion for employees combined with a consequence-oriented approach with strong job-training elements for clients. Social services have been professionalized rather late and remain the most discretion-based of the three welfare services. Employment services have changed the most during the last decades, employing more social scientists, being the most modernized and subjected to competition from private actors.

Over a long period of time, the three welfare services have generally been rather disconnected, with few collaborations and coordinative efforts. Over time, there has been a growing dissatisfaction with this fragmentation, manifested in complaints to the authorities, and in particular the parliament, but this never started a wider reform of the welfare administrative system. Reasons for this lack of political sway were resistance from the different services and their unions, and little interest from the political and administrative leadership. A discussion that led up to the eventual start of the reform process in 2001 was how many users that had problems with the service fragmentation. Researchers indicated that there were around 15 percent multi-service users (Christensen et al. 2007).

The Danish welfare system has traditionally been based on the principle of universalism, supplemented with means-tested additional benefits and differentiated services targeted to people's needs. The principle of universalism has, during the last decades, been challenged by the introduction of more conditional types of benefits (for example, participation in activation and job search activities to be entitled to benefits) and more means-tested benefits (for example, entitlement to benefits being dependent on your partner's assets and income). Hence, 'active welfare state reforms' have created new types of balances between standardized and differentiated welfare benefits and services (Larsen 2013). Such discussions about standardization versus differentiation are also reflected in the ongoing political and administrative discussions about at which level (local, regional or central) responsibility for services should be placed (Larsen 2009). In general terms, the proponents of central control favor standardization, while the more decentralist actors argue that there is a need for flexibility to adjust to local contingencies.

While the municipalities have been the traditional level for the delivery of social services, employment services date back to the end of the 1960s, where a state-run public employment system was launched with the tasks of labor exchange and services for workers covered by unemployment insurance. Municipalities had primary responsibility for social services and for those unemployed who did not qualify for unemployment insurance based on past work history. Hence, Denmark had a two-tier labor market system that functioned until 2009, also making employment and social services quite fragmented. Administrative reforms have subsequently placed responsibility for the main welfare services at the municipal level.

This is also the case with the administration of pensions, which traditionally has been located at the municipal level. However, as part of post-NPM processes, this is now placed in a single semiautonomous organization ('Udbetaling Danmark'), which is jointly owned and operated by all municipalities. This organization has taken over the practical administration of all standardized cases, increasingly administered through digital processes, while the municipalities still have tasks in assessing the individual rights to some types of pensions.

Main features of the development processes

In *Norway*, the parliament in 2001 took the initiative to integrate the three welfare services in an administrative reform. The initiative was unusual in the sense that it came from all political parties, even the parties in government. The government's response was reluctant, but after pressure from the parliament a public committee consisting of academic experts was established. In their report, they mostly sided with the government, but indicated that more coordination between the services locally might be possible. What brought the final solution were two events, the establishment of a new Ministry of Social Affairs, now having the responsibility for all three services, and a new minister (Christensen et al. 2007). He worked out a compromise, consisting of a merging of the pension and employment services into a new central welfare agency, and the establishment of local partnerships between this agency and the social services. This solution did not change the division of authority of the services between the levels. The decision on the reform was made in 2005.

Several features characterized the new structure. It represented a rather seldom and new way of organizing public services locally, combining responsibility from a central and a local political-administrative hierarchy (Askim et al. 2009). It represented a national standardization, in the way that the partnerships were mandatory through a central agreement and implied mandatory inclusion of the three services and co-location. But it also represented some local discretion.

The pooling of the resources in the new organization implied an increased focus on the local level, but also a more coordinated central presence on that level. The major slogan was 'one entrance to welfare services'. Early on, it became evident that the internal division between the services would be more kept in the big cities. This meant that the medium-size and smaller municipalities would be closer to fulfilling the purpose of the reform (Askim et al. 2009).

The dynamic of the reform process changed during the period of establishing the local welfare offices, which was meant to be in the period 2006–2010. The central agency initiated a reorganization of the reform, partly as a result of what they saw as a need to adjust to a large new pension reform established from 2008. The changes made were basically two: six regional pension offices were established, along with 19 county administrative offices. This implied moving a lot of resources from the local to the regional level. The main goals of this reorganization were to increase standardization between counties in the provision of services, to get economy-of-scale effects in larger units, to improve the professional quality of services, and to improve the fairness in treating cases in the same way (Christensen and Lægreid 2012). This reorganization made the decision-making process more complicated, because the local level should advise and receive the applications, the regional level should decide, the central level pay, and the local level implement and help people to get a job. The 'one door' policy changed to a 'three-channel strategy' emphasizing digital communication and installing call centers as two alternative options to reduce the number of face-to-face contacts between citizens and welfare officers (Christensen *et al.* 2013).

In *Denmark*, the preface of reforming the welfare services came when a new center-right government came into power in 2001 and the fragmentation between employment and social services was articulated as a political problem. The first political reaction was to move the responsibility for unemployed social assistance recipients from the Ministry of Social Affairs to the Ministry of Employment. Second, an intention to merge services for insured unemployed and social assistance recipients was formulated in the reform text. However, the intention of creating a 'unified system' and a 'one-stop shop' was highly contested politically, especially as unions and employers' associations were part of state-run public employment services (PESs), and thus had a strong influence on PESs for the insured unemployed (Larsen 2004; Klitgaard and Nørgaard 2010). This type of administrative corporatism is a strong power resource, especially for the unions. Hence, the conservative government preferred a municipally based system while the social democrats wanted to maintain the corporatist structures in the state-run PESs, mainly to protect the interests of the unions. The political compromise of making unified employment and social services was therefore ambiguous.

A window of opportunity, however, opened when the government succeeded to bring the question of an overall administrative local government reform on the political agenda in 2004. As in Norway, a political consensus emerged about the need for an overall administrative reform, helped and legitimized through the work of a public committee consisting of academic experts and stakeholders from ministries, counties and municipalities. The committee identified areas with potential benefits of scale, problems with optimal conditions for the citizens' choice of services and problems of coordination between levels in some policy areas (Strukturkommisionen 2004). However, the emerging political consensus about the need for a local government reform was rather vague (Klitgaard and Christiansen 2008), and only a few observers believed that a reform was politically feasible as vested interests were likely to be mobilized.

Within the employment sector, strong opposition was expected from the social democrats if the corporatist structures were weakened significantly. Similarly, strong resistance was expected from regions if the municipalities were to become larger and take over regional tasks. Finally, the government faced the problem of getting the relatively independent municipalities to accept the mergers into fewer and larger municipalities. However, the 'unlikely' local government reform was decided in 2005 with a narrow political majority. The reform was implemented in 2007, merging the 274 municipalities into 98. The 14 regional counties were replaced with five regions, with healthcare as their main task, while most other responsibilities were transferred to either the central government or the new larger municipalities. Furthermore, the reform paved the way for dissolving the state-run public employment service and transferred their tasks, along with many others, to the municipal level.

Changes in accountability: formal and actual

Formal changes in political accountability were minor in the new merged agency in Norway. It was established with a rather traditional ministry-agency relationship, implying a rather high potential of political control (Christensen *et al.* 2007). This reflected its substantial political importance. In reality, however, the merged welfare agency achieved more actual autonomy, because it was large and complex and represented a challenge for the ministry to control. It was, accordingly, the leadership of the new agency who initiated and implemented the reorganization of the reform in 2008, which implied a partial turning back to some elements of the old agency organization, giving the pension services more internal autonomy and a re-regionalization of resources overall (Christensen and Lægreid 2012).

Through the reform and the establishment of local partnerships, local self-government formally changed because the local welfare offices were a combination of the central and local hierarchies; it was a co-steering arrangement (Fimreite and Lægreid 2009). In reality, the new local welfare offices represented a confirmation of the strength of the central government on the local level. The representatives from the central part of the local partnerships, coming from the new welfare agency, dominated in the new welfare offices, both in numbers, resources, in leadership positions, in the fact that the national standardization measures were strong, etc. Adding to this was the reorganization that weakened the local level and regionalized and centralized the personnel and resources.

Concerning administrative accountability, the formal changes were minor, but the Auditor General's Office was becoming much more active in scrutinizing the new welfare organizations, and made a report along the way that stirred controversy and lead to a hearing in the parliament (Christensen and Lægreid 2012). The managerial accountability also changed somewhat. The central political leadership started to be more active in putting several performance indicators into the annual letter of intent to the welfare agency. The leadership in the agency also became more active using performance indicators (PIs) downwards in the organizations.

Legal accountability was not much influenced by the reform. Formally nothing changed, but in reality there was more focus on the rule of law and equal treatment. These were major arguments for the reorganization of the reform in 2008, creating larger units at the regional level that could secure these considerations (Askim *et al.* 2009).

Professional accountability changed formally through the merger and partnership. In reality, accountability challenges were substantial, not so much at the central level as at the local level. To develop a new local professional 'welfare' identity has been difficult, partly because the three professional groups are rather different (Christensen and Lægreid 2012). An indication of the complexity of the question is that there has not been any political or administrative agreement to establish a new education for people working in the local offices.

Social accountability has changed both formally and actually for groups of users, because the changes in the formal structure have been substantial for most of them and many have lost their traditional contacts and caseworkers. The changes seem to have improved services for the multi-service users, while some of the single-service users have been more left in a limbo. The other aspect of social accountability, the relationship to the interest groups and media, has gone from relatively strong support of the reform to a considerably more critical attitude (Askim *et al.* 2009). Not long after the implementation of the reform, media turned against it, as did many of the crucial interest groups, which has made the scrutiny of the reform stronger.

Political accountability issues are very important to the developments in *Denmark*. First, the strong ministerial responsibility for state-run services has been interpreted by leading political and administrative actors as inefficient and with high risk of attracting blame. This was an important driver for local government reform. Second, key political actors have wanted to reclaim power from the social partners by weakening the corporatist structures. Despite the fact that this has been highly contested politically (primarily by the social democrats), it has not been reversed, even by the social democrat led government that came into power in 2011. In general, the decentralization of services to the local level has decreased formal political accountability for employment services at the central level. Formally, the municipalities are run by democratic councils. Yet, the tighter and more detailed legislation and performance demands create little leeway to design municipal employment services or opt for different levels of service. In this sense, political accountability at the central level has been replaced by a sort of administrative accountability between the local and central level, rather than decentralized political accountability. This is further reinforced by detailed monitoring and benchmarking from the central level. The extent of this indirect central administrative control has been massive, leading to what could be labeled centralized decentralization (Larsen 2013). However, this new type of administrative control has been strongly criticized from both the municipalities and an expert committee for creating a bureaucratic and inefficient system. This has recently resulted in a broad political agreement on giving more discretionary room to the municipalities while maintaining an extensive PI system with economic incentives linked to municipal results.

Legal accountability was formally not much influenced by the municipalization of welfare services. The most striking change was the unusually high number of ministerial powers in the reform legislation, giving the minister authorization to decide upon a number of issues. This, in reality, decreased legal accountability and increased the central administrative power to exercise managerial control over the municipalities. Legislation that followed the reform more rigorously stated the obligations and rights of the citizens, including specific requirements for service delivery. Hence, legal accountability also, to some extent, became part of the new system of a 'centralized decentralization' with decreased political accountability and increased central administrative control.

Professional accountability has been reduced significantly due to central mistrust in front-line workers' ability and will to implement services according to the intention in active welfare state reforms. The merger of the PES and the municipal employment and social services has changed the professional background of staff. As in Norway, no welfare worker identity has been established and there is no joint education for people working in the municipal job centers.

Regarding social accountability, the new municipal job centers have been subjected to harsh criticism in the media for their services and for being too bureaucratic, lacking responsiveness to clients' needs and, in general, being inefficient. The trade unions are among the most vociferous critics in terms of pointing out the shortcomings in the municipal services. Due to the change of accountability relations in general, a blame avoidance game has taken place. The minister, on one hand, supports the critique and blames the municipalities for the shortcomings, and, on the other hand, the municipalities blame the strong central control. There are, however, limits to this kind of blame avoidance, and media, independent experts and a newly established committee have voiced strong critique, which has made the minister react. The result is a new broad political agreement with changes in progress, as mentioned above.

Analyzing accountability changes in the reform processes

In *Norway*, the political accountability relations at the central level didn't change formally through the reform, because political saliency made it feasible to establish a welfare agency of a traditional and not particularly NPM-influenced type. But in reality, political accountability and control changed because of the complexity and size of the new central agency (Christensen and Lægreid 2012). The political leadership was actually against the reform, and it was less politically controversial to say that the implementation of the reform was left to the leadership of the agency. This meant, however, that political control was weakened and administrative accountability at this level became relatively more important than political accountability (Byrkjeflot *et al.* 2014).

Seen from a structural-instrumental perspective, the political executives' attempt at pleasing the parliament by controlling the process of the reform they did not want was partly successful, both process-wise and concerning the end result through the reorganization of the reform. But this implied an instrumental undermining of their influence relative to the welfare agency because of capacity problems. Culturally, this also implied a change pointing towards stronger acceptance of delegation, something that was more inspired by NPM.

Political accountability was also related to the reform, ending up with two competing or collaborating hierarchies, a central and a local one (Christensen et al. 2013). According to the cultural tradition of catering to local self-rule, it was very important for the government to sell the agreement with the municipalities and their organization as a deal between equal partners, combining standardization and local choice. But from an instrumental perspective, the central government had and has the upper hand in the reform and functioning of the local welfare administration.

The formal changes of administrative accountability in a more narrow sense were minor, but actual changes were obvious, particularly in managerial accountability and the increased focus on performance management. This actually helped the ministry regain some control, because they could put more demands into the annual letter of intent/allocation, and also helped the leadership in the agency in their more intensive use of PI downwards in the organization. Overall, from an outside perspective, it contributed in giving the process more legitimacy, but it also changed the culture of interaction in a more NPM direction.

The changes of the legal accountability were formally and actually minor in the reform. But the reorganization of the reform focused more on this. It was argued that larger administrative-professional units would help the rule of law and fairness of casework, something that would support the process and its legitimacy.

As shown, the professional accountability relationship formally changed with the merger at the central level and the partnership on the local level, but in reality it only changed partially since the reform is more implemented outside the larger cities (Byrkjeflot et al. 2014). The complexity at the local level and partial resistance to the reform, struggling to form a new and common 'welfare administrative identity', probably participated in facilitating the reorganization, and in particular the establishment of the regional pension offices, but also the county administrative offices. This reorganization relieved the burden on confronting and collaboration among professional groups and moved many of them into more specialized units with people with the same competence. So both instrumental and cultural intentions to merge were modified by professional forces.

Social accountability has both formally and actually changed a lot through the reform and reorganization. Overall, the user satisfaction has not been that much affected by the larger changes. The original support of the reform by many external stakeholders, including employees' organizations, users' organizations and media, has turned to skepticism and critique (Askim et al. 2009). This has an instrumental side, struggling to achieve main goals behind the reform, but also a cultural-symbolic side, meaning that it is rather easy to stir up a negative debate overdoing the negative effects. But the internal dynamics of the process have overall been much more important than external pressures.

In *Denmark*, political accountability and the authority of state and municipalities in the employment services were at the core of the political negotiations about the overall local government reform. The association of municipalities announced that the municipalities should take over the employment services and the government proposed to establish 'job centers' in each municipality, organized as independent municipal agencies. Although the social democrats did not support the reform, a political agreement was formulated in accordance with concessions given to the social democrats during the negotiations, and the final agreement was far from the clean municipal cut that the government initially proposed. Instead, an experiment with two different administrative solutions was set up. A pure municipal solution was to be tested in 14 municipal job centers, while the remaining job centers were established as joint state and municipal agencies (as in Norway). Seen from a structural-instrumental perspective, two sets of reforms/changes were balanced and related, merging municipalities and reforming employment services, which formally changed the political accountability in a decentralized way. This was, however, the result of interrelated negotiations, resulting in compromises, reflecting cultural features.

However, in 2008, long before the evaluation of the experiment was complete, the government used a finance bill as a legislative vehicle to end the state-run public employment system (PES) and give the municipalities full authority over employment services (i.e. strengthening the instrumentally driven trend), which were to be delivered through municipal job centers. The social partners thereby lost significant influence. In this sense, the changes resulted in a weakening of social accountability.

Seen from the government and leading civil servants, there was a need to reduce political accountability, as well as the influence of the labor market organizations, but also instrumentally to strengthen central administrative accountability. The municipalities were seen as the major obstacle to implementing active welfare reforms, which seems paradoxical in a decentralized reform. The type of legal and administrative (especially managerial) accountability, which was an integrated part of the culture in the former PES system, was introduced to control the municipalities. Managerial accountability was strengthened through new performance benchmarks, output and outcome measurement, and performance incentive mechanisms (i.e. more instruments related to managerial accountability). One may regard these strategies as the 'price' municipal authorities had to pay for being 'allowed' to take over employment services. The central government has sought to strengthen its influence through these monitoring and incentive instruments.

The managerial reforms are designed to limit the discretion of front-line workers, those social workers most mistrusted by central decision-makers (i.e. the reform weakened the professional accountability). This process has been paralleled by a de-professionalization of social work also challenging the former position of professional social workers, traditionally being the primary workforce in the municipal employment and social services (Larsen 2013).

In accountability terms, the reform implies a strengthening of vertical, formal and mandatory accountability relations such as political and administrative/managerial accountability. At the same time, we see a weakening of accountability forms associated with the cultural/institutional perspective such as horizontal, informal, voluntary and soft accountability relations, including professional or social accountability.

Some comparative reflections

Through the local government reform from 2007 and the following municipalization of the employment services in 2009, Denmark took a different path from Norway in the development of the welfare administrative systems. While Norway still struggles to merge its municipal structure (through voluntary processes supported with incentives from the government), Denmark coupled the welfare and municipal structure reform. At the formal level, this development in Denmark is characterized by decentralization and increasing emphasis on the local level. Some of the considerations observed in Norway about the balance between national political-administrative control and local autonomy also apply to the Danish case, leading to a stronger focus on administrative and managerial accountability.

Paradoxically, the transfer of authority from central to local level in Denmark is not so much a story of a new trust-based culture of delegation, but rather a story of applying the former mistrust-based PES culture to the municipalities. The result is that the municipal job centers are exposed to the same criticism as the former PES as being too bureaucratic and inefficient.

Even though the Norwegian case formally is much more about the centralized level having the upper hand on the local level in welfare administration, dominating the locally based social services in the municipal welfare offices, there are important similarities in actual policy. In both cases, there is a stronger emphasis on administrative and managerial accountability relative to political accountability.

Two interrelated changes in professional and social accountability are also similar in the two countries. Professional accountability is weakened in both countries, and both have problems of finding a new professional welfare worker identity. Furthermore, both countries experience a weakening of the employee organizations and their influence, and also intense critique after the reforms from media and other stakeholders.

Why did Denmark choose to make the municipalities responsible for the development of welfare administrative systems, while Norway chose a more hybrid model? The local merging of employment and social services in Denmark illustrates some of the reasons. The formal argument put forward for merging the state-driven PESs and municipal employment services was an attempt to avoid fragmentation and deliver more coordinated services, a reason quite the same as in Norway. However, other rationales seemed to be stronger. The center-right governments and leading civil servants in the Ministry of Employment saw two major problems with the former PES system. One was related to political accountability. As labor market policy issues became more politicized and subject to criticism, the labor minister was constantly blamed for problems with the PES. The more the government took direct control, the more vulnerable it was to criticism as PES was viewed as providing bureaucratic, inefficient and ineffective services (Larsen 2013). This was not an argument in the welfare sector in Norway, even though the dynamic can be seen in other sectors.

Another related issue in Denmark was the corporatist structure, which gave considerable power to the unions. This was both an ideological and political issue, but seen from the central administrative level also a practical problem as this structure made it difficult to force the PES to adapt to new policies as part of active welfare state reforms. In other words, the corporatist structures enabled the unions to protect their members against too-strict work-first and 'activation' initiatives. Also, the unions and employers' associations tended to focus only on core labor. This made it politically and administratively attractive to abolish the PES and devolve authority over employment services to municipalities. In accountability terms, this implies weaker social accountability and stronger vertical accountability. The situation in Norway was different concerning corporatist features. The welfare reform started with the government guaranteeing all employees to keep their jobs, which was popular among the unions. The unions, at least the one from the employment sector, were skeptical towards the reform, but managed to become influential in the new structure, and were more seen as collaborators, but not in a very strong position relative to central political and administrative actors.

The central political and administrative mistrust in the municipal way of implementing employment and social services was, somewhat paradoxically, immense in Denmark. Seen from the central instrumental perspective, the municipalities were 'uncontrollable', with considerable variation across municipalities and limited central knowledge of the services delivered. The municipalities took an approach to services that was based on their social welfare traditions, rather than advancing the policy shift inherent in active welfare state reform. This concern about local implementation was consistent with studies showing that the municipalities in general implemented the formal policies more 'softly' than stated in legislation (Larsen 2009). Many municipalities organized their employment services in 'traditional' ways, with a strong focus on norms of professional social work and wide discretion for front-line workers. Gradually a growing conviction among leading government officials in Denmark developed that municipalities were an obstacle to the active welfare reform agenda.

Elements of the same could be found in Norway concerning locally based social services, but this was not a common trend. The employment and pension sectors, merged in the reform, had a long history of central control, making it less likely to make the municipal take over, but therefore there was also less basis for overall mistrusting the municipalities. But since the central government controlled two-thirds of the sectors participating in the local welfare offices, it was also easier to make the centralized decentralization, based in the regional level, stronger than in Denmark. This also probably made the move from focusing on political accountability to administrative/managerial accountability easier, given the strength and broader scope of the new central welfare agency in Norway.

Conclusion

Comparing the two countries, we see a number of similarities in spite of the formal differences in structural features. Political accountability is formally changed in both countries in the relationship between central and local level. In Denmark, the municipalities become the main locus for delivering welfare services, influenced by municipal mergers that Norway struggles to achieve, and in Norway a combination of local authorities and a central government agency gets the responsibility. However, in both cases, this is accompanied by strengthened administrative and managerial accountability in the relation between state and local authorities. This means that accountability relations move from overt political accountability to somewhat less formal and more opaque administrative and managerial accountability with the national governments as a key actor, but with strong powers to administrative actors to monitor and control the performance of formally independent local and agency delivered services. This is clear in the shift to output and process control (measuring adherence to standardized processes) and in the much-strengthened capacity to govern the economic affairs at the local level.

Another common trend is changes in the professional accountability. In Denmark, we see an increasing distrust in professional accountability, while the weakening in Norway has more to do with a lack of creating a new professional identity based on a new collaboration between three professional groups. In both countries, the trend is to replace this by stronger administrative and managerial control. More strained relationships to stakeholder groups in both countries is also part of this equation.

Legal accountability becomes more important in the relationship between citizens and the employment agencies in both countries as formal demands are sharpened and the basis for allocation of compensation, pensions, etc. change to more standardized forms, leaving less room for professional discretion and less emphasis on social accountability.

Our two case studies also confirmed that accountability relations are complex, with layers from traditional public administration, NPM and post-NPM. It's not the differences in launching new welfare administrative reforms in Norway and Denmark that is the most interesting, but more these similarities that raise new important questions to address: What are the potential consequences of such intermingled accountability structures? How will public trust, and trust between different political levels, be affected by the tendency to replace overt political accountability with more opaque administrative and managerial accountability forms?

References

Askim, J., Christensen, T., Fimreite, A. L. and Lægreid, P. (2009) How to carry out joined-up government reforms: lessons from the 2001–2006 Norwegian welfare reform. *International Journal of Public Administration*, 32(12): 1006–25.

Askim, J., Christensen, T. and Lægreid, P. (2015) Performance management and accountability: the Norwegian hospital, welfare and immigration administrations. *International Journal of Public Administration*, 38(13): 971–82.

Boston, J., Martin, J., Pallot, J. and Walsh, P. (1996) *Public Management: The New Zealand Model*. Auckland: Oxford University Press.

Bovens, M. (2005) Public accountability. In E. Ferlie (ed.), *The Oxford Handbook of Public Management*. Oxford: Oxford University Press, pp. 182–208.

Bovens, M. (2007) Analyzing and assessing public accountability: a conceptual framework. *European Law Journal*, 13(4): 837–68.

Brunsson, N. and Olsen, J. P. (1993) *The Reforming Organization*. London/New York: Routledge.

Byrkjeflot, H., Christensen, T. and Lægreid, P. (2014) The many faces of accountability: comparing reforms in welfare, hospitals and immigration. *Scandinavian Political Studies*, 37(2): 171–97.

Christensen, T., Fimreite, A. L. and Lægreid, P. (2007) Reform of the employment and welfare administrations: the challenges of coordinating diverse public organizations. *International Review of Administrative Sciences*, 73(3): 389–409.

Christensen, T., Fimreite, A. L. and Lægreid, P. (2013) Joined-up government for welfare administration reform. *Public Organization Review*, 36: 556–66.

Christensen, T. and Lægreid, P. (eds) (2001) *New Public Management: The Transformation of Ideas and Practice*. Aldershot: Ashgate.

Christensen, T. and Lægreid, P. (2007) The whole-of-government approach to public sector reform. *Public Administration Review*, 67(6): 1059–66.

Christensen, T. and Lægreid, P. (2012) Competing principles of agency organization: the reorganization of a reform. *International Review of Administrative Sciences*, 78(4): 579–96.

Dahl, R. A. and Lindblom, C. E. (1953) *Politics, Economics, and Welfare*. New York: Harper & Row.

Day, P. and Klein, R. (1987) *Accountabilities: Five Public Services*. London/New York: Tavistock.

Fimreite, A. L. and Lægreid, P. (2009) Reorganizing the welfare state administration. *Public Management Review*, 11(3): 281–7.

Jantz, B., Klenk, T., Larsen, F. and Wiggan, J. (2015) Marketisation and varieties of accountability relationships in employment services: comparing Denmark, Germany and Great Britain. *Administration & Society*, first published on April 22, 2015. doi: 10.1177/0095399715581622.

Klitgaard, M. B. and Christiansen, P. M. (2008) *Den utænkelige reform. Strukturreformens tilblivelse 2002–2005*. Odense: Syddansk Universitetsforlag.

Klitgaard, M. B. and Nørgaard, A. S. (2010) Afmagtens mekanismer: Den danske fagbevægelse og arbejdsmarkedspolitikken siden 1960'erne. *Politica – Tidsskrift for Politisk Videnskab*, 42(1): 5–26.

Larsen, F. (2004) The importance of institutional regimes for active labour market policies: the case of Denmark. *European Journal of Social Security*, 6(2): 137–54.

Larsen, F. (2009) *Kommunal beskæftigelsespolitik – Jobcentrenes implementering af beskæftigelsesindsatsen i krydsfeltet mellem statslig styring og kommunal autonomi*. Frydenlund Academic.

Larsen, F. (2013) Active labor market reform in Denmark: the role of governance in policy change. In E. Brodkin and G. Marsden (ed.), *Work and the Welfare State: Street-Level Organisations and Workfare Politics*. Washington, DC: Georgetown University Press, pp. 103–25.

Malena, C., Forster, R. and Singh, J. (2004) *Social Accountability: An Introduction to the Concept and Emerging Practice*. Social Development Paper 76. Washington, DC: World Bank.

March, J. G. (1994) *A Primer in Decision Making*. New York: Free Press.

March, J. G. and Olsen, J. P. (1983) Organizing political life: what administrative reorganization tells us about government. *American Political Science Review*, 77: 281–97.

March, J. G. and Simon, H. A. (1958) *Organizations*. New York: John Wiley & Sons.

Mulgan, R. (2000) Accountability: an ever-expanding concept? *Public Administration*, 78(3): 555–73.

Mulgan, R. (2003) *Holding Power to Account: Accountability in Modern Democracies*. London: Palgrave Macmillan.

Olsen, J. P. (1983) *Organized Democracy*. Bergen: Scandinavian University Press.

Painter, M. and Peters, B. G. (eds) (2009) *Tradition and Public Administration*. London: Palgrave Macmillan.

Pierson, P. (2004) *Politics in Time: History, Institutions and Social Analysis*. Princeton, NJ: Princeton University Press.

Pollitt, C. and Hupe, P. (2011) Talking about governance: the role of magic concepts. *Public Management Review*, 13(5): 1–18.

Romzek, B. S. and Dubnick, M. J. (1987) Accountability in the public sector: lessons from the Challenger tragedy. *Public Administration Review*, 47(3): 227–38.

Schillemans, T. (2008) Accountability in the shadow of hierarchy: the horizontal accountability of agencies. *Public Organization Review*, 8(2): 175–94.

Scott, W. R. and Davis, G. (2006) *Organizations and Organizing: Rational, Natural and Open Systems Perspectives* (revised 6th edition). Upper Saddle River, NJ: Prentice Hall.

Selznick, P. (1957) *Leadership in Administration*. New York: Harper & Row.

Sinclair, A. (1995) The chameleon of accountability: forms and discourses. *Accounting, Organization and Society*, 20(2–3): 219–37.

Streeck, W. and Thelen, K. (2005) Institutional change in advanced political economies. In W. Streeck and K. Thelen (eds), *Beyond Continuity: Institutional Change in Advanced Political Economies*. Oxford: Oxford University Press, pp. 1–39.

Strukturkommisionen (2004) *Strukturkommisionens betænkning*, Bind I, Hoved-betænkningen, betænkning, nr. 1434.

Van Dooren, W., Bouckaert, G. and Halligan, J. (2010) *Performance Management in the Public Sector*. London: Routledge.

6

PUBLIC SECTOR REFORM AND ACCOUNTABILITY DYNAMICS

The changing welfare administration in Norway and Germany

Bastian Jantz

Introduction

Public organizations have been subject to massive modernization efforts and sometimes to complete restructuring processes within the last decade. The type and character of the implemented reforms differ between countries, but have mainly been influenced by the ideas of New Public Management (NPM) and post-New Public Management (post-NPM). These reform measures have been added to existing forms of steering of the traditional Weberian bureaucracy. This is also true for accountability structures.

Public organizations in an 'era of reform' (Romzek 2000: 21) do not operate in stable accountability environments where the question of who is accountable to whom for what and how can easily be answered, as multiple actors are striving to hold each other to account with different expectations and according to different criteria.

Thus, first, instead of trying to capture accountability relationships by simple principal-agent models, they can be better characterized as an accountability regime, emphasizing the complex nature of multiple stakeholders' expectations and values.

Second, studying accountability means to take the dynamic nature of accountability relations into account. Many accountability studies are conducted in static terms and there is a lack of studies that analyze changes over time (Vibert 2014). Research on how accountability structures evolve, how they are altered, how they influence behavior of the actors involved, and how these actors order and deal with multiple accountability expectations is still limited (Yang 2012).

By taking the recent organizational reforms of welfare and employment administration in Germany and Norway as an example, this chapter will analyze if and how these reforms have affected accountability relations. The chapter will thus address the following question: How does the structure and development of reform processes affect accountability relationships and via what kind of mechanisms?

The chapter is structured as follows. First, it is discussed and outlined how accountability and accountability dynamics can be conceptualized and mapped. Second, the theoretical framework of the article is presented. In the empirical part, the case selection, the reform context and the reform results on accountability relationships will be described. This is followed by an analysis on how the reform process in the two countries has influenced the reform outcome. Finally, the findings are discussed in a comparative perspective.

Conceptualization of accountability and accountability dynamics

Accountability is one of the basic principles upon which societies, and the organizations within them, are constructed implying that if organizations or individuals were not answerable for their behavior, there would be neither shared expectations nor a basis for social order. Accountability relationships guide behavior and stabilize expectations as they allocate resources (such as sanctioning powers), constitute events and debating space (such as annual meetings), empower and constrain actors and make them thus capable of acting according to prescribed rules.

Generally, public organizations in particular are confronted with multiple accountability relationships (Romzek 2000). There are numerous typologies of accountability (for an overview, see Willems and Van Dooren 2012), however there seems to be no common model and no consensus how to classify accountability. One of the most influential definitions of Romzek and Dubnick takes the individual organization as a starting point and states that 'accountability involves the means by which public agencies and their workers manage the diverse expectations generated within and outside the organization' (Romzek and Dubnick 1987: 233). The 'management of expectations' claim reminds us that it is more appropriate to speak of organizations operating in an accountability regime. The degree and nature of accountability from a regime perspective can best be described as emerging from the interactions of multiple actors with differing goals and multiple ties to each other. Therefore, studying accountability requires analyzing the complexity and dynamics of accountability relations and processes (Olsen 2013).

However, there is a lack of studies that are providing a framework for analyzing the dynamics of accountability regimes and that are applying it empirically. Most accountability relationships have evolved over time, are uncontested and routinized. Nevertheless, it might be misleading to assume stability. Especially large-scale reforms, unexpected events or scandals foster political debate and conflict, making accountability relations controversial, political and dynamic (Olsen 2013). Thus, in the following, the relationship between administrative reforms and accountability dynamics will be discussed in more detail.

Public sector reforms and accountability dynamics

All major debates about recent government reforms are also related to accountability. NPM advocates insist that a stronger focus on public sector performance improves government accountability, but opponents refute arguing that there is a tension between managerial and political accountability (Lægreid 2014). Post-NPM believers claim that coordination and network-based delivery lead to better accountability, but others suspect that networks pose significant accountability challenges (Papadopoulos 2010). Hence, the relationship between government reforms and accountability is still contested. The demand and exercise of accountability always implies questions of power. To apply accountability means to define who (forum) has the power to call for an account and who (actor) is obliged to give an explanation for its actions. Rather than assuming a world consisting of predetermined forums and actors and static accountability relationships, there is a need to examine how accountability processes affect the way authority and power are actually organized and exercised. Accountability is a political process in which actors interact and pressure each other with power (Yang 2012).

As accountability implies practices of power, it is rather unsurprising that different accountability mechanisms are promoted, sustained and contested by different forums and actors.

As already mentioned, there are numerous forums of accountability for public organizations. However, the different forums will rarely be equally important. Their respective influence depends on their formal and informal capacity to demand information from the actor and from the possibility to impose sanctions (Biela and Papadopoulos 2014). Reforms can introduce new accountability forums and abolish others or may change the relative weight of different forums, thus empowering some forums while disempowering others. Accountability is not an apolitical project and actors promoting some forums have a political stake. Placing power centrally makes it easier to discern why some accountability forums are privileged over others and why forum constellations change over time.

Apart from changes in the forum constellations, the effects of reforms can also refer to the actor side of accountability, mainly focusing on the interplay between controls exercised on the actor and autonomy that is granted to the actor. Any accountability regime must confront a fundamental issue of how strict controls should be in seeking consistency versus how much discretion should be granted in promoting flexibility and innovation. In this regard, Dubnick and O'Brien (2010) differentiate between two major issues:

1   How specific or detailed is the scrutiny of the activity or behavior of the actor?
2   How much autonomy does the actor have in the fulfillment of its required behavior?

The following four-field matrix gives an overview on the different reform strategies.

The managerial strategy provides considerable discretion in meeting goals or targets set by the accountability forums. The focus is laid on monitoring outputs and results instead of processes or procedures and making those with delegated authority accountable for carrying out their tasks in order to reach agreed (often performance-related) criteria (Day and Klein 1987).

Compliance-based systems design rules and accountability mechanisms to structure incentives and disincentives for actors that will motivate compliance and ensure conformity not only with targets, but also with standard operating procedures. The compliance-based model regards public organizations as a potential source of obstruction to be guarded against by carefully shaping behavior through scrutiny, specifications, incentives and penalties (Philp 2009).

Specificity of Accountable Activity

		low	high
Autonomy of Actor	high	*Integrative* — Development of internalized norms and standards to foster appropriate behavior and probity	*Managerial* — Set 'what' agent is accountable for (targets), allows agent to determine 'how'
	low	*Contrived randomness* — Oversight of actions of the actor ex-post based on unpredictable categories	*Compliance* — Set 'what' agent is accountable for and 'how' to proceed

Figure 6.1 Accountability approaches

An integrity-oriented approach focuses on building professional integrity. It recognizes that accountability cannot be fully motivated by rules and incentives. It is assumed that appropriate behavior results out of intrinsic motivation and probity, rather than simply acting in a response to external incentives. Organizations or individuals are asked how they have exercised the discretion and responsibility associated with their office. Account-giving means accountability for feedback and evaluation (Philp 2009).

Contrived randomness refers to accountability relationships under which accountable bodies face uncertainty, for example by making policies, standards or goals unpredictable and ever-changing through the use of unannounced interference and control or by the assessment of subjective categories of performance (Lodge and Hood 2010). Contrived randomness is inherent in the political logic that politicians can engage themselves in any matter on an ad hoc basis. In addition, outside control, such as the media, represents a strong element of randomness, chance and unpredictability (Bleiklie et al. 2003). Uncertainty establishes some room for maneuvers within which the actors can operate. At the same time, it encourages distrust.

Both facets of reform effects – forum constellations and effect on the actor side – might occur simultaneously or isolated from each other. In order to understand and explain the reform trajectories and the accountability choices in the two countries, two different perspectives from organizational theory on factors enabling and constraining the leeway of political and administrative executives when committing into administrative reform policies will be considered. It will be differentiated between an instrumental (with a hierarchical and negotiation type) and an institutionalist perspective on change (Christensen et al. 2007b). From these perspectives, contrasting expectations about observed effects will be formulated.

An instrumental perspective on accountability change

Accountability can be seen as an instrument of management and reform, where account-giving is perceived as a tool to achieve ends such as better control, increased legitimacy or better performance of public sector organizations (Dubnick 2011). This is in accordance with principal-agent approaches, assuming principals know which institutions are likely to enhance or hamper accountability and that they are able to choose the desired institutions (Olsen 2013). Accountability is mainly a question of organizational design in the hand of powerful reformers. Such a hierarchical-instrumental perspective (Christensen et al. 2007b) sees reforms as a conscious reorganization. This implies that political and administrative leaders are the actors who dominate decisions and the implementation of reforms (March and Olsen 1983). They have unambiguous goals, a clear means-end thinking and choose a structural design for public organizations that fulfills these goals (Christensen and Lægreid 2012). From a hierarchical-instrumental perspective, it is expected that:

1. In situations when leadership is present and uncontested, goals are clear and means are known, a dominant accountability forum will emerge with clear expectations and accountability claims. This includes clear divisions between oversight and execution of tasks, straightforward criteria and measurements for performance, and a logical hierarchy between agents and principals.
2. Leaders acting instrumentally favor clear goals and formal accountability processes, thus either choosing a managerial or compliance-based approach on accountability.

An instrumental-negotiation based perspective sees a reform process as a struggle between different actors, groups and organizations, reflecting the heterogeneity in the public sector and its environment. From this perspective, it can be expected that the focal actors hold different views on and therefore negotiate over the framing of the reform process, the problems and solutions identified, and the organizational structure for the new system. The instrumental-negotiation perspective recognizes that negotiations, conflicts, diverging interests and scarce resources are primary features of political systems. Hence, it can be expected that in these circumstances:

1 Accountability forums and accountability procedures are unstable due to complicated and also constantly changing balances of power between single actors or between coalitions Public organizations are continuously being called to account by several account-holders for their actions and decisions, within different forums with different expectations and through different processes (formal and informal) at the same time.
2 The accountability approach evolving is contrived randomness as goals and expectations are unclear or ambiguous (as actors need to make compromises) and unstable (as they are continuously altered by negotiations).

An institutional perspective on accountability change

From an institutional perspective, accountability regimes are complex and thus cannot easily be designed and reformed at will. Design decisions may often take directions that are unpredictable, imply unanticipated consequences and require that these decisions are continuously adjusted and revised. Accountability regimes have some autonomy and dynamics of their own and some robustness in the face of deliberate reform efforts (Olsen 2013). This does not question the possibility of making interventions in order to change accountability; however, these interventions are mediated through existing accountability relationships. To change accountability relations involves 'a disruption and alteration of existing and ongoing accountability relationships. Reforms designed to make individual actors or agencies more accountable do not fill a vacuum but become part of the accountability space into which they are inserted' (Dubnick 2011: 712). Such an institutionalist perspective on accountability goes beyond the assumption that accountability regimes emerge or change as a result of the deliberate choices of reformers. Rather, the dynamics of accountability regimes are seen as part of complex institutionalization and deinstitutionalization processes. Understood in this way, accountability is an emergent property with a strong influence of informal norms and values, not a given set of rules or tools. Attempts to change accountability relationships are shaped and filtered by institutional legacies, existing traditions and cultural preferences. From this perspective, it can be expected that:

1 Accountability regimes develop informally over time, rather than being established formally by political and administrative leaders. The fate of reform initiatives are thus dependent on the degree of compatibility between the reform and the existing traditions and institutions.
2 The accountability approach evolving is a rather integrative approach focusing on changing or maintaining institutional arrangements and general accountability principles.

In the preceding paragraphs, a conception of accountability dynamics has been described as a starting point to map and analyze how government reforms influence accountability regimes. In the following, the model is applied to the case of the reformed welfare and employment administration in Norway and Germany, showing the dynamics in the accountability regime of two organizations, namely the newly created Norwegian Labour and Welfare Administration (NAV) as well as the reformed German Federal Employment Agency (FEA).

Case selection and method

The case and country selection follows a mixed systems research strategy as advocated by Frendreis (1983), which implies that there are differences between the selected cases, but also important similarities. Norway is a unitary state with a unicameral parliamentary system, whereas Germany is a federal state with strong bicameralism. Overall, Germany is significantly scoring higher on the different indices on veto players and institutional constraints of central state government,[1] thus limiting the degree of governmental influence on policy reforms (Champion and Bonoli 2011).

However, there are also important similarities. In both countries, the principle of ministerial responsibility is entrenched. There is a substantial decision-making space of the ministries with regard to the design of inter-organizational control and accountability relations to subordinate agencies (Bach 2014). Furthermore, both countries have a long tradition of local self-government (Wollmann 2000; Fimreite and Lægreid 2009) and the responsibilities for welfare services have long been fragmented between the central and the local level (Jantz and Jann 2013). This results not only in political influence of the local level when it comes to policy and organizational reforms, but the local level also exert an influence through their participation in the governance structure (Champion and Bonoli 2011).

Furthermore, both countries have implemented reforms that have had a major impact on the respective institutional framework for public employment services, namely the NAV reform starting in 2005 in Norway and the so-called Hartz reforms in Germany starting in 2002. Both reforms combined elements of NPM and post-NPM, thus challenging the previously dominant organization of the welfare state based on clear functional differentiation, hierarchy and compliance-based elements of control. This case selection allows the examination of how a common reform trend in both countries is shaped by country traditions and if similar or different developments in the accountability regime can be observed.

The dynamics and complexity of accountability requires an interpretative in-depth method with attention to context and ambiguities. Qualitative research in this regard is especially suited for the understanding of social phenomena that are changing and shifting, ill-defined, deeply rooted or entailing information that can only be collected from special individuals. Accountability research definitely has to address these issues. The chapter is thus based on in-depth interviews with a variety of actors and secondary data sources. Twenty-six semi-structured interviews in both countries have been conducted. Respondents were selected from a diverse set of actors, including politicians, civil servants in the ministries responsible for welfare services, managers in the welfare and employment services on different levels, public auditors and social partners. These respondents were chosen on the basis of their close involvement in decision-making and implementation of the reforms in the two countries, as indicated by official documents and the literature or by other respondents (snowballing). The analysis of the German reform is additionally partly based on a previous empirical study by the author on the agenda-setting and policy formulation process of the Hartz reforms (Jantz 2004). Secondary data sources include governmental documents and evaluation reports, as well as the scientific literature on the reform trajectory.

The reform trajectories and results in Norway and Germany

Norway

Norway has a two-tier benefit system for the unemployed (unemployment benefits and social assistance). Until 2006, there has been a division of responsibilities between two agencies on the central level and the social services at the municipal level (Christensen *et al.* 2007a).

In 2005, the parliament approved the merger of the 'Social Security Directorate' and the employment service into a single central 'Agency for Employment and Welfare' (NAV). Formally, the new NAV agency was established as a traditional ministry-agency model, implying a close relationship and considerable interaction between the ministry and agency. However, in practice, the patterns of influence have changed in favor of the NAV agency. This can be attributed to the size of the NAV agency, which goes along with an increased task complexity, making it very challenging to hold the agency accountable.

The accountability approach from the political forums is rather ad hoc and driven by political rationalities that lead to changing or layered expectations. For NAV managers, this means constantly anticipating and being responsive to the concerns of elected officials. At the same time, this implies a difficult process of handling different priorities or even having no priorities at all, as a respondent from the NAV agency has reported.

The NAV agency is vertically structured with an administrative accountability chain running down from the ministry and the NAV directorate in Oslo to the regional and local offices, as well as the special units situated across the country. To hold the different levels accountable, a system of management by objectives and result (MBOR) has been implemented with highly detailed (mainly input) targets for each layer. Thus, MBOR in practice is modified and ends up in a combination of target and rule steering as 'result-oriented-rule-steering' (Bleiklie, Lægreid and Wik 2003: 21). Respondents on the different levels have emphasized the loose coupling between their actual working routines and the reporting requirements they have to meet. However, this does not mean that the NAV directorate is not interfering into the operations of the regional and local office, but this takes place outside the formal accountability arrangements on an ad hoc basis.

The reform also introduced formal collaboration between the NAV agency and social services of the municipalities. The NAV offices – situated in each of Norway's 429 municipalities – are organized as a central-local government partnership regulated by local agreements. There are variations between the different municipal governments, but most of them show little interest to hold the local NAV offices into account and rather see them as an affair of the central government. After the implementation of the reform, political accountability through local self-governance came under severe pressure (Christensen *et al.* 2014).

To sum up, the political and administrative accountability reflects both formal hierarchical accountability arrangements and informal accountability dynamics that are based upon implicit and explicit expectations. In practice, two parallel systems of accountability have evolved, one proactive model based on the MBOR system and another reactive model based on a political logic where politicians and top-level administrators are interfering in a more random and ad hoc manner.

The ministry and the administrative leadership are constantly struggling between an accountability approach at arm's length (managerial approach) and immediate interfering (contrived randomness), because of political intervention, reports of misconduct by the Auditor General or the media. Regular informal meetings outside the formal MBOR system between the ministry and the agency make sure that changing priorities are implemented within the agency. Collaboration and coordination between the central and local level play no significant role as joint targets or planning with the municipalities is not in place. Even though the term 'partnership' has played a great role in the reform rhetoric, this is not mirrored in the accountability relationships. As a result of the reform, the NAV agency faces less certainty about the consequences of their actions. It is in an unstable balance between different accountability forums and approaches, and must thus be able to switch between them.

Germany

Prior to the Hartz reforms, Germany had a three-tier benefit system for the unemployed, including unemployment insurance benefit and unemployment assistance. Both were administered by the Federal Employment Agency (FEA), whereas social assistance was administered by the municipalities.

As a result of the reform and the merger of two benefit systems (unemployment assistance and social assistance), the FEA now is solely responsible for the recipients of the insurance-based unemployment benefit I (UB I). The tax-funded and means-tested unemployment benefit II (UB II), as well as active labor market services for all unemployed, that are not eligible for UB I, is usually administered in 'joint facilities' (JFs) where the FEA works together with the municipalities. In the JFs, responsibilities for tasks and funding are clearly separated. Furthermore, 110 municipalities have been licensed to administer the UB II on their own, the so-called opt-out municipalities.

The major political instrument to hold the reformed FEA accountable to the parental Ministry of Labour and Social Affairs (BMAS) are target agreements that are formulated separately for each benefit regime. As in Norway, there are structural asymmetries between the ministry and the FEA. The reorganization has also resulted in three different accountability regimes in place (UB I, UB II divided into joint facilities and opt-out municipalities) with different competencies and power resources to hold the delivery units to account. As a result, the ministry is navigating between central control, autonomy of the FEA as a self-regulated body and the principle of local self-government, creating an accountability regime with limited political accountability. A respondent from the ministry has described the current system as follows:

> Concerning the UB I we only have the legal oversight, that means we are looking if the instructions from the head office of the FEA are in conformity with the law. Everything else, as the control of efficiency and effectiveness is the task of the FEA. [...] Nevertheless, the political responsibility is with us and that is tricky as it is not in our competence. In the realm of the UB II [...] we also have the functional oversight. However, you have to differentiate between the joint-facilities and the opt-out municipalities. For the joint facilities, we have the functional oversight and thus the de facto responsibility for what happens on the ground. For the opt-out municipalities [...], we have the political responsibility but no oversight possibilities at all. This is a lost cause, I would say.

The new organizational model has proven to be a rather unstable and complex institutional solution. The partnership model implies per se a shared accountability between the national and the municipal level. Especially the Federal Court of Auditors has repeatedly criticized accountability and steering problems in both organizational models (Bundesrechnungshof 2006a, 2006b).

The leadership structure of the FEA has also been changed as a result of the reform. Prior to the reform, the operations of the FEA were dominated by what has been called 'welfare corporatism', signifying the intensive involvement of the social partners. The social partners had not only wide-ranging competencies in the supervision of the agency but also for operational measures, budget and staffing policy (Jantz and Jann 2013). After the reform, the responsibility for operational policies has been transferred to a full-time management board. The role of the social partners as accountability forum of the FEA has been reduced drastically as the management board is more or less autonomous in setting internal targets and operational policies. The tripartite administrative board has only a limited influence in the target-setting process (they have to approve the targets ex post).

In contrast to the rather loose political accountability structures, the internal accountability system of the FEA is highly detailed, formalized and target driven for both benefit regimes, UB I and II. A highly complex target system has evolved with procedural indicators (waiting time, duration of benefit application), as well as output and outcome indicators (number of job placements, number of job to job transitions) that are broken down from the management board to the regional and the local level. The target system is combined with a system of pay-for-performance for the senior management at all levels based on target achievement. Through the increased importance of numbers and also because of a new self-confidence of the reformed FEA, there is a constant tension between the political and statutory mandate and the focus on performance and efficiency.

What can be observed for the German case is that a compliance-based model of accountability has emerged with a strong management board that holds the different levels and units of the FEA accountable through a highly formalized controlling system and individual incentives (pay-for-performance). The controlling system is combining bureaucratic principles of input accountability with NPM principles focusing on performance. The 'welfare corporatism' model that has dominated the 'old' FEA has been replaced by a compliance model dominated by the management board. The political accountability is rather weak as the ministry either lacks the instruments (UB I), the resources (JFs) or the formal position and power (opt-out municipalities) to hold the different organizational entities that are providing the services into account. Thus, the changed accountability structures have empowered especially the management board while disempowering the social partners. Even though there are other forums present such as the municipal and regional governments, the Court of Auditors or the media, they are dispersed and rather form a patchwork than a coherent accountability regime (Papadopoulos 2010). They have different concerns, power and procedures that generate competing agendas and capacities.

In both countries, the reforms were radical departures from the original organizational model and represent a complex arrangement and division of responsibility, especially between central and local authorities. In the following, the reform processes, as well as their effects for the accountability relations according to the presented framework, are analyzed.

The reform process in Norway

The reform process in Norway started in December 2001, when the parliament instructed the minority Bondevik II government to give a report on how the welfare bureaucracy could be integrated. Despite the large political consensus regarding the need for reform, there was a strong disagreement on how exactly the different services should be transformed. In fact, the first government white paper, based on the work of an inter-ministerial working group, was rejected by parliament as it proposed that the administration should continue to be divided into three parts (pensions, labor and social services). This resulted in a conflict between the minority government and the parliament, which has been described by a former leading opposition parliamentarian as follows:

> And then we had a very special political situation, because we send that white paper back to government. We just send it back, and said this was not what we asked for. We asked for a white paper discussing one merged NAV [...] When you are a minister in a minority government, you need to discuss things with the people in the parliament before you come with a white paper, and she [the minister] didn't do

that. And therefore why should we use all this time dealing with a white paper with a completely different approach, and we saw it's soon election again, and that the political play was more important.

Thereon, an external expert commission was assigned to resolve the deadlock between the minority government and the parliament. However, the commission reached a similar conclusion as the working group (Christensen et al. 2007a), but the government was reluctant to present a new proposal that was almost identical to the rejected one.

In the end, a political compromise that merged the two national agencies but kept social services as a responsibility of the local level was proposed and finally accepted. The reform also profited from a major reorganization of the ministerial portfolio. In June 2004, the former Minister of Health took over the responsibility for the newly created Ministry of Labour and Social Affairs, encompassing the responsibility for the welfare and the employment administration, as well as the division regulating local governments' social services administration for the first time.

Even though a full-state responsibility had been judged as a better solution by the ministry, this was not feasible because of different veto points, as the former minister had stressed:

> We were all a bit doubtful about what to do with the municipality. This municipal responsibility – because ideally it should have been a part of state responsibility. If I had had total freedom at that time, I would . . . that's what I would have proposed. The reason why we didn't do it was at this time, we had no further appetite on centralization of welfare responsibility [. . .] there was a time of conflict between municipalities and the state. And also about the Minister of Municipalities. She wouldn't go for it.

The partnership model in this regard served as a 'placebo' because it created the illusion that the central and local services were integrated. In reality, however, it consisted of two administrations collaborating with one another (Christensen et al. 2007a).

The reform process in Norway was characterized by a power game between the minority government and the parliament. The combination of an unwilling ministerial leadership without much support in parliament, an inexperienced minister at the beginning of the reform process, resistance from the welfare bureaucracy and a parliamentary initiative that was rather ambiguous regarding how an integrated service should be organized led to a rather low level of rational thinking in the reform process (Aberbach and Christensen 2014). Neither the political nor the administrative leadership had control in the reform phase because the parliament was driving the whole process.

To sum up, the reform process shows clear negotiation-based instrumental features with a high conflict intensity between the government, on the one side, and the parliament, on the other side. The municipalities became later involved, mainly through their interest representation, the Norwegian Association of Local and Regional Authorities (KS). These negotiations were shaped by institutional features, such as the strength of the parliament in a minority-government setting, as well as the strong role of local self-governance in Norway.

The reform process also shed light on the relationship between problems and solutions. The problems induced by the fragmentation of the welfare state were rather diffuse and hard to measure, making their recognition very much dependent on policymakers' political and personal interpretation. The rather limited problem of multi-service users that had to navigate between the different organizations resulted in the wide-ranging solution of a complete merger of 16,000 employees from three very different organizational cultures. It can also be argued that in a garbage can style (Cohen *et al.* 1972), a solution (the one-door policy) was searching for a problem.

The reform process in Germany

The reform process in Germany started at the beginning of 2002 with a report from the German Federal Court of Auditors, which discovered that officials of the Federal Employment Agency (FEA) falsified their placement statistics in order to report higher activity levels. Due to the bad reputation of the FEA regarding its chronic budget deficit and its low level of efficiency, media transformed this revelation into the so-called placement scandal, calling for an immediate political reaction (Kemmerling and Bruttel 2006). However, the importance of the audit report should not be overestimated; it rather functioned as a policy window for a reform-minded group of ministerial bureaucrats and politicians from different parties that have not only been dissatisfied with the performance of the FEA, but also with the inactivity in labor market policies of the red-green government in its first term. Thus, the placement scandal paved the way for policy proposals that have been elaborated among key experts and policymakers prior to the scandal (Fleckenstein 2011). In a first reaction, the red-green government presented a two-stage plan to reform the FEA. In the first stage, the management structure of the FEA was changed and the influence of the social partners significantly reduced, with the aim to reorganize the FEA from a public administration with self-administration into a service provider with private management structures (BT-Drs. 14/8546). In the aftermath of the scandal, neither the social partners nor the opposition parties opposed this bill. A respondent from the German Confederation of Trade Unions had put it that way: 'Self-administration has lost much of its importance since the Hartz reforms. This was also a stated aim of the reform – the intentional disempowerment of the social partner in order to promote governmental targets'.

In the second stage, the introduction of an independent government commission (called the Hartz Commission after its chairman) led to a process that changed the traditional policy formulation process in labor market policies significantly. The introduction of the commission broke with former tripartite reform approaches and thus repealed the de facto veto position of the social partners (Kemmerling and Bruttel 2006). The commission clearly voted for a merger of unemployment assistance and social assistance to a new benefit, the UB II. The idea of a merger of the two benefits regime was thus finally put on the agenda, even though these ideas have been discussed and launched long before the introduction of the commission. Since the commission gave no concrete recommendation on the responsibilities and accountability structures in the new system, one has to look at the reform process following the presentation of the final report and the different interests at stake in this process. It was highly contested who should be in the lead in the new policy regime, the FEA or the local level. A new commission was set up to work inter alia on this question, but the final report only presented three different models on how unemployment and social assistance could be reformed. The initiative was thus returned to the political arena. Here, two opposed reform coalitions have evolved. The social democrats, the trade unions and two umbrella organizations of the local level (the German Association of Cities and the German Association of Towns and Municipalities) were in favor of a responsibility of the FEA, whereas the Christian democrats, the Association of the German Counties and the employer association argued for a municipalization of the responsibility for long-term unemployed (Jantz 2004). The compromise negotiated through the mediation committee of the Bundestag (first chamber) and the Bundesrat (second chamber) then proposed the solution that the FEA should cooperate with the municipalities in the JFs as the basic model and the full municipal responsibility as an optional model.

In Germany, the beginning of the reform process can, to a great extent, be understood from a hierarchical-instrumental perspective. Modernizers from the ministry and the leading governmental party – the social democrats – had a clear goal to reform the leadership structures of the FEA, to transform it into a business-like agency and to disempower the social partners, especially the trade unions. This was possible due to three main reasons:

1 A policy window through the placement scandal that expanded the plausible choices open to powerful actors substantially.
2 A supporting coalition not only of the governmental parties but also from the opposition in the aftermath of the scandal. This process has been facilitated by a disintegration of industrial relations and the corresponding weakening of institutions controlled by the social partners, such as the FEA.
3 An ideal scapegoat as the FEA was for long been seen as a 'large, sleepy and inefficient public bureaucracy'.

(Kemmerling and Bruttel 2006: 94)

However, after the initial consensus, especially among the two major parties (social and Christian Democrats), the reform process entered into a political gridlock. The two parties, as well as the mayor local government organizations, were divisive on who should have the responsibility for the long-term unemployed – the local or the central level. This gridlock was reinforced by institutional constraints, as the approval of the second chamber, where the Christian Democrats had the majority, was necessary. The negotiations resulted in a compromise that opted neither for a central nor for a municipal solution, but a forced partnership. Even though the power fragmentation did not completely inhibit policy changes, the necessary compensation strategies and political compromises made a solution to overcome the organizational fragmentation impossible to achieve.

Comparative discussion

The reform cases analyzed in this article show diverse reform processes in which several driving forces supplement and complement one another, and in combination explain reform trajectories and changing accountability structures. Rather than an either/or explanation, we need to combine different explanatory factors. Reform outcomes cannot be explained in terms of single features – through the free choice of powerful political executives, political compromises or institutional constraints. In Norway, the political-administrative context is crucial for understanding the reform process. Policy formulation and decision-making process had clear negotiated features that constrained hierarchical steering. Initially, the government tried to avoid adapting to the demands from parliament, but non-adaption proved to be a politically unsuccessful strategy under conditions of a minority government and a parliament that wanted to demonstrate its strengths. The administrative leadership in the ministries continued to advocate the fragmented model that the parliament had rejected, but the new minister finally proposed a compromise that was approved. This political entrepreneurship by the minister finally had some of the hierarchical features expected to be observed in reform processes (Aberbach and Christensen 2014) – even though the means-end thinking of the minister rather focused on political goals than on an optimal administrative solution. An interesting feature of the reform process is that the administrative leaders who favored a fragmented solution could not gain acceptance. As expected, the mainly negotiation-based reform process has led to an accountability regime that is unsettled and constantly in flux and negotiated between politicians that expect an anticipation of their political will on an ad hoc basis. The ministry is struggling with the complexity of the structure and activities of the reformed agency and the administrative leadership in the agency has to balance the different priorities. This results in a situation of contrived randomness with the presence of different powerful forums, contradictory expectations and turf battles between different organizations or units.

In Germany, by contrast, the reform at the beginning clearly profited from strong political leadership that abruptly weakened the long-lasting tradition of welfare corporatism in the leadership structure of the FEA. It also installed the management board as new dominant accountability forum with a strong compliance focus. Yet, the longer the reform process lasted, the decisions taken were constrained by re-emerging structural constraints and the institutional factors overlapped and influenced individual action, as well as the strategic negotiation of collective actors. Indeed, the outcome of the organizational arrangement is a prime example of the German political system, which has been described as 'cooperative federalism' (Auel 2010) that distribute financing, decision-making and political accountability across all federal levels. Party majorities in the two legislative chambers were different at the time and the Christian Democrats wanted to demonstrate their strength, and some of their leaders had a clear preference for a municipal responsibility. By setting up the JFs and the opt-out municipalities with rather unclear governance structures, the opportunity for a coherent concept has been missed. Instead, highly complex and sometimes impracticable accountability structures have been created, leading to the fact that different forums (federal ministry, regional and local governments, FEA) mobilize and struggle over who is accepted as accountability forum, over distributions of information, power, and what are legitimate roles. While the reform of the unemployment benefit system was supported by a large coalition of all major political parties and institutions alike, the organizational implementation has revealed strong institutional obstacles.

The following table gives a comparative overview about the reform processes and changing accountability relations in the two countries.

The reform outcomes in both countries are the result of a complex process of powering, puzzling and institutional constraints where different situational interpretations of problems, interests and administrative legacies such as local self-government or 'cooperative federalism' had to be balanced. Reforms have taken place as the legitimacy of old organizational tasks and

Table 6.1 Comparing the dynamics of accountability

	Norway	Germany
Reform process	Conflict and negotiation between the minority government and parliament. Institutional constraints through local self-government.	Instrumental-hierarchical at the beginning – strong institutional constraints and party conflicts over the course of the reform process.
Forum constellations	Parliament more active, marginalization of local government, lacking capacities of the ministry, problems of goal-focus for administrative leadership.	Strong management board evolving, marginalization of social partners, reluctant ministry, separation of the local level.
Dominant accountability approach	Contrived randomness combined with managerial approach by the administrative leadership.	Compliance-based approach within the FEA, contrived randomness for the domain of UB II.

Source: Own compilation.

borders have been challenged. New organizations and relationships have been established, generating new forms of integration and separation, new power relationships and changing accountability forums and mechanisms. These transformations were driven by political ideology and needs for political compromise rather than evidence and analysis producing unintended effects, including unclear accountability relations. Accountability thus results not from a single process of environmental necessity or strategic choice, but from a dynamic interplay between different actors and institutional spheres.

Conclusion

In the emerging multilevel accountability settings studied, dyadic accountability relationships between principal and agent are, to a large extent, replaced by disaggregated modes of accountability. Different forums of accountability – parliament, ministries, central, regional and local agencies, the media, audit offices – are dispersed and do not form a coherent accountability system. The latter would require that forums regularly communicate with each other to coordinate their expectations, instruments and actions. In this regard, the picture of a forum patchwork, as introduced by Papadopoulos (2010), is an adequate description.

Furthermore, the lacking resources of the parental ministries and the increasing organizational complexity of service delivery reduce the accountability capacity of the ministry, and thus political accountability. This is in line with previous research that has shown that a limited government capacity, as well as task complexity, increases the need to loosen control and accountability provisions (Koop 2011). Last but not least, the results are a plea for further research on the dynamics of accountability as it has been shown that accountability is never perfectly institutionalized, fulfilled and static.

Note

1 For an overview on different indices and the German and Norwegian position, see Schmidt (2010: 332–3).

References

Aberbach, J. D. and Christensen, T. (2014) Why reforms so often disappoint. *The American Review of Public Administration*, 44(1): 3–16.

Auel, K. (2010) Between Reformstau and Länder Strangulation? German co-operative federalism reconsidered. *Regional and Federal Studies*, 20(2): 229–49.

Bach, T. (2014) *Autonomie und Steuerung verselbständigter Behörden: Eine empirische Analyse am Beispiel Deutschlands und Norwegens*. Wiesbaden: Springer.

Biela, J. and Papadopoulos, Y. (2014) The empirical assessment of agency accountability: a regime approach and an application to the German Bundesnetzagentur. *International Review of Administrative Sciences*, 80(2): 362–81.

Bleiklie, I., Lægreid, P. and Wik, M. H. (2003) *Changing Government Control in Norway: High Civil Service, Universities and Prisons*. Working Paper, Stein Rokkan Center for Social Studies.

BT-Drs. 14/8546. *Bericht des Ausschusses für Arbeit und Sozialordnung zu dem Gesetzentwurf der Bundesregierung–Drucksache 14/8214*. Berlin: Deutscher Bundestag.

Bundesrechnungshof (2006a) *Durchführung der Grundsicherung für Arbeitsuchende. Wesentliche Ergebnisse der Prüfungen im Rechtskreis des Zweiten Buches Sozialgesetzbuch*. Bonn: Bundesrechnungshof.

Bundesrechnungshof (2006b) *Mitteilung an die Bundesagentur für Arbeit über die Prüfung Handlungsprogram der Bundesagentur für Arbeit*. Bonn: Bundesrechnungshof.

Champion, C. and Bonoli, G. (2011) Institutional fragmentation and coordination initiatives in Western European welfare states. *Journal of European Social Policy*, 21(4): 323–34.

Christensen, T., Fimreite, A. and Lægreid, P. (2007a) Reform of the employment and welfare administrations: the challenges of coordinating diverse public organizations. *International Review of Administrative Sciences*, 73(3): 389–408.

Christensen, T., Fimreite, A. L. and Lægreid, P. (2014) Joined-up government for welfare administration reform in Norway. *Public Organization Review*, 14(4): 439–56.

Christensen, T. and Lægreid, P. (2012) Competing principles of agency organization: the reorganization of a reform. *International Review of Administrative Sciences*, 78(4): 579–96.

Christensen, T., Lægreid, P., Roness, P. G. and Røvik, K. A. (2007b) *Organization Theory and the Public Sector: Instrument, Culture and Myth*. London: Routledge.

Cohen, M. D., March, J. G. and Olsen, J. P. (1972) A garbage can model of organizational choice. *Administrative Science Quarterly*, 17(1): 1–25.

Day, P. and Klein, R. (1987) *Accountabilities: Five Public Services*. London/New York: Tavistock.

Dubnick, M. (2011) Move over Daniel: we need some 'accountability space'. *Administration and Society*, 43(6): 704–16.

Dubnick, M. J. and O'Brien, J. (2010) Rethinking the obsession: accountabilty and the financial crisis. In M. J. Dubnick and H. G. Frederickson (eds), *Accountable Governance: Problems and Promises*, New York: M. E. Sharpe, pp. 282–301.

Fimreite, A. L. and Lægreid, P. (2009) Reorganizing the welfare state administration: partnership, networks and accountability. *Public Management Review*, 11(3): 281–97.

Fleckenstein, T. (2011) *Institutions, Ideas and Learning in Welfare State Change: Labour Market Reforms in Germany*. Basingstoke: Palgrave Macmillan.

Frendreis, J. (1983) Explanation of variation and detection of covariation. *Comparative Political Studies*, 16(2): 255–72.

Jantz, B. (2004) Zusammenlegung von Arbeitslosen- und Sozialhilfe. In W. Jann and G. Schmid (eds), *Eins zu Eins? Eine Zwischenbilanz der Hartz-Reformen am Arbeitsmarkt*. Berlin: Edition Sigma, pp. 38–50.

Jantz, B. and Jann, W. (2013) Mapping accountability changes in labour market administrations: from concentrated to shared accountability? *International Review of Administrative Sciences*, 79(2): 227–48.

Kemmerling, A. and Bruttel, O. (2006) 'New politics' in German labour market policy? The implications of the recent Hartz reforms for the German welfare state. *West European Politics*, 29(1): 90–112.

Koop, C. (2011) Explaining the accountability of independent agencies: the importance of political salience. *Journal of Public Policy*, 31(2): 209–34.

Lægreid, P. (2014) Accountability and New Public Management. In M. Bovens, R. E. Goodin and T. Schillemans (eds), *The Oxford Handbook of Public Accountability*, Oxford: Oxford University Press, pp. 324–38.

Lodge, M. and Hood, C. (2010) Regulation inside government: retro theory vindicated or outdated? In R. Baldwin, M. Cave and M. Lodge (eds), *The Oxford Handbook of Regulation*, Oxford: Oxford University Press, pp. 590–609.

March, J. G. and Olsen, J. P. (1983) Organizing political life: what administrative reorganization tells us about government. *American Political Science Review*, 77(2): 281–96.

Olsen, J. P. (2013) The institutional basis of democratic accountability. *West European Politics*, 36(3): 447–73.

Papadopoulos, Y. (2010) Accountability and multi-level governance: more accountability, less democracy? *West European Politics*, 33(5): 1030–49.

Philp, M. (2009) Delimiting democratic accountability. *Political Studies*, 57(1): 28–53.

Romzek, B. (2000) Dynamics of public accountability in the era of reform. *International Review of Administrative Sciences*, 66(1): 21–44.

Romzek, B. S. and Dubnick, M. J. (1987) Accountability in the public sector: lessons from the Challenger tragedy. *Public Administration Review*, 47(3): 227–38.

Schmidt, M. G. (2010) *Demokratietheorien: Eine Einführung*. Wiesbaden: Springer-Verlag.

Vibert, F. (2014) The need for a systemic approach. In M. Bovens, R. E. Goodin and T. Schillemans (eds), *The Oxford Handbook of Public Accountability*, Oxford: Oxford University Press, pp. 655–60.

Willems, T. and Van Dooren, W. (2012) Coming to terms with accountability. *Public Management Review*, 14(7): 1011–36.

Wollmann, H. (2000) Local government modernization in Germany: between incrementalism and reform waves. *Public Administration*, 78(4): 915–36.

Yang, L. (2012) Further understanding accountability in public organizations actionable knowledge and the structure-agency duality. *Administration and Society*, 44(3): 255–84.

7

THE WELFARE STATE IN FLUX

Individual responsibility and changing accountability relations in social services[1]

Piret Tõnurist and Wouter De Tavernier

Introduction

Increasingly new, experimental and collaborative forms of governance are called for to solve complex social problems (Hartley *et al.* 2013). They illustrate a transition in service principles from universalism to particularism visible in the emergence of personalized and targeted services (Lember *et al.* 2015). In the prior 40–50 years, the welfare state has operated with a certain logic of universality – a concept that can be interpreted in many ways (Goul Andersen 2012) – making services available to the entire population or a large part thereof. Recently, however, there has been a shift away from rights to conditional support (for example, Dwyer 2004), facilitated by the diffusion of information and communication technology (ICT).

Collaborative governance can be seen as part of a larger empowering policy in which the government tries to increase participatory legitimacy when confronted with dissatisfaction with traditional governance methods. However, political debates regarding the introduction of collaborative governance models are mainly dominated by arguments of public sector efficiency, especially since the recent economic downturn. Therefore, it is not surprising that, in practice, the motivation to include citizens in efforts to redefine or redesign services are usually connected to financial cutback strategies (de Vries *et al.* 2015). Consequently, collaborative governance seems to serve two underlying rationales: first, rejuvenating democracy; and second, lessening the (financial) burden of government. In both cases of reasoning, these processes are usually boundary crossing and involve citizens, stakeholders and public officials. This has boosted the academic debate regarding the coordination and network governance of these various stakeholders, but with it the end user is paradoxically left out of the analysis (Surva *et al.* 2016). With the individual level neglected, the effects of personalized and targeted services on the citizen-state relationship within these social innovations are under-explored.

In this chapter, we explore how these transitions change responsibility and accountability relations between the citizen and the state in the field of social welfare. Accountability is usually addressed from the aspect of state and 'non-state' actors mapping the relationships around public agencies (Norris 2014), leaving the citizen-specific perspective aside. This is, of course, understandable, because when 'accountability' is defined in academic literature, it is usually described as the obligation to justify actions to a wider forum and face consequences in the light of outcomes (Bovens 2007: 447). However, if welfare services are becoming increasingly personalized, placing the responsibility on the individual and making self-assessment the norm, would this not weaken accountability? Personal choices of citizens cannot face such scrutiny and the forum of peers can become ineffective in very targeted and specialized topics. Therefore, we ask in this chapter, who is accountable for outcomes when the choice of and participation in services are made by individuals, and how would this possibly change the architecture of the welfare state? We hypothesize that when faced with individual responsibility, a possible coping strategy for these individuals could be to reconsolidate the responsibilities initially put on the individual into advocacy groups and target communities. As such, the individualization of welfare services could mean a shift from political to societal accountability.

Theoretical framework

With the introduction of structural and financial retrenchment in social policy, the golden age of universalism and equal accessibility to welfare has ended. Instead, welfare states are moving towards localized, individualized and targeted interventions and collaborative governance structures to accommodate them (Emerson *et al.* 2012; Jakobsen and Andersen 2013). Bringing the governance of services closer to the 'consumer' is presumed to increase efficiency, productivity and the problem-solving capacity of the public sector, and to improve service quality (Hartley *et al.* 2013). Thus, welfare service reforms across Europe show trends towards new service delivery models that can be categorized by their market orientation (competitive tendering), bureaucratic (expert systems) or collaborative (involvement of autonomous stakeholders) tendencies (Hartley *et al.* 2013). Collaborative governance, defined as the possibility to 'carry out a public purpose that could not otherwise be accomplished' (Emerson *et al.* 2012: 2), could improve the welfare state's performance in terms of dealing with complex, 'wicked' problems. Thus, citizens are directly or indirectly being called to participate in policymaking, to co-create in these new, innovative service delivery approaches (Bekkers *et al.* 2013).

In the theoretical framework, we explain how two core transitions in the welfare state – a movement from universalism to particularism, and the privatization of service provision – can change accountability relationships within social services. Via these processes, the individual is made responsible for his or her own service delivery, and hence for the individual output and outcomes of these services. We claim that this process might lead to societal accountability if these individuals organize into interest and advocacy groups that hold the government accountable not as much for individual outcomes, but for outcomes at the aggregate level. This process is illustrated in Figure 7.1, and it will be explained in the sections below.

Welfare state transitions

Social policies are increasingly based on targeted and individualized approaches, and this is a sign of a transition from universalism to particularism[2] (Lember *et al.* 2015). This process is associated with the spread of ICT solutions, also because many of these technologies include a certain level of self-service, leading to 'self-governance' or a 'self-service democracy' (Eriksson 2012) in which individuals are able to help themselves with limited state interference. This new, personalized model of governance can be described by three different characteristics: user focus, interactive basis and personalized approaches. Moreover, values such as 'self-motivation', 'self-reliance' and 'self-responsibility' are taking center stage (Miller and Rose 2008: 92). This is strongly advocated for in several policy fields, such as activation (Serrano Pascual 2007), self-care policies (Sundsli *et al.* 2012) and housing assistance (Jacobs *et al.* 2014).

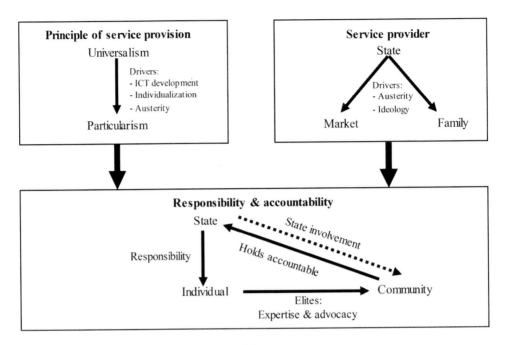

Figure 7.1 Transition in accountability, causal model

These new formats of governance also reflect increasing individualization and respect for the dependent's own preferences. Hence, the guiding principle is that individuals should be able to decide for themselves which services they need and even how they should be provided. This means that there is a renegotiation of the social contract under which welfare is coproduced, that is, citizens produce their own services (Pestoff 2009) or are at least responsible for their own service reception. For instance, active inclusion has been defined as a reinterpretation of the relationship between citizens and the state, redefining the social contract towards individual responsibility (Serrano Pascual 2007). With the increase of citizens' engagement and the state's formal disengagement from responsibility, relations between the public, private and nonprofit sectors and the citizens themselves are fundamentally reshaped.

This process does not simply shift the responsibility for service delivery to the individual, but it also implicates a transition in service providers. If governments retreat from welfare provision, markets would typically fill the gap – at least for those who can afford it. Others (have to) rely on their families for the provision of the service. Hence, 'familization' of policies takes place, for instance in the field of care (Javornik 2014): either policies can explicitly support family care (for example, by paying informal caregivers via cash-for-care schemes or by explicitly making care support dependent on the absence of family), or they can implicitly lead to family care – typically when the dependent person receives insufficient income to purchase care from the private marketplace. A different dynamic, however, could be found in 'familial' countries that start out with limited engagements in certain fields of welfare provision. In the absence of initial universal service delivery, individual responsibility for care is higher to begin with, and thus there is no considerable resistance if social innovation takes place, making it a fertile ground for changes. In this case, the government in its new coordinator function may in fact take new responsibilities through the back door.

Changing responsibility and accountability relationships

Before we move on to discuss how the processes described above influence responsibility and accountability relationships within social service provision, which is the goal of this section, we have to clarify the exact meaning of the concepts of responsibility and accountability. Differentiation between the two is not a straightforward exercise, as many authors use the terms interchangeably (Lindkvist and Llewellyn 2003). According to Bovens (2007: 450), accountability is 'a relationship between an actor and a forum, in which the actor has an obligation to explain and to justify his or her conduct, the forum can pose questions and pass judgement, and the actor may face consequences'. Hence, accountability is essentially about external, retrospective motivation of one's actions (Frees, van Acker and Bouckaert 2015), while responsibility is a pre-assigned duty. In a state setting, formal institutions structure political responsibilities, setting the limits within which the executive power can act (Anderson 2000). Hence, it is important to examine where responsibility is assigned, because this will influence the later accountability relations: one can only be held accountable for issues falling within their responsibilities.

In what follows, we will describe how the personalization of social services leads to a shift in responsibility from the state to the individual – individuals cannot be held accountable for the choices they make in terms of the provision of welfare services to them – while the state remains accountable for policy outcomes not at the individual, but at the aggregate, level.

Personalized social services and the effects of choice

The idea behind social innovation processes is to make users and communities part of planning and delivery through including them in the decision-making process and empowering citizens by sharing knowledge on resources and their allocation (Bovaird 2007). By bringing the governance of services closer to the 'consumer', policymakers hope to gather more insights from the 'street level'. This can happen by giving service users a choice, both at the level of policy design and at the level of individual service consumption. The former usually means that the public sector is opened up and consumers and other stakeholders are involved in service design and innovation. At the individual level, on the other hand, users can be involved via service choice or as the providers of information necessary for service delivery. As such, citizens become more responsible for the 'quality' of the service itself, which leads to an erosion of the responsibility of public institutions (Eriksson 2012). As accountability requires responsibility, this erosion inevitably leads to a decrease in public sector accountability.

The idea that individual choice of services will lead to higher-quality services is based on the assumption that it gives service users a 'voice', giving them the opportunity to raise grievances that otherwise would have been swept under the rug (Jilke and Van de Walle 2013). Choice advocates make no secret that the goal is to shift power from service providers towards the 'clients' (Le Grand 2007), and thus independent consumerism is equalized with personal freedom. However, while user satisfaction can increase with 'personalized' approaches, the evidence on better outcomes has not been conclusive, calling this basic assumption of the marketization literature into question (for example, Vancoppenolle and Verschuere 2012). It is indeed a complex task to gather knowledge about the services provided and compare this to other available services, which has now been assigned to the individual (Breit and Salomon 2015). As a result, the effects of such quasi-markets on citizens have been questioned (Grosso and Van Ryzin 2012; Florio 2013). There is little evidence that users of services actually respond to performance information available to them, and psychological behavioral public administration research shows that citizens experience great difficulties in making decisions based on numeric information and coping with 'choice overload' (Peters *et al.* 2013). Individuals with lower socioeconomic status, the lower educated and the elderly have notably greater difficulties in exercising choice (Meinow, Parker and Thorslund 2011), meaning that market-based providers can become unresponsive to the needs of those precarious groups (Tummers, Jilke and Van de Walle 2013). According to Jilke and Van de Walle (2013), increased marketization and personalization of public services fosters a 'two-track' public service where more vulnerable service users are even worse off.

In sum, it seems that these new social innovation models advance input and throughput legitimacy of the government, but that the effects in terms of output legitimacy are less unequivocally positive. This is especially problematic as the decrease in output legitimacy coincides with the reduction of political accountability – both result from the same processes. This means that it becomes more difficult for those who are worse off after such public service reforms to hold policymakers accountable for the deterioration of their condition. As we explain in the section below, one way to overcome this problem would be to assemble into advocacy groups in order to compensate for the loss of political accountability by an increase in societal accountability – but those groups who are most likely to fall victim to reforms that take services towards particularism and marketization are the ones least likely to get involved in such advocacy initiatives.

The community and emergence of societal accountability

In a world of increasingly collaborative and horizontal forms of welfare governance, asymmetric power relationships may appear, because different stakeholders, especially individual citizens, have different capabilities. Social partners can be marginalized next to more dominant and 'vocal' elites in horizontal decision-making. Indeed, most of these new service provision networks are based on non-elected participatory processes (Mosley and Grogan 2013) and increasingly horizontally governed (Sarapuu *et al.* 2014). These trends can narrow political debate and have very depoliticizing effects: political issues can become the area of separate and specialized personal transaction with the government. The user-driven innovation logic would at the same time assume that at least some people involved in the decision-making process belong to the target group. Coproduction usually refers to a joint action of the provider and end users. Hence, the concept still has a strong element of community-based action in it. While the main question in collaborative governance literature is 'who' should participate, the core principle behind most of these new co-creative social initiatives is that citizens have to actually want to or be able to participate (Jakobsen 2013). This is usually tied to the intrinsic motivation of citizens (e.g. stemming from personal experience with a problem or faith) (Surva *et al.* 2016). As such, collaborative governance processes mean a shift from political accountability to individual responsibility and societal accountability. As outlined above, people with a higher socioeconomic status seem to co-create and coproduce more (Jakobsen and Andersen 2013). Thus, the ability to participate in coproduction (having the necessary resources) is often negatively correlated with the actual need for the service (Jakobsen 2013). Finding individuals from low-income communities to partake in collaborative processes might prove difficult (Mosley and Grogan 2013). And thus, processes usually fail to deliver the intended outcome when engagement is limited (Emerson *et al.* 2012); they might not be a good instrument to deal with wicked problems.

Hence, collaborative governance initiatives tend to become elite-based and professionalized when dealing with specific, targeted problems (Lember *et al.* 2015). These networks can then take over the tasks originally assigned to the individual, in which case the reaction to the shift of responsibility on to the individual level can be a dynamic one, leading to cyclical or iterative governance processes (Emerson *et al.* 2012). Thus, after the wave of self-responsibility endorsement, strategic collaborative management approaches can become the response to individualized obligations. When community-based collaborative actions emerge, they can strengthen a renewed idea of 'government though community' (Miller and Rose 2008: 90), a process leading to a dynamic reshuffling of responsibilities within the modern welfare state from the individual level to target-specific communities advocating individuals' interests. Hence, the initial loss of political accountability now leads to increased social accountability.

Data and methodology

This work is based on the 7th Framework Programme project LIPSE (Learning from Innovation in Public Sector Environments). While the project also covered cases of urban regeneration, we use the data from the seven case studies of co-creation practices in the welfare sector presented in the project report (Voorberg *et al.* 2014). The case studies were conducted in seven countries (the United Kingdom, the Netherlands, Germany, Spain, Denmark, Estonia and Slovakia), following the cross-country comparative case study approach (Yin 2003). The countries were selected to cover different state traditions (for example, importance of central and local governments, reliance on the family or the community for the supply of services). The cases were selected based on the following criteria: citizens' involvement in the co-creation, social innovation project as a co-designer or an initiator, and some derived results to evaluate outcomes. In accordance with the criteria above, the project partners first delivered a sample of five descriptive case studies from the welfare sector per country (35 altogether). During this phase, five open-ended interviews with experts in citizen-state relationships from each country were also carried out. Among the 35 cases, one case from each country was selected for a more thorough analysis. Case diversity and longer-term engagement – to yield some insight into the change in accountability – were prioritized. Next, a minimum of 10 semi-structured interviews with both open and closed questions per case with key stakeholders were conducted for all seven cases in 2014. The interviews were recorded, transcribed and coded in the native language and a case description was prepared in English in accordance with a common case design protocol. The in-depth case descriptions were used for the analysis in this paper. Specific cases will not be discussed in detail, but are presented elsewhere (for example, Nemec *et al.* 2014; Voorberg *et al.* 2014). In the process of the cross-country comparison – after identifying the initial findings based on the protocol – additional factors for analysis were identified. The authors also triangulated data that were available on the cases in other sources after the preparation of the project report and the case descriptions. Hence, the research design can be regarded as explorative.

Results

The case studies were analyzed based on the most important coproduction factors identified in the literature (Voorberg *et al.* 2014), and they include both organizational (risk-aversive/legalistic public sector culture; attitudes of civil servants (professionalism); incentives; compatibility of the public sector) and citizen-relevant factors (willingness; feeling of ownership; social capital). This chapter does not analyze all of the factors individually – this has been presented in Voorberg *et al.* (2015) – but the goal here is to concentrate on the changes that the cases exemplify in terms of universalistic-particular service provision, responsibilization of citizens and accountability relationships.

In Table 7.1, the cases and their characteristics and contexts are presented. The cases cover a wide range of social innovation topics, from organizations supporting social businesses to projects

Table 7.1 Overview of results by case

	The Netherlands Starters4 Communities (S4C)	Germany Dialog macht Schule (DmS)	Estonia Maarja Küla (MK)	Slovakia Social housing Kojatice (SHK)	United Kingdom Dementia Care (DC)	Denmark Cases that Unite (CtU)	Spain Citilab (CL)
Short description	S4C is a booster of social entrepreneurship for starters and inhabitants of Amsterdam East.	DmS is an educational program for public schools facilitating personal and value development of students from migration backgrounds.	MK is a community-based assisted living initiative for youth with disabilities.	Social housing Kojatice focuses on housing for Roma citizens receiving social assistance, and is part of the Slovak People in Need citizen association dealing with social cohesion, humanitarian aid and and human rights.	Initiatives led by the Dementia Network for the inclusion of people with dementia.	CtU is a self-governing institution in Århus working with social businesses. Their goal is to strengthen contacts with healthcare providers and participation in cultural life among socially marginalized and disabled.	Citilab is a center for social and digital innovation in Cornellà de Llobregat, Barcelona.
Type*	New leisure class practices	Delegation practices Community practices	Delegation practices	Social microfinance Community practices	Delegation practices Community practices	Community practices New leisure class practices	Community practices
Welfare state	Rather de-familialist	Rather familialist	Familialist	Familialist	Rather de-familialist	De-familialist	Familialist
Characteristics	Social-entrepreneur-led Platform initiative Risk governance Local necessity	Advocacy-led, state involvement from the beginning Risk governance Target-group-specific	Stakeholder-led, state involvement and introduction of market mechanisms Target-group-specific	Advocacy-led Risk governance Target-group-specific, strong logic of particularism	Community- and municipality-led Target-group-specific Local necessity	Social-entrepreneur-led, community initiatives, minimal state involvement Platform initiative Local necessity	Social-entrepreneur- and state-led Platform initiative

Accountability/ responsibility	Reactionary to missing measures Increase in individual responsibility Accountability not increased	Accountability improvements not visible Accountability hard to determine	Initial increase in individual responsibility State accountability has increased, however services are provided through market mechanisms	Increase in individual responsibility and problem ownership Accountability improvements hard to determine	Individual responsibility Accountability assigned to private service providers through funding, control-led through financial evaluations	Individual action No state accountability	Self-determination, but state-led Participants note an increase in accountability, but awareness is low

★ Based on Lember et al. (2015).

Source: Authors, based on the LIPSE report (Voorberg et al. 2015).

aimed at improving the lives and living conditions of very specific target populations (e.g. individuals with dementia, youth with learning disabilities, Roma receiving social assistance or students from migrant backgrounds). Overall, the initiatives under review can be divided into three groups: advocacy-based initiatives (DC); service implementation initiatives dealing with specific 'risk groups' (DmS, SHK, MK) and 'platform' solutions for self-service citizens to collaborate on (ad hoc) projects (CtU, S4C, CL). The latter include participants with versatile interests who have a possibility to collaborate on different projects. In some cases, the processes are initiated by single social entrepreneurs and can thus be seen in many ways as led by the elite (i.e. new leisure class practices: CtU, S4C); the rest can by and large be characterized as community-led initiatives and delegation practices – where the state has initiated and funded projects (DC) or taken over the practice (MK). In Table 7.1, the cases are also placed within the coproduction typology (new leisure class, delegation, community and social microfinance practices) developed by Lember *et al.* (2015).

The cases develop in very different political contexts, for instance the states' orientations towards the family as the welfare provider. In the Southern and Eastern European countries observed in this study, the family is, to a large extent, relied on with regard to welfare provision. While Denmark is located at the other end of the continuum, the liberal and conservative welfare states in Western Europe (Germany, the Netherlands and the United Kingdom) take intermediary positions with differing levels of reliance on the family.

Several cases in this study (DC, DmS, MK, SHK) are very targeted, and hence adopt a strong logic of particularism. Cases that Unite and Starters4Communities, on the other hand, take a rather universal approach, supporting projects in a wide variety of fields. Citilab falls in-between universalistic and particularistic tendencies as their programs on e-literacy and other related topics have reached out to a larger public than the elderly they were originally designed for. This logic of particularism is connected to individuals' motivations for getting involved. In targeted co-creation cases, personal experience with the problem at hand seems to create a strong, long-term motivation for participating citizens (for example, individuals with a family member suffering from dementia, in the case of DC, or from a learning disability, in the case of MK). Solidarity seemed to be the key factor here. The influence of the origin of cases is, of course, self-evident: stemming from grass roots, they put more emphasis on the willingness and social capital of citizens. In universal cases, this sense of ownership and incentives were much harder to specify.

In some of the projects, the state was either an instigator or an actively involved partner (DmS, DC, CL). In the case of Dementia Care, the project grew out of the concern over the well-being of individuals with dementia in a primarily privatized care system. The others operate independently from the state in an attempt to fill a gap in state policies. Maarja Küla is a combination of both: developed and financed initially by private individuals due to Estonia's limited support for youth with learning disabilities, the government took over the services developed within the project later when they proved to be successful. Hence, the setting in which most of these cases developed is either one where there was no state involvement in a certain niche at all, or one where the market was relied on for service provision. The role of austerity is very prevalent in all these collaborative governance projects, and not only because many have seen a reduction in their public funding; in several cases, the government is not willing to engage in a certain field itself or projects are motivated by the withdrawal of the government and increased citizen responsibility.

As citizens' involvement was one criterion for the selection of cases, all programs entail substantial citizen responsibility. In familialist states, where the government had not taken certain responsibilities for the provision of welfare, the initiative was taken by citizens or civil society (MK, SHK). In the Dementia Care program, on the other hand, the state aimed at citizen involvement from the outset in an attempt to have more control over private care suppliers who take care of individuals with dementia. Finally, certain initiatives had a clear goal to operate completely independently from the state, either out of the determination to 'do better' than the state (CtU) or the conviction that the state cannot solve certain problems (S4C).

As some cases are rather new, it is unclear to what extent they (will) alter accountability relationships with the state. It is clear, however, that target-group-specific initiatives running over a longer period of time begin to act as advocacy groups for their specific populations, and hence entail a certain form of societal accountability. This is most visible in the cases of Dementia Care and Maarja Küla. In both cases, the state did indeed get involved in the projects: in the former case, the state was one of the initiative-takers, even though in the latter case the state only got involved when the project proved to be successful, and finally took it over. In other cases, the effects on accountability have been fuzzier: with increasingly diverse actors involved in service provision, especially in new service areas, it is difficult to assign accountability to specific public organizations.

Discussion

Of all the cases presented, arguably Dementia Care and Maarja Kula fit the process described in the theoretical framework best. That is no coincidence, as they are target-group-specific projects, and hence allow for strong advocacy of a population in need of extra care – which is not the case for the social entrepreneurship platform projects in the study (S4C, CtU, CL). Moreover, the other target-group-specific cases (DmS, SHK) are still in an early phase of development, making it hard to assess their full impact.

Dementia Care and Maarja Küla emerged in very different policy contexts. The former is a government initiative in a largely privatized care market aimed at improving the care for individuals with dementia; the latter is a citizens' initiative that emerged because of the lack of policies supporting youth with learning disabilities. In Estonia, the family is indeed considered to be the main provider of care and welfare. Hence, both cases comply with the initial conditions of our causal scheme (Figure 7.1): the initiatives are target-group-specific and hence have a strong logic of particularism, and they emerge in settings of non-state service provision (the market in the case of Dementia Care, and the family in the case of Maarja Küla).

Both cases involve high levels of individual responsibility. In a largely private care market (DC), individuals are responsible for choosing 'the right' care provider for them. In a situation where the government does not have any policies whatsoever for supporting a specific group of individuals in need of some kind of care (MK), full responsibility lies with the citizens anyway – either with the individual who needs care or with their family or community. In both cases, this situation has indeed led to a community action, signifying an emergence of social accountability. However, the trajectories leading to this community action have been very different in the two cases. Maarja Küla emerged as an elite-led project from the community, whereas in the case of Dementia Care the process was initiated by the state. Either way, both led to advocacy for the target population and ultimately increased the state's involvement in the care for their well-being. As a result of the Dementia Care project, the government began to reward private care providers who gave good care to individuals with dementia. Moreover, it encouraged community organizations to organize activities specifically for individuals with dementia. Thus, the state did not reinstate its direct responsibility for the service, but started to act as an enabler of better market-based services. Hence, government accountability did not increase directly, although public sector involvement did. The direct effect of advocacy was more visible in the case of Maarja Küla, where the state ultimately took over the project, and thus assumed responsibility for the provision of services in the field and opened itself up to more accountability in the field of social services for the disabled.

We could interpret the difference in these transitions in the light of state familialism. In Estonia's highly familialist context, this process of community formation on the basis of individual responsibility led to the involvement of the state, and hence a certain shift of responsibilities away from the family. By holding the state accountable for the lack of support for youth with learning disabilities, the state has finally taken over a task it initially considered a family responsibility. In the United Kingdom, a more de-familialist setting, the state has sought stronger involvement of the family and the community in the care for individuals with dementia by using them in the evaluation of private care providers and encouraging them to organize activities for the target group. As such, the state shifts certain responsibilities back to the family and the community, entailing a – mainly austerity-driven – process of re-familization. Hence, citizen responsibility and government accountability seem to develop in a cyclical manner.

What does the picture look like in the other two target-group-specific cases in this study? Dialog macht Schule seems to be very similar to Dementia Care in its setup. Aimed at improving the personal development of public school students with migration backgrounds, it is a project with a strong state involvement from the very beginning. Moreover, advocacy for the target group is one of the main goals of the project. Social housing Kojatice, on the other hand, has certain traits in common with Maarja Küla. It is a project set up by citizens with the aim of catering for the needs of a specific group of people who are not a subject of government policies – *in casu* housing for Roma receiving social assistance. However, the involvement of the target group (Roma) has been somewhat lackluster in terms of advocacy. Nevertheless, given this setup, it would seem reasonable that both Dialog macht Schule and Social housing Kojatice would lead to similar outcomes in terms of accountability relations and maybe even state intervention, though unfortunately the projects are still at too early a stage of development in order to test this.

The platform initiatives, in contrast, seem to not have led to any changes in accountability so far. Cases that Unite and Starters4Communities have even explicitly stated that they do not want to get involved with the state. In the case of Citilab, where the state is involved, interviewees did declare an increase in accountability, but their awareness on how this increase came about was very low. Platform initiatives as project facilitators combine very different social start-ups, and that also means that there is no center of gravity around which people with similar interests could converge to form a strong forum that would hold the state accountable. Hence, their advocacy capacity seems much weaker, limiting their ability to exert pressure on the government to improve service quality.

Conclusion

In an attempt to increase legitimacy, empower disadvantaged groups or reduce social welfare spending, governments are increasingly making use of collaborative governance strategies to tackle complex social problems. Such a transition could have important consequences in terms of responsibility and accountability relationships, as it increasingly places responsibilities on the individual. Hence, in this chapter, we ask who is accountable for outcomes, when the choices and the participation in services are person-specific and how this could possibly change the architecture of the welfare state. We argue that governments increase individual responsibility by adapting the logic of particularism rather than universalism in service provision and by shifting service provision away from the state on to the market, the family or the community. We hypothesize that when faced with individual responsibility and diluted government accountability, a possible coping strategy could be to reconsolidate the responsibilities initially placed on the individual into advocacy groups and target communities. As such, the individualization of welfare services could mean a shift from political to societal accountability.

Two cases of these targeted organizations, Dementia Care (the United Kingdom) and Maarja Küla (Estonia), have matured and largely confirm our hypotheses. They emerged in a context where the welfare provision for a specific group of people was not (or not any more) a responsibility of the state: the care for individuals with dementia has largely been left to the market of private care providers in the United Kingdom – in which case the responsibility for receiving 'good care' mainly lies with the individual, as it is the individual who chooses the care provider – and support for youth with learning disabilities was considered a family issue in Estonia. In both cases, this individual responsibility led to the formation of community action groups, though via different paths: in the case of Dementia Care, the government initiated the process in order to increase control over private care providers, while Maarja Küla was founded by the elite faced with the problem that youth with learning disabilities were not supported by the government. Both cases, however, successfully managed to act as advocacy groups for these disadvantaged groups, weighing on state policies. In Estonia's case, the government even took over the project once it proved to be successful. In conclusion, even though the responsibility for care and well-being was initially placed on the individual – which entails less political accountability – this resulted in both cases in the regrouping of interests within the community and led to increased societal accountability of the government via advocacy, and ultimately policy change.

Social housing Kojatice and Dialog macht Schule, the two other cases of targeted organizations, have certain characteristics that are similar to Maarja Küla and Dementia Care, respectively, and they emerged in similar contexts, although they are at too early a stage of development in order to analyze whether they will indeed lead to advocacy, societal accountability and policy change. The three platform initiative cases, Cases that Unite, Starters4Communities and Citilab, seem to have little effect on accountability, with two of the three cases even explicitly stating that they want to work independently of the state. Lacking a specific niche, platform organizations probably have too wide a scope to act as an advocacy group on a certain issue.

Our study suggests that welfare states feature certain cyclicality in terms of citizen responsibility, societal accountability and state responsibility. Avoiding political accountability, the state places the responsibility for individuals' well-being on those individuals or their families. When these individuals form a community that advocates for specific social rights, societal accountability can emerge that also creates politically active forums, which might in turn force the state to take up certain responsibilities again. We can see this happen in those cases in the study, which are at different stages in this cyclical process. In the Dementia Care project, the government successfully managed to familialize dementia care by including the family and the community in an otherwise fully marketized care system. Via this initiative, however, the state itself also got more involved in dementia care. Maarja Küla, which was founded in a familialist setting where the state lacked policies for supporting youth with learning disabilities and thus placed the responsibility on their families, managed to demonstrate the need for state intervention to the government. By taking over the services developed by Maarja Küla, the state recognized its responsibility with regard to youth with learning disabilities. As such, the initial societal accountability connected to the citizens' initiative has led to increased political accountability. Hence, collaborative governance can lead to both the de-familization of familialist states and (re-)familization of de-familialist states. This influences both on whom formal institutions place responsibility within given policy fields and if and when governments can be held accountable for failures in these policy fields.

It is important to note, however, that the process described here might lead to different outcomes for different groups in society. In the theoretical framework, we argued that those individuals who are most vulnerable to negative consequences of reforms aimed at the marketization and individualization of public services – the elderly, the low educated and those with lower socioeconomic status – are also the ones who are least likely to get involved in advocacy communities. Hence, for these individuals, the loss of political accountability is unlikely to be compensated for by an increase in societal accountability, perpetuating their disadvantaged position.

Finally, this study has certain limitations. The main weakness of the study lies in its design and case selection. As we describe a process of change here, a longitudinal design would have been more suitable than a cross-sectional one where individuals are asked to answer questions in retrospect. Taking a cross-sectional approach, the study would have benefited from a selection of more mature cases. That way, we would have been able to perform a better test of the process we describe. Given these limitations, the study mainly serves an exploratory purpose, proposing a change mechanism between societal accountability and political accountability that should be tested in further research.

Notes

1. The research is funded by the European Union Seventh Framework Programme under grant No. 320090 (LIPSE).
2. For a thorough discussion on universalism and particularism in the welfare state, see Ellison (1999).

References

Anderson, C. J. (2000) Economic voting and political context: a comparative perspective. *Electoral Studies*, 19(2): 151–70.

Bekkers, V. J. J. M., Tummers, L. G. and Voorberg, W. H. (2013) *From Public Innovation to Social Innovation in the Public Sector: A Literature Review of Relevant Drivers and Barriers*. Rotterdam: Erasmus University Rotterdam.

Bovaird, T. (2007) Beyond engagement and participation: user and community coproduction of public services. *Public Administration Review*, 67(5): 846–60.

Bovens, M. (2007) Analysing and assessing accountability: a conceptual framework. *European Law Journal*, 13(4): 447–68.

Breit, E. and Salomon, R. (2015) Making the technological transition: citizens' encounters with digital pension services. *Social Policy & Administration*, 49(3): 299–315.

de Vries, H., Bekkers, V. J. J. M. and Tummers, L. (2015) Innovations in the public sector: a systematic review and future research agenda. *Public Administration*, 94(1): 146–66.

Dwyer, P. (2004) Creeping conditionality in the UK: from welfare rights to conditional entitlements? *The Canadian Journal of Sociology*, 29(2): 265–87.

Ellison, N. (1999) Beyond universalism and particularism: rethinking contemporary welfare theory. *Critical Social Policy*, 19(1): 57–85.

Emerson, K., Nabatchi, T. and Balogh, S. (2012) An integrative framework for collaborative governance. *Journal of Public Administration Research and Theory*, 22(1): 1–29.

Eriksson, K. (2012) Self-service society: participative politics and new forms of governance. *Public Administration*, 90(3): 685–98.

Florio, M. (2013) *Network Industries and Social Welfare: The Experiment That Reshuffled European Utilities*. Oxford: Oxford University Press.

Frees, W., van Acker, W. and Bouckaert, G. (2015) *The Role of Feedback, Accountability and Learning in Organizational Change and Innovation: A Theoretical Framework*. LIPSE Project Working Paper No. 5.

Goul Andersen, J. (2012) *The Concept of Universalism and Its Operationalisation in a Mixed Economy of Welfare*. CCWS Working Paper no. 81.

Grosso, A. and Van Ryzin, G. G. (2012) Public management reform and citizen perceptions of the UK health system. *International Review of Administrative Sciences*, 78(3): 1–20.

Hartley, J., Sørensen, E. and Torfing, J. (2013) Collaborative innovation: a viable alternative to market competition and organizational entrepreneurship. *Public Administration Review*, 73(6): 821–30.

Jacobs, K. A., Flanagan, K. M., Hulse, K. and Stone, W. (2014) *Individualised Forms of Welfare Provision and Reform of Australia's Housing Assistance System*. Australian Housing and Urban Research Institute Report.

Jakobsen, M. (2013) Can government initiatives increase citizen coproduction? Results of a randomized field experiment. *Journal of Public Administration Research and Theory*, 23(1): 27–54.

Jakobsen, M. and Andersen, S. C. (2013) Coproduction and equity in public service delivery. *Public Administration Review*, 73(5): 704–13.

Javornik, J. (2014) Measuring state de-familialism: contesting post-socialist exceptionalism. *Journal of European Social Policy*, 24(3): 240–57.

Jilke, S. and Van de Walle, S. (2013) Two track public services? Citizens' voice behaviour towards liberalized services in the EU15. *Public Management Review*, 15(4): 465–76.

Le Grand, J. (2007) The politics of choice and competition in public services. *The Political Quarterly*, 78(2): 207–13.

Lember, V., Tõnurist, P. and Kattel, R. (2015) *Co-Creation Practices in Social Innovations: Possibilities and Challenges*. Paper presented at IRSPM conference 'Shaping the Future – Re-Invention or Revolution?' Birmingham, 30 March–1 April.

Lindkvist, L. and Llewellyn, S. (2003) Accountability, responsibility and organization. *Scandinavian Journal of Management*, 19(2): 251–73.

Meinow, B., Parker, M. G. and Thorslund, M. (2011) Consumers of eldercare in Sweden: the semblance of choice. *Social Science & Medicine*, 73(9): 1285–9.

Miller, P. and Rose, N. (2008) The death of the social? Re-figuring the territory of government. In P. Miller and N. Rose (eds), *Governing the Present: Administering Economic, Social and Personal Life*. Cambridge: Polity, pp. 84–113.

Mosley, J. E. and Grogan, C. M. (2013) Representation in nonelected participatory processes: how residents understand the role of nonprofit community-based organizations. *Journal of Public Administration Research and Theory*, 23(4): 839–63.

Nemec, J., Merickova, B. M. and Svidronova, M. (2014) Social innovations on municipal level in Slovakia. Presented at EGPA conference, 10–12 September, Speyer, Germany.

Norris, J. J. (2014) Rethinking accountability in new governance. *Innovation: The European Journal of Social Science Research*, 27(3): 199–219.

Pestoff, V. (2009) Towards a paradigm of democratic participation: citizen participation and co-production of personal social services in Sweden. *Annals of Public and Cooperative Economics*, 80(2): 197–224.

Peters, E., Klein, W., Kaufman, A., Meilleur, L. and Dixon, A. (2013) More is not always better: intuitions about effective public policy can lead to unintended consequences. *Social Issues and Policy Review*, 7(1): 114–48.

Sarapuu, K., Lægreid, P., Randma Liiv, T. and Rykkja, L. H. (2014) Lessons learned and policy implications. In P. Lægreid, K. Sarapuu, L. H. Rykkja and T. Randma-Liiv (eds), *Organizing for Coordination in the Public Sector: Practices and Lessons from 12 European Countries*. Hampshire: Palgrave Macmillan, pp. 263–78.

Serrano Pascual, A. (2007) Reshaping welfare states: activation regimes in Europe. In A. Serrano Pascual and L. Magnusson (eds), *Reshaping Welfare States and Activation Regimes in Europe*. Brussels: PIE Lang, pp. 11–34.

Sundsli, K., Söderhamn, U., Espnes, G. A. and Söderhamn, O. (2012) Ability for self-care in urban living older people in southern Norway. *Journal of Multidisciplinary Healthcare*, 2(5): 85–95.

Surva, L., Tõnurist, P. and Lember, V. (2016) Co-production in a network setting: providing an alternative to the national probation service. *International Journal of Public Administration*, forthcoming.

Tummers, L., Jilke, S. and Van de Walle, S. (2013) Citizens in charge? Public administration reformation: market demand from public organizations. In Y. K. Dwivedi, M. Shareef, S. K. Pandey and V. Kumar (eds), *Public Administration Reform: Market Demand from Public Organizations*. New York: Routledge, pp. 9–27.

Vancoppenolle, D. and Verschuere, B. (2012) Failure in service delivery by public-private networks: the case of Flemish childcare. *Public Policy and Administration*, 27(1): 31–48.

Voorberg, W., Bekkers, V. J. J. M. and Tummers, L. G. (2015) A systematic review of co-creation and co-production: embarking on the social innovation journey. *Public Management Review*, 17(9): 1333–57.

Voorberg, W., Tummers, L., Bekkers, V., Torfing, J., Tõnurist, P., Kattel, R., Lember, V., Timeus, K., Nemec, J., Svidronova, M., Mikusova Merickova, B., Gasco, M., Flemig, S. and Osborne, S. (2015) *Co-Creation and Citizen Involvement in Social Innovation: A Comparative Case Study across 7 EU Countries.* LIPSE Research Report.

Yin, R. K. (2003) *Case Studies Research: Design and Methods.* Thousand Oaks, CA: Sage.

8

DIMENSIONS OF ACCOUNTABILITY IN HEALTHCARE[1]

Karsten Vrangbæk and Haldor Byrkjeflot

Introduction

Several researchers have pointed out that the accountability discourse has expanded and that accountability has become a 'magic word' (Pollitt and Hupe 2011) associated with a multitude of reforms and organizational changes in the public as well as private sector. This has spurred a massive increase in the use of the term, but also a clustering on analyses centered on 'a minimal conceptual consensus', which we will also take as our point of departure (Bovens et al. 2014). A central part of the concept of accountability is the specification of relationships between actors and levels within systems, where actors have obligations to account for their decisions and behavior. Actors in these systems must explain and justify their behavior in forums of different kinds, and their account-giving may actually have consequences (Bovens 2007). Such general accountability frameworks are useful for overall analysis of accountability. Yet, they may not be equally applicable to all sectors and task areas, due to institutional peculiarities and functional differences. The aim of this paper is to explore how this accountability framework can be adapted to a specific sector – healthcare – and explore the usefulness of including concepts of function and direction in order to grasp the complexity of accountability regimes. The guiding question is: *How can existing, general accountability frameworks be adjusted to capture important dimensions within the healthcare sector?*

To answer this question, we first summarize key aspects of the academic debate about accountability in healthcare. Based on this, we discuss a set of possible adjustments to general accountability frameworks to accommodate the specific nature of healthcare.

We use to the two Nordic countries of Denmark and Norway to illustrate selected aspects of this comprehensive framework, and we address the issue of whether the traditional trust-based (Mansbridge 2014) and somewhat informal (Romzek 2014) accountability logics within the public decentralized health systems in Denmark and Norway have changed in terms of form, direction and function. We ask the following question: *Have recent reforms implied a change towards more formalized and sanctions-based accountability forms in Denmark and Norway?*

Accountability concepts for healthcare

Accountability in healthcare is a relatively unexplored field, yet it is possible to find examples of literature at least back to the 1970s that refer to the concept (Etzioni 1975; Day and Klein 1987; Relman 1988; Emanuel and Emanuel 1996; Tuohy 2003; Brinkerhoff 2004; Rosen *et al.* 2012; Denis 2014). The medical profession has been at the core of healthcare, but with the growing attention to patient experiences and perspectives there has also been a change from trusting to checking. External scrutiny and account-giving plays an ever-stronger role compared to trust in the traditional responsibility (Relman 1988). The traditional approach in many health systems was to rely on professional self-regulation, where the state delegated decision-making authority to the professional bodies of medicine. This worked as long as the quality of the relationship between individual doctors and patients was in focus, although it also implied a strong bias in power relations, and limited options for comparing different doctors and delivery organizations. The expansion of health systems implied rising expenditures and demands for health services. At the same time, the culture among users of health systems changed. This meant that both public principals and civic society actors started to demand more insight into the performance of healthcare delivery organizations (Tuohy 2003). Inspiration for such new ways was often found in the toolkit of New Public Management, with its emphasis on measurement, management and markets. The role of indirect instruments and third parties for maintaining accountability was brought forward as many governments developed a policy for information gathering and performance management. One way of framing the issue was to see the new regime as part of an 'audit society' where control was pushed further into organizational structures, inscribing in it systems that could be audited (Power 1997: 42).

Many scholars have pointed to the potentially negative consequences for established trust relations when introducing systematic external scrutiny (Rosen *et al.* 2012). But there are also significant differences among scholars in the way they frame the accountability discussion within healthcare. Some have been more preoccupied with context and how accountability has been related to national and organizational cultures (Saltman 2012) and politics (Mattei 2009), whereas others are more prescriptive in their approach, seeking to develop the ideal model of accountability across national systems, focusing more on the variations among the various domains of the healthcare systems in any country (Emanuel and Emanuel 1996). It is clear from these contributions that accountability is at the nexus of several dilemmas in the current governance of healthcare systems (Thomas 2003). While some researchers see external scrutiny as 'the answer', others see it as a symptom of underlying problems in trust relationships. Still others focus on the potentially negative side effects, including a self-reinforcing dynamic of generating ever more skepticism and control. To analyze developments in accountability, we depart from the framework for studying accountability developed by Mark Bovens and presented in the introduction to this volume. At the core of this framework is a set of formal accountability relationships that represent conscious attempts to establish social expectations and obligations. But accountability also has a more informal and dynamic side, since the formal rules are constantly interpreted and applied in practice. Indeed, some types of accountability primarily rest on informal and normative basis (Romzek 2014), where social sanctions are the main mechanism for ensuring trust-based relationships. Such informal, trust-based accountability (Mansbridge 2014) has been particularly important within the field of healthcare. This can be explained by the high degree of information asymmetry between managerial/public principals and professional agents as well as the relative strength of health professions. Information asymmetry makes it difficult for principals to monitor behavior and makes the cost of monitoring and sanctioning relatively high.

Furthermore, it can be argued that the content of work functions within healthcare requires a high degree of professional, discretionary decision-making. Disease patterns and patients are individual. Some respond well to given treatments; others do not. A significant part of the professional expertise deals with the adaptation of general diagnostic and treatment recommendations to specific situations, and a certain degree of professional discretion is needed in this process. Traditionally, this discretion has been based on trust in the process of selection and socialization through the formal education and subsequent licensing of medical professionals. Individuals that are admitted into the profession – symbolically illustrated by the formal commitment to the professional oath – are entrusted with treating patients and become part of the medical community. Within the medical community, a number of informal norms exist to reinforce a constant focus on applying the most up-to-date evidence in treatment practices. This informal pressure operates through medical communities and on-the-job training within the specific organizational settings for delivering healthcare. It is further reinforced by practice guidelines and more generally by ethical standards within the profession. Ideally, this ensures a high level of professional ethics and quality of practice. However, one might argue that the degree of actual scrutiny of practices in peer-based systems can be relatively weak, and that there are few formal opportunities for sanctioning if things go wrong. Sanctions are often relatively subtle and relate to lack of promotion and gradual exclusion from the social community. The efficiency of this type of accountability scheme is thus based on the premise that there are a significant number of agents with trustworthy internal motivations for delivering high-quality services, and that these internal motivations are backed by widely accepted social norms within the profession to ensure a high level of quality. This premise has been questioned particularly in the past three decades for a number of reasons. First, the availability of information about performance is much greater today than in previous decades. This means that poor performance is much more likely to be discovered by the public. Several highly publicized scandals (e.g. in England and Norway) bear witness to this (Lægreid *et al.* 2014), but discussions about comparative performance have also been important drivers of health policy in the Nordic countries. Second, although the medical profession may consist of many idealistic and intrinsically motivated individuals, their normative orientation tends to be focused on clinical issues for the individual patient and not the broader and sometimes conflicting societal goals within health systems. Healthcare professionals may thus work hard to optimize within their clinical performance, but at the same time the system may fail to live up to broader objectives of cost containment, equity, responsiveness and coordination of care (Papanicolas and Smith 2013). To ensure such broader objectives and to reinforce the internal normative structures within health professions, there has been a pressure to introduce additional accountability structures within healthcare over the past three decades.

A likely result of such changes is that the core of trust-based accountability in regards to the professional staff increasingly become circumscribed by political, administrative/managerial or market-based mechanisms to scrutinize performance and issue sanctions, if particular health professionals or organizational units fail to live up to standards (Mansbridge 2014). Some of these new accountability structures are generated by developments within the healthcare sector itself, while others are a product of general trends in public administration, which has meant that many parts of modern societies have become characterized by a multitude of accountability forms. Such general reforms have introduced new governance forms, which have added to the complexity and ambiguity of the overall accountability structure (Lægreid 2014).

To disentangle the complexity of the new accountability structure, we find it useful to introduce an analytical distinction between several different accountability forms (Mulgan 2000; Willems and Van Dooren 2012). The forms in the typology are meant to be exclusive, but as will be noted below, there may be empirical cases that fall into overlapping subcategories. An example is the use of 'contractual accountability' as part of a public managerial approach. It is thus an empirical matter to further define the concepts in specific cases.

Political accountability refers to the relationship between political leadership and citizens, where citizens come to act as a forum towards political leaders when politics and policies are displayed and performed (Table 8.1). Important political accountability mechanisms include: (a) elections, where voters hold politicians to account; (b) parliamentary scrutiny and questions; (c) the political allocation of budgets and parliamentary budget controls; and (d) transparency rules and administrative policy regulations for steering the bureaucracy. Political accountability is relevant in all health systems due to public involvement in regulation and to varying extent in financing of health services.

By *administrative accountability*, we emphasize accountability relationships inside the administration or by external audit institutions. Important relations are thus between higher- and lower-level administrators in hierarchical relations, and between auditors and public organizations. Internal administrative accountability is particularly relevant in health systems with a high degree of public involvement in delivery and financing of services. In terms of content, administrative accountability often focuses on procedural and formal legal issues such as due processes, compliance with rules and procedures.

Managerial accountability focuses on performance measurement and results. The traditional emphasis on the process and input dimensions has been downplayed as the output and efficiency dimensions of public sector organizations has become more central. Managerial accountability is sometimes institutionalized into contractual relationships, and in such instances overlap with contractual accountability to form a subcategory of managerial public contract accountability. However, managerial public accountability is broader than contracts, and some contracts in healthcare do not involve public actors, as described below.

Professional accountability refers to accountability relationships that are oriented towards clinical procedures, professional standards and (clinical) quality enhancement. Much of this takes place internally within professional ranks, through peer reviews and on-the-job training. Much of it is informal and norm-based, but some elements are formalized in terms of assessments of adherence to clinical guidelines and input to recertification programs. Professional accountability can be external to the organization (e.g. in the form of accreditation programs, whistleblower arrangements and professional bodies that provide input to patient complaints assessment).

Civic society accountability refers to the external scrutiny of healthcare administration and organizations by more or less organized civic society groups, such as patient organizations and mass media. Both play an important role in healthcare, although in a rather ad hoc fashion. Civic society groups also differ significantly in their resources and capacities to exercise this type of accountability. Civic society groups, such as patient organizations, and media can use general transparency regulation to demand information. They have limited formal sanctioning ability, but the reputational effects of poor media coverage and civic society scrutiny can be quite powerful, particularly in systems where patients can choose between different treatment facilities. Media and civic society attention may also generate more formal political or judicial interventions, and can thus feed into the other types of accountability.

Contract accountability is found in health systems where purchasers/insurers can enter contracts with multiple independent delivery organizations. This situation is common in market insurance systems, but increasingly also social health insurance and public health systems. The relationship between purchaser/insurer and provider is based on formalized contracts that include an opportunity for the purchaser/insurer to request information about performance. Sanctions may be specified in the contract and also consist of the threat of deselection for subsequent contracts.

Another type of market accountability exists between shareholders or professional boards and managers in private health delivery organizations and independent public organizations based on an 'enterprise' model. General managers are responsible for organizational performance and adherence to the general strategy of the organization. Boards and general assemblies of shareholders can demand information, and can hold management accountable. They may sanction by interventions in management autonomy or ultimately by firing managers.

As described above, one may also find contractual relationships within the public sector or between a public sector principal and a private sector organization. In such cases, contractual accountability becomes a subcategory of managerial accountability, but with many of the same features as private-private contracts. It is therefore important to declare which type of contract is in focus when using the typology for empirical purposes.

Judicial accountability concerns the use of formal legal interventions through civil and administrative courts. This type of accountability has traditionally played a less prominent role in the Nordic, universalistic health systems than in insurance-based systems, as the legislation typically specifies general obligations for public health systems rather than specific rights. However, there has been a tendency to inscribe more individual rights into the health legislation in recent years (waiting time guarantees, choice of provider, information and informed consent, etc.).

The distinction between political, administrative, managerial, professional, civic society, contractual, and judicial accountability provides a detailed instrument for classifying accountability relationships. Most modern health systems include all of these accountability types, although their importance differs depending on the specific institutional composition of the health systems. The various types of accountability are associated with different types of underlying rationality and support different core values associated with the public sector. We will refer to this as the normative basis for accountability.

Normative basis for accountability

Classical accounts of accountability distinguish between a constitutional, democratic and performance function of accountability (Willems and Van Dooren 2012). Each of these three 'functions' refers to a distinct set of underlying normative ideas of the public sector.

An important set of normative ideas for the public sector revolves around the 'constitutional' safeguards for citizens. This perspective emphasizes procedural rules regarding due process, equal treatment, openness and impartiality. 'Constitutional' rules are meant to provide boundaries for the exercise of public power and to safeguard rights for the individual. Public authorities are held accountable for a variety of well-established rules and procedures to prevent unfairness and abuse of power. Such concerns are also important within healthcare. The principle of equal rights is safeguarded in universalistic health systems, and all European health systems have a set of minimum requirements for healthcare insurers and providers. But the issue of 'policing the boundaries' of professional conduct and safeguarding rights has a deeper meaning within healthcare. This is based on the high degree of information asymmetry between professionals and patients, and by the potentially severe consequences for the individual if professionals fail to live up to general standards. This accountability relationship deals with protection of personal integrity, dignity and safety in all relationships between professionals, pharmaceutical and medical device producers and patients.

The 'democratic' function refers to the interest of citizens (or elected representatives) to be able to control the legislative and executive powers of the state. Citizens should be able to hold representatives accountable for decisions and to select other representatives if necessary. Within healthcare, this means having the means to control and select the formal democratic decision-makers that set the regulatory boundaries for healthcare and determines principles for allocation of public resources in the sector. In public integrated health systems such as the Nordic systems and the UK, this also extends to controlling the public healthcare delivery organizations and their employees.

The normative idea of 'output performance' is based on the underlying understanding of the public sector as primarily responsible for organizing the delivery of services in selected areas. Healthcare is characterized by a set of 'market failures' based on the high degree of information asymmetry between delivery organizations and those in need of care. Furthermore, there are significant externalities associated with healthcare delivery and consumption. This means that public authorities must play a role in safeguarding the performance of delivery organizations, both public and private. Emphasis is therefore on the output dimension of public activities (Scharpf 1999), and accountability is focusing on securing the best possible output performance. Applying this to healthcare means that public authorities, as well as citizens and patients, should be able to hold healthcare providers accountable for the results they achieve. Collectively, we should be able to judge whether we get optimal societal value for the resources allocated to healthcare. The types of measurements to support accountability for output of healthcare organizations range from quality data reported in clinical databases to process data (e.g. waiting times and adherence to standards) and service quality data (e.g. measured as patient perceived quality). Performance data are often made publicly available to allow comparisons and questioning and to support efforts to develop incentive schemes and sanctions by political, administrative or private principals.

The output performance has gained importance as the normative basis for the public sector in general (Hood 1991; Van Dooren *et al.* 2010). This is expressed in a significant growth in monitoring and auditing mechanisms focusing on the three Es of efficiency, economy and effectiveness. Within healthcare, we have seen an explosion in performance-measuring systems focusing on quality, service and efficiency.

Direction of accountability

Schillemans (2011) distinguishes between horizontal and vertical accountability relationships. Vertical accountability refers to situations where a superior demands an account from a subordinate. As with classical hierarchical accountability, a defining characteristic is that authority and distribution of roles are formalized, as is the case between a minister and a ministry. In horizontal accountability mechanisms, the situation is rather an absence of hierarchical relations. Instead, there is an accountability relationship to other organizations within a network or peer group structure. The obligation to provide information is usually based on collaborative norms and the sanctioning mechanisms are usually not clearly specified, and mainly consist of the threat of exclusion from future collaboration and networks. Schillemans emphasizes the voluntary and informal nature of horizontal accountability. We suggest that the situation is a bit more complicated. In a networked society, we see many examples where local or regional organizations enter more formal agreements. In other cases, they are held jointly accountable, and may therefore have stronger interests in holding each other accountable for the joint goals. This represents a situation where vertical and horizontal accountability are combined.

Marc Bovens (2007) introduces an additional possibility of a diagonal arrangement: in diagonal accountability relationships, the forum is not hierarchically superior to the actor, but still has the power to request information and to pass judgment, which may or may not lead to formal sanctions. Ombudsmen or independent complaint boards could be examples of such accountability arrangements. Within healthcare, we also find 'national boards of health' or similar scrutinizing agencies. Such agencies are not superior to the actors they hold accountable, but act on behalf of 'the system' or 'the public interest'.

Summarizing the dimensions of accountability in healthcare

We now have several dimensions to describe accountability within health systems. First, we can distinguish between different accountability *forms*, each with several different forums and account-givers and associated accountability mechanisms. Second, we distinguish between different *normative functions* of accountability. While democratic and constitutional functions have traditionally been closely linked to political, judicial and administrative accountability forms, and performance more closely to market and professional accountability forms, it is important to realize that different forms may include concerns for several different functions. For example, professional accountability typically is concerned with due process, equity and impartiality, as well as performance. Similarly, it can be argued that the performance function of accountability has gained importance in public health systems over the past three decades with the introduction of New Public Management perspectives and tools, and that this is combined with different forms of administrative accountability. Third, we distinguish between different *directions* of accountability. We suggest that horizontal accountability forms have gained importance over time, as more services are delivered in networked structures and as traditional forms of government are giving way to new types of 'governance' relations.

In this sense, there tends to be a dynamic interaction between the different dimensions, as pointed out by Willems and Van Dooren (2012), and accountability regimes can be seen as snapshots of forms, normative basis and direction of accountability in a particular context, at a given point in time (Goodin 2003; Tuohy 2003; Mattei 2009). Reforms can then shift the relative importance of different forms, normative basis and directions over time. This may happen through formal rules, or more implicitly by introducing new institutional structures and relationships. The result can be new configurations of accountability, and specifically within health one may hypothesize that recent reforms have led to new ways of balancing the trust based professional accountability, which has traditionally been at the core of healthcare, and the more formal, sanction-based administrative, political, contract and judicial accountability types (Mansbridge 2014).

The following table summarizes the presentation.

Examples of reforms and accountability changes in healthcare in Denmark and Norway

The health systems in Denmark and Norway are characterized by a high degree of public involvement in financing, planning and delivery of services. Unlike the NHS in England, there has historically been a strong element of decentralized governance based on democratically elected councils at regional (Denmark) and local levels (Denmark and Norway). The decentralized delivery structure in a multilevel system creates particular accountability relations between state, regions and municipalities as regions/municipalities operate in the 'shadow of the hierarchy' and according to political directives and agreements, which sometimes resemble formal contracts.

Professional accountability has traditionally played a central role in the Nordic countries. Professional accountability is nested within the democratic/political and administrative governance structures at national and regional levels. Judicial accountability has been of limited importance, and private sector contract accountability has been of limited relevance due to the

Table 8.1 Dimensions of accountability in healthcare

Accountability form	Accountability forum ↔ account-giver	Account mechanism	Normative function	Typical direction
Political	Voters ↔ parliament Parliament ↔ government Government ↔ administration	Elections Parliamentary scrutiny, questions, votes of no confidence, etc. Budgets and budget control	Democratic Constitutional	Vertical
Administrative	Higher-level ↔ lower-level administrative staff/units (administrative chain of command) Internal audit ↔ public organizations/hospital units External audit ↔ administration/hospital units	Hierarchical scrutiny and intervention Hard or soft contracts Internal or external audit, accreditation, etc.	Democratic Constitutional	Vertical Diagonal
Managerial	Higher-level ↔ lower-level administrative staff/units Administrations ↔ arm's-length agencies or external organizations	Performance monitoring and sanctions Benchmarking Contract management	Performance	Vertical
Professional	Formal or informal profession groups ↔ individual professional Profession-based external committees for evaluation of complaints, malpractice, etc. ↔ individual professionals Administrative bodies ↔ individual professionals	Professional peer review Whistleblowers Profession-based external scrutiny (e.g. through complaint procedures) Administrative examination of professional conduct of individual professionals	Constitutional Performance	Horizontal Diagonal (Vertical)
Civic society	Mass media ↔ health administration, organizations and professionals Organized civic society ↔ health administration, organizations and professionals 'Ad hoc' action groups or individuals (e.g. e-based) ↔ health administration, organizations and professionals	Framing, agenda-setting, information channel, watchdog Monitoring, critical dialogue, petitions, protest campaigns, etc. Growing importance of e-based virtual communities and communication forms	Democratic	Horizontal
Contractual	Purchasers/contracting agencies/insurers ↔ health organizations Shareholders/owners/boards ↔ health organizations	Monitoring adherence to performance targets in contracts – deselection for future contract Performance monitoring Profits	Performance	Horizontal Vertical
Judicial	Judicial courts ↔ health administration, organizations and professionals Administrative courts ↔ health administration, organizations and professionals	Formal judicial trials and procedures	Constitutional	Diagonal

Source: A modified version of this table is presented in Vrangbæk and Byrkjeflot (2016).

dominance of public financing and public provision. This is in stark contrast to, for example, the US healthcare system. Prior to the 1980s, the public had limited insight and limited options for comparing health services, and thus played a relatively indirect role in accountability terms, primarily as voters at local, regional and national levels (political accountability) and, in some cases, as members of civic society groups and interest organizations (civic society accountability).

However, a number of changes have been introduced from the 1980s onwards in the Nordic countries, the UK and most other European healthcare systems (Vrangbæk 1999; Magnussen *et al.* 2009; Byrkjeflot 2011; Olejaz *et al.* 2012; Ringard *et al.* 2013; Lægreid 2014; Peckham 2014). The dominant change trends include the introduction of NPM style reforms from the 1980s onwards, emphasizing choice, economic incentives, performance measurements and transparency (activity, service and clinical quality). NPM reforms have been supplemented by structural reforms changing the balance between central and decentralized governance. A major structural reform was implemented in Denmark in 2007 and a smaller reform in Norway in 2012. These reforms were, among other things, motivated by an ambition to improve coordination of care across sectors and delivery platforms. This is seen as a necessary response to ageing populations with more chronic care needs and higher prevalence of multi-morbidity. The coordination efforts generated more formal horizontal accountability relations between regions and local authorities, and intensified vertical accountability for achieving joint results. The vertical accountability is located within a hierarchical setting in Norway, but with clear managerial traits. In Denmark, the situation is complicated by the fact that regions and municipalities formally have independence, but in reality depend on the state for financing, and also operate in a context where the national authorities may intervene through legislation at any time. In this sense, the accountability relationship is administrative and hierarchical at its core, but with a strong element of managerial accountability based on negotiations and agreements, rather than formal contracts.

Another reform trend in both countries has been ongoing changes in the public/private mix of healthcare by introducing more private providers and encouraging voluntary private insurance. Many of the ongoing reforms have been supported by more extensive digitalization and e-based solutions for communication, monitoring and delivering services.

The many reforms and ongoing changes have led to several changes in accountability relations. At the general level, we have moved to a situation where accountability relations have become more explicit than in the previous era, where many accountability issues remained unarticulated and assumed to be taken care of within the professional ranks or internally in the hierarchical public structure. The overall result is a system that is more complex and layered over time (Bovens and Schillemans 2011). This is seen in the interaction between horizontal and vertical accountability forms. It is also apparent in the ongoing struggles over the boundaries of professional accountability, and in the introduction of managerial accountability, backed by the threat of political/administrative intervention.

One major development trend is thus that administrative accountability has changed to incorporate a more managerial dimension with increasing reliance on performance dimensions and contract/market accountability. In some cases, these NPM-related accountability types have replaced more traditional forms, but more often they have been added on top of existing forms, sometimes creating tensions and lack of clarity for the involved account-givers (Vrangbæk 1999; Byrkjeflot 2011; Lægreid 2014). Examples of increased managerialism can be found in the Norwegian 'enterprise reform', which, in 2002, created semi-independent delivery organizations with boards rather than politically elected management and governed through detailed 'steering documents' with performance demands from the state level (Byrkjeflot and Neby 2008; Mattei *et al.* 2013). In spite of the stated intention to give the Norwegian health enterprises a high degree of autonomy within this framework of managerial goal-based steering, there have been several examples of hierarchical interventions in operational decisions at the hospital level, for example in regard to closure of hospital units.

Denmark has similarly seen experiments with publicly owned 'free hospitals' operating with less tight hierarchical control, and Denmark has also used contracting of private hospitals as part of the national waiting time guarantee.

Performance is monitored in significant levels of detail in both Denmark and Norway, and results are made available on the Internet to support external (civic society) scrutiny and facilitate choice (e.g. www.esundhed.dk). But performance data are also used extensively in the accountability relations between state and regions. Activity data are used for resource allocation in both countries, and performance in regard to implementation of state policy directives, such as guidelines, recommendations and policy directives, are monitored and subject to discussions between state and regional/local level actors.

In both countries, we see indications that professional accountability is increasingly challenged by attempts to superimpose external administrative or contract-/market-based accountability forms. Professional accountability has in itself become more formalized, standardized and transparent (Timmermans 2005). Examples of this development trend include the formulation of clinical treatment guidelines and the surveillance of their implementation through the extensive accreditation program for Danish hospitals, which was implemented between 2007 and 2015 (Burau and Vrangbæk 2008; Vrangbæk 2009), but is currently undergoing reconstruction. Clinical guidelines are also implemented in the Norwegian case along with detailed patient pathway descriptions for particular patient groups.

In both Denmark and Norway, there is a tendency for civic society accountability to play a stronger role. This is enabled by improved transparency and the general development towards a civic society that is more knowledgeable and less inclined to accept variations in quality. Patient organizations continue to play a significant role within health policy (Opedal et al. 2012), but they are increasingly joined by ad hoc e-based virtual interest groups and campaigns that have supplemented traditional civic society interest organizations and mass media in the accountability functions of demanding information and passing judgments.

Judicial accountability in general still plays a minor role, particularly in the two Nordic health systems. Yet, there is a tendency to develop more specific rights within healthcare, for instance in relation to waiting time guarantees, rights to information, etc. Although such rules are not formal judicial rights in all cases, they are still part of a trend towards more explicit formulation of patient rights supplementing the general obligation of the healthcare system. This trend points towards increasing judicialization of healthcare (Hogg 1999). Another driver behind this development is the adaptation to EU legislation, for instance on cross-border healthcare. This creates a new type of mixed judicial and political accountability between citizens, the national health authorities and the EU institutions (Court of Justice and Commission), with the effect of reducing national political sovereignty (Martinsen and Vrangbæk 2008; Vollaard et al. 2013).

Another common trend in the two countries is an increasing importance of horizontal accountability. This can be interpreted as post-NPM efforts to reduce the fragmentation created by previous reforms, and to accommodate the demands from ageing populations with more chronic care needs. Both countries have introduced reforms to encourage more seamless service delivery across different health and social care levels (Rommetvedt et al. 2014). Intergovernmental relationships have become tighter with more formalized mandatory collaboration between regions (hospitals) and municipalities. Regions, municipalities and delivery organizations engage in 'dynamic accountability' relationships based on networks, recursivity, deliberation, innovation, inclusion and publicity (Sabel and Zeitlin 2008; Mansbridge 2014). Interestingly, these horizontal accountability structures are to some extent accompanied by stronger accountability pressures from the state level in terms of monitoring and sanctioning mechanisms for the joint performance of regional and local level delivery organizations. The result is a dynamic interaction between horizontal and vertical accountability involving state, regional and municipal actors.

Based on these observations, we can conclude that there are indications of circumscribing the traditional core of selection and trust-based accountability with a thicker, more complex and more penetrating layer of monitoring and sanctioning accountability (Mansbridge 2014). This can be seen at the clinical level, where traditional reliance on selection and trust-based accountability forms is challenged by IT-based systems for monitoring performance, and by the widespread use of clinical guidelines, standards and operation procedures. In terms of the criteria developed by Mansbridge, this can partly be explained by a reduction in the price of monitoring due to the introduction of IT solutions and collection of 'big data'. Alternatively, one can argue that some of the cost has been shifted to those being monitored, as they are responsible for taking the time to enter data and thus supply the basis for (self) monitoring.

A similar development has taken place in the accountability relations for hospitals and public authorities (regions and municipalities). Rising expectations among patients and in the general population contribute to this development. The authority of healthcare professionals has been weakened and people are less inclined to accept quality differences or failures. In accountability terms, this leads to strengthening of both civic accountability and managerial accountability, in both cases utilizing the increased availability of performance data. A third impetus for the development is thus that politicians and bureaucrats at state and regional levels, as well as hospital managers, are pressured to find effective ways of managing increasing demand for health services. Increasing demand is fuelled by aging populations, rising expectations among citizens and medical technology advances. This has necessitated a tighter control regime and better monitoring of activity and economic performance. This development can also be found in the relationship between the state and regions/municipalities, where the state in both countries have implemented stronger governance of economic performance and tougher sanctions for budget overruns. Productivity increases are mandatory, and failure to deliver such increases results in economic sanctions. In addition, the two Nordic states also use softer means in the form of benchmarking and publication of comparative data in order to hold regions/hospitals accountable and to enable citizens/patients to do the same.

Conclusion

In this chapter, we asked two questions. The first was how existing general accountability frameworks should be adjusted to capture accountability dimensions specific to healthcare. We took Boven's accountability framework as our starting point. Based on this, we argued that there are seven forms of accountability that are particularly relevant in healthcare. Professional accountability has historically been a very important factor in health care based on the strength of health professions and the information asymmetry inherent to the highly technical and complex production of health services. Professional accountability is still very important, but has increasingly become circumscribed and supplemented by other types of accountability relating to public/patient demands for insight into health sector performance and a tightening of the steering relationships between insurers (public and private) and delivery organizations. The configuration of these types of accountability varies somewhat across countries depending on the institutional setup and historical heritage of different healthcare systems. To capture this complexity, we suggested that it is useful to distinguish between political, administrative, managerial, professional, civic society, contractual and judicial accountability, and that understanding the normative basis of each of these is important to go beyond surface labels. Finally, we argued that analysis of the direction of accountability can reveal important information about the actors and the relationship between them within a given accountability regime.

This elaborate framework for studying accountability in healthcare makes it possible to move beyond existing studies, which have tended to focus on the relationship between the medical profession and a few of the other dimensions mentioned (e.g. state or market). Developing a framework is an important step in the process of developing comparative studies of accountability regimes. Until now, there have been few comparative studies of accountability regimes in healthcare (but see Tuohy 2003; Byrkjeflot et al. 2013, 2014). Such studies and also historical case studies of single systems may be useful in understanding the relationship between reforms and accountability relations in theory and practice.

The second main question for our chapter was whether recent reforms have implied a change towards more formalized (Romzek 2014) and sanctions-based (Mansbridge 2014) accountability forms. Using the two Nordic countries of Denmark and Norway as examples, we conclude that a number of reforms have been introduced within healthcare, including: (a) NPM-style reforms from the 1980s and onwards introducing choice, economic incentives, performance measurements and transparency (activity, service and clinical quality); (b) structural reforms changing the balance between central and decentralized governance; (c) changes in the public/private mix of healthcare by introducing more private providers and encouraging voluntary private insurance; (d) various reforms and changes to promote integration of care; and (e) digitalization and e-based solutions for communication, monitoring and delivering services.

These different reforms have resulted in gradual changes of accountability relationships with a growing reliance on formalized transparency measures and a growing emphasis on political, administrative, managerial, contract and legal accountability forms. Yet, within the Nordic systems, this has only partially been accompanied by a clearly articulated sanction-based approach. Sanctions remain somewhat internal, and subject to ad hoc negotiations within the political, administrative and professional steering systems. There is limited upfront definition of criteria and sanctioning levels. The overall result is a rather complex and multidimensional accountability regime where the different actors face increasing scrutiny combined with some uncertainty as to when and how sanctions may be imposed.

Note

1 Parts of this chapter have previously been presented in Vrangbæk and Byrkjeflot (2016).

References

Bovens, M. (2007) Analysing and assessing accountability: a conceptual framework. *European Law Journal*, 13(4): 447–68.
Bovens, M. and Schillemans, T. (2011) The challenge of multiple accountability: does redundancy lead to overload? In M. J. Dubnick and H. G. Friederickson (eds), *Accountable Governance: Promises and Problems*. London: M. E. Sharpe, pp. 3–22.
Bovens, M., Goodin, R. E. and Schillemans, T. (eds) (2014) *The Oxford Handbook Public Accountability*. Oxford: Oxford University Press.
Brinkerhoff, D. W. (2004) Accountability and health systems: toward conceptual clarity and policy relevance. *Health Policy and Planning*, 19(6): 371–9.
Burau, V. and Vrangbæk, K. (2008) Institutions and non-linear change in governance: reforming the governance of medical performance in Europe. *Journal of Health Organisation and Management*, 22(4): 350–67.

Byrkjeflot, H. (2011) Healthcare states and medical professions: the challenges from New Public Management. In T. Christensen and P. Lægreid (eds), *The Ashgate Research Companion to New Public Management*. Aldershot: Ashgate, pp. 147–61.

Byrkjeflot, H., Christensen, T. and Lægreid, P. (2014) The many faces of accountability: comparing reforms in welfare, hospitals and migration. *Scandinavian Political Studies*, 37(2): 171–95.

Byrkjeflot, H. and Neby, S. (2008) The decentralized path challenged? Nordic healthcare reforms in comparison. *Journal of Health Organization and Management*, 22(4): 331–49.

Byrkjeflot, H., Neby, S. and Vrangbæk, K. (2012) Changing accountability regimes in hospital governance: Denmark and Norway compared. *Scandinavian Journal of Public Administration*, 15(4): 3–23.

Day, P. and Klein, R. (1987) *Accountabilities: Five Public Services*. London/New York: Tavistock.

Denis, J. L. (2014) Accountability in healthcare organizations and systems. *Healthcare Policy/Politiques de santé*, 10(SP): 8–11.

Emanuel, E. J. and Emanuel, L. L. (1996) What is accountability in health care? *Annals of Internal Medicine*, 124(2): 229–39.

Etzioni, A. (1975) Alternative conceptions of accountability: the example of health administration. *Public Administration Review*, 35(3): 279–86.

Goodin, R. E. (2003) Democratic accountability: the distinctiveness of the third sector. *European Journal of Sociology*, 44(3): 359–93.

Hogg, C. (1999) *Patients, Power and Politics: From Patients to Citizens*. London: Sage.

Hood, C. (1991) A public management for all seasons? *Public Administration*, 69: 3–19.

Lægreid, P. (2014) New Public Management and accountability. In M. Bovens, R. E. Goodin and T. Schillemans (eds), *The Oxford Handbook of Public Accountability*. Oxford: Oxford University Press, pp. 324–39.

Lægreid, P., Neby, S., Mattei, P. and Feiler, T. (2014) Bending the rules to play the game: accountability, DRG and waiting list scandals in Norway and Germany. *European Policy Analysis*, 1(1): 127–48.

Magnussen, J., Vrangbæk, K. and Hagen, T. P. (2009) *Nordic Healthcare Systems: Recent Reforms and Current Policy Challenges*. Berkshire: World Health Organization/McGraw Hill Open University Press.

Mansbridge, J. (2014) A contingency theory of accountability. In M. Bovens, R. E. Goodin and T. Schillemans (eds), *The Oxford Handbook of Public Accountability*. Oxford: Oxford University Press. DOI: 10.1093/oxfordhb/9780199641253.013.0019.

Martinsen, D. S. and Vrangbæk, K. (2008) The Europeanization of health care governance: implementing the market imperatives of Europe. *Public Administration*, 86(1): 169–84.

Mattei, P. (2009) *Restructuring Welfare Organizations in Europe*. Houndsmills: Palgrave Macmillan.

Mattei, P., Mitra, M., Vrangbæk, K., Neby, S. and Byrkjeflot, H. (2013) Reshaping public accountability: hospital reforms in Germany, Norway and Denmark. *International Review of Administrative Sciences*, 79(2): 249–70.

Mulgan, R. (2000) Accountability: an ever-expanding concept? *Public Administration*, 78(3): 555–73.

Olejaz, M., Juul Nielsen, A., Rudkjøbing, A., Okkels Birk, H., Krasnik, A. and Hernández-Quevedo, C. (2012) Denmark: health system review. *Health Systems in Transition*, 14(2): 1–192.

Opedal, S., Rommetvedt, H. and Vrangbæk, K. (2012) Organised interests, authority structures and political influence: Danish and Norwegian patient groups compared. *Scandinavian Political Studies*, 35(1): 1–21.

Papanicolas, I. and Smith, P. (2013) *Health System Performance Comparison: An Agenda for Policy, Information and Research*. Maidenhead: McGraw-Hill International.

Peckham, S. (2014) Accountability in the UK healthcare system: an overview. *Healthcare Policy/Politiques de santé*, 10(SP): 154–62.

Pollitt, C. and Hupe, P. (2011) Talking about government: the role of magic concepts. *Public Management Review*, 13(5): 641–58.

Power, M. (1997) *The Audit Society: Rituals of Verification*. Oxford: Oxford University Press.

Relman, A. S. (1988) Assessment and accountability: the third revolution in medical care. *N Engl J Med*, 319: 1220–2.

Ringard, Å., Sagan, A., Sperre Saunes, I. and Lindahl, A. K. (2013) Norway: health system review. *Health Systems in Transition*, 15(8): 1–162.

Rommetvedt, H., Opedal, S., Stigen, I. M. and Vrangbæk, K. (2014) *Hvordan har vi det i dag, da? Flernivåstyring og samhandling i dansk og norsk helsepolitikk*. Fakbokforlaget. Bergen.

Romzek, B. (2000) Dynamics of public accountability in the era of reform. *International Review of Administrative Sciences*, 66(1): 21–44.

Romzek, B. (2014) Accountable public services. In M. Bovens, R. E. Goodin and T. Schillemans (eds), *The Oxford Handbook of Public Accountability*. Oxford: Oxford University Press. DOI: 10.1093/oxfordhb/9780199641253.013.0030.

Rosen, B., Israeli, A. and Shortell, S. M. (2012) Accountability in health care reconsidered. In B. Rosen, A. Israeli and S. M. Shortell (eds), *Accountability and Responsibility in Health Care: Issues in Addressing an Emerging Global Challenge* (Vol. 1). London: World Scientific, pp. 7–23.

Sabel, C. F. and Zeitlin, J. (2008) Learning from difference: the new architecture of experimentalist governance in the EU. *European Law Journal*, 14(3): 271–327.

Saltman, R. B. (2012) Context, culture and the practical limits of health sector accountability. In B. Rosen, A. Israeli and S. M. Shortell (eds), *Accountability and Responsibility in Health Care: Issues in Addressing an Emerging Global Challenge* (Vol. 1). London: World Scientific, pp. 189–207.

Scharpf, F. W. (1997) *Games Real Actors Play: Actor-Centered Institutionalism in Policy Research*. Boulder, CO: Westview Press.

Schillemans, T. (2011) Does horizontal accountability work? Evaluating potential remedies for the accountability deficit of agencies. *Administration & Society*, 43(4): 387–416.

Thomas, P. G. (2003) Accountability in modern government. In B. G. Peters and J. Pierre (eds), *Handbook of Public Administration*. London: Sage.

Timmermans, S. (2005) From autonomy to accountability: the role of clinical practice guidelines in professional power. *Perspectives in Biology and Medicine*, 48(4): 490–501.

Tuohy, C. H. (2003) Agency, contract, and governance: shifting shapes of accountability in the health care arena. *Journal of Health Politics, Policy and Law*, 28(2–3): 195–215.

Van Dooren, W., Bouckaert, G. and Halligan, J. (2010) *Performance Management in the Public Sector*. London: Routledge.

Vollaard, H., van de Bovenkamp, H. M. and Vrangbæk, K. (2013) The emerging EU quality of care policy: from sharing information to enforcement. *Health Policy*, 111(3): 226–33.

Vrangbæk, K. (1999) New Public Management i sygehusfeltet – udformning og konsekvenser. In E. Z. Bentsen, F. Borum, G. Erlingsdottir and K. Sahlin-Andersson (eds), *Når styringsambitioner møder praksis – Den svære omstilling af sygehus- og sundhedsvæsenet i Danmark og Sverige*. København: Handelshøjskolens forlag, pp. 33–56.

Vrangbæk, K. (2009) The interplay between central and sub-central levels: the development of a systemic standard based programme for governing medical performance in Denmark. *Health Economics, Policy and Law*, 4(3): 305–27.

Vrangbæk, K. and Byrkjeflot, H. (2016) Accountability in health care. In E. Ferlie, K. Montgomery and A. R. Pedersen (eds), *The Oxford Handbook of Health Care Management*. Oxford: Oxford University Press, pp. 481–95.

Willems, T. and Van Dooren, W. (2012) Coming to terms with accountability. *Public Management Review*, 14(7): 1011–36.

9

ACCOUNTABILITY THROUGH PERFORMANCE MANAGEMENT?

Hospital performance management schemes in Denmark, Germany and England

Karsten Vrangbæk, Tanja Klenk, John Appleby and Sarah Gregory

Introduction

Performance management has developed into a central part of public sector reforms in the last 30 years. It is a tool of governance that may be used for a variety of objectives, such as improving the efficiency and effectiveness of public services, but also for holding organizations delivering public goods and services accountable. While public service providers traditionally have been held accountable for the appropriateness of formal structures and decision procedures, this has changed with the gradual shift towards New Public Management and its focus on outputs. Being accountable is today more and more understood as being answerable for performance. The assumption is that when performance information is publicly available, service providers are more responsive to public accountability claims.

Yet, as is accountability, so is performance management a contested issue and subject to debate: both accountability and performance mean different things to different people. In addition, both accountability and performance management schemes are used for different purposes: to ensure democratic control, to foster organizational learning, or to keep an eye on the economic performance of an organization – to mention only three out of a variety of different purposes. As a result, different performance management models can be distinguished that vary in the way they define performance, deal with poor performance and design accountability instruments to ensure appropriate behavior.

This chapter has an analytical and an empirical objective. In analytical terms, it develops ideal types of performance management in the healthcare sector, focusing on the 'big ideas' behind the systems and on their underlying rationale. Three ideal types are distinguished: a system designed to steer and control, a system considered to support organizational learning, and finally a system that aims at the maintenance of organizational legitimacy. In empirical terms, the chapter's aim is to compare and to explain the institutional design of performance management schemes, taking the field of healthcare as an empirical example. In the healthcare sector, ideas of performance and quality are traditionally contested and split up between a professional and a bureaucratic understanding of accountable service delivery. With the rise of NPM, which has had a considerable impact on the healthcare sector, an additional layer of managerial accountability has been put on the already existing structures. Three countries have been selected: Denmark, Germany and England. The three countries under consideration differ not only with regard to the institutional structures of their healthcare systems, but also in terms of administrative culture and timing of administrative reform.

The chapter contributes to the literature on the complex relationship between accountability and performance management (Halachmi 2002; Dubnick 2005; Pollitt 2010). A comparative empirical case study is provided that indicates that the tensions inherent in these two standard components of public sector reform vary across countries and depend not only on the general public administration system, but also on policy-field-specific traditions, such as the role of professionals and the power of their interest groups. Indeed, the three countries differ not only in terms of whether input, output or outcome data are taken for performance judgments. The locus of power for accountability relations also varies considerably across the three cases.

Performance management and accountability: entangling a complex relationship

Performance management is a cornerstone of recent public sector reform. In parts of the literature, the beginning of the twenty-first century is even characterized as an era of governance by performance management. Performance management has developed to a doctrine: the public sector is not only expected to demonstrate its value, but to constantly push forward the efficiency and effectiveness of its activities (Moynihan 2008). Following Van Dooren, Bouckaert and Halligan (2010: 32), performance in the context of public service delivery can be defined as the realization of public values such as efficiency, effectiveness, equity, robustness, openness and transparency. Performance measurement is the process of acquiring performance information. Performance management again is a sequence of subsequent steps of intentional behavior where either the internal management or external stakeholders (politicians, citizens, civil society organizations such as patient associations) use performance information to decide upon interventions in order to ensure that practices support public values, goals and objectives. Performance management can be understood as a cycle: information concerning performance targets is fed back into organizational goals and programs; the changed organizational goals eventually require the setting of new performance targets, which makes the performance management sequence start over.

Even more than performance management, accountability has developed into a magic concept of public sector reform that everybody agrees with (Pollitt and Hupe 2011). Its attractiveness is grounded in its broad scope, great flexibility and its positive 'spin'. Even though nobody is against it, the precise meaning of accountability is contested. Due to its chameleon-like (Sinclair 1995) and synonymic (Dubnick and Frederickson 2011) nature accountability is often used interchangeably with notions of answerability, responsibility, responsiveness, liability, etc. Sometimes accountability is understood as a virtue, sometimes it is considered as a mechanism (Bovens 2010). In the context of this chapter, accountability is understood as a social relationship where one actor is obliged to explain and justify his or her conduct to the other, while the other, the forum, has means to – positively or negatively – sanction its behavior. The forum can be constituted by a variety of different actors: politicians, bureaucrats, peers and professionals, citizens or users of public services. The relationship can have both a formal and/or an informal character and it does not necessarily imply an active or ongoing engagement (Dubnick and Frederickson 2011: 6). Accountability in practice usually involves three stages (Day and Klein 1987: 5; Bovens 2005: 185). At first, the actor informs the forum about his or her conduct. What follows is the debating phase: the forum might request further information; the actor will answer, and if necessary explain or justify his or her conduct or offer apologies for failure. In the final stage, the forum passes the judgment. Sanctions can either be positive (bonuses or awards) or negative (penalties or termination of contracts).

While both performance management and accountability are expected to contribute to the overall goals of public service delivery, there are competing interpretations concerning their relationship. There is a large strand of literature where the two concepts are equated and used as synonyms. Here, accountability is understood as answerability for performance (Romzek 2000: 22). It is assumed that the very fact that somebody is asked to give reasons for decisions and to explain the results of the actions taken will improve goal attainment. Hence, in both the public and the academic discourse, increased accountability is thought to inherit the promise of increased performance (Dubnick 2005). Vice versa, performance management is considered as a tool to improve accountable behavior. Collecting, comparing and publishing performance data contributes to the transparency of the public sector, which in turn is a precondition for judgments concerning the accountability of actions. Only with such information at hand are stakeholders able to assess public action and evaluate whether it is in line with the goals agreed before.

This positive relationship between accountability and performance management, where one complements the other, is challenged by a more critical strand of literature. While Dubnick (2005) finds that there is not sufficient empirical evidence for the mutually intensifying role of performance management and accountability, and hence questions the suggested causal relationship between the two concepts, others argue that performance management might have a negative impact on accountability. Halachmi (2002), for instance, has pointed to what he calls the accountability paradox, meaning that efforts to improve performance through accountability tend to have the reverse effect. In general, accountability mechanisms slow down or even stop organizational improvements. Thus, instead of being a driver, accountability is a barrier for performance enhancement.

However, the literature on the relationship between accountability and performance management and possible accountability deficits suffers from the problem that most often the assessment criteria are not sufficiently specified (Bovens et al. 2008: 230). When discussing accountability and performance management, one should bear in mind that none of the concepts are ends in themselves, but means to achieve other goals. Reviewing the performance management and accountability literature, we can identify (at least) three major purposes of accountability and performance management schemes. These are learning, steering and control, and gaining or maintaining legitimacy (Aucoin and Heintzman 2000; Bovens et al. 2008; Van Dooren et al. 2010: 97). These purposes are not necessarily exclusive to each other. However, the very fact that accountability and performance management schemes are not designed to pursue only one, but multiple goals creates tensions within and between the schemes that cannot easily be resolved. Trying to attain one of these goals might require neglecting another. The forums where discussions take place, as well as the criteria for assessment, vary depending on the purpose.

Purposes of performance management: three ideal types

Building on research by Aucoin and Heintzman (2000), Bovens, Schillemans and 't Hart (2008) and Van Dooren, Bouckaert and Halligan (2010: 97) the following section describes three ideal types of performance management schemes where either learning, steering and control, or gaining legitimacy is the primary purpose. To clarify the underlying rationale of the three different ideal types, the following dimensions are considered:

- *Forum*: To whom is the organization expected to deliver data? Who constitutes the forum and hence has the right to interpret data and judge about organizational performance?
- *Data*: What type of data is collected and which criteria are applied to judge organizational actions?
- *Assumptions about causality*: What is the central belief about how performance can be improved? How are the data actually used? What mechanisms should increase performance?

Learning: improving the effectiveness of the organization

Performance management schemes with a learning orientation are primarily concerned with the question of what works, what doesn't and why something doesn't work. Applied to the hospital sector, this means that performance management schemes of the learning type are all about improving the quality of the services and the avoidance of malpractice and accidents. In terms of assumptions about causal mechanisms, the learning type of performance management follows the central argument of the implementation literature: organizational knowledge of how things work is first and foremost owned at the street level, which therefore has to be set in the center of learning efforts. Accordingly, this type of performance management scheme primarily addresses an internal audience, in our case first and foremost the professionals working in hospitals. The internal audience is involved in all stages of a performance management cycle: data are typically collected through self-assessment; professionals do not only participate in the interpretation of the results, but also in the design of reform measures. As a result, professionals act in the double role of being accountee and accountor in the same time. Learning models rely on the self-motivation and the professional ethos of those providing services; to ensure a learning stimulating organizational culture, they abstain from hard punitive sanctions for malpractice. Good performance is rewarded with (organizational or individual) autonomy.

Steering and control: power distribution and resource allocation

Performance management schemes designed for the purpose of steering and control are about power distribution and resource allocation. Their main purpose is to prevent the abuse of public resources or public authority and to ensure the financial viability of service providers. In the context of public service delivery, steering and control is traditionally a responsibility of

Table 9.1 The learning perspective: improving organizational effectiveness

Purpose/objectives	• Quality improvement (clinical and patient experience) • Avoidance of accidents, and malpractice incidents
Forum	• Focus on internal actors: professionals
Data	• Data should cover the whole chain of service delivery: input, activities, clinical output, outcome
Assumptions about causality	• Enable self-assessment and support organizational development • Limited disclosure of performance results/publication of only aggregated data in order not to endanger a positive learning climate

Table 9.2 The steering and control perspective: improving organizational efficiency

Purpose/objectives	• Demonstrating value for money (activity/resources or quality/resources) to the immediate principals of the organization • Financial viability and sustainability
Forum	• Politicians and bureaucrats/agencies
Data	• Activities, clinical outcomes, economic performance • Data are collected at the individual or organizational level and related to national standards or predefined targets
Assumptions about causality	• External (hierarchical) scrutiny and threat of interventions • Automatic sanctions • Sanctions: pay for performance, performance budgets

politicians and bureaucrats. However, in the healthcare sector, we have in the insurance-based healthcare regimes also insurance funds as actors with a strong interest in using performance management for the controlling purposes. Hence, this type of performance management scheme expects managers of organizations delivering health services to report to politicians, bureaucrats, to managers from insurance funds, or to all of them. Data are typically collected by 'neutral' external agencies. To stimulate performance improvements, this model relies on external (hierarchical) scrutiny and threat of intervention, combined with positive or negative financial sanctions. Instruments such as pay for performance or performance budgets are characteristic for this model.

Legitimacy: building trust and enhancing public support

Performance management schemes designed to gain or to maintain organizational legitimacy primarily have the purpose of explaining organizational action to the organizations' stakeholders to ensure organizational survival in the long run. Hence, they primarily address an external audience, in particular patients and physicians referring patients to hospitals, but also the general public. To gain public trust, data about clinical outcomes and patient experiences are collected and made easily accessible for the broader public, for instance by obliging hospitals to publish quality reports on their web pages or by compiling hospital rankings that are published in public

Table 9.3 The legitimacy perspective: enhancing trust and public support

Purpose/objectives	• Demonstrating value for money (activity/resources or quality/resources) to the public in general • Maintenance of trust and legitimacy
Forum	• External stakeholders: patients, physicians, the general public
Data	• Clinical outcomes, patient experiences • Data are collected at the organizational level and related to national standards or predefined target
Assumptions about causality	• Comprehensive publication of data • Benchmarking, 'naming and shaming' • Transparency to enable choice or selective contracting

media. Activities and quality are related to organizational resources to allow an assessment of value for money. This ideal type is based on the assumption that performance management works best through reputational mechanisms such as naming and shaming. The core argument is that transparency about activities, quality and organizational resources in itself will enable patients and other decision-makers to deselect particular providers, and that the threat of losing business will incentivize providers to strive for optimal performance.

Methods and case selection

This chapter follows a qualitative approach. The empirical data used have been collected in three different steps. First, written material (government reports, web pages of accountors/accountees, research papers, etc.) has been collected through desk research to compile a country profile along the above presented analytical framework. Second, these descriptions have been validated through presentations before national-level experts and key policy actors. In a final step, the validated country profiles have formed the background for qualitative semi-structured interviews with key policy actors in the three countries to facilitate the interpretation of the different schemes.

Adopting an institutional perspective, we expect different administrative and health policy traditions to have an impact on the development of performance management schemes in the healthcare sector. Hence, we have selected three countries that fall into three different healthcare regimes. Denmark is a public, integrated but relatively decentralized NHS system, with a high degree of public ownership and stewardship and limited application of contracting and internal markets. England is also a public integrated NHS-type system, but with stronger elements of contracting and more private sector provision. Germany is a social health insurance system (SHI) with a relatively weak state stewardship, a high degree of self-governance by 'societal partners' and a heterogeneous ownership structure. In addition, administrative culture and the timing of administrative reforms vary decisively across the countries, with England as the trendsetter and Germany as a late adopter of NPM reforms. Also, when having a closer look at the characteristics of performance management models at the national level, differences between the three countries can be found. Bouckaert and Halligan (2008) argue that the general approach to PM in Germany can be characterized as 'performance administration' (the most fragmented and least comprehensive approach), while the UK is closer to the 'performance management' ideal type (the most integrated and comprehensive type). Denmark, which is not included in the study by Bouckaert and Halligan, comes close to the middle category, 'managements of performances'. We assume that the differences in PM approaches at the national level also impact sector-specific models.

Case studies

England: improving organizational efficiency and enhancing public support

In the literature, the English NHS is typically categorized as the ideal type of a fairly centralized system with much power at the central level due to national-level public financing and state ownership of hospitals (Blank and Burau 2014). However, in the past years, governance structures have been altered profoundly through the introduction of the commissioner/provider split, patient choice, and autonomous foundation trusts. Compared to NHS trusts, foundation trusts enjoy increased managerial and financial accountability. The creation of foundation trusts has further increased the institutional complexity of the NHS as the performance management and accountability structures of both types of trust differ.

In England, healthcare is a field of high political salience. Most citizens have a positive stance towards the NHS and politicians at national level are held accountable for what is going on in the system. Yet, the new governance arrangements provide dilemmas for actors from the central level. As a result of the governance reforms of the last decade, political and administrative powers at the national level are not as strong as might be expected. The traditional vertical lines of political and administrative accountability have been weakened, and politicians no longer have direct control over the commissioning and delivery of services. Instead, lines of horizontal accountability have grown in importance.

Since the 2012 Health and Social Care Act, politicians have influenced the direction of health service provision through an annual mandate issued to NHS England, an arm's-length body directly accountable to parliament. NHS England allocates funds (as agreed by parliament) to clinical commissioning groups (CCGs), which purchase services locally from providers of NHS care, and which must incorporate the performance indicators set out in the mandate to NHS England in their contractual arrangements. CCGs also have powers to fine providers that do not meet these targets. Another key accountee in terms of performance management is the Care Quality Commission, which is a non-departmental government body that regulates and inspects public and private healthcare services and registers providers that demonstrate that they are able to meet the quality criteria. Regarding their financial viability trusts are held accountable by the arm's-length bodies TDA (Trust Development Authority, for non-foundation trusts) and Monitor (for foundation trusts), respectively. In addition to controlling the financial viability of single foundation trusts, Monitor sets the rules that govern the prices paid for services and regulates payments made by commissioners to providers for all NHS services (Government UK 2014). In spring 2016, Monitor and the TDA have merged into a newly created body called NHS Improvement, which will perform the functions of both bodies.

To assess and to judge organizational action, the English performance management model relies primarily on outcome data. The contracts between the clinical commissioning groups and healthcare providers, for instance, include performance indicators that are set out in the so-called outcomes framework (Department of Health 2014). This framework differentiates between five outcome domains: (1) preventing people from dying prematurely; (2) enhancing quality of life for people with long-term conditions; (3) helping people to recover from episodes of ill health or following injury; (4) ensuring that people have a positive experience of care; and (5) finally, treating and caring for people in a safe environment and protecting them from avoidable harm. Mortality rates, the proportion of people feeling supported to manage their condition, or readmission rates are examples for indicators.

Due to the existence of a multitude of accountees, it is hard to point to a single underlying rationale of the English performance management model. As a result of recent healthcare reforms, the different systems reflect different underlying objectives and also a variety of different assumptions about mechanisms and causality. In comparison to Denmark and Germany, however, the explicit focus on financial viability and robustness stands out. But financial viability is not the only purpose of the English PM schemes. An equally important objective is to improve both clinical and patient-experienced quality and to increase value for money.

Dominant assumptions about mechanisms and causality are that performance can be increased by the threat of hierarchical interventions combined with financial sanctions and naming and shaming practices. The TDA, for instance, is characterized by a rather tight de facto hierarchical control system. Monitor operates a licensing scheme with routine evaluations and the threat of replacing executive and nonexecutive board members, and ultimately losing autonomy if the hospital organization does not live up to standards. England has also introduced an offer to patients to choose the hospital of their treatment. For this purpose, quality data are published to support patient choice. However, these instruments have a somewhat symbolic character. Moreover, as the naming and shaming practices have created a number of highly publicized scandals involving poor quality or malpractice, the general trust in the system has been negatively affected. The low-trust environment, in turn, created a climate that has pushed governments to hierarchical interventions introducing new (symbolic) PM institutions and schemes. We have thus seen a string of successive changes, adjustments and additions to the performance management model. New features have been added on top of existing approaches.

Denmark: between the enabling learning and ensuring controlling

The *Danish* approach to performance management in healthcare differs decisively from the hierarchical model in England as it has been introduced stepwise through negotiated procedures reflecting the consensus orientation of Danish politics (Christiansen and Nørgaard 2004), as well as the ongoing struggles for control over healthcare between state and regions (Rommetvedt et al. 2014). The result is a multilevel model, consisting of activity, service and quality measures, and established through a combination of bottom-up and top-down initiatives. While regions and municipalities are responsible for healthcare delivery and quality assurance, the central state sets the general regulation, overall political strategy, and coordination of public finances.

The overall aim of healthcare performance management is to improve quality, reduce the risk of accidents and malpractice incidents, and evaluate that the regions and their hospitals deliver value for money. To achieve these aims, information about activity, productivity, service and quality is collected by national authorities through national patient registries, DRG payment systems, and specific reporting by regional and local authorities. They also feed into a system of indicators covering broad areas of population health, treatment quality, patient experiences and efficiency. These indicators are published on the Internet (Ministry for Health and Prevention 2014). In addition, selected indicators (waiting times and some quality indicators) are published on national-level websites with interactive facilities to enable patients to compare hospitals and to make an informed choice (www.esundhed.dk).

With the introduction of performance management, the steering interactions between state, regions and municipalities have changed profoundly over the past two decades. Activity information is now used to determine the allocation of funds from the national level to the regions. The mechanisms include a target activity level, which must be reached by the individual regions in order to get the full amount of allocated funding. In addition, a minor portion of the funding is allocated through direct activity-based payment. The municipal co-financing of hospital treatment, too, is calculated by using activity information (approximately 20 percent of regional income). Comparative quality performance data are also employed to monitor overall developments and to compare across different regions and municipalities. Furthermore, a system of key indicators has been developed to facilitate a more systematic and multidimensional monitoring of performance in the coordination of care across regions (hospitals) and municipalities (home-based and elderly care). Finally, performance data are used for the internal steering of hospitals. For this purpose, soft contracts between hospital management and regional authorities specify targets (e.g. activity, waiting times, quality indicators). To some extent, performance data are used in activity based payment schemes at the regional level. Quality indicators build a decisive part of the information base for making decisions about which hospitals are allowed to perform highly specialized treatment procedures. A national system of obligatory tri-annual accreditation for hospitals based on performance data was introduced in 2006 and became known as 'The Danish Quality Assessment Model'. National authorities developed standards in collaboration with medical societies, and all hospitals went through two rounds of accreditations between 2007 and 2015.

The data used for monitoring and steering regional and municipal activities are discussed in coordination forums and the official rhetoric behind the Danish Quality Assessment Model was to enable self-assessment. Accordingly, there have been no explicit incentives or sanctions related to service and quality indicators. However, organizational development has been stimulated by a shadow of hierarchy reflecting the implicit threat of interventions if delivery organizations failed the accreditation exercise. Right now, the Danish performance management scheme is experiencing a profound change. The Ministry and the regions have jointly announced a plan to go beyond the traditional 'negotiated' use of quality data by introducing a more 'value-based' scheme with explicit outcome measures and incentives. As a part of the recalibration of the performance management model, the accreditation scheme has been abandoned for hospitals in 2015 as it has now 'served its purpose' of securing a common level of quality. This reform indicates a change in the underlying rationale of performance management schemes from process to outcome. The new focus on outcome also comes to light in a proclaimed turn towards a 'value-based assessment' with according economic incentives. So far, it has been left to the regions to implement this, and several regional-level experiments are currently being implemented.

The readjustment of the Danish performance management model is partly a reaction to complaints from health professionals and hospital managers about the administrative burden of registering information and preparing for the accreditation process. Indeed, performance management schemes within healthcare are exposed to several dilemmas and methodological conundrums. Quality of healthcare is not easy to measure as the final result – the degree of recovery – depends *not* on the actions of healthcare professionals alone (Donabedian 1978). As it is difficult to find good comparative measures for the value creation, performance management in healthcare often has a strong focus on process dimensions, which, however, are not always perceived as relevant by health professionals and patients. In addition, the perceived 'transaction costs' of collecting and processing data might be higher than the perceived benefits. The recalibration the Danish performance management model undergoes at present is accompanied by a centralization of the multilevel model as the national Ministry is supposed to establish 'few, but carefully selected indicators of quality' that the hospitals will be measured up against. Neither this nor the introduction of explicit financial incentives has probably been in the mind of healthcare professionals when criticizing the former model.

Germany: enabling learning

As a result of a weak state stewardship, a strong role of (quasi-)societal associations, and heterogeneous ownership structures, we find in Germany not a coherent approach to performance management, but a variety of mandatory and voluntary initiatives coexisting (Vrangbæk *et al.* 2016).

The most comprehensive national performance management schemes – these are structured quality reports and an industry-wide external quality assessment – are backed by legislation, but are implemented by the societal partners in the Gemeinsamer Bundesausschuss ('Joint Health Commission'), who have the discretion to make appropriate formal arrangements. The performance data for the industry-wide external quality assessment are collected and analyzed by a specialized service deliverer. In the past, these external service deliverers have been private consultancy and research institutes. As a result of recent healthcare reforms, a nonprofit institute has been founded, which took over data collection and analyses on 1 January 2016. This reform measure is thought to improve long-term strategic human resource development and knowledge management in the external industry-wide quality assessment scheme.

Additional performance management schemes on a voluntary basis have been introduced by single health insurance companies. The AOK (Allgemeine Ortskrankenkasse), one of the major statutory health insurance funds, has, for instance, developed the so-called Routine Data Quality Assessment, for which hospitals can register on a voluntary basis. The development of performance management has, to a great extent, also been pushed forward by single hospitals that consider quality management as a mechanism to build trust and gain legitimacy. In particular, for-profit hospitals, which are of growing importance in the governance of the German hospital sector (Stumpfögger 2009), play a proactive role in this respect. Finally, the Medical Review Board of the Statutory Health Insurance Funds is a decisive actor in the governance of performance management schemes. This board is responsible for identifying and processing cases of malpractice or misconduct. For this purpose, the quality of service provision is assessed through on-site quality checks. Information about the total number of complaints and decisions are published regularly, however again only on an aggregated level.

The prior objective of performance management in the German hospital sector is to improve quality and to avoid accidents and malpractice incidents. The idea to control and steer the hospital system via performance management is not strongly developed, neither at the level of the overall hospital system nor at the level of single hospitals. However, in 2015, the government has passed the so-called hospital structure law (Krankenhausstrukturgesetz), which became effective on 1 January 2016, and which aims at strengthening the resource allocation and control dimension by feeding back performance information into the political decision-making process. Hospitals with above-average quality will receive additional resources; poorly performing hospitals will have to face deductions.

In terms of the assumptions about causality, the difference to England is striking: the idea of pushing quality improvement by practices of naming and shaming is completely absent. The results of performance management are mainly addressed to internal forums, first and foremost to the hospital management and the professionals. This is true for the obligatory industry-wide external quality assessment as well as for voluntary initiatives such as the AOK routine data assessment. While the results of the latter are not made transparent at all, the wider public is informed about the results of the industry-wide external assessment, however only on an aggregated level. Hence, patients know how many problems have occurred – but not in which region, let alone in which hospital. The structured quality reports, which hospitals are required to publish regularly, address the wider public and patients as an accountability forum. These reports allow assessments of single hospitals, but are not designed for direct comparison between hospitals. Moreover, only input and process parameters are collected and published. Thus, the quality reports allow patients only partly to act as informed consumers. Health insurance funds and umbrella organizations of the outpatient sector, in turn, are allowed to compare hospitals, to give recommendations for patients on the basis of the quality reports, and to publish their recommendations on their home pages. Up to now, however, health insurance funds are reluctant with the publication of hospital rankings, which reflects the corporatist style of governing the German health system.

Instead of naming and shaming, the performance management scheme is based on the idea of enabling self-assessment in the shadow of hierarchy. Sanctions such as fees or revoking the license to practice medicine do exist. When the external industry-wide quality assessment reveals, for example, that hospitals are underperforming, they are invited to enter a so-called structured dialogue (§ 10 QSKH-RL), meaning that the hospitals have the possibility to explain their behavior and negotiate with the account-holding agency. Thus, a fierce control and sanctioning philosophy, which is characteristic of the English NHS, is lacking in Germany. Instead, the assumptions about causality point towards the corporatist nature of the German hospital sector with its consensus-oriented decision-making style. However, while so far sanctions related to poor quality results have been rather rare in the German performance management scheme, this might change with the new hospital structure law that became effective in January 2016. The new law strives, as explained above, to strengthen the control and steering dimension of the performance management scheme by introducing pay for performance mechanisms.

Discussion

The objective of this chapter was to elucidate the multitude of goals associated with performance management schemes and accountability measures. Being interested in the 'big ideas' underlying performance management and accountability, the chapter has presented three ideal-typical models that differ with regard to the type of data collected, the assumptions about causality, and the related disclosure practices and sanction mechanisms. The three ideal types have been used to assess the development of performance management in Denmark, Germany and England. Needless to say, the reality is always hybrid and the three countries under consideration do not easily fall into one of the three ideal types. Accountability mechanisms in the British hospital sector have a strong focus on control and sanctioning, but there is also the idea of enhancing public trust, and hence legitimacy, by making performance results transparent. The German scheme is supportive of organizational learning, while both the controlling and the legitimacy perspective are less developed. Denmark is somehow in the middle between the steering and control and the learning model, combining powerful actors at the central level with the encouragement for individual organizational learning at the regional and hospital levels. Legitimacy plays an important role as both regions and the state are struggling to maintain legitimacy for the public health system in the eye of an evermore-demanding population, with a growing appetite for private sector solutions (Vrangbæk 2015). Furthermore, the regions and their hospitals have, since the structural reform in 2007, existed under the threat of being reorganized. They are therefore keen on maintaining legitimacy by demonstrating responsiveness towards state demands and adherence to performance standards (Rommetvedt *et al.* 2014).

The different paths the development of performance management schemes has taken in the three countries can be explained by both differences in the national administrative culture and differences in the governance at the sectoral level. The steering and control type relies heavily on hierarchical means of governance (Van Dooren *et al.* 2010). Hence, it seems plausible that countries with a high acceptance of a hierarchical administrative culture, such as England (Bendix 1974), come closest to this ideal type of performance management. Sector-specific characteristics, namely the still highly centralized governance style of the English NHS (Blank and Burau 2014), have contributed to the cultivation of the steering and control type of performance management as well (Pollitt 2010: 88). Germany, on the contrary, can be considered as the most dissimilar case in terms of national administrative culture (Bouckaert and Halligan 2008; Pollitt and Bouckaert 2011), but also regarding the governance structures at the sectoral level. Professionals and their associations are powerful players with a considerable amount of discretion, even if the German healthcare sector has experienced a shift to marketized and centralized governance in the last decade (Gerlinger 2010). Accordingly, we find the evolving performance management scheme shaped by collaboration and dialogue at eye level, hence by mechanisms that are typical for professional governance. Denmark in the middle has, like England, an integrated National Healthcare System, but at the same time also a tradition of decentralized decision-making, which gives professionals room to maneuver and makes the system similar to the German one (Mattei *et al.* 2013). However, as a result of recent centralization reforms, the possibility of hierarchical intervention is more likely than in Germany.

As the case studies have shown, accountability relations have indeed been altered in all three countries as a result of the introduction of new performance management instruments. However, judgments whether the two concepts support or hinder each other cannot be easily made. First of all, the three different models of performance management are not neutral in terms of power distribution, but empower different accountability forums. In *England*, the most important accountees are external stakeholders, in particular arm's-length agencies such as TDA and Monitor, but also citizens through means of choice. However, the patients' possibilities to choose healthcare providers, despite having been improved, are still limited in practice and cannot generate the disciplinary force of a competitive market (Newman and Vidler 2006; Forster and Gabe 2008; Pollitt 2010: 88). As a result, accountability towards citizens remains rather symbolic and we do not find a real citizen empowerment. In *Denmark*, we observe increasing political and administrative accountability as a result of the growing importance of the central level in the governance of the healthcare system (Rommetvedt *et al.* 2014). As in England, there is the rhetoric of increased patient choice, which, however, again does not unfold sufficient sanctioning power to shape everyday hospital management in a decisive way. In *Germany*, finally, it is difficult to talk about a real power shift. Professionals *were* and *are* held accountable mainly by professionals. Even the industry-wide quality assessment – the most important external assessment scheme – is designed by the actors of self-governance, and hence primarily by professionals. Thus, traditional professional accountability continues to be the strongest accountability mechanism, even if the intensity of assessments and their degree of formalization have been intensified through the introduction of new performance management instruments.

When assessing the impact of performance management on accountability, we also have to bear in mind that performance management can have both positive and negative effects on behavior (van de Walle and Cornelissen 2014), and that these positive and negative effects differ with respect to the different models of performance management. The *learning model* considers trust as a prerequisite for organizational learning, and hence abstains from strong external pressure. While there is empirical evidence that the learning model contributes to increased performance (Van Dooren *et al.* 2010: 152–4), it should also be taken into consideration that the learning model requires a second prerequisite: highly intrinsically motivated actors. When the latter is lacking, the learning model of performance management very likely results in reform backlog and status quo preservation. The *steering and control perspective* on performance management considers the possibility of self-motivation as a myth and thus restricts the autonomy of street-level bureaucrats involved in service provision. Again, there is empirical evidence that performance management understood as steering and controlling can improve goal attainment (Van Dooren *et al.* 2010: 154–6). However, there is also an intense debate about the dysfunctional effects of the steering and control model, such as gaming the system by manipulating the performance measurement or the output data (Aucoin and Heintzman 2000: 47–9; Van Dooren *et al.* 2010: 158). The positive effect of the *legitimacy perspective*, finally, is that it reminds managers of public service providers of the ultimate purpose of their work: to serve the needs of citizens as the final accountability forums in democratic systems. However, the positive effect can easily turn to dysfunctional behavior when the accountability means used are not appropriate. This might be the case when rankings are merely based on uncontextualized output data, when mass media sensationalize cases of misconduct in order to promote themselves, or when processes of account-holding are mainly driven by partisan competition to improve electoral turnout (Aucoin and Heintzman 2000: 53). In these cases, accountability through performance management is likely to simplify decision-making instead of promoting serious dialogue between accountor and accountee (Van Dooren et al. 2010: 153) – and hence the willingness of managers and professionals to take assessments into account very likely will be rather low.

Conclusion

From our case studies, we can conclude that both positive and negative effects of performance management can be found in all three countries. Our experts reported during the interviews about quality circles eager to critically reflect the processes of service provision in German hospitals, which, however, were blocked by unmotivated key actors that couldn't be removed due to lacking sanctions; they reported about improved resource allocation within regions in Denmark, and about taking patient-experienced quality more seriously in English hospitals. However, there have also been manifold episodes reported about cheating in the process of data collection and about decoupling inside procedures from outside presentation.

So far, we do not have the appropriate data to assess the relative weight of the positive and negative effects of performance management in our three countries. We thus end this chapter with proposing future research directions. Van Dooren et al. (2010: 167) suggest that there is a close relationship between the intensity of pressure and the intensity of effects: the higher the external pressure, the higher the intensity of effects – including, however, both negative and positive effects. Applied to our cases, this would imply that we would find in England, with its steering and control-oriented perspective, a high degree of dysfunctional behavior (Bevan and Hood 2006), but also a high degree of functional effects. In Germany, the learning-oriented performance management scheme would come along with less intense dysfunctional effects. The price, however, might be that we also see less positive effects. It is easier for street-level bureaucrats to ignore such an approach. Denmark, again, would range in the middle, which can ideally lead to a situation where you get the benefits from both sides. However, it might just as well lead to a murkier picture, where the actors become uncertain about the goals of the performance system, and therefore do not participate actively. These – against backdrop of the mainstream literature rather counterfactual – working hypotheses would be a good start to take a closer look at the relationship between accountability and performance management in a follow-up publication.

References

Aucoin, P. and Heintzman, R. (2000) The dialectics of accountability for performance in public management reform. *International Review of Administrative Science*, 66(1): 45–55.

Bendix, R. (1974) *Work and Authority in Industry: Ideologies of Management in the Course of Industrialization.* Berkeley, CA: University of California Press.

Bevan, G. and Hood, C. (2006) What's measured is what matters: targets and gaming in the English public health care system. *Public Administration*, 84(3): 517–38.

Blank, R. H. and Burau, V. D. (2014) *Comparative Health Policy* (4th edition). Basingstoke: Palgrave Macmillan.

Bouckaert, G. and Halligan, J. (2008) *Managing Performance: International Comparisons.* London: Routledge.

Bovens, M. (2005) Public accountability. In E. Ferlie (ed.), *The Oxford Handbook of Public Management.* Oxford: Oxford University Press, pp. 182–208.

Bovens, M. (2010) Two concepts of accountability: accountability as a virtue and as a mechanism. *West European Politics*, 33(5): 946–67.

Bovens, M., Schillemans, T. and 't Hart, P. (2008) Does public accountability work? An assessment tool. *Public Administration*, 86(1): 225–42.

Christiansen, P. M. and Nørgaard, A. S. (2004) Konsensusdemokrati og interesseorganisationer. *Politica*, 36(4): 418–29.

Day, P. and Klein, R. (1987) *Accountabilities: Five Public Services.* London/New York: Tavistock.

Department of Health (2014) *NHS Outcomes Framework 2015 to 2016.* Available at: www.gov.uk/government/uploads/system/uploads/attachment_data/file/385749/NHS_Outcomes_Framework.pdf (accessed 22 July 2016).

Donabedian, A. (1978) The quality of medical care. *Science,* 200(4344): 856–64.

Dubnick, M. (2005) Accountability and the promise of performance: in search of the mechanisms. *Public Performance and Management Review,* 28(3): 376–417.

Dubnick, M. J. and Frederickson, H. G. (2011) *Public Accountability: Performance Measurement, the Extended State, and the Search for Trust.* Washington, DC: National Academy of Public Administration & The Kettering Foundation.

Forster, R. and Gabe, J. (2008) Voice or choice? Patient and public involvement in the National Health Service in England under New Labour. *International Journal of Health Services,* 38(2): 333–56.

Gerlinger, T. (2010) Health care reform in Germany. *German Policy Studies,* 6(1): 107–42.

Government UK (2014) *About – Monitor.* Available at: www.gov.uk/government/organisations/monitor (accessed 22 July 2016).

Halachmi, A. (2002) Performance measurement, accountability and improved performance. *Public Performance & Management Review,* 25(4): 370–4.

Mattei, P., Mitra, M., Vrangbæk, K., Neby, S. and Byrkjeflot, H. (2013) Reshaping public accountability: hospital reforms in Germany, Norway and Denmark. *International Review of Administrative Sciences,* 79(2): 249–70.

Ministry for Health and Prevention (2014) *Indblik i sundhedsvæsenets resultater.* Available at: www.sum.dk/Aktuelt/Publikationer/Indblik-i-sundhedsvaesenets-resultater-maj-2014.aspx (accessed 22 July 2016).

Moynihan, D. P. (2008) *The Dynamics of Performance Management: Constructing Information and Reform.* Washington, DC: Georgetown University Press.

Newman, J. and Vidler, E. (2006) Discriminating customers, responsible patients, empowered users: consumerism and the modernisation of health care. *Journal of Social Policy,* 35(2): 193–209.

Pollitt, C. (2010) Performance blight and tyranny of light? Accountability in advanced performance measurement regimes. In M. J. Dubnick and H. G. Frederickson (eds), *Accountable Governance: Problems and Promises.* New York: M. E. Sharpe, pp. 81–97.

Pollitt, C. and Bouckaert, G. (2011) *Public Management Reform: A Comparative Analysis – New Public Management, Governance, and the Neo-Weberian State* (3rd edition). Oxford/New York: Oxford University Press.

Pollitt, C. and Hupe, P. (2011) Talking about government. *Public Management Review,* 13(5): 641–58.

Rommetvedt, H., Vrangbæk, K., Opedal, S. and Stigen, I. M. (2014) *Hvordan har vi det i dag, da? Flernivåstyring og samhandling i norsk og dansk helsepolitikk.* Bergen: Fakbokforlaget.

Romzek, B. (2000) Dynamics of public accountability in the era of reform. *International Review of Administrative Sciences,* 66(1): 21–44.

Sinclair, A. (1995) The chameleon of accountability: forms and discourses. *Accounting, Organizations and Society,* 20(2–3): 219–37.

Stumpfögger, N. (2009) Wenn die Gründerzeit zu Ende geht. In N. Böhlke, T. Gerlinger, K. Mosebach, R. Schmucker and T. Schulten (eds), *Privatisierung von Krankenhäusern: Erfahrungen und Perspektiven aus Sicht der Beschäftigten.* Hamburg: VSA, pp. 199–219.

van de Walle, S. and Cornelissen, F. (2014) Performance reporting. In M. Bovens, R. E. Goodin and T. Schilemans (eds), *The Oxford Handbook of Public Accountability.* Oxford: Oxford University Press, pp. 441–55.

Van Dooren, W., Bouckaert, G. and Halligan, J. (2010) *Performance Management in the Public Sector.* London: Routledge.

Vrangbæk, K. (2015) Denmark. In A. Sagan and S. Thomson (eds), *Voluntary Health Insurance in Europe: Country Profiles.* Copenhagen: WHO Regional Office for Europe on behalf of the European Observatory on Health Systems and Policies, pp. 38–42.

Vrangbæk, K., Appleby, J., Klenk, T. and Gregory, S. (2016) Comparing the institutionalisation of performance management schemes for hospitals in Denmark, Germany, and England. In R. Pinheiro, F. Ramirez, O. Francisco, K. Vrangbæk and H. Byrkjeflot (eds), *Towards a Comparative Institutionalism? Forms, Dynamics and Logics Across the Organizational Fields of Health and Higher Education.* Bingley: Emerald, pp. 81–106.

10
ACCOUNTABILITY, LEGITIMACY AND IMMIGRATION CONTROL

The inclusion of social actors in asylum regulation in Norway, Denmark and Germany

Tord Skogedal Lindén, Ina Radtke and Karsten Vrangbæk

Asylum systems under pressure

Immigration constitutes a profound challenge to public administration as it can be labeled a 'wicked issue' (Rittel and Webber 1973; Head 2008) characterized by high levels of uncertainty, ambiguity and complexity. For example, there is no definitive knowledge on the impact of immigrants on the welfare system or a consensus on whether immigration should be a human right (Boswell 2000; Guild 2006) within the multilevel, cross-sectoral and multi-actor environment. Thus, the maintenance of legitimacy as basis for the support of stakeholders is a continuous and particularly difficult quest (Head 2008: 102). This chapter focuses on the regulation of asylum seekers where policy formulation and implementation is torn between demands of restriction and liberalization. Public opinion tends to favor restrictive policies in the stage of policy formulation but has a more liberal opinion in the stage of implementation when individual fates are concerned (Ellermann 2006). Thus, the asylum process has been criticized from both sides with a sometimes devastating overall 'impression of governmental incompetence and incapacity' (Crisp 2003: 83). The current refugee crisis accentuates the high political salience of asylum policy.

Norway, Denmark and Germany have addressed the criticism in several reforms in the last decades with varying degrees of policy and organizational change. In all three countries, new appeals bodies that include social actors were set up. Social actors (laypeople) are actors connected to interest organizations. We ask: What legitimacy concerns led to the introduction of such appeal bodies and hardship commissions, respectively, in Norway, Denmark and Germany? And second: How are accountability relations affected by these changes? The chapter follows a neo-institutionalist and comparative perspective. We hereby aim to contribute to legitimacy literature where it is said that 'non-elected domestic bodies' have not been studied sufficiently (Maggetti 2010), as well as to accountability literature, which has hardly analyzed the policy field of immigration (Reichersdorfer *et al.* 2013). With such a focus on legitimacy and accountability, our comparative analysis contributes to explaining institutional reforms and also to investigating their effects on the influence of certain actors in the policy field (Bovens 2007; Byrkjeflot et al. 2014).

The chapter proceeds by outlining the theoretical perspective as well as the working assumptions for the analysis. We then describe the case selection and data. Next, we apply the developed working assumptions to the Norwegian Immigration Appeals Board (IAB), the Danish Refugee Appeals Board (RAB) and the German hardship commissions (HCs). This is followed by a comparative discussion and conclusion.

Legitimacy and accountability

Coping with ambiguity is central to establishing and maintaining legitimacy. From a neo-institutionalist perspective, legitimacy is the core concern of organizations seeking to ensure their survival (Meyer and Rowan 1977; DiMaggio and Powell 1983). It is a 'generalized perception or assumption that the actions of an entity are desirable, proper, or appropriate within a socially constructed system of norms, values, beliefs, and definitions' (Suchman 1995: 574). Legitimacy thus is the basis for the support of stakeholders. Suchman's definition hereby refers to output legitimacy. It has been contrasted by the term of input legitimacy (Scharpf 1970; Magetti 2010), which points to structures and processes. The overall legitimacy of a policy field can be challenged by *institutional crises* induced by a scandal or more often by an incremental process, which may lead to a situation where core actors 'have come to realize that traditional structures and processes are no longer effective and appropriate' (Alink et al. 2011: 289). Crises may in turn lead to reforms to regain legitimacy. Empirically, input and output legitimacy can be difficult to disentangle, and scholars differ in their opinions about whether they constitute trade-offs or are mutually reinforcing (Lindgren and Persson 2010). Within this context, the setup of new bodies that include social actors can be understood as an attempt to increase input legitimacy. Based on Suchman (1995), input legitimacy can be further operationalized into three analytical dimensions. Our first research question is thus guided by the following assumption: *The setup of new bodies in the context of increasing input legitimacy is based on pragmatic, moral and cognitive legitimacy concerns.*

(a) *Pragmatic legitimacy* is based on considerations regarding the relationship with stakeholders. The setup of new bodies can be seen as an attempt to increase pragmatic legitimacy by ensuring greater predictability (Maggetti *et al.* 2013: 3) of such interactions and at the same time as a delegation of power, which increases the influence of stakeholders. Three indicators point to pragmatic legitimacy concerns as the reason for the establishment of these bodies. First, the composition of the new bodies, in particular the inclusion of stakeholders that did not have influence within the asylum system beforehand. Included stakeholders then grant legitimacy as responsiveness to their interests (Suchman 1995: 578). Second, decision-making power of the new bodies that indicate that they are not purely symbolic, and rather constitute a channel of influence for the stakeholders (Suchmann 1995: 584). Third, the bodies being autonomous entities. Only then, 'dispositional spillovers' (Suchmann 1995: 588) from a positive image of new bodies to the policy field are possible.

(b) *Moral legitimacy*: If structures and processes of the new bodies are in accordance with socially accepted ideas, the moral legitimacy of the policy field is said to increase. Moral legitimacy is composed of procedural legitimacy and consequential legitimacy (Suchman 1995: 580), with the latter being focused on output judgements. Again, three indicators can be identified that point to the importance of moral legitimacy concerns as the reason for the establishment of new bodies. First, articulations in the documents that try to draw an image of the new bodies as being positively connoted within the asylum system (e.g. picturing them as 'human', 'fair', etc.). It is hereby shown that 'altruistic ideals' (Suchmann 1995: 588) of the environment are incorporated in the organization. Second, arguments in the documents that point to securing and increasing knowledge within the decision-making process (e.g. by the inclusion of experts in the bodies) (Maggetti *et al.* 2013: 3). Third, transparency about the output (i.e. number of cases and individual decisions that are the bases for judgements in regard to consequential legitimacy).

(c) *Cognitive legitimacy*: Here, predictability and plausibility is at the core. When this form of legitimacy is threatened, failures of meaning appear. The establishment of new bodies can be interpreted as 'creation of monitors and watchdogs' or as 'disassociation' (Suchman 1995: 598) as a repairing strategy. Indicators that point to cognitive legitimacy being a concern for the establishment of new bodies are thus twofold. First, and related to the strategy of disassociation, blame shifting could be indicated in the documents. It would be expressed as the delegation of tough decisions and problems and would result in reducing the vulnerability to electoral punishment (Maggetti *et al.* 2013: 3). Second, a monitoring function of the new bodies, which would be in the realm of the 'watchdog' strategy to repair legitimacy.

The subsequent analysis investigates the effect of the introduction of new bodies with social actors on the policy field's actor constellation. The establishment of new bodies can be purely symbolic at extreme or can have an actual impact. The concept of accountability is hereby helpful as it forms the analytical lens for the influence of certain types of actors, and thus also of change within a policy field's actor constellation. Bovens defines accountability as 'a relationship between an actor and a forum, in which the actor has an obligation to explain and justify his or her conduct, the forum can pose questions and pass judgment, and the actor may face consequences' (Bovens 2007: 450). Based on the forums to which actors must give an account, Bovens distinguishes between different forms of accountability. They form the analytical dimension for the chapter's analysis of types of actors and their influence on other forums after the establishment of new bodies. The second research question thus focuses on the relationships between the new and established actors. Answering this second research question is guided by this assumption: *The new bodies lead to weakening of administrative accountability and strengthening of social and legal accountability.*

Social accountability concerns the role of interest organizations, NGOs (nongovernmental organizations) and social actors in holding public authorities and agencies accountable (Bovens 2007). Stakeholders usually have limited opportunity to sanction actors (Bovens 2007: 457; see also Schillemans 2011). The setup of new bodies formalizing social accountability by including social actors might strengthen this forum.

Legal accountability (Bovens 2007: 456) is how courts and court-like bodies hold authorities to account. Legal accountability has traditionally enjoyed more importance in countries with administrative courts (e.g. Germany). In regard to our analysis, an increase of legal accountability must be stated if the bodies are granted independence, the decisions of the new bodies are binding and noncompliance can be sanctioned.

Administrative accountability is often visible in the hierarchical relationships among administrative actors but can also have the form of contracts between public and private ones. For our investigation, the dependence of the bodies from other administrative actors is crucial to observe the strength of this forum.

Case selection and data

Germany is receiving most asylum applicants among the 32 EU/EEA countries, with Denmark and Norway as numbers 11 and 12 (Eurostat 2015). Ranking countries based on applicants relative to inhabitants, Norway and Denmark have the fifth-highest rates in Europe, closely followed by Germany. Yet, Norwegian and Danish immigration policy has become more restrictive over the last two decades (Reichersdorfer *et al.* 2013). The same is true for Germany (Thränhardt 2007; Löhlein 2010), although in the recent asylum crisis there was a temporary extensive liberalization observable. All three countries have seen many immigration reforms since 2000, resulting in policy and institutional change. Thus, Christensen and Lægreid (2009: 174) refer to Norway as 'an eager immigration administration reformer'. Also, Denmark has, since 2000, experienced several changes in its immigration law and the ministries and agencies responsible in this field (Reichersdorfer *et al.* 2013: 280). In Germany, immigration policy has generally gained a more prominent status since the beginning of the millennium (Mushaben 2011; cf. Reichersdorfer *et al.* 2013).

The establishment of new bodies that include social actors took place within this overall reform context. In Norway, an Immigration Appeals Board has handled appeals of rejections since 2001. Since 1983, Danish cases of appeals have been handled by the Refugees Appeals Board. In Germany, all federal states have established hardship commissions, mostly in the context of the immigration reform of 2005.

The investigation is based on document studies of primary sources such as bills, parliamentary debates, ordinances and annual reports of the bodies under investigation, as well as press and online releases of political, administrative and societal actors in the policy field. Additionally, secondary sources such as expert evaluations, journal articles and other public sources are taken into account. Admittedly, official sources may not be completely open and might be biased in their statements regarding legitimacy and accountability. However, official documents state reasons for the introduction and composition of new bodies, and careful analysis of such documents, as well as taking secondary sources into account, allows us to shed light on these.

Norway: the Immigration Appeals Board

The IAB has handled appeals of rejections by the Norwegian Directorate of Immigration (NDI) since 2001. The IAB is a public administrative body described as court-like due to its extended independence and dominance of legally trained board leaders. Yet, it is not fulfilling all characteristics of a court. Cases are most often processed by the board leader and/or the legal secretariat. However, in around 5–10 percent of the cases, decisions are reached in appeals board meetings where one of three board members is appointed on the basis of suggestions from humanitarian organizations, meaning that social actors are involved. Decisions are binding, but it is possible to appeal to ordinary courts.

Christensen *et al.* (2006) provide a full account of Norwegian IAB reforms, but focus less on interest organizations and social actors. They identify overload, blame avoidance, legal safeguards, justice and confidence as important arguments in these reforms (Christensen *et al.* 2006: 67–8, 173). When investigating why social actors are included in the processing of appeals, and how this affects accountability relations, the bills on changes in the Immigration Act from 1996, 1999 and 2005 are of particular relevance.

Legitimacy concerns

Our analysis of these documents confirms a claim found in several official studies: according to Harborg (2008), the composition of boards has never been properly justified. Harborg interprets the composition as an expression of wanting to secure legitimacy and avoid criticism (Harborg 2008: 25). A green paper says the role of board members is vague and that parliamentary documents do not treat this question thoroughly (NOU 2010: 77, 93). The documents give more information on why an independent body is needed than explaining its composition. However, we find traces of Suchman's (1995) three concerns for legitimacy.

In the first reform phase in 1996, pragmatic and moral legitimacy concerns are evident. In the parliamentary treatment, it is emphasized how confidence in the board presupposes independence, and that this is also influenced by its composition. It is argued that a broad composition, including people suggested by humanitarian organizations, will secure the independence of the board and access to expert knowledge (Innst.O. nr. 24 1996–1997: 3). Legal safeguards are also seen as a benefit of this composition (St.forhandl. 1996–1997: 226). The bill was not adopted, though, and the parliament asked the government to prepare a new bill.

The second reform phase resulted in the introduction of the IAB in 2001, with board members appointed on suggestions from the Ministry of Justice, Ministry of Foreign Affairs, the Norwegian Bar Association/the Norwegian Association of Lawyers, and humanitarian organizations. Documents in this phase include arguments such as legal safeguards, public confidence and how the IAB is expected to increase the legitimacy of decisions (Ot.prp. nr. 17 1998–1999). Less explicitly, however, this expected increase in legitimacy of decisions and confidence in the immigration administration is connected to the composition. The Ministry argues that a broad composition resembles the Danish solution and that this composition works well there (Ot.prp. nr. 17 1998–1999). The Standing Committee of Justice of the Storting notes that there could be a potential challenge of integrity for humanitarian organizations. The committee stresses that it is important that these organizations are seen as independent and free, and not considered an alibi for decisions, but the committee does not see this as a big problem (Innst.O. nr. 42 1998–1999: 10).

In 2005, the Immigration Act was changed again, but this reform is less relevant for the issue of the inclusion of social actors. However, the reform establishes a Grand Jury of the IAB to handle matters of principle, and its arguments on composition are interesting. The laypersons form the majority, and this may be considered to strengthen democracy and the confidence in the board (Ot.prp. nr. 31 2004–2005: 40). And: 'The ministry attaches importance to securing high legitimacy of decisions in the Grand Jury. This is expected to be ensured best through increased interest organization representation' (Ot.prp. nr. 31 2004–2005: 48).

In sum, the laypeople element is not given thorough discussion in public documents. However, referring back to Suchman (1995), all the three concerns for legitimacy expressed in assumption 1 seem to apply to the Norwegian case. Pragmatic (autonomous entities, social actors with influence) and moral legitimacy (legal safeguards with equal treatment of cases, expertise of social actors and system confidence) are most visible. Cognitive legitimacy is also evident, including efficiency by relieving the ministry and informally blame shifting by reducing political responsibility, but not so clearly connected to social actors. An additional argument is the reference to Danish experiences.

Effects on accountability relations

The inclusion of laypeople appointed based on the suggestion of humanitarian organizations contributes to the body's hybridity. The fact that 'ordinary people' participate in decisions on whether asylum seekers should be allowed to stay or not seems to imply a clear strengthening of social accountability. However, since few appeal cases are handled in board hearings where these laypeople are present, and due to the dominant position of the board leader and the IAB secretariat in preparing cases, as well as other limitations, the influence may be rather limited. According to Byrkjeflot *et al.* (2014: 14), the inclusion of laypeople is symbolic. Being included in so few cases suggests that social actors may provide legitimization more than quality assurance of the processing of appeals. Critical voices, though, worry that comprehensive social actor inclusion has implications and may result in liberalization of immigration policy (e.g. Innst.O. nr. 68 2004–2005: 12).

An obvious observation is that the court-like IAB increases legal accountability. The NDI is accountable to the IAB, and the IAB is accountable to the ordinary court(s). When appeals are handled by the IAB rather than the Ministry of Justice, political and administrative accountability is weakened, in line with our second assumption (see also Christensen and Lægreid 2006: 24–5). Decisions of the IAB are almost equal to judicial decisions. However, the IAB is hybrid in character: it is only a court-like, administrative body, and this may result in unclear accountability relations.

The developments also illustrate how accountability relations are 'multiple and complex' (Byrkjeflot *et al.* 2014: 4). An expert committee discussing how the appeal system is and should be organized (NOU 2010: 24) nicely presents dilemmas of balancing different considerations. Legal safeguards and the correct use of law may secure legitimacy of decisions. However, legitimacy is also influenced by the extent to which decisions correspond to the views of the general public, parliament and government (NOU 2010: 24, 81). This tension between control and autonomy is clearly present in the different reforms, between political and administrative accountability.

Political accountability may be suffering from the reforms, and establishing a board may 'negatively complicate the government's responsibility towards the Storting' (Innst.O. nr. 42 1998–1999: 6). This was the background for the reform in 2005, which increased the scope for political control (Christensen *et al.* 2006). Balancing political control and the legitimacy and confidence of the IAB is challenging (Christensen *et al.* 2006).

The Danish Refugee Appeals Board

Since 1983, Danish cases of appeals have been handled by the Refugees Appeals Board. As in Norway, this is a court-like public administrative body. It is headed by judges and with members appointed by relevant ministries (Justice and Foreign Affairs), a professional organization (the Danish Bar and Law Society) and a humanitarian NGO (Danish Refugee Council). Decisions of the Refugee Appeals Board are legally binding and cannot be appealed to other courts, except for claims about procedural errors (cf. udlændingelovens § 56, stk. 8). Decisions are made by simple majority voting, and each member has one vote. Contrary to Norway, the social actors participate in all cases handled by the board.

Legitimacy concerns

The Danish Refugee Appeals Board was established in 1983 with the first Danish law that explicitly addressed refugees and the treatment of refugees. The incoming conservative-led government put the new law for foreigners (Udlændingelov) forward in response to the growing need to establish judicial control over this area (Udlændingelov nr. 226 af 8. juni 1983).

The law ended up getting broad support in parliament as only the anti-immigration protest party 'Fremskridspartiet' voted against the law.

The procedures established with the law from 1983 became the backbone of policy practice in this field, and the Danish Refugee Appeals Board maintained its role and organization throughout the 1980s during the reign of the conservative-led government. The social democratic coalition government from 1992 to 2002 also maintained the broad representation in the Board, including representatives from the humanitarian organization Danish Refugee Council and the Danish Bar and Law Society. Meanwhile, there was a growing critique in the population of the rather liberal asylum policies in Denmark at the time, and this found a strong resonance in the anti-immigration party the Danish People's Party, which was established in 1995 (Bille and Rüdiger 2009).

After the election in 2001, a center-right minority government was established, led by the liberal party Venstre and relying on the Danish People's Party for parliamentary support. This led to a decade of successive tightening of immigration. The gradual tightening involved changes to practice and changes to the organization of immigration administration in Denmark. One of the first moves was a major package of laws in 2002. This 'package' also affected the Danish Refugee Appeals Board. The composition of the Board was changed, and both the representative appointed by the humanitarian organization Danish Refugee Council and the representative from the Ministry of Foreign Affairs were removed from the Board. Furthermore, the government established an independent Ministry for Refugees, Immigrants and Integration, which was charged with pursuing tighter immigration policies. This Ministry replaced the Ministry of Justice on the Board. These changes in the representation signaled a stronger emphasis on the political goal of reducing the inflow of immigrants. Furthermore, it weakened the importance of the type of country expertise represented by the Ministry of Foreign Affairs. All in all, this organizational change can be interpreted as an attempt to increase the government's influence on the practices of the independent RAB.

In legitimacy terms, one might interpret the changes in asylum policies as an attempt to gain legitimacy by providing results that were in line with the growing skepticism in the population about the increasing inflow of immigrants, and the problems in integrating these immigrants into Danish society.

The restrictive policies pursued by the center-right government from 2001 onwards found broad support even within the social democratic opposition party. However, as time progressed and the administration of the restrictive policies brought Denmark into potential conflicts with international conventions (Reichersdorfer, Christensen and Vrangbæk 2013), more and more members of the opposition came to see the policies as problematic. The election in 2011 created an opportunity to articulate this, and the incoming social democratic minority coalition implemented several changes to the immigration and asylum policy. The Ministry for Immigration was dismantled and the composition of the Danish Refugee Appeals Board was changed so that the Ministry of Foreign Affairs and the Danish Refugee Council were once again given the right to appoint members of the Board. The government argued that these changes would strengthen the concerns for 'due process' and unbiased evaluation of asylum cases (Retsinformation: Forslag til lov om ændring af Udlændingeloven 2012).

Referring to assumption 1 and Suchman (1995), it is possible to find references to all three types of legitimacy in the Danish debate. Pragmatic (independence) and moral legitimacy (legal safeguards with equal treatment of cases, expertise of laypeople and system confidence) are clearly relevant. Cognitive legitimacy is also evident in the initial argumentation for establishing the Board as a way to deal with a difficult and growing problem by establishing an institution with arm's length from ministries and politicians. It is noticeable that legitimacy arguments are used in different ways in the highly politicized debate in Denmark. Immigration-skeptical politicians refer to legitimacy as bringing the operation of the Board into alignment with the general mood in the population – a sort of political legitimacy. Other politicians emphasize the pragmatic and moral legitimacy of maintaining independence and including laypeople and independent experts.

Effects on accountability relations

The Danish case shows many of the same accountability issues as the Norwegian case. Introducing an independent Refugee Appeals Board introduces legal accountability into the administration of asylum policies. However, in contrast to the Norwegian case, there are no further appeals options within the civil court system within Denmark. The only option for asylum seekers that are denied in the Appeals Board is to refer their case to the international human rights court if they can argue that the decision is in conflict with relevant international conventions.

Asylum cases are first treated by the Ministry of Justice, and thus subject to political and administrative accountability. However, the use of an independent appeals board creates a new relation with the purpose of protecting asylum seekers from the political interests embedded in the state ministries. As a consequence, the (formal) political accountability is weakened by definition (Christensen and Lægreid 2006: 24–5).

Legal accountability is also strengthened by the fact that the Board is headed by judges who are independent from the state administration. The inclusion of representatives, which are appointed by a humanitarian NGO and by a professional organization increases social accountability.

This tension between control and autonomy is clearly present in the different reforms, between political and administrative accountability.

Germany: hardship commissions

The hardship commissions (Hügel 2000; Schneider 2012) have been established based on §23a of the Residence Act of the immigration law of 2005 but had existed in Berlin and North Rhine-Westphalia since the 1990s. The purpose of hardship commissions is to deal with single cases of foreigners with no legal right of residence. Initially, hardship commissions were set up for only five years with a follow-up evaluation and a respective decision on their continuity. However, the time limitation was abandoned by the German government in 2008 (Schneider 2012: 45). Social actors are included in HCs in different ways.

Legitimacy concerns

The reasons for the establishment of hardship commissions reflect two of three legitimacy dimensions of Suchman's concept: pragmatic and moral legitimacy. Regarding pragmatic legitimacy concerns, all three indicators are present. First, the composition of bodies indeed includes stakeholders that did not have influence within the asylum system beforehand. The composition of the hardship commission is, however, very diverse, ranging from five to 23 members. The background thereby varies. There are always administrative representatives. In all federal states (except for Hamburg), head associations of the non-statutory welfare sector, as well as Protestant and Catholic churches, choose members of the hardship commissions. Also, a variety of social migrant organizations are represented in the bodies. Thus, social actors, which have not been formally included in the decision process on asylum seekers, are now represented within this system. Second, the decision-making power of the new bodies is indeed not purely symbolic, and can thus be considered to constitute an actual channel of influence for the stakeholders. It must, however, be stated that the hardship commissions can only recommend that a hardship is granted to an individual. The final decision is taken by the respective minister of interior of the federal state. The hardship commissions' activity reports, however, show that recommendations followed by the authorities of interior exceed 80 percent in most of the federal states. This points to the normative power of the bodies despite the absence of formal authority. Third, the bodies are autonomous entities. This is at least true in a formal sense. Due to their organizational affiliation to the ministries of interior or integration, they are required to follow general procedural rules from the respective supreme authority. Yet, hardship commissions decide independently on individual cases. Further, the hardship commissions' decisions are not contestable in court. To some extent, their independence can, however, be doubted based on loyalty issues that members of the commission might experience due to their dual linkage to the organization they represent and the new body.

Regarding moral legitimacy concerns, most operationalized indicators are visible in the case of hardship commissions as well. The first indicator of 'altruistic ideals' (Suchmann 1995: 588) of the environment being represented in the organization's structure and processes is reflected in the very conditions for a decision of hardship by the hardship commission: urgent humanitarian or personal reasons. Second, the increase in knowledge is reflected in the reports of these bodies. Here, it is stated that these bodies are regularly consulted in regard to temporary bans of deportation. Third, an increase of transparency as an attempt to increase moral legitimacy is observable. Numbers of enquiries and recommendations that a hardship should be granted are made publicly. And also, cases regularly get – mostly at a local and regional level – media attention, which also stipulates more transparency about decision-making criteria of the regular process on asylum.

In regard to the dimension of cognitive legitimacy, however, the operationalized two indicators cannot be found in the case of the hardship commissions. First, blame shifting is not visible because the decisions and problems are not really delegated to the new bodies. The Ministry of Interior still holds the power of the final decision on individual cases. Thus, hardship commissions only constitute additional bodies, which is also represented in the number of cases they deal with. It is a low percentage of denied asylum applications. Second, a monitoring function in form of a 'watchdog' strategy to repair cognitive legitimacy is also not present in the case of the hardship commissions as their decisions do not state that the decision to deny the application by authorities is (legally) wrong.

Effects on accountability relations

In line with the working assumption, the new bodies indeed strengthen social accountability. However, they have a rather weakening effect on legal accountability and do not have any effect on administrative accountability within the asylum system. Thus, the assumption holds only partly true in the German case. These findings are based on the position of hardship commissions as new bodies within the German asylum system, their procedures as well as their affiliation to one or more accountability fora and their relationship to other fora.

The administration of asylum policies takes place in the multilevel environment of the German federal system (Groß 2006; Schneider 2012). Decisions on asylum are made centrally by the Federal Office for Migration and Refugees (BAMF) and its decision-makers in its outposts and special envoys, respectively. In the case of rejection, the asylum seeker can appeal to the administrative court and has to leave Germany if the rejection is upheld. Decisions on deportation are the responsibility of the federal states, hence the reason for hardship commissions being established at this level. Hardship commissions make their decisions on individual cases in non-public meetings. There is no formal right of an asylum seeker to appeal to the hardship commissions. Only members of the body are allowed to put cases on the agenda. However, the hardship commissions of some federal states mainly gather information on potential cases through their offices to which asylum seekers can turn. If it is classified as a case of hardship, a recommendation to grant a residence permit is formulated. Subsequently, the ministry or senator of the interior of the federal state has to decide if it is accepted. If this is the case, the responsible foreigners' registration office is ordered to follow the decision. Only in North Rhine-Westphalia, the recommendation is directly passed on to the foreigners' registration office.

The hardship commissions hereby constitute hybrids of accountability fora. The social and administrative fora are represented in the bodies. Their 'accountability identity' varies based on their composition across the federal states. Formally, however, they belong to the administrative accountability forum with them being organizationally located at the ministries of interior of the federal states. Social accountability is strengthened in those federal states where respective representatives are included in the composition as they are given a formal voice within the system. Most of the cases have already been appealed against in front of a court and rejected. When subsequently the hardship commissions decide that it should be recommended that the applicant should be granted a residence permit and the ministry of interior agrees, the decision of the court is overruled. Thus, legal accountability is weakened, which is remarkable as the legal forum had some sort of final decision power on individual cases before the establishment of the hardship commissions.

Comparative discussion

Two assumptions guided our analysis. First, we expected the establishment of new bodies that include social actors *to be justified with pragmatic, moral and cognitive legitimacy concerns* (Suchman 1995). In all three cases, pragmatic (autonomous entities, social actors with influence) and moral legitimacy (humanitarian or personal reasons, legal safeguards, expertise, confidence, transparency) dominate. The Danish debate is the most politicized in this respect; social actors have been included, excluded and then invited back again. The Danish case also illustrates how the legitimacy concept may mean different things to different actors in a politicized context. Cognitive legitimacy concerns are perhaps less visible in our cases, but evident for the IAB and RAB (e.g. with respect to having boards with arm's length from ministries, thus relieving the ministry of work and allowing blame shifting). Overall, involving actors who are commonly seen as spokespersons for adherence to due process and protection of the rights of asylum seekers makes it more difficult to dismiss the process as biased and illegitimate.

Our second assumption, expecting the new bodies to weaken administrative and to strengthen social and legal accountability, is only partly supported. In Germany, the legal accountability within the arrangement has always been quite strong. The hardship commissions actually weakened this forum. In Denmark and Norway, in contrast, administrative accountability has been weakened and legal accountability strengthened. However, as the two Scandinavian countries start from a low level of legal accountability, this increase should not be overestimated. The IAB and the RAB are *court-like* but still public *administrative* bodies. In many respects, they do not work in the way an ordinary court would work. While we consider the increase in legal accountability to make the three countries more similar, we do not claim that this reflects a high level of convergence. Furthermore, while both the IAB and RAB are court-like, one could argue that the Norwegian solution is to maximize judicial-based legitimacy, whereas the process in Denmark is partly politically controlled because central civil servants take part in the decision-making process. Accountability balances are thus different. In Norway, the attitude seems to be that the law and legal practitioners should decide, securing an independent body. In Denmark and Germany, there has been more emphasis on maintaining the political and democratic influence. The Norwegian and German approaches are more focused on input legitimacy, the Danish one on output legitimacy. Moreover, legal actors have a stronger position in Norway since the opportunity to bring the appeals bodies' decisions to ordinary courts is more restricted in Denmark.

Social accountability is strengthened in all countries, but the overall position and influence of social actors remains weak. In Germany, the HCs only have advisory capacity. An important difference between Norway and Denmark is that in the latter social actors are present in all cases, meaning that among our three countries, social actors probably enjoy most influence in Denmark.

Using a broader neo-institutionalist frame, we may interpret our observations from instrumental and cultural-organizational perspectives (Christensen, Fimreite and Lægreid 2007). A *structural-instrumental perspective* is based on the concept of bounded rationality (March and Simon 1958). It takes for granted that reforms are based on rational calculation and clear organizational thinking (Dahl and Lindblom 1953; March and Olsen 1983). The perspective includes a hierarchical and a negotiational version. The hierarchical perspective would lead to expectations of a political/administrative center that is able to introduce policy changes based on rational calculations of goals and means. In our analysis, we found support for this perspective in the sense that the initial introduction of appeals boards represents a solution to capacity, administrative and legal issues, arising from the growing number of refugees. Yet, it is equally clear from the three cases that the hierarchical instrumental perspective is insufficient in itself. Otherwise, we would expect very similar organization forms in response to similar problems in the three countries. Instead, we find considerable differences in timing and organization of the appeals boards. One explanation for this can be found in the negotiational perspective. In this case, the different constellations of stakeholders and political interests determine the national solutions, and the changes over time. The Danish case provided a particularly good example of how different political interests lead to restructuring of appeals boards with new combinations of stakeholders involved in different time periods.

However, our analysis also indicates that national perceptions of moral obligations, *Rechtsstaat* principles, legal and political traditions are important for understanding the national configurations (Olsen 1983). The appeals boards can be seen as symbolic representations of organizational forms that are perceived as legitimate in the three countries at particular times. This is in line with a *cultural-institutional perspective* emphasizing that public organizations develop as a result of adaptation to internal and external pressure through natural processes (Selznick 1957; Scott and Davis 2006). Public institutions reflect cultural traditions that filter norms and values, and the implementation of reforms is likely to depend on the degree of compatibility between the reform and the organizational-cultural tradition (Brunsson and Olsen 1993; Painter and Peters 2009).

Conclusion

This chapter has discussed two questions: Why did Norway, Denmark and Germany include social actors in asylum appeals systems? And how are accountability relations affected by these changes? For the first research question, we find that particularly increasing pragmatic and moral legitimacy was an important motive for the inclusion of social actors. Policymakers wanted to ensure independence, legal safeguards, expertise, system confidence and transparency. This means that the first guiding assumption is confirmed. For the second research question, we conclude that the inclusion of social actors has weakened political and administrative accountability but strengthened social and legal accountability. In Germany, however, legal accountability is reduced. Our second guiding assumption is thus partly confirmed, and we argue for a twofold convergence among the cases. First, we find traces of recently formalized social accountability within these new bodies in all three countries. And second, we identify an increase of legal accountability in the two Nordic cases, which thus move their characteristics towards the German approach. However, Germany starts from a much stronger legal tradition than Norway and Denmark. And the formalization of social accountability does not imply that societal actors have gained a strong position. In Norway, social actors are included to a low degree, and in Germany they are part of an advisory body only. Social accountability thus seems strongest in Denmark, although social actors for a period were completely excluded here. However, does the inclusion of social actors create a 'stable environment', taking pressure of governments and administrations? Is legitimacy secured by the inclusion of social actors? And what about the relationship between accountability, legitimacy and performance: Are there systematic differences between the three bodies under investigation in processing time and outcome of the appeals, and how can potential differences be explained? These are important issues for further research.

References

Alink, F., Boin, A. and 't Hart, P. (2011) Institutional crises and reforms in policy sectors: the case of asylum policy in Europe. *Journal of European Public Policy*, 8(2): 286–306.
Bille, L. and Rüdiger, M. (2009) Dansk Folkeparti. In *Den store danske encyclopedi*. Available at: www.denstoredanske.dk/Samfund,_jura_og_politik/Samfund/Danske_politiske_partier_og_bevægelser/Dansk_Folkeparti (accessed 25 September 2015).
Boswell, C. (2000) European values and the asylum crisis. *International Affairs*, 76(3): 537–57.
Bovens, M. (2007) Analysing and assessing accountability: a conceptual framework. *European Law Journal*, 13(4): 447–68.
Brunsson, N. and Olsen, J. P. (1993) *The Reforming Organization*. London/New York: Routledge.
Byrkjeflot, H., Christensen, T. and Lægreid, P. (2014) The many faces of accountability: comparing reforms in welfare, hospitals and migration. *Scandinavian Political Studies*, 37(2): 171–95.
Christensen, T., Fimreite, A. L. and Lægreid, P. (2007) Reform of the employment and welfare administrations: the challenges of coordinating diverse public organizations. *International Review of Administrative Sciences*, 73(3): 389–409.
Christensen, T. and Lægreid, P. (eds) (2006) *Autonomy and Regulation: Coping with Agencies in the Modern State*. Cheltenham: Edward Elgar.
Christensen, T. and Lægreid, P. (2009) Organizing immigration policy: the unstable balance between political control and agency autonomy. *Policy and Politics*, 37(2): 161–77.
Christensen, T., Lægreid, P. and Ramslien, A. R. (2006) *Styring og autonomi; organisasjonsformer i norsk utlendingsforvaltning*. Oslo: Universitetsforlaget.
Crisp, J. (2003) Refugees and the global politics of asylum. *The Political Quarterly*, 74: 75–87.
Dahl, R. A. and Lindblom, C. E. (1953) *Politics, Economics and Welfare*. New York: Harper & Brothers.
DiMaggio, P. J. and Powell, W. W. (1983) The iron cage revisited: isomorphism and collective rationality in organizational fields. *American Sociological Review*, 48: 147–60.
Ellermann, A. (2006) Street-level democracy: how immigration bureaucrats manage public opposition. *West European Politics*, 29(2): 293–309.
Eurostat (2015) *Asylum in the EU*. Eurostat newsrelease 53/2015, 20, March.
Groß, T. (2006) Die Verwaltung der Migration nach der Verabschiedung des Zuwanderungsgesetzes. In M. Bommes and W. Schiffauer (eds), *Migrationsreport 2006. Fakten – Analysen – Perspektiven*. Frankfurt/Main: Campus, pp. 31–62.
Guild, E. (2006) The Europeanisation of Europe's asylum policy. *International Journal of Refugee Law*, 18(3–4): 630–51.

Harborg, H. (2008) *Uavhengig gjennomgang av Utlendingsnemndas (UNE) praksis i valg av avgjørelsesform i asylsaker*. Rapport på oppdrag av AID.
Head, B. W. (2008) Wicked problems in public policy. *Public Policy*, 3(2): 101–18.
Hügel, V. M. (2000) Härtefallkommissionen. In WOGE e.V. and Institut für soziale Arbeit e.V. (eds), *Handbuch der sozialen Arbeit mit Kinderflüchtlingen*. Münster: Votum, pp. 172–81.
Innst.O. nr. 24 (1996–1997) Innstilling fra justiskomiteen om lov om endringer i lov av 24. juni 1988 nr. 64 om utlendingers adgang til riket og deres opphold her (utlendingsloven) – klagenemnd i utlendingssaker m.v.
Innst.O. nr. 42 (1998–1999) Innstilling fra justiskomiteen om lov om endringer i utlendingsloven og i enkelte andre lover (klagenemnd for utlendingssaker m.v.).
Innst.O. nr. 68 (2004–2005) Innstilling fra kommunalkomiteen om lov om endringer i utlendingsloven m.m. (styringsforhold på utlendingsfeltet).
Lindgren, K.-O. and Persson, T. (2010) Input and output legitimacy: synergy or trade-off? Empirical evidence from an EU survey. *Journal of European Public Policy*, 17(4): 449–67.
Löhlein, H. (2010) Fluchtziel Deutschland. In P. Dieckhoff (ed.), *Kinderflüchtlinge. Theoretische Grundlagen und berufliches Handeln*. Wiesbaden: VS Verlag, pp. 27–33.
Maggetti, M. (2010) Legitimacy and accountability of independent regulatory agencies: a critical review. *Living Review in Democracy*, 2: 1–9.
Maggetti, M., Ingold, K. and Varone, F. (2013) Having your cake and eating it, too: can regulatory agencies be both independent and accountable? *Swiss Political Science Review*, 19(1): 1–25.
March, J. G. and Olsen, J. P. (1983) Organizing political life: what administrative reorganization tells us about government. *American Political Science Review*, 77: 281–97.
March, J. G. and Simon, H. A. (1958) *Organizations*. New York: John Wiley & Sons.
Meyer, J. W. and Rowan, B. (1977) Institutionalized organizations: formal structure as myth and ceremony. *American Journal of Sociology*, 83(2): 340–63.
Mushaben, J. M. (2011) Citizenship and migration policies under Merkel's Grand Coalition. *German Politics*, 20(3): 376–91.
NOU (2010) 12. Ny klageordning for utlendingssaker.
Olsen, J. P. (1983) *Organized Democracy*. Bergen: Scandinavian University Press.
Ot.prp. nr. 17 (1998–1999) Om lov om endringer i utlendingsloven og i enkelte andre lover (klagenemnd for utlendingssaker m.v.).
Ot.prp. nr. 31 (2004–2005) Om lov om endringer i utlendingsloven m.m. (styringsforhold på utlendingsfeltet).
Painter, M. and Peters, B. G. (eds) (2009) *Tradition and Public Administration*. London: Palgrave Macmillan.
Reichersdorfer, J., Christensen, T. and Vrangbæk, K. (2013) Accountability of immigration administration: comparing crises in Norway, Denmark and Germany. *International Review of Administrative Sciences*, 79(2): 271–91.
Retsinformation. Forslag til lov om ændring af Udlændingeloven (2012) Available at: www.retsinformation.dk/forms/R0710.aspx?id=141575 (accessed 23 September 2015).
Rittel, H. and Webber, M. (1973) Dilemmas in a general theory of planning. *Policy Sciences*, 4(2): 155–69.
Scharpf, F. W. (1970) *Demokratietheorie zwischen Utopie und Anpassung*. Konstanz: Universitätsverlag.
Schillemans, T. (2011) Does horizontal accountability work? Evaluating potential remedies for the accountability deficit of agencies. *Administration and Society*, 43(4): 387–416.
Schneider, J. (2012) *The Organisation of Asylum and Migration Policies in Germany*. Study of the German National Contact Point for the European Migration Network (EMN). Nürnberg: BAMF.
Scott, W. R. and Davis, G. (2006) *Organizations and Organizing: Rational, Natural and Open Systems Perspectives* (6th revised edition). Upper Saddle River, NJ: Prentice Hall.
Selznick, P. (1957) *Leadership in Administration*. New York: Harper & Row.
St.forhandl. (1996–1997) Sak 5: Innstilling fra justiskomiteen om lov om endringer i lov av 24. juni 1988 nr. 64 om utlendingers adgang til riket og deres opphold her (utlendingsloven) – klagenemnd i utlendingssaker. 10.12.1996.
Suchman, M. C. (1995) Managing legitimacy: strategic and institutional approaches. *The Academy of Management Review*, 20(3): 571–610.
Thränhardt, D. (2007) Einwanderungs- und Flüchtlingspolitik. In S. Schmidt, G. Hellmann and R. Wolf (eds), *Handbuch zur deutschen Außenpolitik*. Wiesbaden: VS Verlag für Sozialwissenschaften, pp. 684–91.

11
WELFARE REFORMS, ACCOUNTABILITY AND PERFORMANCE

Per Lægreid and Kristin Rubecksen

Introduction

The main theme of this chapter is the dynamics between administrative reforms in welfare states and accountability, as well as the relationships between accountability and performance. Both relationships are ambiguous and contested (Lægreid 2014). First, we address the relationship between administrative reforms and accountability. Better accountability has been a main driver of the reforms in the welfare state, but in practice the reforms have tended to make accountability relations more complex (Thomas 1998; Christensen and Lægreid 2015). An important question is what kind of accountability the executives perceive as appropriate (Romzek 2000). We want to examine how comprehensive reforms have affected the relationship between political, administrative, professional and social accountability. Second, we ask to what extent different accountability types affect perceived performance. Is there a clear relationship between accountability and better performance or is it loose and contested (Dubnick 2011)?

The chapter addresses these relationships in the area of administrative reforms in the welfare administration and hospitals in Norway, Denmark and Germany. All three countries have recently been subject to large-scale transboundary administrative reforms within these policy areas. In Norway, there were major reforms in the hospital administration (2002) and in the welfare administration (2005). In Denmark, the structural reform (2006) implied major reorganization of the hospital and welfare administration and Hertz reform (2004) reorganized the labor and employment services in Germany. We ask how different accountability relations and performance relations are perceived as seen from the top administrative executives in central government and how different accountability types affect different types of performance. The focus is on accountability to whom and the problem of many eyes and on a broad set of accountability indicators.

More specifically, the following research questions will be addressed:

1   What is the prevalence of different accountability types?
2   How do accountability types vary with country, policy areas and structural features?
3   What are the effects of different accountability relations on public sector performance?

Theoretically, we will apply a structural perspective, a task-specific perspective and a cultural perspective, drawing on a broad range of explanatory factors in order to shed light on the observed patterns of accountability relations in and between the three countries. Such factors include, first, historical traditions and national political-institutional legacies. The countries have both similarities and differences that are likely to promote some types of accountability over others. They are all well-established Western parliamentary democracies, but diverge in political-administrative systems and administrative traditions.

Second, task-specificity related to the reform areas (political salience of tasks, degree of professionalization and complexity in service delivery, acceptance of local variation in task execution) might matter. The reforms have had a major impact on the respective institutional frameworks in both sectors in all three countries. Furthermore, the welfare and hospital sectors in these countries display important differences in bureaucratic capacity, specialization and representation of users and citizens (Lægreid and Mattei 2013). Third, structural affiliations of the executives might matter, such as their positions or if the executives are in a ministry or a central agency.

Regarding the effects of accountability on performance, we distinguish between an instrumental hypothesis on a tight and positive relationship between accountability and performance and a cultural-based hypothesis underlining the loose connection between accountability and performance. When studying the impacts of accountability on performance, we control for the effects of country, tasks and structural features.

The empirical data are based on a comprehensive survey to top civil servants in different European countries conducted in 2012–2013 by the COCOPS project (Coordinating for Cohesion in the Public Sector).[1] Core questions are, first, to what extent the executives refer issues upwards in the hierarchy, to political actors or bodies, and to what extent they consult civil society/interest groups or experts; and, second, their perceived effects on performance along the following dimensions: cost and efficiency, service quality, policy effectiveness, policy coherence and coordination, citizen participation, social cohesion, equal access to services, fair treatment, and citizens' trust in government.

First, we will give an introduction to core concepts, as well as theoretical approaches, and derive some expectations regarding empirical findings. Second, we give a brief outline of the relevant reform context in the three countries that we compare. Third, we outline the data basis. Fourth, we present the empirical findings, and finally we discuss the findings and draw some conclusions.

Concepts and theoretical approaches

Accountability

After three decades of reforms in the welfare state, it is rather evident that we have to operate with a multidimensional accountability concept going beyond hierarchical principal-agent accountability (Christensen and Lægreid 2015). This is especially clear in the ambiguous and unsettled situations that often characterize reform periods (Olsen 2013). Bovens (2007) distinguishes between an information phase, a discussion phase and a consequence regarding accountability relations. Our proxy mainly focuses on the information and discussion phase. Many different processes of accountability are taking place at the same time, involving a vast array of actors. In each process, different kinds of information will be demanded and different kinds of discussions will occur. Governments are continuously being called to account by several account-holders for their actions and decisions, within different forums at the same time (Willems 2014).

Public organizations face the problem of many eyes, and their leaders are accountable to a number of different forums and ways of categorizing who is accountable to whom (Romzek and Dubnick 1987; Bovens 2007; Willems and Van Dooren 2011). *Political accountability* is mainly a vertical one in which hierarchical relationships give the forum formal power over the actor. Administrative executives are expected to refer issues upwards to political actors and bodies. *Administrative accountability* is related to a person's position in a hierarchy whereby a superior calls a subordinate to account for his or her performance of delegated duties (Sinclair 1995). We examine internal administrative accountability relations focusing on bureaucratic accountability issues that are referred upwards in the administrative hierarchy. *Professional accountability* denotes the importance of professional peers or peer review. Particularly in typical public organizations concerned with professional service delivery, the executives tend to rely on the technical knowledge of experts (Romzek and Dubnick 1987). We address this by examining to what extent the administrative executives consult relevant experts (e.g. scientists and consultants). *Social accountability* arises out of the existence of social stakeholders in the environment. This produces pressure on public organizations whereby they feel obliged to consult civil society organizations and interest groups. Giving account to various stakeholders in society occurs normally on a voluntary basis and has been labeled horizontal accountability (Schillemans 2008).

All four types of accountability will be included in our analysis, and our particular interest is in the prevalence of accountability types and their effect on public sector performance.

Theoretical perspectives

Tasks or policy area matter: political salience, professionalism and standardization

The requirements and constraints inherent in the primary tasks of different public organizations influence the decision-making of these units (Pollitt *et al.* 2004; Byrkjeflot *et al.* 2014). The main idea is that tasks matter and that we cannot discuss accountability structures and processes without taking into account the particular activities to which they apply (Pollitt 2008; Verhoest *et al.* 2010). Task-specificity and the nature of the actual work are important to understand variations in accountability (Wilson 1989). Important considerations are to what degree the tasks can be standardized, whether their consequentiality is high or low, whether they are politically sensitive or not, whether they involve major financial resources and whether they are subject to market competition (Pollitt 2003).

The two reforms studied are dealing with different types of tasks and service deliveries, and there are both similarities and variations among them in political salience, level of professionalization and complexity, as well as the degree of acceptance of local variation. It is then necessary to ask if tasks matter for the accountability relations we see. First, both reforms aim at strengthening administrative accountability and constraining political accountability. At the same time, both policy areas are of high political salience, which makes us expect that political accountability is still central. The welfare services are continuously brought into the limelight of the media and politics, and are thus 'politicized'. In the hospital reform, professional accountability is critical and potentially challenging to political accountability. High political salience may also make social accountability challenging.

Second, we expect that the degree of professionalism and complexity in service delivery matters. Day and Klein (1987) argue that services with high levels of professionalism and specialization are likely to be more complex. The complexity of a given service area relates to how many kinds of skills it has to coordinate in order to deliver, as well as to how many services it has to provide. We would thus expect that professional accountability would be associated with complexity in areas with diversity in service delivery, such as in hospitals, whereas social services will be more standardized and less professionalized.

Third, we expect that the acceptance of local variation in service delivery would make a difference (Byrkjeflot *et al.* 2014). If there are strong norms of impartiality and equal services for the same kind of users or clients all over the territory, we would expect that standardization of services and administrative accountability will be strong, such as in health cases. For service deliveries that accept more local variations, such as the employment area, we would expect that social accountability would be more addressed.

- Overall, we expect that the major tension in both fields will be between political accountability, on the one hand, and administrative and social accountability, on the other hand.
- We expect that professional accountability will be more up front within the health area than within the welfare administration area.

Culture matters: the importance of administrative culture in different countries

Different national political-institutional legacies may thus be important with respect to explaining variations in accountability (Painter and Peters 2010). The three countries differ along important political-institutional background variables but nonetheless share some key characteristics, the most important one being that all countries are mature Western European parliamentary democracies with a bureaucratic state infrastructure that have faced big administrative reforms in the selected policy areas over the past decade. All of them have undertaken administrative reforms that have had a major impact on the respective institutional frameworks for welfare services, but the scope and depth varies between countries, administrative levels and welfare state sectors.

The countries also differ in administrative tradition (Painter and Peters 2010; Pierre 2011). Norway and Denmark are both small unitary states, belonging to a West-Nordic Scandinavian collaborative tradition with big professional welfare states and ministerial responsibility with strong line ministries and semiautonomous subordinate agencies. A citizen-oriented, participatory approach is stronger in these countries than in Germany (Pollitt and Bouckaert 2011). Germany is a large federal state, and represents a tradition with special interlocking coordination problems as a result of the federalist system (Scharpf 1988). Germany's welfare state regime is based on the continental corporatist Bismarck model. Reforms in federal Germany have a stronger focus on flexibility and professionalism, and Germany has often been viewed as a 'laggard' with regard to welfare reforms (Jann 2003). The Scandinavian countries have, in recent decades, been more active and receptive.

The *Rechtsstaat* orientation of the German administrative system may render vertical accountability types easier, but will at the same time produce significant horizontal accountability problems. The German relationship between political and administrative executives is also fairly politicized (Pollitt and Bouckaert 2011), which might result in increased use of political accountability mechanisms. The strong consensus orientation and collaborative decision-making style of the Nordic countries might further horizontal coordination and also accountability with stakeholders outside government. The same might be the case with Germany, which also has a strong corporative tradition. Both the Scandinavian countries and Germany also have strong professional bureaucracy that will enhance professional accountability. It is therefore interesting to investigate whether there is still a Scandinavian model of welfare state administration or whether that model is breaking up (Byrkjeflot and Neby 2008).

Historical tradition in the state and in the public administration constrains and enables the reform trajectory and matters for the reform path chosen. National administrative tradition is important, but it does not determine reform choices and it needs to be understood as one of several factors affecting the way administrative reforms develop (Painter and Peters 2010). Based on country-specific and cultural features, we will expect that:

- The differences in the use of different accountability tools will be greater between Norway and Denmark, on the one hand, and Germany, on the other.
- Political accountability will be stronger in the Scandinavian countries, whereas administrative accountability will be more up front in Germany.

Structure matters: the importance of positions and administrative level

Political accountability plays out according to a structural perspective. The formal structure of public organizations will channel and influence the models of thought and the actual decision-making behavior of the civil servants (Egeberg 2012). A major precondition for such effects is that the leaders must have relatively clear intentions and goals, choose structures that correspond with these goals and have insight into the potential effects of the structures chosen. Luther Gulick (1937) stressed the importance of vertical specialization. The argument is that public sector units' external organizational ties to other public sector organizations, the form of affiliation, will make a difference.

As one such type of affiliation, state agencies are an important part of central government in all three countries. Each state agency sorts politically under one parent ministry, and the principle of ministerial responsibility is strong. Delegating autonomy to agencies can have advantages for the ministry in charge. Delegation frees up capacity to focus on political and strategic tasks and may enable ministries to blame agencies for undesirable policy effects (Dunleavy 1992; Hood and Lodge 2006: 182). 'Agencification' potentially reduces ministerial control and may allow state agencies to develop interests that diverge from those of their principal ministries (Binderkrantz and Christensen 2009: 290). To ensure that agencies behave in the ministries' interest, ministries use various control instruments.

A core hypothesis from this perspective is that organizational forms affect the accountability mechanisms. Our expectations are that political accountabilities are weaker and administrative, professional and social accountability are stronger in semiautonomous agencies than in ministerial departments (Egeberg and Trondal 2009). We will also expect that political accountability is stronger for top civil servants than for other administrative executives, which will pay more attention to administrative accountability. Hence, we expect:

- Social accountability will be stronger in semiautonomous agencies than in ministerial departments, and for political accountability it will be the other way around.
- Top civil servants will prioritize political accountability while administrative executives will prioritize administrative accountability.

Accountability and performance

Both accountability and performance have been central aspects of administrative reforms in the public sector during the last decades. Despite this, their relationship is yet understudied and public managers increasingly complain about negative effects of accountability (Ossege 2012). The causal linkages between accountability and performance have yet to be proved and the relationship between them is contested. Thus, the question of what the mechanisms are, if any, that link account-giving to individual leaders and organizational performance is still disputed. The reforms in the two welfare state areas have to a large part been based on arguments of an instrumental relationship; that 'greater accountability will mean improved performance' (Dubnick 2005). The assumed linkage between accountability and performance is so powerful that the two are often used as indicators of each other: to be accountable is to live up to expected performance, and to be performing up to standards is a clear sign of being accountable (Dubnick and Frederickson 2011).

However, another strongly held position is that there are tensions between accountability and performance due to incompatibility with each other (Ossege 2012). The accountability dilemma (Behn 2001) and the accountability paradox (Dubnick 2005) have been mentioned in the literature. The former signifies a trade-off between accountability and efficiency as expenses of time and resources devoted to account-giving are resources that could have been used to improve performance. In the accountability paradox, organizations are held to account for how well they implement formal accountability processes and procedures rather than for how well they actually perform their primary tasks and duties (Dubnick and Frederickson 2011). Another variant of this argument is what Dubnick (2011) labels the 'reformist paradox', in which efforts to improve accountability through reforms generates consequences that might alter, complicate or undermine existing forms of accountability. Public organizations typically face multiple sources of legitimate authority and competing expectations for performance. The existence of multiple and often competing accountability relationships may thus result in negative organizational outcomes (Romzek and Dubnick 1987; Romzek and Ingraham 2000). Even though the relationship between accountability and performance may not be as clear as we want it to be, it is not any less important to reconsider the effect of accountability on performance, because accountability can be understood as 'answerability for performance' (Romzek 2000), and that more accountable government will perform better as it responds to pressures for improved service. Hence, the following hypotheses:

- The paradox/dilemma hypothesis: there will be a loose coupling between accountability types and performance (culture matters).
- The instrumental hypothesis: use of different accountability types will tend to enhance performance (structure matters).

Reform context

Since 2002, all three countries have had administrative reforms in the areas of labor/employment and hospital administration that might affect different accountability relations (Table 11.1). All these reforms have a whole-of-governance flavor aimed at reducing fragmentation and increasing integration and coherence between administrative levels, and also between policy areas, by enhancing both horizontal and vertical coordination. But they also have NPM components focusing on efficiency and performance management. The content of the reforms varies, however, between policy areas and between countries producing different trade-offs and tensions between accountability types, both formally and in practice.

Table 11.1 Administrative reforms in labor/employment and hospital administration in Norway, Denmark and Germany

	Norway	Denmark	Germany
Labor/ employment	Big administrative reform 2005–2011. Merging employment and pensions and partnerships with municipalities regarding social services. Local one-stop shops but also regional specialized units.	The structural reform in 2006 resulted in shared job centers between municipalities and central government. In 2009, municipalities got full responsibility on this policy area, but under central government regulation and supervision.	The Hertz reform of 2004 was a mixed policy and administrative reform. A combined model of local customer centers organized by the Federal Employment Service provided insurance-based unemployment benefits and 'joint facilities' with municipalities regarding means-end tested unemployment benefits and active labor market services.
Hospital	Big administrative reform in 2002 transferring the ownership of hospitals to central government and reorganizing the hospitals into health enterprises. Administrative decentralization.	The structural reform in 2007 transferred the responsibility of hospitals to the regions governed by directly elected politicians. Political decentralization.	No big reform but a corporatist system with third-party payers (sickness funds) and also an increasing privatization of hospitals. A dual system of federal and state responsibility.

Norway

Welfare

In 2001, the parliament asked the government to come up with a unified solution for the welfare administration. In 2004, this resulted in a partial merger, in order to get more people off benefits and into the workforce, offer more user-friendly and coordinated service, and be more efficient. The reform entailed, first, a merger of the agencies for employment and the national pensions system, creating a big new welfare agency. Second, it established local partnership agreements between this new agency and the municipalities responsible for locally based social services. In 2008, the reformed system underwent a significant reorganization. Six regional pension offices were established together with county-based administrative back offices.

Hospitals

In 2001, the parliament decided to change the status of hospitals from public administration agencies to health enterprises and to transfer the ownership for the hospitals to the central government. New management principles were introduced for the hospitals based on a decentralized enterprise model. The Minister of Health assumed full responsibility for conditions in the health sector, but the enterprises were given enhanced local autonomy with their own executive boards and general managers with powers of authority to set priorities and manage the health enterprises. This was a big reform that tried to centralize the ownership and decentralize the management of hospitals through administrative decentralization.

Denmark

Welfare

The structural reform in Denmark in 2007 introduced a multilevel one-stop shop called a shared job center. The tasks and clients were divided between municipalities and the state. The unions lost the strong influence that they traditionally held. In 2009, the government decided that municipalities should take over responsibility for all services, and all job centers are now run by the municipalities but are subject to central regulation. Four regions monitor the work of the job centers and coordinate regional needs. Since responsibility for most of the services in question has now been gathered in one polity, there has been a movement towards more distinct political accountability in this reform area in Denmark.

Hospitals

The hospital reform in Denmark in 2007 gave the new regional level responsibility for hospitals. The Danish reform was more 'balanced' than the Norwegian, in the sense that there is now an overlap between administrative and political accountability at the regional level. The regional bodies are still governed by directly elected politicians, unlike in Norway. In order to ensure coordination between the administrative levels, binding partnerships between municipalities and regions have been created through health coordination committees.

Germany

Welfare

A comprehensive reform was launched in 2003. The reform aimed to reorganize the central level and promote strong central steering of local welfare administrations. It produced a complex system with ambiguous accountability relations. It has not been possible to introduce a one-stop agency solution in Germany for all unemployed persons. Thus, there are numerous lines of ambiguous political and managerial accountability relations between the major central government actors and the local level (Jantz and Jann 2013).

Hospital

In contrast to the Norwegian and Danish systems, with national health services that are owned, run and funded by the public sector, the German system is of a more diverse, corporatist nature. German hospitals have historically been more autonomous, and a large-scale privatization of hospitals has taken place. The hospital sector is managed in a dual system of federal and state responsibilities where considerable financial decision-making power is devolved to individual states. But corporatist actors may exert considerable pressures on the relevant decision-making processes.

Data basis

The survey was conducted in 2012–2013 as part of the comparative COCOPS project. The overall response rate was 23 percent in Germany, 19 percent in Denmark and 28 percent in Norway. Here, we employ data from top civil servants who work in the policy area of 'employment services' and 'health', which can be considered to be the most relevant policy areas to survey for our purposes: trying to tie the countries' accountability types in the two policy areas closer to top administrative executives' perceptions of performance in the fields. All in all, 219 top administrative executives in these policy areas answered the questionnaire in the three selected countries: 119 from Germany, 28 from Denmark and 72 from Norway. Overall, 13 percent of respondents were from ministries, 76 percent from central agencies and 11 percent from other governmental levels. Our quantitative analysis employs indices that depict the typical use of different accountability types when their organization's responsibility or interests conflict or overlap with that of other organizations. Based on their experience, the respondents were asked to rank the following accountability forums on a scale from 1 (strongly disagree) to 7 (strongly agree) (various forums are not mutually exclusive):

- Refer the issue upwards in the hierarchy (proxy for administrative accountability).
- Refer the issue to political actors and bodies (proxy for political accountability).
- Consult civil society organizations or interest groups (proxy for societal accountability).
- Consult relevant experts (e.g. scientists or consultants) (proxy for professional accountability).

Regarding performance, we use the answer on the following question as a proxy: 'Thinking about your policy area over the last five years, how would you rate the way public administration has performed on the following dimensions?' on a scale from 1 (deteriorated significantly) to 7 (improved significantly) (various dimensions are not exclusive). The following dimensions are included: 'cost and efficiency', 'service quality', 'policy effectiveness', 'policy coherence and coordination', 'citizens' participation and involvement', 'social cohesion', 'equal access to services', 'fair treatment of citizens' and 'citizen trust in government'.

The strength of this analysis is that we have comparative data from three countries. But there are also some obvious limitations to this analysis. First, we see accountability from the top administrative executives' point of view, which might not be in line with those working in lower positions and in local service-providing units. Second, the response rate is low, making it somewhat disputable about the representativeness of the answers. This is especially the case regarding Denmark. Third, we mainly have data on perceptions that might be different from actual accountability and performance. Fourth, there is not a total overlap between the area covered by the reforms and the policy areas that we examine. The welfare and employment reform has a bigger scope than the 'employment' field and the hospital reform has a more narrow scope than the 'health' area. Fifth, our proxy for accountability is rather rough. It focuses on organizational accountability and it is about relations between actors and different forums, and it might include information, discussion and answerability, but it focuses mainly on the initial phases of accountability and does not directly include the retrospective ex post and consequential features of accountability (Bovens et al. 2014). It is important to keep this in mind when interpreting empirical findings and drawing conclusions. In spite of these limitations, we argue that the data sources employed in this chapter provide a rich empirical backdrop against which the theoretical arguments outlined above can be assessed.

Accountability types: culture, tasks and structure

Table 11.2 reveals that administrative accountability is considered by far the most common accountability type by top civil servants. This shows that the administrative hierarchy is still very much alive and kicking, even in these policy fields that have been the aim of comprehensive 'whole-of-government' reforms over the past decade. This pattern confirms a general finding

Table 11.2 Types of accountability (percent)

	Disagree	Indifferent	Agree	N = 100%
Administrative accountability – refer issues up the hierarchy	27	20	53	204
Political accountability – refer issues to political actors/bodies	55	19	26	203
Social accountability – consult civil society/interest groups	65	19	16	198
Professional accountability – consult relevant experts	46	18	36	200

Note: Accountability types are based on a seven-point scale: 1–3 = disagree, 4 = neutral/indifferent, 5–7 = agree.

that hierarchical governance remains dominant (Hill and Lynn 2005). Also, professional accountability is rather common, reflecting the importance of professionals such as medical doctors and nurses, but also professional social workers. One out of four points to political accountability, while social accountability is the least common among the four accountability types, somewhat surprising since increasing user, client and patient participation were part of the reforms. Overall, we see a multidimensional and complex accountability pattern (Christensen and Lægreid 2015).

There is positive and significant bivariate correlation between political and administrative accountability (Pearson's R .39★★), reflecting that both accountability types are hierarchical and partly overlapping. There is also a significant correlation between professional and social accountability (Pearson's R .53★★), indicating that these accountability relations are more voluntary and horizontal. So, what we see is more a divide between the vertical hierarchical mandatory accountability relation, on the one hand, and the horizontal and voluntary accountability relations, on the other hand.

There are no significant correlations between the independent variables and political and administrative accountability. In unsettled, transformative periods when there are major reforms going on, such vertical accountability relations come under pressure and the relationships become more blurred, ambiguous and uncertain (Olsen 2014). Social accountability varies with policy area. It is stronger in the area of employment than in health. When controlling for other variables (Table 11.3), we see that professional accountability varies with country and policy area. It is weaker in Germany than in the Scandinavian countries, and stronger in welfare administration than in health.

Table 11.3 Summary of multivariate regression analysis (beta coefficients, linear regression)

	Professional accountability
Germany	–.17★
Policy area	.23★★
Administrative level	.07
N	191
R2	.08
Adjusted R	.066
F statistics	5.095
Significance of F	.002

★ Sign at the .005 level
★★ Sign at the 0.01 level

Accountability and performance

The top civil servants have generally a very positive attitude towards the perceived impacts of the reforms in their own policy area (Table 11.4). Regarding cost and efficiency and service quality, two of the main goals of the reforms, three out of four report that they have seen improvement over the last five years and only a very little minority observe deterioration. Also, when it comes to equal access to services and fair treatment of citizens, the perceptions of top civil servants are rather positive. The picture is, however, more mixed with regard to policy coherence and coordination, and citizens' participation and involvement. For social cohesion and citizens' trust in government, we see deterioration more than improvement.

We will, in the following regression analysis (Table 11.5), only include those independent variables that showed significant bivariate correlations with our selected dimensions for performance.

When controlling for the cultural, task-specific and structural features, a main pattern is that horizontal accountability relations such as social and professional accountability have greater impact on performance than vertical accountability relations.

From the regression analysis, we see some country-specific differences with reference to our performance dimensions. In the case of Norway, top civil servants perceive social cohesion to have significantly improved in the past five years, but they also report a significant deterioration in cost-efficiency in the same period. In Germany, top civil servants perceive both policy effectiveness and policy coherence and coordination to have significantly worsened. There is no significant improvement found for our performance dimensions in the Danish case, but service quality is reported to have significantly deteriorated during the last five years. Also, policy areas have an impact. In the area of employment, there are more positive perceived effects on equal access to services and fair treatment of citizens in the last five years, compared to top civil servants in the health area.

We find several significant and positive relations between the administrative level and our performance measures, especially for cost-efficiency and service quality, but also for policy effectiveness – meaning that governmental units closer to the state core perceive these items to have improved more than those further away. In addition, position in the organization matters – the higher up in the organizational hierarchy you are, the more perceptions of improvement in fair treatment increase.

Table 11.4 'Thinking about your policy area over the last five years, how would you rate the way public administration has performed on the following dimensions?' (percent)

	Deteriorate	Indifferent	Improve	N = 10
Cost and efficiency	7	17	76	197
Service quality	9	15	76	197
Policy effectiveness	18	44	38	191
Policy coherence and coorodination	25	39	36	188
Citizen participation and involvement	25	41	34	192
Social cohesion	28	48	23	192
Equal access to services	9	37	54	192
Fair treatment of citizens	8	37	55	194
Citizen trust in government	34	34	32	191

Note: Performance dimensions are based on a seven-point scale: 1–3 = deteriorated, 4 = neutral/indifferent, 5–7 = improved.

Table 11.5 Summary of multivariate regression analysis (beta coefficients, linear regression)

	Cost and efficiency	Service quality	Policy effectiveness	Policy coherence and co-ordination	Citizen participation	Special cohesion	Equal access to services	Fair treatment of citizens	Citizen trust in government
Germany	–	–	–.16*	–.19*	–.11	–	–	–	–.25*
Norway	–.29**	–	–	–	.12	.23**	–	–	.10
Denmark	–	–.19**	–	–	–	–	–	–	–
Administrative level	.26**	.25**	.10*	.05	–	–	–	–	–.12
Policy area	.04	–	–	–	–	–	.14*	.16*	–
Position	–	–	–	–	–	–	–	.16*	–
Administrative accountability	–	–	–	–	–.21**	–.18*	–	–	–
Political accountability	–	–	–	–	–	–	.08	–	–
Social accountability	–	–	.15	.18*	.24**	.24**	–	–	.12
Professional accountability	–	.15*	.09	.00	.08	.15*	.25**	.26**	.20*
N	188	188	181	178	181	182	174	173	182
R2	.3	.12	.09	.07	.16	.19	.11	.13	.20
Adjusted R2	.11	.10	.07	.05	.14	.17	.09	.12	.18
F statistics	8.794	8.157	4.242	3.365	6.781	10.415	6.809	8.565	8.717
Significance of F	.000	.000	.003	.011	.000	.000	.001	.000	.000

* Significance at the 0.05 level
** Significance at the 0.01 level

Discussion

This analysis shows, first, that there are multiple accountability types in action in the policy areas of health and employment, but their importance varies. Administrative accountability is up front, but also professional accountability is much used. Political accountability is not that important, which might reflect that many of the reforms have aimed at reducing the political accountability by stronger delegation to semi-independent agencies and enterprises. Social accountability is present, but is normally used by a minority of the administrative executives.

Second, the task-specific perspective is only partly supported. As we expected, administrative accountability would be more up front than political accountability in both policy areas. But it does not seem to be a strong tension between political and administrative accountability seen from the top of the administrative hierarchy. In contrast to our expectations, professional accountability is not more important in health than in labor. Also, policy area has an impact on fair treatment of citizens and equal access to services.

Third, the cultural perspective gets little support. Except for professional accountability, there seems to be little variation between the three countries. Here, Germany is scoring less than the Scandinavian countries. In contrast to our expectations, political accountability is not more up front in the Scandinavian countries than in Germany. Administrative accountability is more important in Germany than in Denmark but less important than in Norway. Country makes a stronger difference when it comes to performance. Germany seems to do more poorly than the Scandinavian countries on policy effectiveness, policy coherence and citizens' trust in government. Norway is scoring high on social cohesion but low on cost-efficiency, and Denmark is doing relatively poorly on service quality.

Fourth, the structural perspective also gets very weak support. There is no variation according to positions and administrative level. This has probably to do with the fact that there are little variations in positions and administrative levels since the majority of respondents are from top positions in ministries and central agencies. But top civil servants in the ministries generally perceive more improvement in cost-efficiency, service quality and policy effectiveness than those working in central agencies. And those in the very top positions have also a more positive assessment of fair treatment of citizens than managers that are not at the very top.

Fifth, we have revealed that the administrative executives generally have positive perceptions regarding the performance along several dimensions in their own policy area some years after compressive reforms have been implemented. The relationship between accountability types and performance is, however, rather uncertain and varies between accountability types. The relationship between accountability and performance is rather complex. Performance is not only related to accountability, but also to country differences, structural features and policy areas. Overall, the findings support the findings that the relationship between accountability and performance is ambiguous and contested (Pollitt 2011). There is no effect of any accountability type on cost-efficiency. Especially, there is a loose coupling between vertical administrative and political accountability and different performance indicators. This reveals that in unsettled transitional periods, the accountability relations become blurred and the relations between accountability and performance are more ambiguous and uncertain (Dubnick 2011; Olsen 2014). For administrative accountability, there even seems to be a negative impact on citizens' participation and social cohesion. Horizontal accountability relations such as professional and social accountability seem to enhance social cohesion, and there is also a positive effect of professional accountability on social cohesion and equal access to services, as well as fair treatment of citizens and citizens' trust in government. Thus, the paradox/dilemma hypothesis gets more support than the instrumental hypothesis. The support of the dilemma and the instrumental hypothesis varies with different accountability types, and the instrumental hypothesis gets little support regarding vertical administrative and political accountability. But this is seen from the top civil servants' point of view. If we had asked the service providers in the two reform areas, the picture might have been different.

Summing up, we have revealed that uncovering the linkages between administrative reforms, accountability and performance is more complex than it appears at first sight (Jann and Lægreid 2015). The accountability obligations faced by public bureaucrats are multiple and varied and often represent tensions (Mulgan 2014). Administrative reforms create new institutional and accountability structures, which influence service delivery, but not necessarily in the direction expected by the reform agents. This implies that reforms may affect accountability relations but also that different accountability relations may influence the performance of reforms. There seems to be a loose coupling between administrative reforms and accountability types and also between accountability and performance. This supports the reformist paradox (Dubnick 2011), which states that efforts to improve accountability through reforms might alter, undermine or complicate existing forms of accountability (Flinders 2014). Public accountability is about management of expectations in settings when there are multiple expectations, and in unsettled situations the accountability tends to become ambiguous (Olsen 2014).

Conclusion

To conclude, we have, first, shown that different complex, dynamic and layered accountability forms are emerging in the two policy areas that have been through comprehensive reforms. Vertical accountability relations are supplemented by other accountability types and accountability relations are blurred and ambiguous. Our database is, however, cross-sectional and only covers assessments at one point some years after the reforms, which makes it difficult to examine changes over time.

Second, we have revealed that the relationship between performance and accountability is rather ambiguous, contested and loosely coupled. The reforms have affected accountability relations and the relationships between performance and accountability, but not in a straightforward way. There are attribution problems, meaning also that other factors than the reform are important to understand how accountability relations play out and how performance is perceived. Our argument that different reform patterns and different country features matter for both performance and accountability, and for the relationship between performance and accountability, is only partly supported and has to be modified.

There is little evidence of a particular Scandinavian style, and in some respects there are more similarities between Germany and Norway, or between Denmark and Germany, than between Norway and Denmark. It is important to acknowledge, however, that there are both similarities and differences in concrete reform steps chosen between these three countries that might be of importance. For example, within the policy area of health, all three national governments have asserted influence through recent reforms, but the reforms have been more comprehensive in Norway and Denmark than in Germany and have been more centralized in Norway. Long-term factors associated with country-specific tradition, culture and history also have to be taken into account, along with intermediating factors. Rather than a straightforward replacement of the old welfare state administration in the different countries, we see a combination of old welfare administration, New Public Management features, and joined-up or post-NPM government measures coexisting and adding up to rather complex and hybrid systems that have implication for accountability relations, as well as relations between accountability types and perceived performance. Blurred reforms might also result in blurred relations between reforms and accountability, and between accountability and performance. Accountability design has not been up front in the administrative reforms studied in this chapter. One lesson is that there might be a need for a stronger focus on meaningful accountability design and on when to choose what type of accountability (Bovens and Schillemans 2014).

Note

1 The research leading to these results received funding from the European Union's Seventh Framework Programme under grant agreement No. 266887 (Project COCOPS) (www.cocops.eu/), Socio-Economic Sciences & Humanities.

References

Behn, R. (2001) *Rethinking Democratic Accountability*. Washington, DC: Brookings Institution Press.
Binderkrantz, A. S. and Christensen, J. G. (2009) Delegation without agency loss? The use of performance contracts in Danish central government. *Governance*, 22(2): 263–93.
Bovens, M. (2007) Analyzing and assessing public accountability: a conceptual framework. *European Law Journal*, 13(4): 837–86.
Bovens, M. and Schillemans, T. (2014) Meaningful accountability. In M. Bovens, T. Schillemans and R. E. Goodin (eds), *The Oxford Handbook of Public Accountability*. Oxford: Oxford University Press, pp. 673–82.
Bovens, M., Schillemans, T. and Goodin, R. E. (2014) Public accountability. In M. Bovens, T. Schillemans and R. E. Goodin (eds), *The Oxford Handbook of Public Accountability*. Oxford: Oxford University Press, pp. 1–22.
Byrkjeflot, H., Christensen, T. and Lægreid, P. (2014) The many faces of accountability: comparing reforms in welfare, hospitals and migration. *Scandinavian Political Studies*, 37(2): 171–95.

Byrkjeflot, H. and Neby, S. (2008) The end of the decentralized model of health governance? Comparing development in the Scandinavian hospital sector. *Journal of Health Organization and Management*, 22(4): 331–49.

Christensen, T. and Lægreid, P. (2015) Performance and accountability: a theoretical discussion and an empirical assessment. *Public Organization Review*, 15(2): 207–25.

Day, P. and Klein, R. (1987) *Accountabilities: Five Public Services*. London/New York: Tavistock.

Dubnick, M. (2005) Accountability and the promise of performance: in search of the mechanisms. *Public Performance and Management Review*, 28(3): 376–417.

Dubnick, M. (2011) Move over Daniel: we need some 'accountability space'. *Administration and Society*, 43(6): 704–16.

Dubnick, M. J. and Frederickson, H. G. (2011) Introduction. In M. J. Dubnick and H. G. Frederickson (eds), *Accountable Governance: Problems and Promises*. London: M. E. Sharpe, pp. xiii–xxxii.

Dunleavy, P. (1992) The globalization of public services: can government be 'best in world'? *Public Policy and Administration*, 9(2): 36–64.

Egeberg, M. (2012) How bureaucratic structure matters: an organizational perspective. In B. G. Peters and J. Pierre (eds), *The Sage Handbook of Public Administration* (2nd edition). London: Sage, pp. 157–68.

Egeberg, M. and Trondal, J. (2009) National agencies in the European administrative space: government driven, commission driven or networked. *Public Administration*, 87(4): 779–90.

Flinders, M. (2014) The future and relevance of accountability studies. In M. Bovens, T. Schillemans and R. E. Goodin (eds), *The Oxford Handbook of Public Accountability*. Oxford: Oxford University Press, pp. 661–72.

Gulick, L. (1937) Notes on the theory of organization. In L. Gulick and L. Urwick (eds), *Papers on the Science of Administration*. New York: Institute of Public Administration.

Hill, C. and Lynn, E. (2005) Is hierarchical governance in decline? Evidence from empirical research. *Journal of Public Administration Research and Theory*, 15(2): 173–95.

Hood, C. and Lodge, M. (2006) *The Politics of Public Sector Bargain*. Oxford: Oxford University Press.

Jann, W. (2003) State, administration and governance in Germany: competing traditions and dominant narratives. *Pubic Administration*, 81(1): 95–118.

Jann, W. and Lægreid, P. (2015) Introduction: welfare state reforms – managerial accountability and performance. *International Journal of Public Administration*, 38(13): 941–6.

Jantz, B. and Jann, W. (2013) Mapping accountability changes in labour market administrations: from concentrated to shared accountability? *International Review of Administrative Sciences*, 79(2): 227–48.

Lægreid, P. (2014) New Public Management and public accountability. In M. Bovens, T. Schillemans and R. E. Goodin (eds), *The Oxford Handbook of Public Accountability*. Oxford: Oxford University Press, pp. 324–38.

Lægreid, P. and Mattei, P. (2013) Introduction: reforming the welfare state and the implications for accountability in a comparative perspective. *International Review of Administrative Sciences*, 79(2): 197–200.

Mulgan, T. (2014) *Making Open Government Work*. London: Palgrave Macmillan.

Olsen, J. P. (2013) The institutional basis of democratic accountability. *West European Politics*, 36: 447–73.

Olsen, J. P. (2014) Accountability and ambiguity. In M. Bovens, R. E. Goodin and T. Schillemans (eds), *The Oxford Handbook of Public Accountability*. Oxford: Oxford University Press, pp. 106–23.

Ossege, C. (2012) Accountability – are we better off without it? *Public Management Review*, 14: 585–607.

Painter, M. and Peters, B. G. (eds) (2010) *Tradition and Public Administration*. London: Palgrave Macmillan.

Pierre, J. (2011) Stealth economy? Economic theory and the politics of administrative reform. *Administration & Society*, 43(6): 672–92.

Pollitt, C. (2003) *The Essential Public Manager*. Maidenhead: Open University Press.

Pollitt, C. (2008) *Time, Policy, Management: Governing with the Past*. Oxford: Oxford University Press.

Pollitt, C. (2011) Performance blight and the tyranny of light? Accountability in advanced performance measurement regimes. In M. J. Dubnick and H. G. Frederickson (eds), *Accountable Governance: Problems and Promises*. New York: M. E. Sharpe, pp. 81–97.

Pollitt, C. and Bouckaert, G. (2011) *Public Management Reform: A Comparative Analysis, New Public Management, Governance and the Neo-Weberian State*. Oxford: Oxford University Press.

Pollitt, C., Talbot, C., Caulfield, J. and Smullen, A. (2004) *Agencies: How Governments Do Things Through Semi-Autonomous Organizations*. Basingstoke: Palgrave Macmillan.

Romzek, B. (2000) Dynamics of public accountability in the era of reform. *International Review of Administrative Sciences*, 66(1): 21–44.

Romzek, B. S. and Dubnick, M. J. (1987) Accountability in the public sector: lessons from the Challenger tragedy. *Public Administration Review*, 47(3): 227–38.

Romzek, B. S. and Ingraham, P. W. (2000) Cross pressures of accountability: initiative, command, and failure in the Ron Brown plane crash. *Public Administration Review*, 60: 240–53.

Scharpf, F. W. (1988) The joint decision trap: lessons from German federalism and European integration. *Public Administration*, 66: 239–78.

Schillemans, T. (2008) Accountability in the shadow of hierarchy: the horizontal accountability of agencies. *Public Organization Review*, 8(2): 175–94.

Sinclair, A. (1995) The chameleon of accountability: forms and discourses. *Accountability, Organizations and Society*, 20(2–3): 219–37.

Thomas, P. G. (1998) The changing nature of accountability. In B. G. Peters and D. J. Savoie (eds), *Taking Stock: Assessing Public Sector Reforms*. Quebec: Canada Centre for Management Development, pp. 348–93.

Verhoest, K., Roness, P. G, Verschuere, B., Rubecksen, K. and MacCarthaigh, M. (2010) *Autonomy and Control of State Agencies: Comparing States and Agencies*. Basingstoke: Palgrave Macmillan.

Willems, T. (2014) Democratic accountability in public-private partnerships: the curious case of Flemish school infrastructure. *Public Administration*, 94(2): 340–58.

Willems, T. and Van Dooren, W. (2011) Lost in diffusion? How collaborative arrangements lead to an accountability paradox. *International Review of Administrative Sciences*, 77(3): 505–30.

Wilson, J. Q. (1989) *Bureaucracy: What Government Agencies Do and Why They Do It*. New York: Basic Books.

PART III

Accountability in unsettled situations

12

ACCOUNTABILITY, TRANSPARENCY AND SOCIETAL SECURITY[1]

Tom Christensen and Martin Lodge

Introduction

In December 2014, the US Senate Select Committee on Intelligence published a summary report into the CIA's interrogation methods that highlighted the various ways in which interrogation had used questionable methods to limited effect. The report also suggested that the agency had misled its political masters and noted how the CIA had exploited loopholes in international arrangements (*Guardian* 2014). The report's publication coincided with the final weeks of Democrat dominance as it was feared that a Republican-controlled Congress would not publish such a condemning report.

Earlier, in late November 2014, the *Financial Times* revealed a leaked letter in which a former head of the UK's GCHQ called on ministers to release guidelines regarding the way UK intelligence was sharing information with US agencies to support drone strikes against militants. The letter suggested that such openness would reduce public concerns as to whether the UK government was breaking the law in assisting US drone strikes. The official response by the UK's Foreign Office was 'to follow convention' in not commenting on this particular issue, but to highlight that 'our intelligence agencies operate under the law and in accordance with our values' (*Financial Times* 2014).

At the very same time, the former head of New Zealand's Security Intelligence Service was criticized for responding to a freedom of information request by a right-wing blogger with ill-informed information about the then-leader of the opposition, Phil Goff (Labour) (*Dominion Post* 2014). In Germany, continued concern about its federal- and land-level intelligence services surrounded their approach towards extreme right activities. In Norway, the Norwegian Police Security Service's decision to heighten threat levels in the summer of 2014, and subsequently to publish further alerts, was criticized as unnecessary scaremongering. However, these heightened threat levels were used to justify the first ever general (temporary) permission for police staff to carry guns (PST 2014). In the meantime, *The Economist* reported on the ways in which various spyware attacks on private companies were traceable to national espionage activities (*Economist* 2014). This was followed by the alleged hacking of Sony's internal data management system by North Korea.

These examples highlight that the accountability and transparency of organizations tasked with 'societal security' is central to contemporary political discourse, even before the tragic events in Paris in early 2015 triggered a return to debates about introducing 'snooper's charters' in a number of countries. This concern with holding agencies to account builds on multiple agendas and problems, whether it is because of diagnosed intelligence failures of the 'imagination' and 'initiative' kind (as noted by 9/11 and Katrina investigation reports, respectively), because of alleged lack of political neutrality, or because of an increased awareness regarding trade-offs between privacy and surveillance following the revelations by Edward Snowden.

Societal security poses a challenge to Bentham's central maxim that 'secrecy, being an instrument of conspiracy, ought never to be the system of a regular government' (Bentham, cited in Hood 2006: 9). Indeed, Bentham's patron, the Earl of Shelbourne, noted how transparency of all government activities was to be encouraged, with the exception of the 'secret service' (cited in Hood 2006: 10). Such concerns have also found their way into the OECD's principles regarding 'high level risks' that endorse 'accountability and transparency' while acknowledging potential limitations (OECD 2014). However, such expressions of 'good governance' thinking rarely acknowledge different forms of accountability and transparency, for example differences in political, administrative, legal, professional and social accountability (Bovens 2007). Such questions are centrally important, given the interest in procedural and structural devices in holding bureaucratic agents under control (Balla 2015).

However, societal security goes beyond the 'deep state' of intelligence services. This chapter considers, in addition to intelligence, the environment (flood defenses) and essential supply chains, namely food safety. All three domains deal with risks and uncertainties. They raise issues of trust as incidents of organizational or individual wrongdoing or failure may have wider implications for the legitimacy of the wider industry or sector, if not the state at large. There are also inherent tensions: although the publication of flood or earthquake maps may be somewhat less problematic than the issuing of bespoke terror warnings, being transparent about calculations regarding flood or earthquake risk may not be particularly welcome to homeowners in affected areas.

More broadly, societal security and the ways activities are organized and executed is intrinsic to public management research and practice. In the wider public administration perspective, the literature on (civilian) societal security has mostly focused on issues of turf (see Wilson 1989) and reorganization (Hammond 2007; Christensen *et al.* 2013; Lægreid and Rykkja 2013). Furthermore, societal security cannot easily be shoehorned into 'settled' or 'unsettled' contexts – it deals with expected and surprising moments of 'unsettleness' while seeking to reassure the wider public about the 'settled' nature of organizational arrangements. Societal security therefore represents a particular type of 'wicked issue'; it is multidimensional, it is of high and low salience at the same time, and it deals with inherent value trade-offs.

This chapter explores social accountability and transparency-related provisions in three societal security sectors in six countries: Australia, Germany, New Zealand, Norway, the United Kingdom and the United States. Its focus is on: (a) identifying literatures that provide for expectations as to ways in which organizations tasked with societal security give account and are making themselves transparent to external scrutiny; and (b) by using these literatures, accounting for the commonalities and variations in observed patterns across agencies and countries.

Mulgan (2014: 3–6) suggests that transparency could be seen both as a wider and more narrow concept than accountability. We follow this more narrow definition in terms of seeing transparency as related to the informational part of accountability, which, together with debate/interaction and consequence, are the central parts of accountability (Bovens 2007). Accountability is defined as the obligation to report to certain standards, where the failure to do so may lead to the imposition of sanctions (Bovens 2007). Transparency is defined as requirements to expose procedures and outputs/outcomes to external scrutiny. The next section considers questions of accountability and transparency more extensively. Then, this chapter discusses its research design and explores the empirical similarities and variations. The concluding section accounts for the observed patterns.

Accountability, transparency and societal security

Transparency and accountability have become part of the global vocabulary of 'good governance' (Grimmelikhuijsen and Klijn 2015; Reynaers and Grimmelikhuijsen 2015). How 'transparency' or 'accountability' are established, and whether they are compatible with each other, is, however, contested (Hood 2006). Limitations and side effects of demands of account-holding and account-giving have been recognized (Mashaw 2006; Hood 2010; Lodge and Stirton 2010).

While account-giving and being transparent might be seen as normatively desirable, the actual exercise of account-giving is shaped by reputational concerns, regardless of whether these activities are based on mandatory requirements or voluntary commitments (Goffman 1959; Bovens 2007; Wittington and Yakis-Douglas 2012; Koop 2014). In the area of societal security in particular, where success in terms of outcome is largely invisible (and 'failure' highly visible), reputation management is particularly important as actors seek to persuade their audiences about their competence (Elsbach 2012; Rhee and Kim 2012), whether this is on the basis of technical, procedural, performative or moral dimensions (Carpenter 2010). Having a reputation for competence enhances societal acceptance, thereby reducing the need for coercion in ensuring compliance (Watson 2007).

Such reputational concerns are of particular interest in an era of declining public trust, and consequently growing pressure on public organizations to verify their performance and to account for themselves. Being accountable and transparent becomes an essential part of an organization's strategy to sustain an organization's reputation. Social constructivist and cultural theories offer one set of explanations as to how organizations seek to manage reputation(s) (Selznick 1957; Meyer and Rowan 1977). According to Selznick (1957), organizations evolve through a process of mutual adaptation to internal and external pressures from their task environment (Thompson 1967). This leads to the institutionalization of a set of informal norms that characterize an organization and its reputation (Brunsson and Olsen 1993). The area of societal security offers scope for probing further into the ways in which accountability and transparency understandings are being incorporated in public organizations' appearances. We consider these in the light of a number of strains in the literature, namely those emphasizing task and structural considerations, and those pointing to the significance of managerialist and neoliberal doctrines.

The first strain in the literature suggests that variations in accountability and transparency relate to *tasks*, in particular task-specificity, the characteristics of the target population and the nature of the actual work (Pollitt et al. 2004; Pollitt 2011). One way to explore how tasks matter is to adopt Wilson's distinction between measurability of outputs and outcomes (Wilson 1989). Societal security organizations vary significantly on these two dimensions. In the case of the intelligence services, outputs and outcomes are difficult to measure (qualifying them as 'coping' agencies).

In contrast, food-safety-related agencies represent examples of 'procedural organizations' (as defined by Wilson): outputs are observable, such as the number of inspections, enforcement actions and such like; however, whether these activities advance overall food safety outcomes is less certain. Similarly, agencies dealing with the risk of flooding are of a procedural kind. In the absence of extreme weather events, it is possible to measure activities such as expenditure, protection work and inspections; however, there is no immediate link to actual prevention or mitigation of flooding in the event of actual extreme weather events, but probably in more moderate crisis events.

In addition, there are also differences in terms of political salience. Failure is, in all three cases, likely to result in a 'minister/top civil servant over board' scenario. However, on a day-to-day basis, flood defense is arguably less politically salient than food inspections or the intelligence services. All three sectors involve substantial financial and organizational commitment in terms of administration. Food safety largely operates in parallel with private production chain arrangements, whereas flood defense, and in particular intelligence work, have as yet mostly not been privatized or witnessed the emergence of private intelligence-gathering chains. Public intelligence nevertheless relies on information gleaned from private networks. Similarly, para-public self-governing institutions exist, for example in the management of Dutch polders. Table 12.1 summarizes the argument above.

These contrasting profiles have consequences on the ways we expect agencies to seek to present themselves to external scrutiny. In the case of intelligence services, we expect a particular emphasis on ex post review and ongoing monitoring through political oversight committees and specific watchdogs. Judicial accountability is likely to exist in the form of procedural requirements. However, actual 'real time' information about activities and priorities is unlikely to be forthcoming, with the exception of 'most wanted' messages and other general public alert messages.

Both the food safety and flood defense areas are likely to feature considerable political, legal and judicial accountability. In both sectors, we expect to witness fewer specific watchdogs and political oversight arrangements to provide for secrecy. It is likely that the food sector is characterized by more transparency towards the wider public, for example in publishing inspection reports or numbers, in issuing detailed warnings and guidance. Flood defense can similarly be expected to feature considerable information about areas prone to flooding, weather warnings, and reports on investment and inspections.

The second strain in the literature points to *variations in organizational and institutional diversity*. As studies in the UK on the 'government of risk' have suggested (Hood *et al.* 2001), risk is rarely handled by one agency alone. Coproduction, and coordination more broadly, is always prone to issues of over- and underlap, information exchange difficulties and inconsistent approaches. In other words, all three sectors are likely to suffer from the 'many hands problem' (Thompson 1989). Intra- and inter-organizational dispersion in a vertical and horizontal sense therefore matters (Gulick 1937; Egeberg 2012). Table 12.2 illustrates the argument.

Table 12.1 Task-related characteristics in intelligence, food safety and flood defense*

	Intelligence	*Food safety*	*Flood defense*
Visibility of output and outcome	Low/low	High/medium	High/medium
Political sensitivity	High	Medium (outside times of acute incident/crisis)	Low (outside times of acute incident/crisis)
Public resource commitment	High	High	High
Private sector presence	Low	High	Low
Public resource commitment	High	High	High
Private sector presence	Low	High	Low

* The first score is for output and the second for outcomes

Table 12.2 Forms of specialization and coordination

	Intra-public specialization and coordination	External specialization between public and private sector
Vetical specialization and coordination	(I) Specialization and coordination between public sector levels – central, regional and local.	(III) Specialization and coordination between public and private sector (i.e. private actors in a provider role).
Horizontal specialization and coordination	(II) Specialization and coordination between public sector entities on the same level (i.e. among ministries, agencies and units on lower levels).	(IV) Specialization and collaboration between public and private units related to public regulation and services.

Category I deals with public sector internal vertical separation of authority, which could range from highly centralized to varieties of decentralization and delegation. In most countries, intelligence security related organizations are centralized, even though there may be regional and local branches of separate subnational services. Food safety will normally have a central agency with standard-setting responsibilities. However, enforcement is often in the realm of local and regional governments (especially in European countries). In addition, information gathering depends on the speed and quality of specialist laboratories. Similarly, in flood safety, actual operational responsibilities are usually found at the local and regional level, with some degree of central government involvement. Overall, we expect that accountability- and transparency-related features will be more centralized in the area of intelligence than food safety and flooding.

Category II deals with the horizontal dispersion of authority among public organizations, and therefore also with 'horizontal accountability' (Schillemans 2008), let alone with questions of redundancy (Landau 1969) and specialization among 'stand-alone' bodies (Gregory 2003). Category III emphasizes vertical collaboration and coordination with private providers. Organizing societal security in collaboration with for-profit or nonprofit organizations may involve outright privatization, competitive tendering, contractualization or 'public-private partnerships'. Category IV points to horizontal public-private collaboration and coordination among actors at the same level. Our analysis mostly deals with arrangements that are represented by category I.

The third strain in the literature emphasizes the significance of *managerialist doctrines* in shaping accountability and transparency-related arrangements, as illustrated by the literature on the 'audit society' (Power 1997), the 'performance mindset' (Radin 2006) and 'New Public Management' more broadly (Hood 1991; Pollitt and Bouckaert 2011). We should expect some aspects of more 'managerialist' understandings of accountability and transparency to creep into agency activities in the societal security domain, such as the acknowledgement of particular services and activities in the first place, the growing visibility and personalization of agency leadership, or the display of supposed 'threat levels'. The spread of managerialist doctrines should be expected to accompany (rather than displace) more traditional conventions of how societal security is being held to account (such as via special parliamentary committees, watchdogs or tribunals). In particular, we expect the intelligence domain to be least exposed to managerialist ideas regarding accountability and transparency, as noted. In contrast, food safety could be expected to display managerialist ideas, if only to display inspection activities and reports, announce recalls and issue warnings. Flood defense could be expected to be less exposed, as responsibilities are dispersed across sectors and levels of government and not easily fitting with performance management. However, we expect some information on floodplains and about warnings to feature.

The final strain in the literature suggests that transparency and accountability-related features will be shaped by the idea of *'neoliberal' risk management*, namely the idea that individuals are responsible for their own fate. Accordingly, the shifting of responsibility away from the state means that individuals are to be put in a position in which they can make informed choices, depending on their risk appetite. We are living in an age of 'neoliberalism'; we therefore should expect to observe the provision of information to support individual choice, for example in offering information about products, ingredients or inspections (in food safety) or about flood-related risks to certain areas. In intelligence, such information for (domestic) choice is less likely to exist ('most wanted' lists and 'travel advice' represent long-standing communication features). In the area of intelligence, the provision of information regarding the suspected whereabouts of subversive elements (such as extremists of all kinds) is unlikely to be regarded as helpful by the organizations in question. Indeed, the perception of being overwhelmed by risk- and threat-related information may reduce rather than enhance trust in public organizations (Etzioni 2004).

Table 12.3 summarizes our expectations based on the four strains.

Methodology

As noted, this chapter investigates accountability and transparency relationships in three core areas of societal security, flood defense, food safety and intelligence, in four Anglo-Saxon settings (the US, the UK, Australia and New Zealand), as well as in Norway and Germany. The three areas of societal security have been chosen to maximize difference in terms of dispersion, functional demands and observability of activities. The country selection is similarly based on commonality and difference. Most states in our sample have witnessed major terror incidents (the exceptions, at the time of final drafting, late 2015, being New Zealand and Germany, the latter having, however, witnessed terrorist activities and failed attempts). All of them have been exposed to flooding, and all of them are part of international food safety regimes. The allocation of responsibilities varies between those jurisdictions characterized by more formal federal constitutions than others, although intergovernmental relationships matter across all countries in our sample. For example, local actors are closely involved in flood defense and food safety inspections. The German federal government's powers in the area of flood control are, for example, highly restricted given its constitution, which guarantees the Länder far-reaching powers (which are, in turn, highly dependent on local authorities). The different countries also reflect difference in terms of their openness to managerialist principles and legal traditions. In other words, our research design allows us to probe into a neglected area that potentially offers insights regarding functional and institutional differences.

In terms of approach, this study primarily relies on a 'Web census' (and limited direct communication where we required clarification) (Lodge 2015). A website is a central tool for reputation management, and therefore should provide information about how different services account for their own activities and how they make their activities transparent. Such an approach does not offer any insights into actual effectiveness of the different agencies. The presence of a special secretive oversight committee is hardly evidence that it can exercise challenging oversight in practice, especially as governments are often able to withhold information from such committees. This chapter also does not deal with the actual degree of 'real life' accountability relationships and transparency; in particular, we do not deal with responses to information provision. In this chapter, we also do not deal with change over time. For example, US accountability provisions were considerably altered following the Watergate scandal in the mid-1970s.

Table 12.3 Expectations related to accountability, trust and transparency

	Intelligence	Food safety	Flood defense	Empirical indicator
Political accountability – overall	High	Medium/high	Medium/low	Emphasis on formal requirement to report to the executive/ legislative committees/ special watchdogs
Tension between levels	Low	Low/medium	High/medium	Emphasis on highlighting limits of competency
Tension related to public-private relationship	Low	Medium	Medium	Emphasis on highlighting limits of competency
Administrative/managerial accountability	Low	High on both	Medium on administrative	Emphasis on operational and performative information
Judicial accountability	High	High	Low/medium	Emphasis on precedural requirements and codes of conduct
Professional accountability	High	High	Medium/low	Emphasis on staff qualifications
Social accountability to general public	High	High	High/medium	Emphasis on publicness of organizational activities
Reputation management typical	Medium/low	High	Medium	Overall extent and tone of information provided
Tension between individual and collective concerns	High/medium	Medium	Medium/low	Emphasis on non-trade-off between individual and state interests
Horizontal accountability	Medium	Medium	Medium/high	Emphasis on collaborative efforts
Tension between public units on same level	High	Medium	High/medium	Emphasis on highlighting limits of competency
Tension between public and private organizations	Low/medium	Medium	Medium	Emphasis on highlighting limits of competency
Overall focus on trust	High	High	High/medium	Emphasis on ex ante and ex post controls
Overall focus on transparency	Low	High	Medium	Overall extent and tone of information provided

* Categories in *italics* are subcategories of the main accountability types

Table 12.4 Number of societal security organizations

	UK	USA	New Zealand	Australia	Norway	Germany
Intelligence	5	3	2	6	3	3
Flooding	1	1	2	1	1	1
Food safety	1	2	2 (1)	1 (1)	1	3

This study focuses on a number of dimensions involving legal and political accountability relationships, as well as more managerialist dimensions. These dimensions were grouped into four broad categories, namely *resources* available to the various organizations (agency leadership, staffing and funding levels, address), *operational* information regarding the activities of the various agencies, *oversight* activities over the activities of these agencies (legislative committees, executive controls), and information regarding *alternative channels* that hold these organizations to account (specific watchdogs, codes of conduct, complaint channels).

As noted, the research involved six countries and three sectors. The jurisdictional competencies of different organizations vary, and so does their number in any national jurisdiction. Table 12.4 provides a brief overview. The numbers reflect the typical distinction between domestic and external espionage activities, and some bodies are mainly tasked with coordinative rather than operational activities. Germany had instituted, following its own BSE (mad cow) crisis in the early 2000s, a distinction between risk assessment and risk management activities. One agency operates cross-jurisdictionally, the Food Standards Agency for Australia and New Zealand. We focus solely on agencies operating at the national level of government.

Sectoral patterns

Intelligence

The area of espionage has witnessed considerable moves towards greater transparency over the recent decade or so. In the UK, for example, the identity of security services was finally acknowledged, and the names of agency leaders have become public, with heads of security services even making public appearances. Similarly, in the German case, there has been a growing supply of 'transparency', such as the introduction and the creation of a website (in 2013) in the case of the military intelligence service, or the publication of historical studies into the immediate post-Second World War establishment of intelligence organizations and potential linkages to Nazi regime officials. In light of concern about torture and surveillance activities, the primacy of parliamentary oversight over intelligence services was entrenched in the constitution (Art 45d GG). In the Norwegian Police Security Service, the head of the organization was using her blog actively and the organization was also using Twitter to enhance transparency.

Across the six countries, agencies reported on their broad thematic objectives and concerns. All agencies offered information and images of their leader(s). However, they did not offer any detailed account of their activities. Some agencies, such as the German domestic intelligence service, offered an annual evaluation of 'threats'. However, there were differences in terms of agencies making transparent their staff numbers, their address, and their funding. In addition, variation existed in political accountability mechanisms, related to the complexity and composition of oversight and scrutiny bodies.

In the United States, our sample includes the Department of Homeland Security (a coordination agency), the FBI and the CIA. The CIA website offered information about different organizational priorities, its leadership, and political accountability mechanisms. However, it did not provide information regarding its funding, its headquarters' precise location, its actual operations or its staffing levels. It has specific legislative oversight, as well as specific (in-house) 'trustee'-type control, namely the President-appointed Inspector General and the White House's Intelligence Oversight Board and the President's Intelligence Advisory Board. The FBI did provide information on staffing and funding, as well as its address. It also provided a 'most wanted' display (unlike any other agency). The FBI was overseen by the Department of Justice's Inspector General, whereas the Department of Homeland Security had its own Inspector General. The CIA's Inspector General's jurisdiction was more broadly defined than those of the other two agencies, with the two latter emphasizing audit functions.

In the UK, MI6's ('Secret Intelligence Services') staff numbers were also absent, and specific funding provisions were difficult to establish. However, a picture of the (central London) headquarters featured centrally on the agency's website (as did its address). Specific fora holding the SIS to account were Parliament's 'Intelligence and Security Committee', the Intelligence Service Commissioners and, for complaints, the 'investigatory powers tribunal', whose leadership has to consist of individuals with a background in high legal office. In the case of MI5, the same oversight and review units were in place; however, staff numbers were disclosed. MI5 also disclosed a threat level. The same applied to GCHQ (the UK government's 'communication detection agency'). The military's intelligence operation, 'Defense Intelligence', offered hardly any information as it operated within the defense budget. The coordinating and decision-making body, the National Security Council, was part of the cabinet government system, including senior ministers and civil servants.

New Zealand's Security Intelligence Service and the Government Communications Security Bureau were overseen by the parliamentary Security and Intelligence Committee. The former was also accountable to the Ombudsman. Both agencies informed on their staff numbers and their address, but not on their funding levels. In Australia, the Secret Intelligence Service's budget was decided by a parliamentary joint committee on intelligence and security. The address was available on the website, but not staff numbers. This contrasted with Australian National Security, which did disclose funding and staff numbers. Less information was available in the case of the Defense Intelligence Organization, the Signals Directorate or the (coordinating) Office of National Assessments. Australia also featured an Inspector-General for Intelligence and Security that offered annual reports on the operation of Australia's intelligence services.

Two Norwegian agencies, the Norwegian Police Security Service and the National Security Authority, reported on their staff numbers, their funding, and their address. They were overseen by different parliamentary committees – the control and constitution committee and the foreign affairs and defense committee, respectively. The former was overseen by a specific independent committee that also included members drawn from outside parliament. In contrast, the Norwegian Directorate for Civil Protection, which coordinated, audited and advised on emergency preparedness work in ministries, county governors and municipalities, was subordinate to the Ministry of Justice and Public Security.

An oversight committee, the so-called G-10 committee, was involved in holding the German agencies, the Bundesnachrichtendienst and the Bundesamt für Verfassungsschutz, to account. Furthermore, there was further parliamentary oversight, but the executive could refuse the provision of certain information to the committee. Hardly any information existed in relation to the military intelligence service ('MAD'), apart from an indication the military's inspectorate performed oversight functions.

Flood defense

The public management of flood control was characterized by intergovernmental relationships across the six different jurisdictions, regardless of whether countries were federal or not. That is, across countries there was a reliance on local-, regional- and national-level actors. There was, furthermore, a difference in terms of type of agency, ranging from the political appointment of the head of FEMA in the US (as part of the Department of Homeland Security) to the executive agency, the Environment Agency, in the UK, to subordinate administrative bodies, such as in Norway and Germany. Again, across agencies, leaders were identified. Agencies' tasks could be distinguished between those preparing for potential emergencies, and those dealing with actual emergencies. Accountability was to respective legislative committees. General ombudsmen offices were involved in cases of complaints regarding administrative actions. Conforming to our expectations, central agencies did provide for flood maps (the US, the UK and Norway). In other systems, such flood maps were provided by local or regional governments (New Zealand, Australia and Germany).

Food Safety

Across the three sectors, transparency-related provisions featured most prominently in the area of food safety. Information ranged from the provision of inspection reports, warnings and alerts, to information about agency leadership, funding and organization, as well as broader performance data, especially in the case of the US agencies, the FDA and the USDA. New Zealand and Australia shared a standard-setting agency for food (food safety inspection being a subnational issue in Australia). New Zealand's Food Safety Authority had become part of the Ministry of Primary Industries. Actual inspections were the responsibility of local authorities. The Norwegian Food Safety Authority, which relates to three ministries, did not only give information about its rules/standards and actual activities/inspections to businesses and other authorities, but also issued advice and guidelines to consumers.

The UK Food Standards Agency offered information on the 'food scores' of different establishments across the UK, even though these inspections had been conducted by local authority staff. The website also allowed owners of these establishments to challenge results and require a new inspection. The German food safety system was characterized by a division in risk assessment and risk management. The Bundesamt für Verbraucherschutz und Lebensmittelsicherheit was in charge of warnings and alerts, especially via the website www.lebensmittel.de, which was operated in conjunction with the federal states. The Bundesanstalt für Landwirtschaft und Ernährung was in charge of certification. Finally, the Bundesinstitut für Risikobewertung was in charge of investigating the potential contamination of diverse foodstuff. The two later offered information about their activities, but little direct user engagement.

Comparative analysis

One of the key findings is the broad similarity in the way agencies tasked with different aspects of societal security seek to be transparent about their activities. All of them offered information about their leadership, and only a few agencies (in intelligence) do not provide postal address, information on staffing numbers or funding arrangements, reflecting more formal constraints on what information they can reveal. All of the agencies offered links to press offices and press notices. Therefore, it is likely that this study reflects the outcome of considerable pressure on agencies for more transparency and that a similar study, if conducted over a decade ago, would have led to bigger contrasts. As such, this may give rise to the conclusion that the age of 'managerialist' doctrine has left an imprint on societal security.

Some key features are summarized in the following Tables 12.5 and 12.6. Table 12.5 points to the different aspects of transparency and accountability that were explored across the various dimensions.

The focus on websites potentially biased our attention towards particular emphases in terms of reputation management. For example, judicial features were emphasized in the area of intelligence, professional standards in the area of food safety, whereas social relationships featured in the area of flood defenses. Websites sought to reassure: This was particularly noticeable in the area of intelligence where attempts at reassurance were rarely backed by actual information about activities. Overall, food safety scored most highly when it came to transparency.

Given these observed patterns, we suggest that cross-sectoral differences outweigh differences generated by national constitutional features. These are illustrated in Table 12.6.

As noted, some differences across agencies involved in 'security' and intelligence could be linked to differences in tasks; some were directly involved in operations, others primarily involved in coordinating different agencies. However, there are some key features that stand out. Across agencies, the emphasis was on offering some broad statements about the key aspects of intelligence activities, without offering information on specific 'engagements'. Norway, the UK and Australia offered an explicit 'threat level' indication. New Zealand did not display a 'threat

Table 12.5 Sectoral characteristics of accountability and transparency provisions in societal security

	Resources	*Operations*	*Oversight*	*Alternative channels*
Intelligence	Information about leadership and appointment, location (with exception), limits to funding and staffing levels.	Broad indications of activities and central themes; no information on actual operations. Stressing domestic and international collaboration.	Government chief executive/specific parliamentary committees, 'trustee' type committees and inspector generals/ auditors.	Comprehensive reporting on relevant laws giving authority. Procedural controls/complaint channels/ombudsman (privacy commissioners).
Flooding	Details about leadership, financing, location and staffing. Varied use of social media.	Information about activities, anticipatory warning systems and emergency responses. Focus on domestic/ local collaboration.	Executive and legislative controls, especially departmental parliamentary committees.	Procedural controls and complaints, ombudsman.
Food safety	Details about leadership, financing, location and staffing (with exceptions), limited by constitutional differences. Focus on professional competence. Varied use of social media.	Comprehensive and detailed information about activities, PIs, food alerts and inspection reports. Stressing international and domestic collaboration.	Executive and legislative controls.	Explicit listing of relevant laws and rules. Administrative procedures.

Table 12.6 Overview of similarities and differences

	Dominant sectoral characteristics	Main cross-national difference	Comparing expectations with observed patterns
Intelligence	Mostly information about broad areas of activities; specific legislative oversight committees; lower level of transparency in relation to military intelligence.	Differences in use of threat alerts. Role of oversight/ scrutiny committees, including non-parliamentarians.	Yes – emphasis on procedural and political accountability, some emphasis on administrative and judifical oversight, limited on administrative/ managerial. Limited explicit boundary drawing.
Flood defense	Emphasis on flood maps and emergency preparation/management.	Presence of centralized information, likely due to constitutional/structural differences.	Yes – emphasis on legal and administrative transparency, limited cross-jurisdictional information; reliance on 'normal' administrative oversight.
Food safety	Emphasis on product warnings and safety information.	Presence of inspection reports/labels, likely due to constitutional/structural differences.	Yes – emphasis on consumer warnings; limited cross-jurisdictional information; reliance on 'normal' administrative oversight.

level', although such an indicator did officially exist. The US had abandoned its threat level system in April 2011 and replaced it with the Department of Homeland Security's 'National Terrorism Advisory System' that was supposed to offer a more specific indication as to level, geographical and nature of threat. Furthermore, legislative oversight was conducted by specific committees that operate on the basis of specific secrecy arrangements and (often) select membership. Furthermore, various 'trustee' type committees existed, which involved members from outside parliament, and, at times, were required to have a legal background.

In contrast, both flood defense and food safety were characterized by a high degree of similarity: agencies reported on their activities, offered advice on preparing for emergencies or on avoiding food contamination. In flood defense, some agencies offered flood warnings and maps. In food safety, agencies offered information on product recalls and, in some cases, information about inspection results. Differences here reflected largely constitutional differences, for example the German food product recall warning system operated on a specific website jointly run by the federal agency and its equivalents at the land level. In this respect, both fields had moved towards an understanding of risk management that offered consumers material to inform their choices. In short, task-specific and organizational conditions seemed to explain most of the variation in transparency across agencies tasked with societal security.

Comparing the observed patterns in the light of the expectations formulated earlier (Table 12.3), some key arguments can be put forward. One is that political salience was reflected in the extent to which specific oversight and other scrutiny bodies existed in different domains. In other words, specific bodies existed only in intelligence. Flood defense and food safety featured 'normal' political and legal accountability provisions. The relationship among different levels of state and non-state actors, as well as issues of horizontal dispersion, were also critical for the extent to which agencies reported on activities in the field. Agencies with coordinating functions featured far less information than those dealing with operational activities. Constitutional jurisdictions arguably explain why certain information was available on some agencies' websites rather than others, although it does not explain the contrasting experience of inspection reports in New Zealand and the UK, with the latter having information on inspections despite both relying on local authorities for the information displayed.

Conclusion

Societal security is central to public management. However, it also poses particular challenges for accountability and transparency. Our study may be accused of a certain degree of naivety. After all, we focus on the appearance on public (websites) only, without focusing on the level of detail and effectiveness of such provisions, or on contextual or situational factors. However, as noted earlier, websites are critical for establishing and maintaining reputation, and therefore exercising social accountability (Busuioc and Lodge 2016). They are therefore critical even if they reflect voluntary rather than mandatory provisions (Koop 2014).

One of the critical aspects affecting all societal security related agencies is to establish 'trust', not just in the activities of particular agencies (i.e. tolerating infringements in civil liberties in the name of security), but also in the functioning of critical infrastructures (such as food supply chains). Being transparent and accountable therefore matters. However, such requirements can also prove disruptive to the core activities of particular agencies as it invites critical scrutiny. Exposing societal security-related activities to public scrutiny and requiring it to report therefore highlights that such measures might be 'trust building' in the sense of seeking to gain greater acceptance for agencies and activities, but it might also invite hostility and decreasing acceptance. Our focus on websites has also focused on operations during 'normal times'; a different study would focus on agencies' attempts to appear transparent and accountable during periods of acute crisis, whether this is during or after security incidents, food-related scandals or flooding.

This study expected to establish differences in terms of transparency and accountability across tasks, on the basis of the distinct profiles of intelligence, flood defence and food safety activities. The expected variations were confirmed when investigating the respective agencies' websites. There was, furthermore, a certain degree of similarity across all agencies and countries, pointing to a rather homogeneous set of demands on agencies on what kind of information should be provided on websites. These similarities reflected on leadership, resources, and notifications by agencies. In the intelligence sector, political salience and difficulties in monitoring outputs and outcomes led to an emphasis on political and judicial accountability and a complex web of oversight and scrutiny bodies. This complexity may reflect the particular 'wicked issues' in this sector.

Food safety, in contrast, offered more information on inspection activities, and was mostly directed towards offering individual consumer information, especially in the UK. Emphasis was placed on high degrees of expertise. Finally, the area of flood defence scored somewhere between the patterns observed in food safety, on the one hand, and intelligence, on the other. That is, despite some information about areas prone to flooding and advice on how to deal with emergencies, there was a strong emphasis on professional competence and the importance of inter-organizational relationships.

Our study highlights what agencies do. Ultimately, however, our study cannot establish whether transparency and accountability provisions matter for societal security (Bovens 2007). The need to appear transparent does represent a normative commitment, and it is therefore likely to have some implications for organizational behavior (as organizations are expected to seek to minimize too much disparity between public announcements and actual activities).

However, it should also be noted that a focus on the presence of transparency and accountability provisions only goes so far; it neither tells us much about residual powers of executives (and agencies) in withholding information, nor about actual operations. Accountability and transparency are not ends in themselves. Whether the public management of societal security is operated in constitutionally appropriate ways is therefore more about normative orientations, about the acceptability of intrusive measures (e.g. surveillance or torture), continuous public attention, and organizational self-reflection.

Note

1 We are grateful for the comments received on an earlier version of this chapter during the SOG Conference 'Accountability and Welfare State Reforms', University of Bergen, 19–20 February 2015. We are indebted to Isobel Green and Vilja Ohr Iversen for research assistance.

References

Balla, S. J. (2015) Political control, bureaucratic discretion, and public commenting on agency regulations. *Public Administration*, 93(2): 524–38.

Bovens, M. (2007) Analyzing and assessing public accountability: a conceptual framework. *European Law Journal*, 13(4): 837–68.

Brunsson, N. and Olsen, J. P. (1993) *The Reforming Organization*. London/New York: Routledge.

Busuioc, E. M. and Lodge, M. (2016) The reputational basis of public accountability. *Governance*, 29(2): 247–63.

Carpenter, D. (2010) *Reputation and Power: Organizational Image and Pharmaceutical Regulationa at the FDA*. Pinceton, NJ: Princeton University Press.

Christensen, T., Lægreid, P. and Rykkja, L. H. (2013) *Wicked Problems and the Challenge of Transboundary Coordination*. COCOPS Working Paper 11. Available at: www.cocops.eu/wp-content/uploads/2013/05/COCOPS_workingpaper_No11.pdf (accessed 19 July 2016).

Dominion Post (2014) 'Dirty politics' report directs harsh criticism at SIS. *Dominion Post*, 25 November. Available at: www.stuff.co.nz/national/politics/63505210/Dirty-politics-report-directs-harsh-criticism-at-SIS (accessed 17 August 2015).

Economist (2014) The spy who hacked me. *The Economist*, 29 November, p. 65.

Egeberg, M. (2012) How bureaucratic structure matters: an organizational perspective. In B. G. Peters and J. Pierre (eds), *Handbook of Public Administration* (2nd edition). London: Sage, pp. 116–26.

Elsbach, K. D. (2012) A framework for reputation management over the course of evolving controversies. In M. L. Barnett and T. G. Pollock (eds), *The Oxford Handbook of Corporate Reputation*. Oxford: Oxford University Press, pp. 466–84.

Etzioni, A. (2004) *How Patriotic is the Patriot Act? Freedom versus Security in the Age of Terrorism*. New York: Routledge.

Financial Times (2014) Publish guidance on lethal drone strikes, says former GCHQ chief. *Financial Times*, 26 November. Available at: www.ft.com/cms/s/0/c9a38848-73ea-11e4-92bc-00144feabdc0.html#axzz3j4lPUG9W (accessed 15 August 2015).

Goffman, E. (1959) *The Presentation of Self in Everyday Life*. New York: Doubleday.

Grimmelikhuijsen, S. and Klijn, A. (2015) The effects of judicial transparency on public trust. *Public Administration*, 93(4): 995–1011.

Gregory, R. (2003) All the king's horses and all the king's men: putting New Zealand's public sector back together again. *International Public Management Review*, 4(2): 41–58.

Guardian (2014) The Senate intelligence committee's report on CIA torture. *The Guardian*, 9 December. Available at: www.theguardian.com/us-news/ng-interactive/2014/dec/09/-sp-torture-report-cia-senate-intelligence-committee (accessed 15 August 2015).

Gulick, L. (1937) Notes on the theory on organizations. With special reference to government. In L. Gulick and L. Urwin (eds), *Papers on the Science of Administration*. New York: A. M. Kelley, pp. 1–45.

Hammond, T. (2007) Why is the intelligence community so difficult to redesign? *Governance*, 20(3): 401–22.

Hood, C. (1991) A public management for all seasons? *Public Administration*, 69(1): 3–19.

Hood, C. (2006) Transparency in historical perspective. In C. Hood and D. Heald (eds), *Transparency: The Key to Better Governance?* Oxford: British Academy/Oxford University Press.

Hood, C. (2010) Accountability and transparency: Siamese twins, matching parts, awkward couple? *West European Politics*, 33(5): 989–1009.

Hood, C., Rothstein, H. and Baldwin, R. (2001) *Government of Risk*. Oxford: Oxford University Press.

Koop, C. (2014) Theorizing and explaining voluntary accountability. *Public Administration*, 92(3): 565–81.

Landau, M. (1969) Redundancy, rationality, and the problem of duplication and overlap. *Public Administration Review*, 29(4): 346–58.

Lægreid, P. and Rykkja, L. H. (2013) *Coordinating for Internal Security and Safety in Norway*. Available at: www.cocops.eu/wp-content/uploads/2013/06/Norway_CGov_Internal-Security.pdf (accessed 19 July 2016).

Lodge, M. (2015) Accountability and consumer sovereignty. In A. Bianculli, X. Fernandez-i-Marin and J. Jordana (eds), *Accountability and Regulatory Governance*. Basingstoke: Palgrave Macmillan, pp. 235–64.

Lodge, M. and Stirton, L. (2010) Accountability in the regulatory state. In R. Baldwin, M. Cave and M. Lodge (eds), *Oxford Handbook of Regulation*. Oxford: Oxford University Press, pp. 349–70.

Mashaw, J. L. (2006) *Accountability and Institutional Design*. Available at: http://papers.ssrn.com/sol3/papers.cfm?abstract_id=924879 (accessed 19 July 2016).

Meyer, J. W. and Rowan, B. (1977) Institutionalized organizations: formal structure as myth and ceremony. *American Journal of Sociology*, 83(2): 340–63.

Mulgan, R. (2014) *Making Open Government Work*. Basingstoke: Palgrave Macmillan.

OECD (2014) *OECD Recommendations on the Governance of Critical Risks*. Available at: www.oecd.org/gov/risk/recommendation-on-governance-of-critical-risks.htm (accessed 15 August 2015).

Pollitt, C. (2011) Performance blight and the tyranny of light? Accountability in advanced performance measurement regimes. In M. J. Dubnick and H. G. Frederickson (eds), *Accountable Governance: Problems and Promises*. New York: M. E. Sharpe, pp. 81–97.

Pollitt, C. and Bouckaert, G. (2011) *Public Management Reform: A Comparative Analysis* (2nd edition). Oxford: Oxford University Press.

Pollitt, C., Talbot, C., Caulfield, J. and Smullen, A. (2004) *Agencies: How Governments Do Things with Semi-Autonomous Organizations*. Basingstoke: Palgrave Macmillan.

Power, M. (1997) *The Audit Society*. Oxford: Oxford University Press.

PST (2014) *Terror Threat Against Norway*. Available at: www.pst.no/media/pressemeldinger/terror-threat-against-norway/> (accessed 15 August 2015).

Radin, B. (2006) *Challenging the Performance Movement*. Washington, DC: Georgetown University Press.

Reynaers, A.-M. and Grimmelikhuijsen, S. (2015) Transparency in public-private partnerships. *Public Administration*, 93(3): 609–26.

Rhee, M. and Kim, T. (2012) After the collapse: a behavioral theory of reputation repair. In M. L. Barnett and T. G. Pollock (eds), *The Oxford Handbook of Corporate Reputation*. Oxford: Oxford University Press, pp. 446–65.

Schillemans, T. (2008) Accountability in the shadow of hierarchy: the horizontal accountability of agencies. *Public Organization Review*, 8(2): 175–94.

Selznick, P. (1957) *Leadership in Administration*. New York: Harper & Row.

Thompson, D. F. (1989) Moral responsibility of public officials: the problem of many hands. *American Political Science Review*, 74(4): 905–16.

Thompson, J. (1967) *Organizations in Action*. New York: McGraw-Hill.

Watson, T. (2007) Reputation and ethical behavior in a crisis: predicting survival. *Journal of Communication Management*. 11(4): 317–84.

Wilson, J. Q. (1989) *Bureaucracy: What Government Agencies Do and Why They Do It*. New York: Basic Books.

Wittington, R. and Yakis-Douglas, B. (2012) Strategic disclosure: strategy as a form of reputation management. In M. L. Barnett and T. G. Pollock (eds), *The Oxford Handbook of Corporate Reputation*. Oxford: Oxford University Press, pp. 402–20.

13
ACCOUNTABILITY UNDER INQUIRY

Inquiry committees after internal security crises

Julia Fleischer

Introduction[1]

When crises occur, governments face accountability pressures. They are held accountable for the causes leading to the critical event, as well as their crisis management and handling of its consequences. The growing literatures on blame management (see Hood *et al.* 2007, 2011) and crisis management (Boin *et al.* 2008, 2009) argue that actors may engage in blame games exploiting these accountability pressures, in political games focusing on officeholders and institutions, and in policy games over policy instruments (Boin *et al.* 2009). For political games, these scholars claim that governmental actors are primarily interested in keeping the status quo, whereas their political opponents act as change advocates (Boin *et al.* 2009: 101). Yet, it is puzzling that certain crises seem to generate a consensus between government and opposition, whereas others cause severe controversy.

This study argues that such partisan consensus is not only related to the nature of the crisis, but may also be mitigated through ad hoc accountability forums set up after critical events. These ad hoc accountability forums shape the capabilities of governmental actors to accept or deny responsibility, as well as of opposition actors to generate and apply blame. As a consequence, they influence the likelihood and scope of changes to the status quo (see Boin *et al.* 2009). The mitigation of accountability pressures through ad hoc forums is influenced by their mandate and composition, determining which actors and activities they inquire (and thus hold into account) and with what consequences for the status quo.

The empirical analysis examines the ad hoc accountability forums set up after critical events in the area of internal security. It compares the various forums created in the aftermath of the terrorist attacks in Norway in July 2011 and the disclosure of a Nazi terrorist cell (National Socialist Underground, NSU) in Germany in November 2011. The study examines these accountability forums and the evolving political games in which blame is raised and consequences are discussed. The mandate and composition, but also the interactions between different ad hoc accountability forums, explain the political games emerging in both countries, mitigating partisan consensus over the origins of the crises but also over its consequences for the status quo. The analysis is based on an extensive document and media coverage analysis, especially those primary sources issued by the various inquiries.

The accountability dilemma after crises

The scholarly literatures on accountability and crisis management accelerated over the past years; only recently, they intersected (e.g. Boin *et al.* 2009; Kuipers and 't Hart 2014). Since the seminal work of Romzek and Dubnick (1987), authors have discussed the multiple accountabilities that public sector organizations face, also in ordinary times (Simon *et al.* 1991: 513–61). Accordingly, accountability is defined more broadly as the 'means by which public agencies and their works manage the diverse expectations generated within and outside the organizations' (Romzek and Dubnick 1987: 228). Building upon this work, Bovens (2007: 467) defines accountability as 'a relationship between an actor and a forum, in which the actor has an obligation to explain and to justify his or her conduct, the forum can pose questions and pass judgment, and the actor may face consequences' (see also Bovens 2010). More importantly, Bovens introduced five types of accountability, where different actors are held into account by different forums, distinguishing administrative, professional, legal, social and political accountability. For this study, particularly administrative and political accountability are crucial because they refer to the part of the chain of delegation linking cabinet ministers with parliament, but also where political parties and the media may act as forums (Bovens 2007: 455).

The crisis management literature argues that governing after critical events generates debates about accountability and blame, depending upon actor constellations and political strategies, and expressed in political games holding officeholders and institutional arrangements into account (see Hood *et al.* 2007, 2011; Boin *et al.* 2008, 2009). Such political games 'centre around the clash between government and opposition' (Boin *et al.* 2009: 88), distinguished as four ideal types along two dimensions. On the one hand, oppositional forces may or may not blame officeholders for the occurrence of the crisis, its causes and consequences, as well as their handling of the acute post-crisis phase and long-term effects. In case they blame the government, they may further claim for its removal or only damage the government's reputation. On the other hand, officeholders may accept or reject these allegations of responsibility for the critical events.

In general, political games deal to a great extent with political accountability but are also linked to other types of accountability. They may investigate preexisting arrangements for administrative and professional accountability and their potential failures leading to the critical episode. Likewise, they may be linked to legal and social accountability; the latter is often dealt with in the media coverage of the critical episode. This analysis focuses on political blame games unfolding alongside ad hoc accountability forums set up after a critical incident that are most relevant for political accountability.

The reverse chain of delegation in parliamentary systems describes the relations of political accountability, connecting the bureaucracy with cabinet ministers, prime ministers, parliaments and voters. After critical episodes, ad hoc accountability forums may be created between parliamentary and governmental actors in this chain of accountability (Schillemans 2011). On the one hand, they may originate in the *legislative arena* in the form of a parliamentary inquiry committee. These inquiry committees are widely regarded as a core instrument for the opposition to hold governments accountable (Helms 2013). As a consequence, most formal rules of procedures in Western parliaments require a threshold for setting up these inquiries that can be met with the votes of the opposition. These ad hoc accountability forums consist of acting MPs and may involve external experts and witnesses in their inquiring activities. In addition, parliamentary inquiries often contextualize the gathering of evidence as quasi-legal in the sense that witnesses can be asked to testify under oath, also explicitly allowing future legal prosecution. Despite the variety of possible mandates for parliamentary inquiries, the very nature of this instrument (controlling government) tends to lead to some 'past bias': (opposition) MPs aim to identify malevolent behavior and failures of the government, and therefore invest a considerable part of their inquiring activities 'into the past', reconstructing who did what, when, and why.

On the other hand, ad hoc accountability forums may originate in the *executive arena* as external expert commissions or internal evaluations. External expert commissions come in many different forms and are comparably less formalized than parliamentary inquiries. To be sure, several countries have established formal rules or strong conventions as to how such expert commissions or internal evaluations are established and operate. Nevertheless, the empirical variation is broader. One possible difference is the installing actor (i.e. whether the expert commission is set up by the government as a whole or by individual cabinet ministers). They often consist of experts appointed by this sponsoring actor, and also hold hearings of witnesses and experts, but rarely allow a straightforward usage of any testimonies in court. Besides, such expert commissions and internal evaluations can be regarded to have some 'future bias': experts participating in a temporary commission created by the executive are most often tasked to reconstruct the causes of a critical episode but also to formulate recommendations as how to change the status quo – ideally, in a neutral but still manageable way for the government or minister in office.

In many cases, legislative and executive actors create ad hoc accountability forums to address the same critical episode and add to the preexisting accountability regime a special emphasis on political accountability. It is very likely that those ad hoc forums influence each other, and partly such a 'duplicating' of forums is also very much intended.

Ad hoc accountability forums in internal security crises in Norway and Germany

This analysis compares the ad hoc accountability forums created in the aftermaths of recent internal security crises in Norway and Germany. Despite the similar policy area, the scope of the crises differs. In Norway, the terrorist attacks in Oslo and Utøya on 22 July 2011 presented the worst violence in the country's history since the Second World War; eight people died in a bomb attack at the government quarter, and 69 young party members were killed during a party summer camp on Utøya island; a total of 172 persons were injured. Therefore, one may regard this internal security crisis in Norway as a 'dual attack', simultaneously addressing the government (and its quarter in the capital), as well as a distinct political party (and many members of its youth organization).

In contrast, the German critical episode unfolded accidentally, when a bank robbery went bad and the police detected that the bank robbers were part of a terrorist cell (NSU) responsible for various crimes that had been committed over almost a decade, including a murder series of nine shop owners with migration backgrounds, the murder of a policewoman and attempted murder of her colleague, a pipe bombing in a popular business area for migrants, injuring over 20 people, and a series of 14 bank robberies. Therefore, the internal security crisis in Germany can be regarded as 'attack series' (i.e. it was triggered by an unrecognized series of crimes committed over a rather long time period).

Despite these differences in scope, both internal security administrations came under severe accountability pressures after these critical events. In both countries, no politicians resigned, and instead top officials were removed from office. In Germany, the internal security crisis resulted in the largest number of dismissed agency heads in history, including the head of the Federal Office for the Protection of the Constitution and his counterparts in four German state agencies.

Table 13.1 Ad hoc accountability forums set up in the aftermath of the two crises

	Norway	Germany
Executive arena	22 July Commission (08/2011–08/2012 = one year)	BMI Internal Expert Commission (11/2011–02/2012 = three months) BMI + LMI Expert Commission (BLKR) (02/2012–05/2013 = 15 months)
Evaluations	• Justice Ministry: Project Group • Police (Sønderland Commission) • Directorate for Civil Protection (internal evaluation) • Health administration (internal evaluation *and* external evaluation)	• Interior Ministry: Project Group
Legislative arena	Stortinget's 22 July Committee • created approx. three months after the executive ad hoc forum • 17 MPs (from all parliamentary parties) • approx. four months' tenure	Bundestag's Inquiry Committee • created approx. two months after the executive ad hoc forum • Eight MPs (from all parliamentary parties) • approx. 19 months' tenure

Source: Own illustration

Besides, executive and legislative actors responded by creating various ad hoc accountability forums (see Table 13.1). These ad hoc accountability forums played a vital role in providing an arena for potential blame games, as well as guiding the subsequent changes of the institutional and policy status quo.

The supremacy of the 22 July Commission in Norway

The Norwegian Prime Minister (PM) announced a 'Norwegian government inquiry' (NOU) three weeks after the critical incident in August 2011, formally put forward under a royal resolution. Initially, some minor controversies occurred between the governing parties, being in power for six years, and the opposition parties complaining that the PM did not consult them for their feedback on the mandate and composition. However, eventually they agreed and supported the Commission's mandate and members. The mandate of the 22 July Commission aimed:

> to examine the ability of the authorities *and* society as a whole to:
> • disclose plans of attacks and prevent such attacks,
> • protect themselves against and reduce the consequences of a future attack, and
> • deal with the situation during and after such events, including taking care of the injured and relatives of those killed or injured.
>
> *(PM press release, 12 August 2011)*

Put differently, the Commission was supposed to answer three major questions: 'What happened 22/7? Why did it happen? And more fundamentally: How could our society allow this to happen?' (NOU 2012: 13). As such, the 22 July Commission was tasked with a rather broad mandate, mixing the immediate fact-finding of responsibilities and accountability in the preexisting internal security administration with the more general notion of societal resilience and societal awareness of terrorist tendencies. At the time of its inception, the government's intention was to cover all potential aspects that had caused the severe incident, as well as what should be taken into account for the future to prevent similar attacks. After the finalization of its tasks, however, a more nuanced view may conclude that its broad mandate limited a clear identification of responsibilities within the internal security administration, providing various actors in the field with leeway to, for example, establish their own internal evaluations (see also Christensen and Lægreid 2012; Christensen et al. 2013) that reduced the Commission's focus on evaluating their contribution, or, in other words, their answers to the first two major questions noted above.

The Commission was set up as independent of the government and the PM; it was mandated to complete its work by 10 August 2012 and report to the PM, therefore providing a limited tenure of one year. The Commission was asked to appoint its own secretariat. Despite the official notion to aim to put together a Commission with a broad range of expertise, the impartiality of the Commission members was concern for some debate – but eventually an independent evaluation by a lawyer concluded that no problems of impartiality existed (Advokatfirmaet Hjort 2011). The Commission members were selected by cabinet and included a high share of legal expertise (Christensen 2013: 246). Besides, this dominant legal background overlapped to some extent with police competence (i.e. three members had former occupations in the police, including two foreign members). What is most striking is the strong background in the private sector of several Commission members, including the chairwoman with previous working experience at Statoil, another member who was previously the CEO of the Norwegian Railways, and a secretariat member who had served as President of Hydro. In addition, the Commission also included two members with an academic background in terrorist studies and history, respectively. Some private sector experience may have been related to their former experience with resilience and preparedness issues, including, for example, the management and prevention of train accidents. Others, however, may have been related to the government's objective to bring together a broader range of experience. It has been part of the debate after the final report was issued, whether the absence of public sector experience and knowledge in political science and organization studies may have contributed to the alleged misguidance of the 22 July Commission in some of its results and subsequent recommendations (see Christensen 2013).

Much has been said about the findings of the 22 July Commission, the failures of the government authorities that it identified and the recommendations that it put forward (Christensen et al. 2011, 2012, 2013; Fimreite et al. 2012). Among the key critical stances of the report is the overall observation of a mismatch between the alleged 'illnesses' in the Norwegian internal security sector and its proposed 'medicine' (Christensen et al. 2011, 2013; Lango et al. 2011) (i.e. that the Commission acknowledged that the formal organizations had failed in prevention and crisis management, but also concluded that organizational changes are not essential, and instead the culture and leadership of these governmental organizations need adaptation) (Christensen et al. 2011, 2013; Fimreite et al. 2012).

In addition to the major inquiry by the 22 July Commission, executive actors established their own evaluations, including the police (Sønderland et al. 2012), the fire departments (DSB 2012) and the health services (KAMEDO 2012; Lereim et al. 2012; see also Christensen and Lægreid 2012). Likewise, the crisis management center submitted an evaluation to the 22 July Commission (JD 2012a, 2012b). Partly, these evaluations complemented the findings and assessments of the 22 July Commission. Partly, however, they may have also contributed to additional concerns over accountability and blame (see below).

Although not receiving as much scholarly attention as the external expert commission set up by the government, the Norwegian parliament also created an ad hoc accountability forum.

Table 13.2 Key executive ad hoc accountability forums in Norway and Germany

	Norway: 22 July Commission (Gjørv Commission)	Germany: Federal-State Commission on Right-Wing Extremism (BLKR)
Tenure	12.08.2011–13.08.2012 (365 days)	08.02.2012–25.03.2013 (470 days)
Mandate	<ul><li>to examine the ability of the authorities *and* society as a whole to: – disclose plans of attacks and prevent such attacks – protect themselves against/reduce the consequences of a future attack – deal with the situation during/after such events, including taking care of the injured and relatives</li><li>to propose measures to improve preparedness in the future</li><li>free to consider other factors/measures that its review shows as relevant</li></ul>	<ul><li>analyze and evaluate the coordination between the various authorities in the area of internal security</li><li>formulate recommendations for the future internal security administration</li><li>recognize the following evidence: – interim results of the investigation by the Attorney General – expertise of the intelligence agencies – findings of the parliamentary inquiries and special envoys (at federal/state level) – decisions by the Ministers of Interior (IMK) on measures for improved coordination – results of the IMK working group on police and intelligence</li></ul>
Chair Members	(1) Lawyer and former Hydro executive (2) Former head of the Norwegian armed forces' intelligence services (3) Former Police Chief of Hordaland (4) Former Police Commissioner in Copenhagen (5) Former CEO of NSB (Norwegian railways) (6) History professor (7) Political scientist, terrorism (8) Vice President Norwegian Red Cross (9) Chief County Medical Officer	None (1) Former State Minister of Interior (Hamburg) (2) Former State Minister of Interior (Berlin), replaced by former State Minister of Interior (Rhineland-Palatine) (3) Former Federal Prosecutor General (4) Law professor
Key findings	<ul><li>inappropriate organizational culture</li><li>poor leadership and attitudes</li></ul>	<ul><li>lacking exchange of information and collaboration</li><li>weak oversight capabilities inside ministries</li></ul>
Changes of status quo	<ul><li>various institutional measures</li><li>various organizational reforms</li><li>stronger legislation on terror planning, prohibition of semi-automatic weapons</li></ul>	<ul><li>mostly institutional: Federal Intelligence Agency as hub for coordinating state authorities</li><li>joint analyses and information exchange centers</li></ul>

Source: Own illustration.

Following the statements of the Ministers of Interior and of Defense in parliament in November 2011, it established a '22 July Committee' to investigate their assessments and to formulate recommendations (Stortinget 2011). It is relevant to note that the parliamentary inquiry committee stated in its mandate explicitly that its purpose was 'to provide a broader basis for parliamentary consideration of any need for legislative and budgetary priorities *before the 22 July Commission has finalized its work* and evaluations that have been initiated in the Police Directorate (POD) and the Norwegian Police Security service (PST) are completed' (Stortinget 2011: 5, emphasis by the author). An explicit paragraph in the mandate set out the boundaries between the parliamentary inquiry and the external expert commission, highlighting the principle of the separation of powers and acknowledging the mandate of the 22 July Commission. Consequently, the parliamentary inquiry completed its work within four months and issued its report in February 2012, several months before the 22 July Commission had published its final report.

The major evidence informing the parliamentary inquiry were two rounds of written questions sent to the various ministries and a hearing in February 2012 in which the Ministers of Justice and of Defense, the former chief of the Police Security Service (PST) and the acting police director were questioned.[2] Its key recommendations address mostly the police services and the police security service.

The dominance of the federal parliamentary inquiry in Germany?

The Federal Minister of Interior issued the first response to the NSU crisis in Germany by creating an external expert commission three weeks after the terrorist cell's accidental disclosure. The commission consisted of a former President of the Federal Office for the Protection of the Constitution and of the Federal Intelligence Service, a former President of the Federal Criminal Police Office, and a former Conservative MP and expert in internal security (BT-Drs. 17/9463). This commission was asked to examine all relevant files of the police and the intelligence services from the federal and state level related to the NSU and draw conclusions (i.e. to propose changes to the status quo of the German internal security administration) (FAZ 2011a). In practice, though, the expert commission never met – because simultaneous debates in Parliament and in several German states about an appropriate accountability forum persuaded the minister to wait (FAZ 2011c).

The initial option debated in Parliament as how to respond to the crisis was to nominate a special envoy, formally by the Parliament's Control Board (PKGr) that supervises the intelligence services at federal level (PKGrG; see also Art. 45d GG).[3] However, this initiative failed because the board lacked the necessary two-third majority due to the Social Democrats' refusal to vote with the other two opposition parties (and the Left Party's representative being absent). The Social Democrats rejected the initiative because they wanted to clarify the responsibilities and competences of the various accountability forums before commissioning a special envoy, also taking the Minister's announced external expert commission into account (FAZ 2011b).

Similarly, the Social Democrats rejected the second option to create an official parliamentary inquiry committee. One major concern was the involvement of the authorities at state level in the critical episode – which could not be directly investigated by a parliamentary inquiry at federal level.[4] This opinion was also followed by MPs from the Conservatives and some MPs of the Liberal Party. Partly, though, the rejection of an inquiry committee was related to the general notion among MPs from all parties that they had already spent a lot of time in other inquiry committees, and recognizing that such a committee would meet well until the general election in 2013 (expert interviews; FAZ 2011a). The Social Democrats therefore pledged for a joint legislative-executive accountability forum, including representatives from federal and state level, nominated by the two major parties and the Green Party as well as the Liberal Party, and incorporating the three experts commissioned by the Federal Minister of Interior already. The Left Party and several MPs of the Liberal Party rejected such an expert inquiry because it would blur the lines of political accountability between the legislative and the executive and would therefore not suffice the parliament's claims in elucidating the events; eventually, this third option was dropped as well.

Nevertheless, the other opposition parties pressed on; the Green Party issued a discussion paper entitled 'Determined Against Right-Radicalism', claiming for the creation of an inquiry committee, and laid out its mandate (Green Parliamentary Party 2011). Also, the Left Party supported the creation of a parliamentary inquiry committee from the beginning. Together, though, both opposition parties failed to reach the quota to set up such a committee (a quarter of all MPs, i.e. 155 MPs). In mid-January, the chief whip of the Conservative parliamentary party initiated meetings with the chief whips of the other parliamentary parties, responding to the increasing public pressure to investigate the causes of the critical event. Eventually, the political parties agreed to set up both a parliamentary inquiry committee at federal level and a joint external expert commission with members appointed by the federal and the state governments (see below).

The final mandate of the parliamentary inquiry committee at federal level was to:

> get an overall picture of the terrorist group 'National Socialist Underground', its members and crimes, their environment and their supporters, as well as to *why they could commit their serious crimes undetected for so long*. On the basis of these findings the inquiry committee *should draw conclusions* for the structure, cooperation, training and competencies of the security and law enforcement agencies and *make recommendations* for an effective combat against right-radical extremism.
>
> *(BT-Drs. 17/74539, emphasis by the author)*

Moreover, the Inquiry Committee recognized the parallel investigations by the Federal-State Expert Commission (see below), as well as parliamentary inquiry committees set up at state level (BT press release, 09.02.2012; FAZ 2012a) (see below). It proactively aimed to avoid a duplication of work, albeit many files of the various internal security authorities at state and federal level had to be exchanged between the different ad hoc accountability forums.

The final report highlighted several issues regarding the preexisting accountability regime; it mainly addressed: (a) administrative and (b) professional accountability, considering horizontal and vertical relations between the various internal security authorities, as well as (c) professional accountability by acknowledging the relevance of the professional standards and dominant norms, whereas (d) political accountability was rather neglected.

In the executive arena, the Federal Minister of Interior appointed, together with his counterparts at state level, a Federal-State Expert Commission in February 2012, commissioned to investigate the causes of the crisis and to formulate reform proposals (BMI 2012), summarized as performing a 'bundling, analysis, and evaluation function' (BM Friedrich, cited in FAZ 2012b: 4). In fact, it was supposed to cut across the different authorities at the different state levels in order to get a general overview on the shortcomings and failings of the preexisting internal security architecture, but also to make recommendations on how to improve it with regard to the challenges triggered by the critical event as well as others. It issued two interim reports and its final report was published in May 2013 (BLKR 2012, 2013). Moreover, the expert commission was not limited in its tenure, albeit the upcoming general election was widely regarded as a critical circumstance for such an ad hoc accountability forum and the debate about its findings and results should not coincide with the electoral campaign.

The four members of the so-called 'Federal-State Expert Commission Right-Wing Terrorism' (BLKR) were appointed by both the federal and the *Länder* level: the federal government appointed a law professor and a former Federal Prosecutor General, and the *Länder* appointed two former State Ministers of Interior (BMI 2012). The expert commission was supported by a secretariat of six officials from the Federal Ministry of Interior (FAZ 2012b) (see Table 13.2). The changing composition of the BLKR in comparison to its predecessor, which had been set up by the Federal Minister himself, could be interpreted as an indication for the helpful but also problematic involvement of previous officeholders with accountability forums set up to take a general overview over several years and holding a system into account to which they contributed in their previous professional occupations.

The BLKR published its report in May 2013, highlighting the relevance of the strong normative and factual separation of intelligence and police work in Germany as a cause for regular frictions over information gathering, analyses and adequate responses between the various authorities. Besides, it stressed legal requirements limiting an inadequate horizontal information exchange. As a consequence, its report recommended strengthening the exchange of information within the network of intelligence services, and also acknowledging the Federal Office for the Protection of the Constitution as a hub.

In sum, the external expert commission set up after the German internal security crisis addressed mainly administrative and professional accountability. Accordingly, the reform proposals refer to reorganizing competencies within and between the criminal police offices and the intelligence agencies. Its focus on formal rules was oriented towards legal frameworks and the current and future ways to hold the various German internal security authorities legally accountable. The final report mostly neglects political accountability and avoids blaming incumbent or former political or administrative officeholders.

In comparison, in both countries, the executive initiated the creation of an ad hoc accountability forum in gestalt of an external expert commission rather quickly after the critical episode. Later, executive actors also commissioned evaluations, as internal project groups or external evaluations. The mandate of the two ad hoc accountability forums set up by the governments differ: whereas in Norway the 22 July Commission was explicitly commissioned with an almost impossible task, namely to investigate the authorities' *and* the society's contribution to the causes of the critical events, as well as to recommend improvements for Norwegian internal security policy and administration, the German expert commission was mainly focused on the failures within and between governmental authorities leading to the critical episode, as well as recommendations for reforming the status quo. Besides, the Norwegian 22 July Commission was explicitly mandated to finish its tasks within one year, whereas the German BLKR commission was not formally limited despite the upcoming general election. Most striking, the composition of the two ad hoc accountability forums differs considerably, arguably related to the government's motives for setting up the accountability forum in the first place and the 'audience' the accountability forum was supposed to talk to. The severe scope of the Norwegian terrorist attack required a strong dialogue between the external expert commission and society (in fact, societal causes and consequences were part of its official mandate), and therefore a broad range of expertise was incorporated, although expertise in public sector organizations is missing. In contrast, the composition of the German BLKR commission seems to solely focus on such expertise (i.e. the federal and state governments appointed strong experts in the field of internal security, arguably with strong ties to those authorities whose alleged failures the accountability forum were tasked to identify).

More importantly, in both countries, the legislative arena followed the government and established their own ad hoc accountability forums. The mandates of both forums are rather similar, but the Norwegian parliamentary inquiry has been more limited in its scope, also with regard to the evidence and information that it gathered. Consequently, the Norwegian 22 July Committee in Parliament finished its task within four months, whereas the German NSU Inquiry in Parliament lasted for more than 19 months.

Next to the sequencing, the interplay of these ad hoc accountability forums is also of interest. While in Norway the (succeeding) parliamentary inquiry noticed the necessity to demarcate boundaries in their mandate in relation to the external 22 July Commission and explicitly departed itself from this ad hoc accountability forum, the German (succeeding) external expert commission's mandate declared the findings of the parliamentary inquiry as an integral source of its own evidence and did not distance itself from the other ad hoc accountability forum (in fact, the political parties decided simultaneously to set up an inquiry in parliament and turn the initial external expert commission of the Federal Minister of Interior into a federal-state expert commission).

The blame games in Norwegian and German ad hoc accountability forums

The inception of the 22 July Commission and the comparatively more limited and short-term parliamentary inquiry in Norway followed a strong convention of relying upon governmental expert commissions (NOUs) to investigate critical incidents but also other major policy issues of interest. Also, due to the scope of the crisis in Norway, the creation process was not accompanied by partisan conflicts over appropriate ad hoc accountability forums.

To some extent, the broad mandate of the 22 July Commission omitted a stronger focus on political accountability and associating blame with distinct political and bureaucratic actors and their potential failures leading to the critical incident but also managing the crisis and its aftermath. Presumably, this was expected and intended by the government as sponsoring actor, aiming to address the general public and thus providing a political assessment but also offering a broader 'societal evaluation'. Yet, the simultaneous self-evaluations conducted by various executive actors, ranging from the police to the health services, were therefore necessary to complete the fact-finding and evidence provision – as well as to assess accountability issues. All self-evaluations were published before the Commission issued its final report. More importantly, these self-evaluations differed considerably with regard to identifying failures and proactively taking responsibility (and thus blame) for them: the internal evaluation of the police services concluded that the police forces could not have done anything different, therefore neglecting any failures or mistakes (Sønderland et al. 2012). This may reveal the 'organizational survival' mode of the Norwegian police forces in the aftermath of the crisis, reducing blame and accountability pressures that may have led to changes in their status quo. In contrast, the health services not only issued an internal evaluation (Lereim et al. 2012), but also an external evaluation by foreign evaluators (KAMEDO 2012), acknowledging failures that had been made. More importantly, the health services did not become a major concern of the 22 July Commission (in fact, the Commission recommended the evaluations as further readings), but the police services and their self-evaluated good performance became a major issue of debate within the Commission – and this attention informed the parliamentary inquiry focusing on the police services and their reforms as well.

The biggest chance for blame games emerged after the 22 July Commission issued its final report in August 2012. Despite severe criticism in parliament and a controversial hearing of the PM and several cabinet ministers, the opposition did not take the opportunity to blame the government. Next to the scope of the crisis, one possible explanation might have been its dual nature (i.e. it was not only an attack on the government (quarter), which may have raised issues of accountability for the various government authorities involved in preventing terrorist attacks and managing a terrorist attack, but also an attack on many members of one of the ruling parties' youth organizations).

In Germany, all parliamentary parties supported the parliamentary inquiry committee and its findings and recommendations, but the initial process leading to its creation already revealed some conflicts over the appropriate ad hoc accountability forum. Yet, their ultimately consensual exercise of holding governmental authorities to account, almost neglecting to participate in a blame game, is rather surprising. Although one may explain this cross-party consensus with the strong societal relevance of the issue (i.e. right-radical extremism is widely regarded as one of the most crucial threats for German democracy), and therefore MPs from all political parties prefer consensus upon the causes of the critical episode, as well as its consequences for the preexisting status quo. However, it is also caused by partisan motives.

Four of the five parliamentary parties at federal level have been in office over the past decade when the NSU committed their crimes. Therefore, blaming the responsible minister (of interior) would inherently mean self-blame. In addition, the Left Party, which has been in opposition at federal level ever since, participated in government at state level and has accordingly also a rather limited interest to focus its blame towards incumbents and former officeholders. In addition, party-specific motives further lowered the interest in blaming the current government. The Conservative Party has a long self-understanding to be responsible for 'law and order' despite its aims to reach out for new voters (e.g. among migrants). Hence, a strong blaming of incumbents and former officeholders acting as ministers of interior would address their own senior party figures. The Social Democrats feared a similar experience as with the parliamentary inquiries investigating the visa affair and the BND affair, putting their own Ministers of Interior and for Foreign Affairs under severe pressure – and would rather avoid similar pressures, especially heading up to a general election. Moreover, it holds strong ties with the police trade unions, and therefore its MPs focused rather strongly on how to reform the criminal police offices and, more importantly, how to reorganize their interrelations with the intelligence services. The Green Party took several initiatives to support the creation of a parliamentary inquiry committee in the first place, but did not behave as oppositional as could have been expected and instead joined the other parties in rather modest usage of blame.

In contrast, the external expert commission set up by the German ministers of interior revealed stronger blame game dynamics. This became visible when a position paper by the Federal Office for the Protection of the Constitution on three potential future scenarios for the set of intelligence agencies in Germany was leaked in May 2012 (*Der Spiegel* 2012). Almost immediately, the actors in the field defended the status quo or the proposed changes, blaming lacking resources or the authorities for their failures. More importantly, the reform proposals were assessed for their consequences for parliamentary accountability (i.e. how to ensure that MPs at federal and state level are better equipped to control and oversee how the various criminal police offices and intelligence agencies perform their tasks). Hence, the BLKR Commission was less concerned with political accountability and much more concerned with administrative and professional accountability, raising issues of resources and oversight capabilities within the German internal security sector, claiming failed budget allocations and lacking or misguided priorities (investing too much into detecting and prosecuting left-wing and Islamic terrorism) by previous governments.

Conclusion

This chapter argues that partisan consensus after a critical incident is not only related to the nature of the crisis, but may also be mitigated through ad hoc accountability forums. It examined the ad hoc accountability forums set up by legislative and executive actors in the aftermath of the terrorist attacks in Norway and the disclosure of a Nazi terrorist cell in Germany, which put both internal security administrations under severe pressure.

The analysis shows that the parliamentary and governmental ad hoc accountability forums differ with regard to their nature and outcomes. The parliamentary inquiries are, by and large, surprisingly consensual, especially the classic divide between governing and opposition MPs after critical episodes is nearly absent. As a result, though, blame minimization was easy to accomplish by the political incumbents. In addition, their reform proposals contrast with the mandate of inquiry committees – to accomplish political accountability – and address instead mostly administrative and professional accountability (i.e. they suggest moderate changes of organizational structures and stress the relevance of professional standards and norms). In contrast, the external expert commissions set up by the Norwegian and German governments appear, as expected, rather consensual, providing opportunities for blame minimization by focusing mostly on administrative and professional accountability. Their reform proposals are congruent to their mandate and objectives (i.e. they do not hold ministers accountable and avoid allocating political blame).

Moreover, the empirical analysis reveals the relevance of sequence and interaction between ad hoc accountability forums set up by legislative and executive actors. Despite the differences with regard to the scope and origins of the crisis, in both countries the executive actors reacted first by creating internal evaluations and expert committees, thus responding towards the increasing accountability pressures emerging after the crisis. Soon thereafter, parliaments reacted and created their own inquiries as ad hoc accountability forums in order to join or check the accountability – and thereby enable to play political games allocating responsibility and blame. However, the nature of both types of ad hoc accountability forums may also explain this particular sequencing in setting up additional devices for accountability after crises: whereas the ad hoc forums created by executive actors are more often oriented towards recommendations on the future, thus blurring to some extent the allocation of blame and responsibility for the origins and causes of the critical event, the legislative ad hoc accountability forums investigate more strongly the past and aim exactly at attributing accountability to former and current officeholders.

Lastly, this study shows that the scope and nature of both crises led to some 'de-politicization dynamics', limiting the capabilities of actors to exploit ad hoc accountability forums for political games. Instead, executive and legislative actors avoid utilizing the critical episode for short-term gains in party-political competition. Yet, it is also a matter of time and the researcher's analytical focus. Just recently, all parliamentary parties in Germany set up a second parliamentary inquiry on the NSU, further investigating aspects that have been partly examined by parliamentary inquiries at the state level, as well as the court case against one of the alleged NSU members (BT-Drs. 18/6330). Put differently: for some crises unfolding in particularly salient areas calling for party-political consensus and unity in the direct aftermath, the time for playing political games alongside ad hoc accountability forums may just come a little later.

Notes

1   I would like to thank Tom Christensen, Per Lægreid, Helge Renå, Line Marie Sørsdal and the participants of the SOG 2015 Annual Conference in Bergen for their comments on an earlier draft. All remaining errors are mine.

2   In addition, the parliament held a separate hearing after the 22 July Commission's final report was published.
3   It includes 11 MPs who are elected by the plenary at the beginning of the legislative period.
4   Yet, the Green Party commissioned the Bundestag administration to examine the matter, which also concluded that 'state officials have to appear and witness before federal parliamentary committees' (cited in FAZ 2012a).

References

Advokatfirmaet Hjort (2011) *Kommisjonens vurdering av medlemmenes habilitet*. August 2012, Oslo.
Boin, R. A., McConnell, A. and 't Hart, P. (2008) *Governing After Crisis: The Politics of Investigation, Accountability and Learning*. Cambridge: Cambridge University Press.
Boin, R. A., McConnell, A. and 't Hart, P. (2009) Crisis exploitation: political and policy impacts of framing contests. *Journal of European Public Policy*, 16(1): 81–106.
Bovens, M. (2007) Analyzing and assessing public accountability: a conceptual framework. *European Law Journal*, 13(4): 837–68.
Bovens, M. (2010) Two concepts of accountability: accountability as a virtue and as a mechanism. *West European Politics*, 33(5): 946–67.
Bundesministerium des Innern (BMI) (2012) *Friedrich stellt Bund-Länder-Regierungskommission Rechtsterrorismus vor*. Press release, 8 February.
Bundestagsdrucksache (BT-Drs.) 17/14600 [2013]. Beschlussempfehlung und Bericht des 2. Untersuchungsausschusses, 22.08.2013, Berlin.
Bundestagsdrucksache (BT-Drs.) 18/6601 [2015]. Beschlussempfehlung und Bericht zu dem Antrag der Fraktionen CDU/CSU, SPD, DIE LINKE. und BÜNDNIS 90/DIE GRÜNEN, Einsetzung des 3. Untersuchungsausschusses, 09.11.2015, Berlin.
Bund-Länder-Kommission Rechtsextremismus (BLKR) (2012) *2. Zwischenbericht der Bund-Länder Expertenkommission Rechtsterrorismus*, 27 November 2012.
Bund-Länder-Kommission Rechtsextremismus (BLKR) (2013) *Abschlussbericht der Bund-Länder Expertenkommission Rechtsterrorismus*, 30 April 2013.
Christensen, J. (2013) 22. juli-Kommisjonen. Perspektiver på en felles fortelling. *Nytt Norsk Tidsskrift*, 30(3): 243–54.
Christensen, T., Fimreite, A. L. and Lægreid, P. (2011) Crisis management: the case of internal security in Norway. *Administration and Society*, 43(5): 561–94.
Christensen, T. and Lægreid, P. (2012) Reputation management in times of crisis. In A. Wæraas and M. Maor (eds), *Organizational Reputation in the Public Sector*. London: Routledge, pp. 95–117.
Christensen, T., Lægreid, P. and Rykkja, L. H. (2013) After a terrorist attack: challenges for political and administrative leadership in Norway. *Journal of Contingencies and Crisis Management*, 21(3): 167–77.
Der Spiegel (2012) Anarchos im Amt, No. 30/2012, 20–24.
DSB (2012) *Evaluering av krisehåndteringen etter hendelsene i Regjeringskvartalet og på Utøya 22. juli 2011, innenfor DSBs ansvarsområder*. Tønsberg: Direktoratet for samfunnssikkerhet og beredskap.
Fimreite, A. L., Lango, P., Lægreid, P. and Rykkja, L. H. (2012) 22. juli-kommisjonen. Organisering, styring og ansvar. *Nordiske Organisasjonsstudier*, 14(4): 49–58.
Frankfurter Allgemeine Zeitung (FAZ) (2011a) Friedrich setzt Kommission ein, 25.11.2011, p. 6.
Frankfurter Allgemeine Zeitung (FAZ) (2011b) Untersuchung zur NSU spatter, 16.12.2011, p. 6.
Frankfurter Allgemeine Zeitung (FAZ) (2011c) Alles eine Frage der Aufklärung? 27.12.2011, p. 8.
Frankfurter Allgemeine Zeitung (FAZ) (2012a) NSU-Untersuchungsausschuss soll 'Doppelarbeit' vermeiden, 10.02.2012, p. 4.
Frankfurter Allgemeine Zeitung (FAZ) (2012b) Kompetenzgerangel bei Aufklärung des NSU-Terrors, 09.02.2012, p. 4.
Green Parliamentary Party (2011) Entschlossen gegen Rechts, Fraktionsbeschluss 13. Dezember 2011, Berlin.
Helms, L. (ed.) (2013) *Parliamentary Opposition in Old and New Democracies*. London: Routledge.
Hood, C., Jennings, W., Hogwood, B. and Beeston, C. (2007) *Fighting Fires in Testing Times: Exploring a Staged Response Hypothesis For Blame Management in Two Exam Fiasco Cases*. CARR Discussion Paper No. 42. London: LSE, Centre of Analysis of Risk Regulation.
Hood, C., Jennings, W., Hogwood, B. and Beeston, C. (2011) Blame avoidance and accountability: positive, negative, or neutral? In M. J. Dubnick and H. G. Frederickson (eds), *Accountable Governance: Problems and Promises*. Armonk, NY: M. E. Sharpe, pp. 167–79.

Justis- og beredskapsdepartementet (JD) (2012a) *Intern rapport. Justis- og beredskapsdepartementets ansvar for samfunnssikkerhet og beredskap*. Oslo: Justis- og beredskapsdepartementet.

Justis- og beredskapsdepartementet (JD) (2012b) *Evaluering. Justisdepartementets håndtering av hendelsene 22. juli 2011. Intern rapport*. Oslo: Justis- og beredskapsdepartementet.

Katastrofmedicinska observatörsstudier (KAMEDO) (2012) *Bombattentatet i Oslo och skjutningarna på Utøya 2011*. Västerås: Socialstyrelsen.

Kuipers, S. and 't Hart, P. (2014) Accountability and crises. In M. Bovens, R. E. Goodin and T. Schillemans (eds), *The Oxford Handbook of Public Accountability*. Oxford: Oxford University Press, pp. 589–602.

Lango, P., Lægreid, P. and Rykkja, L. H. (2011) Organizing for internal security and safety in Norway. In G. Nota (ed.), *Risk Management Trends*. Rijeka: InTech, pp. 167–88.

Lereim, I., Prietz, R., Strand, M., Klinkenberg, E., Ellefsen, M., Misvær, G. and Jamtli, B. (2012) *Læring for bedre beredskap: helseinnsatsen etter terrorhendelsene 22. juli 2011*. Oslo: Helsedirektoratet.

NOU (2012) *14. Rapport fra 22. juli-kommisjonen*. Oslo: Statens forvaltningstjeneste. Informasjonsforvaltning.

Romzek, B. S. and Dubnick, M. J. (1987) Accountability in the public sector: lessons from the Challenger tragedy. *Public Administration Review*, 47(3): 227–38.

Schillemans, T. (2011) Does horizontal accountability work? Evaluating potential remedies for the accountability deficit of agencies. *Administration and Society*, 43(4): 387–416.

Simon, H. A., Thompson, V. A. and Smithburg, D. W. (1991) *Public Administration*. New Brunswick, NJ: Transaction.

Sønderland, O., Dahl, B. K., Eriksen, E., Frøyland, E., Krogstad, T. and Paulsen, Ø. S. (2012) *22. juli 2011: evaluering av politiets innsats*. Oslo: The Police, the Norwegian Directorate of the Police.

Stortinget (2011) *Innstilling fra Den særskilte komité om redegjørelse fra justisministeren og forsvarsministeren i Stortingets møte 10. november 2011 om angrepene 22. juli*. Oslo.

14
ACCOUNTABILITY RELATIONS IN UNSETTLED SITUATIONS

Administrative reforms and crises

Tom Christensen and Per Lægreid

Introduction

Accountability is often studied in stable situations where relationships between actors are rather clearly defined. In this chapter, however, we will examine multiple accountability relations in ambiguous and unsettled situations (Olsen 2013). In theoretical terms, we will argue for the need to go beyond instrumental perspectives in general or principal-agent models more specifically, and also adopt an institutional approach to understand how accountability plays out under such conditions. Rational top-down approaches have to be supplemented by approaches that take account of broader sociocultural processes, path-dependencies, symbols and contextual constraints. Conceptually, we follow the Utrecht school of accountability, with its focus on multiple accountability types (Bovens 2007). We ask who is accountable for what, to whom, when and why.

Empirically, we will address two different types of unsettled situations: administrative reform and crisis management, both of which typically handle 'wicked issues' characterized by complexity, uncertainty, ambiguity and transboundary challenges. Wicked issues require a holistic approach that goes beyond conventional linear vertical relationships and one that has the capacity to work across organizational boundaries (Clark and Stuart 1997). This implies a new style of accountability. We will analyze the ambiguous relationship between reform and accountability, as indicated by Dubnick's (2011) reformist paradox – namely, that reform may undermine rather than improve accountability relationships – and also look at how dealing with crises raises questions such as the role of different forums in handling post-crisis accountability, the strategies used by different actors and the outcomes of accountability processes.

Our research questions are accordingly:

- What characterizes accountability relationships in unsettled situations related to reforms and crisis management?
- How is accountability handled in circumstances that go beyond 'business as usual'?

We illustrate our analysis using the Norwegian welfare administration reform from 2005, as well as the crisis management related to the terrorist attack in 2011. The two examples display core characteristics of public accountability. They address matters of public concern and public interest where openness and transparency are key issues.

The main data on the Norwegian welfare reform are taken from interviews with the political and administrative leadership and some members of parliament (Byrkjeflot *et al.* 2014). Concerning crisis management, we use interviews with core political and administrative executives conducted by the inquiry commission (NOU 2012: 14). We also use public documents, such as governmental proposals to parliament, reports from public committees and from the inquiry commission, and the minutes of parliamentary sessions. Finally, we draw on secondary sources, such as research publications on the subject.

We will start by discussing different dimensions of accountability, going on to relate them to the specific challenges of accountability in unsettled situations by adding an institutional approach to instrumental considerations. Second, we will address the relationship between accountability, reform and crisis generally. Third, we will illustrate the relationship the accountability challenges in the two specific Norwegian cases. Fourth, we will discuss our results in relation to the broader issues of unsettled situations and 'wicked issues'. Finally, we will draw some conclusions.

Accountability

Schillemans (2013) emphasizes that a minimum definition of accountability should include answerability and adds that it is a relational concept and a layered process. The core factors in accountability relations are information, debate and consequences (Bovens 2007: 447; Reichersdorfer *et al.* 2013). In contrast to responsibility, which is about entrusting someone with a task, accountability is generally retrospective (Day and Klein 1987). A person or an organization is systematically held to account or has to answer for what happened. If they fail to carry out their tasks, they are accountable for the consequences.

Public organizations face the *problem of many eyes* or who subordinate actors are supposed to *account to* and which criteria should be used to judge them (Bovens 2007). The more complex and hybrid a public apparatus is, the more difficult judgment is. Public organizations also face the problem of *many hands* (Thompson 1980). Actors may potentially be held to account by a number of different forums, and there are different ways of categorizing who is accountable to whom (Romzek and Dubnick 1987; Bovens 2007; Willems and Van Dooren 2011).

Political accountability is built on a hierarchical chain of superior/subordinate relationships (i.e. voters delegate their sovereignty to elected bodies, who further delegate authority to the cabinet and the civil service, and the latter are then held accountable back up the chain). *Administrative accountability* is related to an administrative superior calling a subordinate to account for his or her performance of delegated duties (Sinclair 1995). Traditional administrative accountability has a process or procedure focus. *Managerial accountability* is a modern version of administrative accountability related to performance management, which monitors output and results according to agreed performance criteria (Askim *et al.* 2015).

Professional accountability denotes the importance of professionals or peer review. Different professions are constrained by professional codes of conduct – a system marked by deference to expertise (Mulgan 2000) and a reliance on the technical knowledge of experts (Romzek and Dubnick 1987). *Social accountability* pressurizes public organizations to account for their activities vis-à-vis the public at large, stakeholders or (civil) interest groups and users' organizations, via public reporting, public panels, information on the Internet or through the media (Malena *et al.* 2004). It is often connected with image-building, reputational management and externally oriented legitimacy (Maor 2010; Carpenter and Krause 2012; Wæraas and Byrkjeflot 2012).

Bovens *et al.* (2010) distinguish between mandatory *vertical accountability* and voluntary *horizontal accountability*. In the first instance, the forum has formal power over the actor, as in political, administrative and managerial accountability. In the second instance of horizontal accountability, the 'accountee' is not hierarchically superior to the 'accountor' (Schillemans 2011: 390). There is more room for choice and moral convictions about duty with no direct intervention from leaders, as in social and professional accountability based on informal and voluntary accountability relations.

Accountability has different purposes (Bovens *et al.* 2008) or functions (Willems and Van Dooren 2014), which may overlap in several ways (Aucoin and Heintzman 2000). Dubnick and Frederickson (2011) identify three different 'promises' that accountability mechanisms should fulfill: control, legitimacy and performance. Actors might be responsible for processes, procedures and compliance with rules or for finances, performance and outcomes (Behn 2001; Bovens *et al.* 2010).

Accountability in unsettled situations: a supplementary institutional approach

Characteristics of unsettled situations

Traditionally, accountability literature has been anchored in instrumental approaches, such as the principal-agent model (Bovens *et al.* 2014; Gailmard 2014). Typically, it has addressed routine and settled situations with clear goals, strong means-end knowledge and predetermined superior and subordinate actors in hierarchies where it is pretty clear who is accountable to whom and for what. Political, administrative and managerial accountability are primary. The information and reporting phase and the consequences and punishment phase of accountability are crucial. The degree of political salience is normally low, and decision-making is largely delegated to managers in semi-independent institutions. A logic of consequences and dyadic, monocentric relationships between certain leaders and subordinates – or in the principal-agent terminology, opportunistic agents and their principals interested in specific results – are at the forefront (March 1994; Knott and Hammond 2012).

In contrast, unsettled situations require us to address the complexity and dynamics of accountability relations using a supplementary institutional approach. In multilevel, transboundary and hybrid circumstances, accountability channels are normally multiple (Bovens *et al.* 2008). Goals and means are ambiguous, participation is more fluid, authority is more contested and experiences are less transparent (Olsen 2014). Accountability relations become more interpretive, interactive and reflexive in nature. Who is accountable to whom and for what is not stable, but is evolving and changing. Who is to blame does not necessarily depend on a strong causal understanding and hard evidence, but rather on ambiguous and contested interpretations by different actors and forums in different contexts, where myths or symbols may prevail (Meyer and Rowan 1977). Societal norms and expectations of appropriate behavior and approval from social constituencies are important (March and Olsen 1989). Motivation and control are more internal, based on traditional cultures and socialization into a professional ethic and public ethos, and actors and forums are supposed to behave in a more altruistic and integrative way (Selznick 1957).

Actors often face wicked issues that transcend different levels and policy areas and are characterized by uncertainty and ambiguity. In unfamiliar situations, new accountability relations are added to traditional ones, making them more complex and multidimensional. Formal and vertical accountability relationships are supplemented with informal and horizontal accountability relations in 'living' institutions. New accountability relations are added to old ones, creating complex layers and combinations of coexisting institutions (Romzek 2000; Streeck and Thelen 2005; Lægreid and Verhoest 2010; Olsen 2013).

In unsettled situations, the empirical evidence for a positive relationship between accountability, reform and crises is often inconclusive. There may be both agency drift and forum drift due to lack of motivation, time and energy, knowledge and capabilities (Schillemans and Busuioc 2014), and the balance between institutional autonomy and accountability is problematic. Rather than assuming predetermined principals and agents, there is a need to examine how accountability relations play out in relation to the way authority is actually organized, exercised and controlled (Olsen 2013). Public administration is involved in policy advice, interpretation, implementation and enforcement, and its relations to stakeholders are discretionary and multiple. This challenges traditional hierarchical and vertical accountability relations in which the hierarchical political leadership is supreme.

Summing up, a supplementary institutional approach delves more into broad sociocultural processes and informal norms and values (Selznick 1957; Meyer and Rowan 1977). Unsettled situations, such as reforms and crises, may be characterized by cultural path-dependency and manipulation of symbols, which makes accountability relationships more contested, complex, hybrid and ambiguous. We see competing instrumental and institutional logics in accountability processes.

Accountability and reform

The relationship between accountability and reform is still contested and we have to operate with a multidimensional accountability concept going beyond vertical accountability forms (Christensen and Lægreid 2015). This is especially clear in the ambiguous and unsettled situations that often characterize periods of reform (Olsen 2013, 2014). Many different accountability processes take place at the same time, involving a vast array of actors, information, discussions and consequences. Governments are continuously being called to account by several account-holders for their actions and decisions and within several different forums simultaneously (Willems and Van Dooren 2014). The driving forces behind this process may be attempts to engage in hierarchical structural design, negotiation processes, cultural path-dependency and compatibility concerns, or else reform myths and fashions/fads (March and Olsen 1983; Brunsson 1989).

Studying accountability in reform processes therefore requires us to analyze the complexity and dynamics of accountability relations and processes (Olsen 2013). By their very nature, reforms imply that the patterns of influence and accountability inherent in existing structures and cultures will be redefined, creating new dynamics. Rather than just asking whether government officials are more or less accountable after reforms, one should focus on what kind of accountability is perceived as appropriate (Romzek 2000). Reforms driven by ideology or wishful thinking rather than by evidence-based knowledge may produce unintended effects and make accountability relations difficult. Reform processes do not always happen as deliberate design and institutional engineering, but are often ambiguous and conflict-driven, producing accountability challenges.

Contemporary administrative reforms foster both change in basic government arrangements and new forms of accountability relations. One dimension is changes in vertical specialization and coordination, balancing the need for central political control with institutional and leadership autonomy (Egeberg 2012). Another is the structural changes in horizontal specialization and coordination, balancing the need for unambiguous roles with the need for coordination and a more holistic approach. Combining these two dimensions creates a continuum from integrated to fragmented, alluding, respectively, to post-NPM and NPM reforms, both of which added to and partly modified Old Public Administration features. Public reforms may also partly focus on cultural changes, trying to develop subcultures or changing cultures, for example NPM's focus on service cultures, or the more holistic cultures espoused by post-NPM reforms, but increased cultural complexity or hybridity are also evident in some reforms (Christensen and Lægreid 2007).

Under NPM, accountability came to rely to a greater extent on non-majoritarian semi-independent agencies populated by public officials who were neither directly elected nor managed by elected representatives. Leaders would often receive less information from and have less influence over subordinate institutions and leaders, but would still be accountable to parliament and the general public, with no change in the ministerial accountability principle (Brunsson 1989). Politicians have a strategic, goal-setting role, and civil servants are supposed to be autonomous managers held to account through contracts, performance arrangements, reporting and incentives (Barberis 1998). There is a built-in inconsistency in NPM. The reformers claim to empower customers, free managers and strengthen political control, but these three aims are difficult to achieve simultaneously, making accountability more ambiguous (Pollitt and Bouckaert 2011).

Over the past two decades, the NPM model has been challenged by post-NPM reform measures characterized by an increased focus on integration and coordination, as well as by a renewed emphasis on the rule of law and stronger central government capacity (Christensen and Lægreid 2007). Post-NPM reforms represent centralization but also seek to improve the horizontal coordination of governmental organizations and to enhance coordination between the government and other actors, alluding to New Public Governance and governance network (Osborne 2010; Lodge and Gill 2011; Klijn 2012; Klijn and Koppenjan 2016). The trend in the post-NPM reforms is apparently to bring political accountability to the fore once again, which may potentially influence the complex system of relationships between different types of accountability. Under post-NPM, politicians are guarantors of compromise deals between multiple stakeholders, while civil servants are more often network managers and partnership leaders. Post-NPM governance-inspired reforms have been more inter-organizationally and collaboratively oriented and have tried to enhance cross-sectoral collaboration strategies (Sørensen 2012). Post-NPM has supplemented and modified NPM, resulting in increased complexity and hybrid organizational forms, as well as new accountability challenges (Christensen and Lægreid 2007).

The effects of contemporary reforms on accountability are often inconclusive (Lægreid 2014). Emphasizing output and outcomes at the expense of inputs and procedures does not necessarily mean more or less accountability. Rather, it means that different accountability relationships should be addressed. Dubnick (2011) addresses this coupling between reforms and accountability by introducing the 'reformist paradox', in which efforts to improve accountability through reforms generate consequences that might alter or complicate existing forms of accountability. One may focus on what kind of accountability is related to different reforms and their dynamics (Romzek 2000). Accountability in a multifunctional public sector means being responsible for the achievement of multiple and often ambiguous objectives.

Accountability and crises

Societal crises always involve public organizations in one way or another, so their level of competence, preparedness, organization and trust are crucial (Christensen *et al.* 2013). Crises may be man-made or occur naturally, so that crisis management is likely to involve ex ante preparedness/prevention, handling the crisis itself and post-crisis accountability. How political and administrative leaders organize for crises ex ante is important, and concerns both the use and allocation of resources and how organizations deal with specialization and coordination both internally and vis-à-vis other organizations (Hutter and Power 2005). When a major crisis strikes that transcends organizational boundaries, leaders must define and interpret the crisis, paying attention to both the internal and external dimensions. This means deciding how to prioritize resources internally and how to communicate with stakeholders in the environment (Boin et al. 2005). Crises and external shocks may reveal weaknesses in public organizations, but are also challenging because the leadership must improvise and delegate to develop the necessary flexibility.

Post-crisis accountability processes tend to differ from accountability processes in settled situations because they are more political and strategic and often accompanied by different accountability management efforts (Kuipers and 't Hart 2014). Rational learning processes after crises are constrained by the symbols of blame avoidance, political survival strategies and exploitation, but also path-dependency factors. One important forum is the mass media, which report, monitor and judge the performance of the various public actors involved in the crisis, but formal forums such as regulatory bodies, audit offices, investigation commissions, judicial authorities and the parliament may also be activated. Actors often become involved in blame allocation by denying the problem, defending themselves or passing the buck (Hood 2014). But their actions can also be more ritualistic or symbolic in other ways. They may show solidarity and empathize, offer reassurance, apologize or simply be responsive. Indeed, actors are more likely to apologize, express regret, reframe, justify or defend their actions than simply allowing themselves to be called to account (Dubnick 2005; Olsen 2014).

While there is often a strong wish to learn from a crisis, dramatic crises may produce incremental rather than radical policy and structural changes, because of cultural path-dependency and resistance (Boin et al. 2008). Reputation management is often important in times of crises, because the system is exposed, but lack of cultural compatibility may hamper changes and reforms (Carpenter 2010; Maor 2010; Rhee and Kim 2012). Accountability might be more about political communication than about learning and improvement. Communication strategies may be either accommodating or defensive (Coombs 1998). Post-crisis accountability tends overall to be complex, ambiguous and uncertain, and to have a political flavor, where successful reputation management may mask the true nature of the crisis (Watson 2007).

Crisis management is often a response to typical wicked issues. Transboundary crises cannot be solved by any organization in isolation, but require cooperation, collaboration and coordination between organizations, ministerial areas and administrative levels. Their complexity, ambiguity and uncertainty often puts pressure on accountability relations. Crisis management involves various critical tasks such as accountability and learning (Boin et al. 2005; Boin and 't Hart 2012; 't Hart 2014). Recovery and aftermath politics is not only about addressing resilience and the capacity to return to 'normality' or to 'bounce back', but also about reviewing and learning from the event, which may differ between types of crisis and contexts. This reviewing/learning phase often involves accountability processes and blame games. A key challenge is to restore trust in governance capacity during and after crises. Accountability is a major challenge – one that implies looking back and requiring people and organizations to judge their performance, which limits the potential for change (Boin et al. 2008). Officeholders have to account to public forums for their actions prior to and during a crisis.

What are the potential similarities and differences between processes of reform and crisis management? First, both represent unsettled situations, and as such are likely to be complex, hybrid and ambiguous – all the more so in comprehensive reforms and major crises. Second, they both put political-administrative systems under strain and stress (i.e. the systems are open and exposed), leading actors to want either to change or to defend the status quo, depending on the pattern of influence. Third, reforms imply conscious efforts to bring about structural or cultural change, while crisis management has an element of system containment and reaction based on the existing organization, but also potential for change and organizational improvisation.

Accountability, reform and crisis in Norway

The welfare administration reform

Traditionally, Norway had a tripartite welfare administration system with tasks divided between the National Pension and Insurance Agency, the National Employment Service and the social services based at municipal level (Fimreite and Lægreid 2009). After a conflict-ridden process, the parliament approved the merger of the Pensions and Insurance Agency and the Employment Service into a single central Agency for Employment and Welfare (NAV) in 2005. The reform also introduced formal collaboration between the central NAV agency and the social administration in the municipalities. The NAV collaborative offices – situated in each of Norway's 428 municipalities – constitute a one-stop shop system where NAV services are integrated with local social services. This front-line office is organized as a central-local government partnership regulated by local agreements. The merger and partnership arrangements are typically post-NPM features designed to enhance vertical and horizontal coordination, but the reform also applies an NPM-related performance management system, meaning that overall, the reform is hybrid (Christensen *et al.* 2013).

The establishment of the one-stop shops and partnerships locally in the *welfare administrative reform* reallocated tasks and changed the division of labor through typical central hierarchical means. It established new, and changed existing, lines of control and authority. The main goals were consciously designed and controlled from the top. However, the reform also introduced some typical network elements. The partnership agreement alluded to an equal relationship between the state and the local authorities, representing a joining up at the base. The NAV reform also implied joining up at the top, through the establishment of the newly merged NAV agency under the Ministry of Labour. In 2008, new management and pension bodies were added at the regional level, moving tasks and resourses from the one-stop shops and representing a re-centralization and a re-specialization. Even though the horizontal integration between employment and pensions was challenging, it worked better than the vertical relationship between central and local government (Christensen *et al.* 2013).

The reform challenged the traditional vertical hierarchical elements of accountability. The balance between vertical political and administrative accountability, which worked in favor of the central agency after the reform, was blurred by enhanced efforts to introduce managerial accountability, which turned out to be difficult to implement. But horizontal accountability relations, such as social and professional accountability, were part of the equation too, making those relations ambiguous, multiple and complex. The way the coupling between formal accountability relations and actual accountability relations played out in practice was rather loose. And overall accountability relations were constrained by important contextual features such as the salience of the policy area and task-specific features reflecting cultural features (Byrkjeflot *et al.* 2014).

The terrorist attack

Two shocking terrorist attacks occurred in Norway on 22 July 2011. First, a car bomb destroyed several buildings in the central government complex in the capital, Oslo, including the office of the prime minister. Eight people were killed and nine seriously injured. Two hours later, 69 young people from the Labour Party's youth organization attending a summer camp on Utøya Island were shot and killed; 33 others were injured. Both attacks were carried out by an ethnic Norwegian citizen. One year later, his trial demonstrated that he had operated alone. The 22 July 2011 attacks dealt a terrible blow to Norway, which is generally regarded as a peaceful, open and robust democracy and has had limited experience of terrorism (Rykkja *et al.* 2011). They were quickly characterized as the most devastating in the country since the Second World War. Government structures for preventing and handling crises were put to a severe test.

Within the area of *internal security*, the 2011 terrorist attacks revealed a long-standing need for more focused attention, central leadership, authority and coordination. Providing the necessary powers in the form of adequate tools and sanctions to ensure control, follow-up and implementation, as well as rewards to ensure commitment, turned out to be crucial assets, although this was barely reflected in the official commission's report, which focused on a culture and leadership narrative (NOU 2012: 14). Even though no one was formally held accountable or punished, political and administrative leaders at a high strategic level fared better in the commission's evaluation and in the media than the police leading the actual crisis management did, reflecting a cleverer use of symbols. The parliamentary inquiry did not point to individuals or organizations as accountable, but vaguely blamed 'the authorities'.

Examining developments over time shows that the primary structures of crisis management still stand strong, even though the call for more and better coordination has been loud – especially after the terrorist attacks in 2011. In an incremental effort, the government tried to weaken the silo effect of the doctrine by building secondary structures through two complementary strategies (Christensen *et al.* 2015): first, by establishing collegial network arrangements for cross-boundary information sharing and discussion; and second, by introducing a lead agency approach. A general problem with network arrangements is that they largely involve part-time participants with a loyalty to their primary position. Furthermore, they often lack a clear mandate, appropriate resources, and authority and potent governance tools. Their meetings are often irregular and infrequent. The Ministry of Justice has gradually moved towards becoming a lead ministry in crisis management, making it a driving force in policy development and responsible for coordination.

Comparative discussion

The two cases portray some important similarities (Table 14.1). They are both examples of unsettled situations and governmental efforts to tackle wicked problems and solve central accountability problems in situations where the problem structure does not seem to fit the organizational structure.

Both the reform and the crisis situation represent a government system in transition with a lot of ambiguity and uncertainty. Organizational arrangements are hybrid and complex in various ways, which tends to produce multiple accountability challenges that tended to change over time.

The welfare administration reform tried to solve the tension between the two hierarchies (i.e. the principle of ministerial responsibility and local self-government) by introducing the one-stop shop at the local level and merging central agencies in order to increase both vertical and horizontal integration with a view to handling wicked transboundary issues, but it ran into complex accountability problems. Finding a close relationship between the goals of the reform, how the organizational arrangements work in practice and how accountability relations play out has been difficult.

Table 14.1 Accountability changes – reform, crisis and interpretations

	Reform	Crisis
Main similarities	Increasing complexity, hybridity, uncertainty and ambiguity. Multiple and dynamic accountability relations, including vertical and horizontal, mandatory and voluntary accountability. The problems of many hands and many eyes are obvious.	
Differences	Competing political accountability on national and local level. Administrative and managerial. Accountability challenging political accountability on central level. Learning by reorganizing.	Ambiguity and conflict in both vertical and horizontal accountability in central crisis prevention. Handling of crisis focused on managerial accountability and operational failures. Crisis aftermath characterized by attempts at blame avoidance. Incremental structural learning.
Instrumental-structural factors	Post-NPM features dominate, but NPM elements too.	Instrumental-operational challenges most important.
Institutional cultural and symbolic factors	Difficult to reconcile central and local cultures. Holistic central symbol. Partnership symbol on local level.	Main narrative is cultural interpretation. Incremental change. Democratic symbols used by central political leadership. Blame-avoidance symbols used by police.

The same applies to preparedness for crisis management, how crisis management pans out when a crisis actually occurs and how accountability relations are handled. Both before and after the crisis, the handling reflected conflicts and ambiguities related to vertical and horizontal accountability, initially highlighting competing political accountability relations, and later revealing a tension between political and administrative/managerial accountability. In general, when vertical accountability relations compete or have to be supplemented by horizontal arrangements, accountability becomes more multidimensional and challenging, and the relationships between formal and actual accountability become more ambiguous and uncertain in unsettled situations.

There are also important differences. The reform mainly highlighted conflicts between central and local political accountability as they played out locally in the partnerships, while the crisis played out more at the central level, but with critique about local action. The conflicts and ambiguities of accountability on the central level are definitely more vertical in the reform (ministry-agency) than in the crisis, where horizontal components are obvious (between ministries), especially in the prevention phase. Blame avoidance had a bigger role to play in the aftermath of the crisis than in the reform. And the reform was more of a 'big bang' reform, although eventually reorganized, while in the area of internal security and crisis management change has been rather incremental and cautious.

How can we interpret the reform and crisis, based, respectively, on instrumental and institutional approaches? First, both the reform and the crisis management had instrumental ambitions that turned out to be difficult to fulfill due to uncertainty and ambiguity. Second, the reform revealed the difficulties of reconciling central and local political-administrative cultures, while the main official narrative in the crisis was culture and leadership. Third, in the reform, a holistic symbol was used on the central level and a similar partnership symbol was used locally; in the crisis, the central political executives used democratic symbols while the police chiefs used blame-avoidance symbols.

The two cases have revealed that in unsettled situations, the 'wicked problems' being dealt with are typically multidimensional, poorly bounded, vaguely formulated and not easily broken down. This makes it difficult to evaluate the success of the relevant arrangements. New forms of cooperation pose new challenges with regard to accountability, and consequently the legitimacy of decision-making and institutions. Accountability relationships become increasingly complex and hybrid in situations where the government acquires a more horizontal and multilevel character, which was typical for the crisis management (Michels and Meijer 2008).

In transitional situations, the information, deliberation, discussion and debating phase of accountability is more relevant and important because the standards for accountable behavior are ambiguous, which was most typical for the crisis. Dialogue about behavior might be more important than formal reporting and information or imposing formal punishment based on defensive compliance. In complex and transitional reform periods or in unexpected and changing crisis situations, accountability standards are not clearly defined by stable external criteria, but have to be formulated in an endogenous process. Thus, an open and transparent debate about who is accountable for whom and for what is a core element in unsettled situations. Often one faces compound and composite arrangements in dynamic contexts (Bovens and Schillemans 2014), where there is a need to be sensitive to complex contextual constraints.

The discussion about accountability might also be turned from a demand to increase accountability, to one to reduce it or else a combined approach (Flinders 2014). In unsettled situations, the normal response is often to reduce the accountability gap by introducing new types of accountability. But one can also address this problem by trying to reduce accountability requirements. In crisis and reform processes that are complex, ambiguous and uncertain, unrealistically high demands are often made of accountability. In situations that are not easy or straightforward, unrealistically high expectations can easily lead to negative assessments of accountability (Willems and Van Dooren 2011). Adopting a strategy to explain fragmentation, complexity and ambiguity indicates that public accountability is also about the management of expectations in situations where these are multiple and conflicting (Romzek and Dubnick 1987; Dubnick 2011). In our cases, the expectations towards the reform and the crisis were jointly furthered by the political leadership, the professional leadership and the media, and the media turned eventually against the (lacking) effects of the reform and the poor handling of the crisis.

We have revealed that uncovering the links between comprehensive administrative reforms and major crises, on the one hand, and accountability, on the other, is more complex than it appears at first sight. The accountability obligations faced by public actors are multiple and varied, and often represent tensions and deficits (Mulgan 2014). In unsettled situations, accountability types are in flux and tend to become blurred. This supports the reformist paradox (Dubnick 2011), which states that efforts to improve accountability through reforms might alter, undermine or complicate existing forms of accountability (Flinders 2014).

We have shown how complex, dynamic and layered accountability forms emerge in two unsettled situations that are partly similar and partly different. Vertical accountability relations are supplemented by other accountability types, and accountability relations become more ambiguous, contested and loosely coupled. Reforms and crises may affect accountability relations but not in a straightforward way. Our argument is that in unsettled situations, different coexisting accountability arrangements unfold, producing rather complex and hybrid systems.

Conclusion

We have argued that in unsettled situations, one has to go beyond an instrumental approach to accountability and supplement it with an institutional approach. This makes the accountability discussion less elegant but hopefully more realistic. In unsettled transboundary situations, the context is dynamic and evolving. We have illustrated our argument by addressing two unsettled situations: administrative reform and crisis where it is not obvious who is accountable to whom, for what and why, and where the relationships between accountability reform and crisis are blurred.

The complex and hybrid welfare state reforms moved vertical accountability relations towards managerial accountability. Accountability for output and outcomes increased and accountability for process was reduced; there was also a rise in horizontal accountability. Our crisis case also reflected the more general pattern of complex accountability relations and inter-organizational activities that generate important challenges for accountability (Mulgan 2014). Shared responsibilities will tend to blur accountability relations. The different accountability mechanisms have to be treated as supplementary and complementary in a mixed political order that combines and blends different modes of governance (Olsen 2010). In unsettled situations, accountability faces ambiguous obligations that are both complex and conflicting in a context of dynamic change and evolving situations (Mulgan 2014). Difficult dilemmas need to be handled to which there are no easy answers.

We have revealed a multiple accountability regime in which the different accountability mechanisms do not substitute for each other (Schillemans 2008), but are overlapping and complementary (Scott 2000). In such cases, a new accountability regime with more layered accountability forms emerges. A key challenge is how to handle hybrid accountability relations embedded in partly competing institutional logics. It is often claimed that such different conceptions of accountability may undermine organizational effectiveness. But this might not always be the case (Schillemans and Bovens 2011). Multiple accountability may present an appropriate solution for an increasingly pluralistic system of governance. In unique and unsettled situations with a fluid, complex, flexible, semiautonomous and fragmented multilevel governance polity, one has to go beyond the traditional hierarchical models of political accountability (Flinders 2011). We have to rethink democratic accountability in ways that resonate with the new reality of transitional governance systems.

Reform processes as well as crises represent dynamic and unexpected situations. Often reform agents and crisis managers have limited power and also weak means-end knowledge. Thus, we need to study the dynamic relationships between reforms, crises and accountability, and how multiple and hybrid accountability relations interact and change over time. In other words, a multidimensional accountability approach is needed to handle accountability in a pluralistic political-administrative system.

The relationship between administrative reform, crises and accountability has highlighted the need for new accountability mechanisms to supplement formal vertical accountability relations. But it is also important to address the need to reduce new accountability measures by promoting reforms less concerned with blame avoidance, low trust and skepticism towards politics (Flinders 2014). A third focus might be the design of relevant accountability mechanisms and the conditions and contexts in which they will work well (Bovens and Schillemans 2014). Accountability design has not been a prominent feature of administrative reforms and crisis management, so a stronger focus on meaningful accountability design, and on what type of accountability to choose when, might be in order.

References

Askim, J., Christensen, T. and Lægreid, P. (2015) Accountability and performance management. The Norwegian hospital, welfare and immigration administration, *International Journal of Public Administration*, 38: 971–82.

Aucoin, P. and Heintzman, R. (2000) The dialectics of accountability for performance in public management reform. *International Review of Administrative Science*, 66(1): 45–55.
Barberis, P. (1998) The New Public Management and a new accountability. *Public Administration*, 76(3): 451–70.
Behn, R. (2001) *Rethinking Democratic Accountability*. Washington, DC: Brookings Institution Press.
Boin, A. and 't Hart, P. (2012) Aligning executive actions in times of adversity: the politics of crisis coordination. In M. Lodge and K. Wegrich (eds), *Executive Politics in Times of Crisis*. London: Palgrave Macmillan, pp. 179–96.
Boin, A., 't Hart, P., Stern, E. and Sundelius, B. (2005) *The Politics of Crisis Management*. Cambridge: Cambridge University Press.
Boin, A., McConnell, A. and 't Hart, P. (eds) (2008) *Governing After Crisis: The Politics of Investigation, Accountability and Learning*. Cambridge: Cambridge University Press.
Bovens, M. (2007) Analyzing and assessing public accountability: a conceptual framework. *European Law Journal*, 13(4): 837–68.
Bovens, M., Curtin, D. and 't Hart, P. (2010) *The Real World of EU Accountability*. Oxford: Oxford University Press.
Bovens, M., Goodin, N. R. E. and Schillemans, T. (2014) Public accountability. In M. Bovens, R. E. Goodin and T. Schillemans (eds), *The Oxford Handbook of Public Accountability*. Oxford: Oxford University Press, pp. 1–22.
Bovens, M. and Schillemans, T. (2014) Meaningful accountability. In M. Bovens, R. E. Goodin and T. Schillemans (eds), *The Oxford Handbook of Public Accountability*. Oxford: Oxford University Press, pp. 673–82.
Bovens, M., Schillemans, T. and 't Hart, P. (2008) Does public accountability work? An assessment tool. *Public Administration*, 86(1): 225–42.
Brunsson, N. (1989) *The Organization of Hypocrisy*. Chichester: Wiley.
Byrkjeflot, H., Christensen, T. and Lægreid, P. (2014) The many faces of accountability: comparing reforms in welfare, hospitals and immigration. *Scandinavian Political Studies*, 37(2): 171–97.
Carpenter, D. P. (2010) *Reputation and Power: Organizational Image and Pharmaceutical Regulation at FDA*. Princeton, NJ: Princeton University Press.
Carpenter, D. P. and Krause, G. A. (2012) Reputation and public administration. *Public Administration Review*, 12(1): 26–32.
Christensen, T., Fimreite, A. L. and Lægreid, P. (2013) Joined-up government for welfare administration reform. *Public Organization Review*, 36: 556–66.
Christensen, T. and Lægreid, P. (2007) The whole of government approach to public sector reform. *Public Administration Review*, 67: 1059–66.
Christensen, T. and Lægreid, P. (2015) Reputation management in times of crisis: how the police handled the terrorist attack in 2011. In A. Wæraas and M. Maor (eds), *Organizational Reputation in the Public Sector*. New York/London: Taylor & Francis.
Christensen, T., Lægreid, P. and Rykkja, L. H. (2015) The challenges of coordination in national security management: the case of the terrorist attack in Norway. *International Review of Administrative Sciences*, 81(2): 352–72.
Clarke, M. and Stewart, J. (1997) *Handling the Wicked Issues: A Challenge for Government*. Birmingham: INLOGOV.
Coombs, W. T. (1998) An analytical framework for crisis situations: better responses from a better understanding of the situation. *Journal of Public Relations Research*, 10(3): 177–92.
Day, P. and Klein, R. (1987) *Accountabilities: Five Public Services*. London/New York: Tavistock.
Dubnick, M. (2005) Accountability and the promise of performance: in search of the mechanisms. *Public Performance and Management Review*, 28(3): 376–417.
Dubnick, M. (2011) Move over Daniel: we need some 'accountability space'. *Administration and Society*, 43(6): 704–16.
Dubnick, M. J. and Frederickson, H. G. (2011) Introduction. In M.-J. Dubnick and H. G. Frederickson (eds), *Accountable Governance: Problems and Promises*. London: M. E. Sharpe, pp. xii–xxxii.
Egeberg, M. (2012) How bureaucratic structure matters: an organizational perspective. In B. G. Peters and J. Pierre (eds), *The Sage Handbook of Public Administration* (2nd edition). London: Sage, pp. 157–68.
Fimreite, A. L. and Lægreid, P. (2009) Reorganization of the welfare state administration: partnerships, networks and accountability. *Public Management Review*, 11(3): 281–97.

Flinders, M. (2011) Daring to be a Daniel: the pathology of politicized accountability in a monitory democracy. *Administration & Society*, 43(5): 1–25.
Flinders, M. (2014) The future and relevance of accountability studies. In M. Bovens, R. E. Goodin and T. Schillemans (eds), *The Oxford Handbook of Public Accountability*. Oxford: Oxford University Press, pp. 661–72.
Gailmard, S. (2014) Accountability and principal-agent theory. In M. Bovens, R. E. Goodin and T. Schillemans (eds), *The Oxford Handbook of Public Accountability*. Oxford: Oxford University Press, pp. 90–105.
't Hart, P. (2014) *Understanding Public Leadership*. London: Palgrave Macmillan.
Hood, C. (2014) Accountability and blame-avoidance. In M. Bovens, R. E. Goodin and T. Schillemans (eds), *The Oxford Handbook of Public Accountability*. Oxford: Oxford University Press, pp. 603–16.
Hutter, B. M. and Power, M. (eds) (2005) *Organizational Encounter with Risk*. Cambridge: Cambridge University Press.
Klijn, E. H. (2012) New Public Management and governance: a comparison. In D. Levi-Faur (ed.), *The Oxford Handbook of Governance*. Oxford: Oxford University Press, pp. 242–57.
Klijn, E. H. and Koppenjan, J. (2016) *Governance Networks in the Public Sector*. London: Routledge.
Knott, J. H. and Hammond, T. H. (2012) Formal theory and public administration. In B. G. Peters and J. Pierre (eds), *Handbook of Public Administration* (2nd edition). London: Sage.
Kuipers, S. and 't Hart, P. (2014) Accounting for crisis. In M. Bovens, R. E. Goodin and T. Schillemans (eds), *The Oxford Handbook of Public Accountability*. Oxford: Oxford University Press, pp. 589–602.
Lægreid, P. (2014) Accountability and New Public Management. In M. Bovens, R. E. Goodin and T. Schillemans (eds), *The Oxford Handbook of Public Accountability*. Oxford: Oxford University Press, pp. 324–38.
Lægreid, P. and Verhoest, K. (2010). *Governance of Public Sector Organizations: Proliferation, Autonomy and Performance*. London: Palgrave Macmillan.
Lodge, M. and Gill, D. (2011) Towards a new era of administrative reform? The myth of post-NPM in New Zealand. *Governance*, 24(1): 141–66.
Malena, C., Forster, R. and Singh, J. (2004) *Social Accountability: Social Development Papers no 40*. Washington, DC: World Bank.
Maor, M. (2010) Organizational reputation and jurisdictional claims: the case of the U.S. food and drug administration. *Governance*, 23(1): 133–59.
March, J. G. (1994) *A Primer in Decision Making*. New York: Free Press.
March, J. G. and Olsen, J. P. (1983) Organizing political life: what administrative reorganization tells us about government. *American Political Science Review*, 77: 281–97.
March, J. G. and Olsen, J. P. (1989) *Rediscovering Institutions: The Organizational Basis of Politics*. New York: Free Press.
Meyer, J. W. and Rowan, B. (1977) Institutionalized organizations: formal structure as myth and ceremony. *American Journal of Sociology*, 83(2): 340–63.
Michels, A. and Meijer, A. (2008) Safeguarding public accountability in horizontal government. *Public Management Review*, 10(2): 165–73.
Mulgan, R. (2000) Accountability: an ever-expanding concept? *Public Administration*, 78(3): 555–73.
Mulgan, R. (2014) Accountability deficits. In M. Bovens, R. E. Goodin and T. Schillemans (eds), *The Oxford Handbook of Public Accountability*. Oxford: Oxford University Press, pp. 545–59.
NOU (2012) *Rapport fra 22. juli kommisjonen* [Report from the 22 July Commission]. Oslo: Ministry of Justice.
Olsen, J. P. (2010) *Governing Through Institution Building: Institution Theory and Recent European Experiments in Democratic Organizations*. Oxford: Oxford University Press.
Olsen, J. P. (2013) The institutional basis of democratic accountability. *West European Politics*, 36(3): 447–73.
Olsen, J. P. (2014) Accountability and ambiguity. In M. Bovens, R. E. Goodin and T. Schillemans (eds), *The Oxford Handbook of Public Accountability*. Oxford: Oxford University Press, pp. 106–23.
Osborne, S. (ed.) (2010) *The New Public Governance: Emerging Perspectives on the Theory and Practice of Public Governance*. London: Routledge.
Pollitt, C. and Bouckaert, G. (2011) *Public Management Reform: A Comparative Analysis* (2nd edition). Oxford: Oxford University Press.
Reichersdorfer, J., Christensen, T. and Vrangbæk, K. (2013) Accountability of immigration administration: comparing crises in Norway, Denmark and Germany. *International Review of Administrative Sciences*, 79(2): 271–91.

Rhee, M. and Kim, T. (2012) After the collapse: a behavioral theory of reputation repair. In M. L. Barnett and T. G. Pollock (eds), *The Oxford Handbook of Corporate Reputation*. Oxford: Oxford University Press, pp. 446–65.

Romzek, B. (2000) Dynamics of public accountability in the era of reform. *International Review of Administrative Sciences*, 66(1): 21–44.

Romzek, B. S. and Dubnick, M. J. (1987) Accountability in the public sector: lessons from the Challenger tragedy. *Public Administration Review*, 47(3): 227–38.

Rykkja, L. H., Lægreid, P. and Fimreite, A. L. (2011) Attitudes towards anti-terror measures: the role of trust, political orientation and civil liberties support. *Critical Studies of Terrorism*, 4(2): 219–37.

Schillemans, T. (2008) Accountability in the shadow of hierarchy: the horizontal accountability of agencies. *Public Organization Review*, 8(2): 175–94.

Schillemans, T. (2011) Does horizontal accountability work? Evaluating potential remedies for the accountability deficit of agencies. *Administration and Society*, 43(4): 387–416.

Schillemans, T. (2013) *The Public Accountability Review*. Working Paper. Utrecht University School of Governance.

Schillemans, T. and Bovens, M. (2011) The challenge of multiple accountability: does redundancy lead to overload? In M. J. Dubnick and H. G. Frederickson (eds), *Accountable Governance: Problems and Promises*. London: M. E. Sharpe.

Schillemans, T. and Busuioc, M. (2014) Predicting public sector accountability: from agency drift to forum drift. *Journal of Public Administration Research and Theory*, 25: 191–215.

Scott, C. (2000) Accountability in the regulatory state. *Journal of Law and Society*, 76: 539–58.

Selznick, P. (1957) *Leadership in Administration*. New York: Harper & Row.

Sinclair, A. (1995) The chameleon of accountability: forms and discourses. *Accountability, Organizations and Society*, 20(2–3): 219–37.

Sørensen, E. (2012) Governance and innovation in the public sector. In D. Levi-Faur (ed.), *The Oxford Handbook on Governance*. Oxford: Oxford University Press, pp. 215–27.

Streeck, W. and Thelen, K. (2005) Introduction: institutional change in advanced political economies. In W. Streeck and K. Thelen (eds), *Beyond Continuity: Institutional Change in Advanced Political Economies*. Oxford: Oxford University Press, pp. 1–39.

Thompson, D. F. (1989) Moral responsibility of public officials: the problem of many hands. *American Political Science Review*, 74(4): 905–16.

Wæraas, A. and Byrkjeflot, H. (2012) Public sector organizations and reputation management: five problems. *International Public Management Journal*, 15(2): 186–206.

Watson, T. (2007) Reputation and ethical behavior in a crisis: predicting survival. *Journal of Communication Management*, 11(4): 317–84.

Willems, T. and Van Dooren, W. (2011) Lost in diffusion? How collaborative arrangements lead to an accountability paradox. *International Review of Administrative Sciences*, 77(3): 505–30.

Willems, T. and Van Dooren, W. (2014) Coming to terms with accountability: combining multiple forums and functions. *Public Management Review*, 14(7): 1011–36.

15
ACCOUNTABILITY IN TIMES OF AUSTERITY
Democratic and constitutional gains but learning loss?

Hanne Foss Hansen and Mads Bøge Kristiansen

Introduction

In the last decades, the quest for stronger accountability has been a driver of many public sector reforms (Lægreid 2014). Whereas public accountability research in many years was dominated by studies of accountability deficits (Bovens and Schillemans 2014), such deficits may thus not be the primary problem anymore (Bovens and Schillemans 2014; Mulgan 2014). Deficits may have been transformed into overloads as the increased focus on accountability has produced excessive costs, red tape and negative effects on other important public values, such as effectiveness, efficiency, trust and learning (Bovens and Schillemans 2014: 674). In the present context of austerity, accountability arrangements aimed at controlling public expenditure and securing efficient use of scarce resources become of special interest. This chapter analyzes how such accountability arrangements are changed in times of austerity and what the effects of the changes are.

The analysis concerns reforms of accountability arrangements aimed at controlling public expenditure and securing efficient use of resources in Danish central government. Like other countries, Denmark was hit by the 2008/2009 financial, economic and fiscal crisis. As a result hereof, the pressure on the public finances increased and public sector reforms have been launched. One kind of reform comprises changes in public sector systems for budgeting, spending controls and financial management. In 2012, a Budget Law for the public sector was approved, and in 2011 new requirements for financial management and accounting in central government were launched. Together, these initiatives resulted in a regime shift in the Danish budget and financial management system. Interesting questions are how this regime shift has changed accountability relations and whether the new regime works as intended. The empirical analysis investigates three research questions: (1) How do the Budget Law and the new requirements for financial management change accountability relations? (2) What are the effects of this? (3) Why do these effects occur? The analysis has focus on central government.

The analysis of the new regime is based on an analytical framework developed by Bovens *et al.* (2008) covering three different theoretical perspectives on public accountability – a democratic, a constitutional and a learning perspective. Each of these perspectives gives different answers to why public accountability is important, and when accountability regimes are effective. The empirical basis is documentary material and interviews with civil servants who have either designed or implemented the initiatives.

The chapter is structured in five sections. Section 2 looks into the accountability literature, deduces a theoretical analytical framework and outlines the research method. Section 3 presents the reform initiatives and holds the analysis of how accountability relations have changed. Section 4 discusses the effects hereof. Section 5 holds the conclusions and reflects on what can be learned from the analysis.

Theoretical, analytical framework and method

Accountability is an elusive concept. Originally, it was related to bookkeeping (Bovens 2005: 182, 2007: 448). Later it became a bureaucratic concept (Kearns 2003: 583). Today, the concept of accountability is often used in a very broad sense, making it difficult to maintain clear distinctions to concepts such as transparency, responsiveness, responsibility, answerability and liability (Bovens 2007: 449; Dubnick 2014: 26). As the broad conceptualization is inappropriate for analytical aims, it is proposed to define the concept more narrowly as a social relation:

> Accountability is a relationship between an actor and a forum, in which the actor has an obligation to explain and to justify his or her conduct, the forum can pose questions and pass judgment, and the actor may face consequences.
>
> *(Bovens 2007: 450)*

The analysis is based on this definition.

Accountability: overloads and deficits

Accountability conveys an image of transparency and trustworthiness (Bovens 2007: 448), which is why politicians, public employees, journalists and taxpayers support the need for more public accountability (Halachmi 2014: 560). Thus, it might seem like the more accountability, the better (Bovens *et al.* 2008: 225).

Historically, the accountability literature has focused on accountability deficits and the need for introducing accountability arrangements (Mulgan 2014). In recent years, it has, however, been argued that the benefits of adding new layers to the existing accountability requirements are small and add evermore red tape (Bovens *et al.* 2008: 228; Schillemans and Bovens 2011, Halachmi 2014). The result may be an accountability overload possibly to occur if an accountability regime is characterized by large opportunity and transaction costs (Halachmi 2014), a focus on short-term success, while disregarding future goals (Halachmi 2005), a discouragement of innovation (De Bruijn 2007), and a motivation to gaming and manipulation (Smith 1995). Thus, when arrangements to assure accountability become dysfunctional and end up undermining effectiveness and efficiency, *accountability paradoxes* appear (Halachmi 2014). In order to be able to discuss how to get a proper balance between accountability overload and deficit, criteria for assessing accountability systems are needed. In the following, such criteria are discussed.

Criteria for assessing accountability

Bovens *et al.* (2008) have developed an analytical framework for assessing accountability containing a range of criteria deduced on the basis of three different normative perspectives: a democratic, a constitutional and a learning perspective. Each of these perspectives gives different answers to questions such as why public accountability is important, and how we can determine whether public accountability systems are effective. In the following, the three perspectives are discussed. For each perspective, distinct criteria for assessing accountability practices are deduced and an integrated analytical framework is presented.

In the democratic perspective, the political-administrative system can be described as a range of principal-agent relationships. In the democratic chain of delegation, (1) the citizens can keep an eye on the politicians; (2) the politicians can keep an eye on the civil servants; and (3) civil servants can keep an eye on the front-line personnel (Vedung 2000: 104–6). The most important issue in the democratic perspective is whether the accountability arrangement increases the possibilities to control executive power, which is why accountability arrangements should provide democratically legitimized principals with correct, timely and relevant information about the behavior of their agents (Bovens et al. 2008: 233). Based on this perspective, the quality of the new accountability regime is related to its ability to consolidate and reaffirm the democratic chain of delegation.

In the constitutional perspective, the main concern is to prevent tyranny by rulers, elected leaders, or by the executive power. From the constitutional perspective, accountability systems should prevent or at least reveal and amend abuse of power and fight corruption (Bovens *et al.* 2008: 231–2). Accountability forums should therefore have enough investigative powers to reveal mismanagement, and their available sanctions should be strong enough to make potential offenders reconsider before acting (Bovens *et al.* 2008: 233). Based on this perspective, the quality of the new accountability regime will arise from a dynamic equilibrium between various powers and the organization of institutional countervailing powers (Bovens *et al.* 2008: 231).

In the learning perspective, accountability is seen as a tool to make and keep governments, agencies and civil servants effective in achieving their goals and more responsive to the needs of their stakeholders. In this perspective, the purpose of accountability is to induce the executive branch to learn (Bovens *et al.* 2008: 232). From the learning perspective, accountability systems motivate public authorities and civil servants to search for more intelligent ways of organizing their operations (Bovens *et al.* 2008: 232). On the basis of this perspective, the essential question is whether the new accountability regime offers the right information and incentives to officials and agencies to reconsider their actions. If the new accountability regime is to produce reflection and learning, it has to be focused on issues that matter to stakeholders at the same time as it has to be experienced as safe and non-threatening in order to minimize the risks of defensive, anti-learning actions (Bovens *et al.* 2008: 233).

In order to develop an *integrated analytical framework*, Bovens et al. (2008: 234) disaggregate the definition of accountability as a social relation (presented above) into its three components – (1) information provision (2) debate; and (3) consequences – and deduce evaluation criteria in relation to the three perspectives. Since the three perspectives do not point in the same direction, what is considered effective from one perspective may be assessed as the opposite from another (Bovens *et al.* 2008: 233). The integrated analytical framework forming the basis of the analysis of the new regime is presented in Table 15.1.

The integrated analytical framework of Bovens *et al.* (2008) is fruitful as a means to describe and conceptualize specific accountability arrangements seen through the lenses of the three perspectives, and this is how we will use it below.

Method

The analysis is based on documentary material such as ministerial circulars, reports and guidelines, and interviews with civil servants who have been designing and/or implementing the initiatives.

Table 15.1 Analytical framework for assessing accountability

Perspective Components	Democratic	Constitutional	Learning
Information provision	Democratic chain of delegation is informed about the conduct and consequences of executive actors.	Forum gains insight into whether agent's behavior is in accordance with laws, regulations and norms.	Information gathering and provision routines yield an accurate, timely and clear diagnosis of important performance dimensions.
Debate	Interaction concentrates on conformity of action with principal's preferences.	Interaction concentrates on conformity of actions with laws and norms.	Ongoing, substantial dialogue with clients and other stakeholders about performance feedback.
Consequences	Ability of democratic chain of delegation to modify the actor's policies and/or incentive structures.	Forum should be able to exercise credible 'deterrence' vis-à-vis the actor.	Sufficiently strong outside interests to make actors anticipate, yet sufficiently 'safe' culture of sanctioning to minimize defensive routines.

Source: Bovens et al. (2008: 238).

The analysis focuses on central government. Interviews were carried out in two rounds. From January to April 2013, interviews were carried out in 15 ministries. Five ministries are not represented in the study. Very small ministries without subordinate agencies, such as the Prime Minister's Office and the Ministry of Ecclesiastical Affairs, were not contacted. A few other ministries didn't reply to our request for an interview. Because most of the ministries chose to send more than one person, all in all 28 civil servants were interviewed. The group of informants includes a permanent secretary, several heads of divisions, a managing director in an agency, and heads of departments and employees in departments with responsibility for financial management, budgets and planning. An interview guide was developed on the basis of the analytical framework presented above, focusing especially on how the reform initiatives affected accountability relations and the potential consequences of the initiatives. Each interview lasted one hour to one hour and a half. A second round of interviews was carried out in August and September 2015. Interviews were done in three ministries to follow up on whether there had been changes after the initiatives had settled, so to speak.

The interviews were coded with point of departure in the theoretical framework, whereby it was possible to identify patterns in the empirical data. In the analysis, quotations are used in order to illustrate these patterns.

Accountability arrangements in times of austerity: changes in relations

This section holds the analysis. After a brief introduction to the Danish context, the initiatives taken are presented and it is shown how accountability relations have changed using the analytical framework introduced above. Hereafter follows the analyses of the effects, and the explanations hereof.

Accountability in central government

Several overall accountability mechanisms are built into central government in Denmark. One is ministerial responsibility, implying that ministers are accountable for their entire jurisdiction and possess the power to exercise control over the civil service, which similarly has a duty of obedience towards the minister (within the law). The parliament has mechanisms such as parliamentary committees and consultation arrangements to hold ministers accountable. Further, on the political dimension, it may adopt a motion of censure (mistillidsdagsorden), and on the judicial make a decision to hold an inquiry or initiate impeachment proceedings (rigsretssag) (Finansministeriet 2006: 26).

The portfolio principle emphasizes the autonomy of the minister relative to other ministries and establishes limits for coordination across ministerial fields. Coordination at government level takes place through government committees and cross-coordinating ministries. The Ministry of Finance has cross-coordinating competencies related to the budget, financial management, human resource management, etc. The Minister of Finance launches the government's budget proposal for the parliament and ministries have to obtain approval from the Ministry of Finance before in-year supplement appropriations due to new unfinanced policy initiatives (aktstykker) are presented for the Finance Committee in the parliament (Finansministeriet 2010: 18). The Ministry of Finance monitors the ministries' use of their appropriations, and at the end of the fiscal year ministries render an account (Jensen et al. 2008: 145). The Public Accounts Committee appointed by parliament (Statsrevisorerne) and the Auditor General's Office (Rigsrevisionen) take care of auditing.

Within ministries, ministers of course delegate authority to departments, agencies and public organizations. In this hierarchical chain of principals and agents, there are several accountability mechanisms such as performance contracts and budget and financial accountability arrangements.

Historically, the Ministry of Finance's budgetary procedure consisted of a detailed control demanding a lot of resources without giving much overview. In line with what later became discussed as New Public Management (NPM) reforms, a budget reform was launched in 1984–1985 with the purpose of fixing weaknesses such as inflexibility and a lack of incentives for efficient operation. Ministries and agencies were given increased autonomy and flexibility in budgetary affairs (Ginnerup et al. 2007: 3; Hansen 2011). If a ministry economized resources, it was rewarded through the carry-forward system. At the same time, decisions on expenditure policy were centralized, with the Ministry of Finance setting next year's overall limit for the state's expenditures, as well as expenditure limits for each individual ministry. Through a reporting system, the Ministry of Finance monitored in-year compliance and ministries were obliged to take action in order to prevent or repair overspending (Jensen and Nielsen 2010: 204).

The recent regime shift

In 2012, a Budget Law proposed by the Minister of Finance passed the parliament. The law came after a period where successive governments had experienced difficulties in controlling public expenditure and where the accession to the EU Fiscal Compact demanded a more responsible financial policy. The purpose of the law was to strengthen expenditure control and realize targets for financial and expenditure policy (Finansministeriet 2012). The law implies that the budget has to be in balance or surplus. In case of deviations, a correction mechanism is activated. Each year, in August, the Minister of Finance has to make up the structural balance for the following fiscal year. If the Minister of Finance's control indicates a fundamental deviation (>0.5% of GDP) of the balance requirement, a corrective action must be carried out (Finansministeriet 2012: 6).

Moreover, budget ceilings for central and local government were introduced. The ceilings include a rolling four-year period and must be approved by the parliament. The central government ceiling is split into two: one for operating expenses and one for non-cyclical income transfers (e.g. pensions, student grants/loans). These ceilings cover about 60 percent of total central government spending. In this study, we primarily look into the operational expenses. At the end of 2012, the Ministry of Finance presented *Government Circular on the Testing of the Provisions of the Budget Law in Central Government in 2013* (Retsinformation 2012a). It contained a new rule related to allocation of savings, in which it appears that a specific agency to spend savings must have approval from its parent ministry, and that net spending of savings must be neutral or negative in total for the minister's range of portfolio in the fiscal year. These rules are subsequently insisted on (Finansministeriet 2014: 35).

Related to the Budget Law, the Ministry of Finance launched a project called 'Sound Financial Management in Central Government' at the end of 2011 (Moderniseringsstyrelsen 2011). The purpose was to ensure that spending ceilings were being observed, as well as to increase opportunities for achieving a more efficient performance of tasks and prioritizing of resources (Finansministeriet 2012). Agencies and parent ministries should obtain exact knowledge of what they get out of the money being spent and of their effectiveness, and a more solid foundation for making spending forecasts (Regeringen 2012).

The first step toward the realization of these objectives was the introduction of *Guidance on Budgeting and Budget and Accounting Controls* from 22 December 2011. It contains three overall themes:

1. *A shared basis of figures and budget transparency*. Agencies have to feed a core budget into the shared financial system. This must reflect the agency's internal budget at an aggregated level. Thereby a basis for a permanent reporting frame for the expenditure control during the year is established.
2. *Periodizing*. The core budget and the forecast for spending throughout the year must be periodized in months or quarters depending on the type of appropriation and a risk assessment. This increases transparency, establishes a more precise basis for the budget and makes it possible to identify deviations between budget and spending.
3. Standard cadences for budget and accounting control focusing on explaining deviations and describing corrective action if relevant.

(Moderniseringsstyrelsen 2013)

As the aim of the new regime is to centralize and tighten expenditure control, it can be seen as a post-NPM reform aimed at increasing political accountability (Lægreid 2014: 333). Also, the new regime has changed accountability relations, as will be shown beneath.

Democratic perspective: changes

In the new regime, the democratic chain of delegation is clearly better informed about the conducts of executive actors at all levels. Budget targets and expenditure ceilings are clearly communicated and spending monitored and controlled in a range of processes before, during and immediately after the fiscal year. The principles of core budgets, periodized forecast and explanations of deviations provide a lot of information shared between the different levels of delegation. Accountability in the chain of delegation is strengthened and clarified by the approval of core budgets and forecasts, and not least in the ongoing spending control. The fact that reports have to be signed by the permanent secretary underlines the strengthening of accountability mechanisms.

As the amount of information, the level of detail in the information, the frequency of reporting and the opportunity for the forum to pose questions increases, the accountability arrangement becomes more comprehensive and parent ministries get instruments to ask questions to the agencies. Agencies have to report why there are deviations and why these have occurred. Moreover, the changes of the accountability arrangement change the role of the parent ministry and the interaction between parent ministry and agency:

> We (parent ministries) will have to play a much more active role, we now have to enter the engine room in each single agency, and with the new regime the agencies will have to present, what they are spending their money on, how much they have spent at this time of the year? They will to a higher degree be held accountable for their prognoses [. . .] In that sense we get a better impression of where and when they are spending money.

As argued above, the parent ministry must, in the spending reports, assess whether the ministry's final accounts are expected to exceed the appropriations for the fiscal year. Furthermore, the minister must find specific financing within the ministry if the prior spending control shows that the appropriations are likely to be exceeded. The result hereof is that the parent ministry must coordinate across the ministry's portfolio to ensure that the total net spending of savings in the ministry is either neutral or negative. If necessary, the parent ministry must reorder priorities in order to ensure that the net spending of savings is reduced to zero, before the result of the prior spending control is reported to the Ministry of Finance (Retsinformation 2012a). Thus, the demand for coordination and information within the minister's range of portfolio has increased, as parent ministries must allocate reduced spending in one part of the ministry to other parts. The parent ministry receives more information on spending developments and parent ministry and agencies debate these issues more often. This means that the parent ministry moves closer to the operations in their agencies:

> If an agency wants to make investments, then other agencies will have to spend less than budgeted corresponding to the amount of the investments. The result hereof is that the steering relations between parent ministries and agencies changes and become more intense, as we (parent ministries) have to be some kind of a bank manager.

Constitutional perspective: changes

In the constitutional perspective, the Ministry of Finance can be seen as balancing the power between the legislatures (the parliament approving the expenditure ceilings) and the executives (the ministries). The Ministry of Finance's power for controlling the executives has been enhanced with the new regime. Thus, from a constitutional perspective, accountability relations are also strengthened, as the information provided and the interaction between the forum (the Ministry of Finance) and actor (the ministries) increases. The interaction between forum and actor focuses on conformity of action with the expenditure ceilings and explanations of deviations: 'The Ministry of Finance has a very narrow focus on whether we are keeping the budgetary framework'.

The Minister of Finance's coordination responsibility is, moreover, strengthened, because expected reduced spending must be reported to the Ministry of Finance in the spending controls with the purpose of redistribution (Retsinformation 2012a).

With the Budget Law, the Ministry of Finance has got more leeway for sanctioning. If the Minister of Finance's spending control during the fiscal year shows indications of central government expenditure ceilings not being observed, counter-arrangements must be launched. If there is a risk of exceeding the central government expenditure ceiling, the Minister of Finance is obliged to carry out initiatives preventing this. In addition, the Minister of Finance must carry out a subsequent spending control after the end of the year. If the central government expenditure ceiling is exceeded, a reduction in its ceiling for the following year corresponding to the excess has to be implemented (Finansministeriet 2012: 8).

In addition to the Budget Law, the law on the Economic Council[1] and the Environmental Economic Council was changed in order to further strengthen the reliability of the expenditure ceilings (Retsinformation 2012b). With the amendment to the act, the Economic Council as an independent fiscal institution must assess whether the expenditure ceilings are aligned with fiscal objectives for the public finances (Finansministeriet 2012: 3). Thus, the Economic Council now has a more prominent role in the appraisal of fiscal and expenditure policies. In addition to this, it must assess whether the approved expenditure ceilings are being observed in the planning phase ex ante, as well as when the accounts are available ex post (Retsinformation 2012b). Hereby, the Economic Council has got extended capacity and competencies for holding the Ministry of Finance accountable in both the planning phase and throughout the fiscal year. The Ministry of Finance has an obligation to explain their actions, and the Economic Council can pose questions to the Ministry of Finance and pass judgment (e.g. see Det Økonomiske Råd 2013; Finansministeriet 2013). In short, the Economic Council receives competencies and capacity to guard the guardian.

Learning perspective: changes

From a learning perspective, it is important to yield an accurate, timely and clear diagnosis of important performance dimensions. Whether this happens with the Budget Law is not clear. The intention is that reporting routines should provide more detailed information related to the spending development. But information on ministries' performance is very limited as it has focus on whether or not expenditure ceilings are being observed. As argued above, the interaction between the agencies and their parent ministries and between the parent ministry and the Ministry of Finance increases, but it focuses on control rather than learning, and it focuses on observing the expenditure ceilings within a year, rather than on long-term organizational outcomes.

Whereas the learning potential related to the Budget Law seems to be limited, Project Sound Financial Management might yield an accurate, timely and clear diagnosis of important performance dimensions. The majority of the informants in the ministries argue they have gained further insight into the financial situation in the minister's range of portfolio, and that this insight is obtained in a timely manner:

> If we have to find out where in the organisation there is reduced spending [. . .] then we need a more precise oversight of our finances much earlier in the year. In that context this thing about periodizing the budget is after all very sensible.

Thus, it seems that Project Sound Financial Management might contribute towards generating learning in some ministries. The new requirements give a new set of interaction routines, leading to an ongoing dialogue related to the agencies' performance. The interaction is, however, related to a narrow focus on performance and primarily goes on within the ministries and between these and the Ministry of Finance. Clients and other stakeholders are not in focus.

Accountability arrangements in times of austerity: effects and explanations

Based on the three perspectives, we will now look into the effects of the new regime, and why they occur.

Democratic perspective: effects

Seen through the lenses of the democratic perspective, changes have taken place in relation to information provision as well as debate, and these changes have had consequences. In the new regime, information provision in the delegation chain has increased considerably and debate and interaction have been intensified. The effects are tightened accountability relations in the democratic chain of delegation from the parliament that approves the expenditure ceilings, to the responsible minister, who has to observe the ministry's expenditure ceiling, and to the agency director, who has to observe their budget frame. The demand for more central steering and increased coordination from the parent ministry leads, in several ministries, to giving a higher priority to corporate management. As a consequence of the increased amount of information and transparency in the budgets, forecasts and in the spending development, the parent ministry moves closer to their underlying agencies, and the information asymmetry between parent ministry and their agencies decreases:

> We have to approve core budgets, we have to approve revised forecasts and explanations of deviations. We are supposed to be re-allocating the opportunity of spending savings. We can't do that without being close to the operations in the agencies. So you can say that, seen from here (a parent ministry) it might be a positive thing, that we are more in touch with what is going on.

The new regime enhances focus on finances and financial management in the entire organization. Attention towards budgeting, periodizing, controlling, etc. reinforces the democratic chain of delegation according to financial management all the way from every single employee in an agency to the permanent secretary.

Constitutional perspective: effects

Seen through the lenses of the constitutional perspective, changes have also taken place in both information provision and debate, having several consequences. Both an existing (the Ministry of Finance) and a new forum (the Economic Council) gain insight into ministries' behavior. Interaction with the ministries concentrates on conformity to the Budget Law, and the Ministry of Finance is able to sanction the ministries. From the constitutional perspective, the effect of the new accountability regime is the introduction of countervailing powers. With the new accountability regime, the opportunities of the Ministry of Finance to observe the ministries have increased. The Ministry of Finance increases its insight into the ministries' and their agencies' economy and financial management:

> The consequences [...] is that you share data in a much more extensive way than before. That means – all other things being equal – that the Ministry of Finance gains a better insight into the priorities that normally have been the ministries' own responsibility. Time will show what they can actually use this for, but in principle they have gained a lot more insight and oversight of what is going on.

Thus, the Ministry of Finance has a stronger position as expenditure guardian, because the amount of information flowing to it is increased in frequency as well as in scale. This will presumably increase the Ministry of Finance's oversight of the ministries' operations and reduce the level of asymmetry. The Ministry of Finance's increased insight into the budgets, combined with economic sanctions, give incentives to keeping within the expenditure ceilings approved by the parliament. Economic sanctions are, however, rare and the informants emphasize instead the importance of the introduction of central government comparable key figures for the precision of spending forecast. The 'naming and shaming' that follows from the comparable key figures increases the incentive to hit the spending forecast, and today it is seen as inappropriate for budget managers not hitting the spending forecasts.

With the introduction of the Budget Law, a new powerful watchdog and a new accountability forum was, moreover, introduced in the central government budget system, as the Economic Council got a new role, extended capacity, competencies and opportunities to observe the Ministry of Finance and to hold them accountable. The new accountability arrangement, however, to some extent also restricts the Economic Council. Whereas it formerly could speak more freely, it is now obliged to have opinions on the budget ceilings proposed by the Ministry of Finance. The relationship between the two actors have become more complicated as they both run long-term economic forecasts but based on slightly different economic models with different assumptions. This situation has politicized the debate on expenditure policy.

Learning perspective: effects

Whereas the strengthening of the accountability relations in the new regime is very effective from a democratic and a constitutional perspective, the consequences and effects may be dysfunctional and create an accountability overload when seen through the lenses of the learning perspective. An example hereof is that net spending in total for ministries has to be either neutral or negative in the new regime. This is an appropriate requirement when seen from a democratic and a constitutional perspective, as agencies in central government have generated large savings in recent years. If ministries and agencies had the opportunity to spend their savings, it would be very difficult to ensure that the ceilings were being observed. The majority of the informants therefore argue that a lot of the elements in the Budget Law are reasonable when seen from a macro-political point of view focusing on controlling the expenditures. Despite this, it is argued that the changed arrangement for spending savings gives some incentives at the organizational level that might create dysfunctional behavior and effects.

Different kinds of dysfunctional effects are emphasized in the interviews. The first is a risk for establishing buffers in the budget with the intention of avoiding sanctions. The fear of exceeding the ceilings might thus lead to caution in spending at the beginning of the year. At the same time, it is expected that the new rules for savings give incentives for the agencies to spend their entire appropriation before the end of the year, whereas incentives for practicing cost-effectiveness vanish. At the end of the year, money might therefore be spent on initiatives, which are not strictly necessary. These behavioral changes are described in various ways in the interviews: as a kind of 'stop-go' management, and as 'intelligent petrol burning':[2]

> You have to be cautious at the beginning of the year, and then you can spend the appropriation later in the year, but then it is often too late [. . .]. There is a risk that it might be some kind of a stop-go management, which is not very appropriate.

> There is an element of this that is 'petrol burning' in some sense [. . .]. So you will do things that normally would not have been done. It might be that [these things] are not totally irrational – they might be fairly well-founded [. . .], but things that normally would not have been prioritised will pass.

Therefore, there is a risk that the central government ceiling at macro-level for operating expenses might be converted into a range of ceilings at the micro-level in which a security saving is made at the beginning of the year in respect to keeping to the budget. At the end of the year, 'petrol burning' might be the case, because there is no prospect of spending the funding after the end of the year.

The risk of 'petrol burning' might be illustrated through behavioral changes in central government agencies immediately following the more stringent procedures for expenditure savings in the autumn of 2012. Normally, the public purchase of goods is greater in the fourth quarter than in the rest of the year, because of ordinary cautious financial management. In the fourth quarter of 2012, the public purchase of goods was, however, exceptionally large, especially in central government. The Economic Council (Det Økonomiske Råd 2013: 133) see the rise in the purchase of goods in the fourth quarter of 2012 as a reaction to the announced more stringent procedures for expenditure savings in central government. The purchase of goods might be reasonable transactions that in any circumstances would have been carried out at some point, but there is a risk that more inappropriate transactions were also carried out. In relation to this, several informants pointed to a third dysfunctional effect, as increased control leads to a more short-term-oriented management. The main focus is on keeping to the budget framework within a year, and this leads to decreased flexibility in the spending.

In relation to Project Sound Financial Management, it was argued above that the interaction concerns a very narrow focus on performance. Although the dialogue is narrow, it might contribute to secure more systematic procedures and more reflections on the spending development. It is, however, still unclear for several informants whether the increased transparency results in learning and increased effectiveness and not solely in increased control.

Although the informants argue that several of the elements in the new regime are quite reasonable, at the same time they argue that it contains many unnecessary and too detailed requirements. The spending control is argued to be too comprehensive, too frequent, too focused on details and not sufficiently supported by IT systems:

> Sometimes we have had to explain why a small bill in an agency with a very big budget was received in March instead of April, so they (the Ministry of Finance) still need to figure out how detailed the explanations of deviations have to be.
>
> It is a hell of forms [. . .] It is a reporting hell in a very detailed way which does not serve any purposes.

Standardized procedures such as periodizing and the requirements for explanations of deviations lead to detailed regulation, but no learning. The proliferation of requirements gives a more voluminous accountability arrangement, whereby the resources spent on financial management increase. Enhanced transparency is undoubtedly achieved, but it is still unclear whether learning is achieved. From a learning perspective, Project Sound Financial Management contains appropriate initiatives, but in order to reduce the administrative burdens and make the accountability system more meaningful, an appropriate – or a more differentiated – level of requirements still needs to be found.

Effects overall

Table 15.2 provides an overview of the effects of the new regime according to the analytical framework suggested by Bovens *et al.* (2008: 238) and presented above in Table 15.1.

Conclusions

The aim of the analysis has been to investigate how recent changes of financial accountability systems in the form of the Budget Law and Project Sound Financial Management, implemented in a time of austerity, affect accountability relations in central government, what the potential effects hereof are, and why they occur.

The analysis has shown that, from a democratic perspective, the accountability regime has led to enforced accountability mechanisms, as the accountability relations throughout the democratic chain of delegation are strengthened, among other things, by an increased amount of information reported more frequently upwards, as well as the information being discussed more frequently between forums and actors. The increased transparency has reduced the

Table 15.2 Effects of the new regime as seen from the three perspectives on accountability

Perspective Components	Democratice	Constitutional	Learning
Information provision	Increased transparency in budgets, the use of resources and deviations from forecasts.	Increased transparency in expenditure policy.	Increased transparency in how the budget is spent, but narrowly related to short-term spending control.
Debate	Intensified debates between parent ministry and agencies/state institutions, etc.	Intensified debates between the Ministry of Finance and the ministries. The Economic Council as a new forum observing the Ministry of Finance and debating expenditure policy.	Interaction focuses on observing the expenditure ceilings within a year, rather than on learning and long-term organizational outcomes. Do not support dialogue with clients and other stakeholders about performance feedback.
Consequences	Financial and corporate management strengthened. Vertical coordination intensified.	Countervailing powers strengthened. Ministry of Finance has become a more powerful watchdog. Actors are disciplined due to the risk of being sanctioned and through ranking of precision in spending forecasts. The Economic Council guards the guardian.	Risk of dysfunctional effects such as petrol burning and stop-go practices. A risk of growing administrative burdens related to financial management.

information asymmetry between principals and agents and increased vertical coordination. Due to this, the attention towards financial management has increased from the bottom to the top in the democratic chain of delegation.

The accountability mechanisms have also been strengthened when seen from a constitutional perspective. The new accountability regime has introduced countervailing powers ensuring conformity of actions with laws and norms. The Economic Council observes the Ministry of Finance and the Ministry of Finance observes the ministries. The Ministry of Finance has gained a stronger position as expenditure guardian, as the amount of information flowing to it has increased. As a result hereof, the Ministry of Finance's oversight of the ministries' operations has increased, and the level of asymmetry decreased. Combined with economic sanctions and ranking of precision in spending forecast, this regime has strengthened the incentives to keep within the expenditure ceilings and to hit the spending forecasts. The strengthened accountability mechanisms seem to have increased the opportunity for meeting the macro-political targets and create credibility for the Danish economy, but they have also politicized the debate about expenditure policy.

From a learning perspective, the consequences of the new regime, with its centralized and standardized procedures for financial management, may, however, be questioned. There is a risk that the implementation of the accountability regime might create a range of dysfunctional effects such as buffers in the budget, 'stop-go' management and a risk of a lack of flexibility in spending the appropriation because a short-term perspective is adopted. Although some of the requirements in Project Sound Financial Management might contribute towards gaining increased learning and effectiveness, it is, however, argued that the new regime contains unnecessary and very detailed requirements that do not contribute to increased learning or the efficient use of resources.

Based on the analysis, there seems to be a difficult balance and a trade-off between democratic and constitutional accountability, on the one hand, and learning aims, on the other. The analysis shows that an accountability system that strengthens the accountability relation will be very effective for the budget compliance, but it might also have a range of dysfunctional side effects that potentially might weaken the operative economy locally in the agencies and ministries. It raises the question as to whether the same accountability system can satisfy several demands. Is it possible to find a balance between democratic and constitutional control and organizational learning, or do we have to design an accountability system with the point of departure in the main purpose, with the risks that it will crowd out other purposes?

Regardless of the answer to this question, the implication of the analysis is that it seems reasonable to periodically carry out assessments of the effects of accountability systems with an eye to whether they could be adjusted towards more appropriate designs, and whether dysfunctional effects could be avoided.

Notes

1 The Economic Council is an economic advisory body headed by a chairmanship consisting of four independent economists and served by a secretariat with approximately 30 employees. The other 25 members of the Council are representatives of labor and business, the Danish central bank and government organizations.

2 In Denmark, spending money on non-essential activities at the end of the year is in popular terms often referred to as 'petrol burning'. This is a reference to the 1970s before the budget reform in the mid-1980s, where Danish Defence in particular was said to burn off petrol in December to spend the entire budget and avoid cutbacks the following year.

References

Bovens, M. (2005) Public accountability. In E. Ferlie, L. E. Lynn Jr. and C. Pollitt (eds), *The Oxford Handbook of Public Management*. Oxford: Oxford University Press, pp. 182–208.

Bovens, M. (2007) Analysing and assessing accountability: a conceptual framework. *European Law Journal*, 13(4): 447–68.

Bovens, M. and Schillemans, T. (2014) Meaningful accountability. In M. Bovens, R. E. Goodin and T. Schillemans (eds), *The Oxford Handbook of Public Accountability*. Oxford: Oxford University Press, pp. 673–82.

Bovens, M., Schillemans, T. and 't Hart, P. (2008) Does public accountability work? An assessment tool. *Public Administration*, 86(1): 225–42.

De Bruijn, H. (2007) *Managing Performance in the Public Sector*. London/New York: Routledge.

Det Økonomiske Råd (2013) *Dansk Økonomi Efterår 2013* [Danish Economy Autumn 2013]. Albertslund: Rosendahls-Schultz Grafisk.

Dubnick, M. J. (2014) Accountability as a cultural keyword. In M. Bovens, R. E. Goodin and T. Schillemans (eds), *The Oxford Handbook of Public Accountability*. Oxford: Oxford University Press, pp. 23–38.

Finansministeriet (2006) *Centraladministrationens organisering – status og perspektiver* [Central Government Organization – Status and Perspectives]. Albertslund: Schultz Information.

Finansministeriet (2010) *Budgetvejledningen 2011* [Budget Instruction 2011]. Albertslund: Rosendal Schultz Information.

Finansministeriet (2012) *Handouts vedrørende budgetlov* [Handouts Concerning the Budget Law]. København: Finansministeriet.

Finansministeriet (2013) *Skriftligt indlæg til DØRs rapport Dansk økonomi – Efterår 2013 – Notat* [Written Contribution to the Economic Council's Report Danish Economy – Autumn 2013 – Memo]. København: Finansministeriet.

Finansministeriet (2014) *Budgetvejledningen 2014* [Budget Instruction 2014]. Albertslund: Rosendal Schultz Information.

Ginnerup, R., Jørgensen, T. B., Jacobsen, A. M. and Refslund, N. (2007) Performance budgeting in Denmark. *OECD Journal on Budgeting*, 7(4): 1–24.

Halachmi, A. (2005) Performance measurement: test the water before you dive. *International Review of Administrative Sciences*, 71(2): 255–66.

Halachmi, A. (2014) Accountability overloads. In M. Bovens, R. E. Goodin and T. Schillemans (eds), *The Oxford Handbook of Public Accountability*. Oxford: Oxford University Press, pp. 560–73.

Hansen, H. F. (2011) NPM in Scandinavia. In T. Christensen and P. Lægreid (eds), *New Public Management*. Farnham: Ashgate, pp. 113–29.

Jensen, L., Andersen, T. S. and Henneberg, S. (2008) Statens budget: Processer, rammer og aktører. In P. M. Christiansen (ed.), *Budgetlægning og offentlige udgifter*. Århus: Systime Academic, pp. 108–46.

Jensen, L. and Nielsen, D. F. (2010) Budget reform in Denmark. In J. Jensen, J. Wanna and J. D. Vries (ed.), *The Reality of Budgetary Reform in OECD Nations*. Cheltenham: Edward Elgar, pp. 193–220.

Kearns, K. P. (2003) Accountability in a seamless economy. In B. G. Peters and J. Pierre (eds), *Handbook of Public Administration*. London: Sage, pp. 581–90.

Lægreid, P. (2014) Accountability and the New Public Management. In M. Bovens, R. E. Goodin and T. Schillemans (eds), *The Oxford Handbook of Public Accountability*. Oxford: Oxford University Press, pp. 324–38.

Moderniseringsstyrelsen (2011) *Kom godt i gang med de nye krav til økonomistyring i 2012. Vejledning til Projekt god økonomistyring i den offentlige sektor* [Getting Well Under Way with the New Requirements for Financial Management in 2012. Gudiance to Project Sound Financial Management in the Public Sector]. København: Moderniseringsstyrelsen.

Moderniseringsstyrelsen (2013) *Vejledning om budgettering og budget- og regnskabsopfølgning* [Guidance on Budgeting and Budget and Accounting Controls]. København: Moderniseringsstyrelsen.

Mulgan, R. (2014) Accountability deficits. In M. Bovens, R. E. Goodin and T. Schillemans (eds), *The Oxford Handbook of Public Accountability*. Oxford: Oxford University Press, pp. 545–59.

Regeringen (2012) *Danmark i arbejde – udfordringer for dansk økonomi mod 2020* [Denmark in Employment – Challenges for the Danish Economy Towards 2020]. København: Finansministeriet.

Retsinformation (2012a) *Cirkulære om afprøvning af budgetlovens bestemmelser i staten i 2013* [Government Circular on the Testing of the Provisions of the Budget Law in Central Government in 2013]. CIR nr. 85 af 29/11/2012.

Retsinformation (2012b) *Lov om ændring af lov om Det Økonomiske Råd og Det Miljøøkonomiske Råd* [Act on the Changes of the Act on the Economic Council and the Environmental Economic Council]. 2011/1 LSV 167.

Schillemans, T. and Bovens, M. (2011) The challenge of multiple accountability: does redundancy lead to overload? In M. J. Dubnick and G. H. Frederickson (eds), *Accountable Governance: Problems and Promises*. New York: M. E. Sharpe, pp. 3–21.

Smith, P. (1995) On the unintended consequences of publishing performance data in the public sector. *International Journal of Public Administration*, 18(2/3): 277–310.

Vedung, E. (2000) *Public Policy and Program Evaluation*. New Brunswick, NJ: Transaction.

16

REGULATORY REFORM, ACCOUNTABILITY AND BLAME IN PUBLIC SERVICE DELIVERY

The public transport crisis in Berlin

Tobias Bach and Kai Wegrich

Introduction

Among the many promises of reforms of the 'regulatory state' type, the clarification of accountability relations features prominently. While not always using the language of accountability, a major argument against the state as direct provider of a range of public services was that accountability relations were unclear: state providers of services such as telecommunications and transport were hybrids between commercial enterprises and public service providers that were largely self-regulatory in terms of service provision and technical safety (Lodge and Wegrich 2012). The governance of such enterprises allowed political logics to trump economic rationales, and it was unclear in how far the management of these companies should follow either a political or a managerial logic, as they had to provide 'essential public services' in an economically efficient way.

The regulatory state solution to this problem of accountability, manifest in both quality and cost problems of these services, was a clear separation of roles, the introduction of market-driven incentives, and a clarification of distinct types of accountability: the provision of services had to be opened up for competition and the state had to change its role from a service provider to a regulator (Majone 1997). When social objectives of essential public services had to be met, the state needed to regulate prices, quality, service levels, etc. But such regulatory tasks were to be delegated to agencies insulated from the purview of fickle, myopic politicians (Majone 1997; Gilardi 2008); contracts with providers would be based on competitive tendering and franchising arrangements with a clear specification of service levels and quality.

This chapter explores the realities of accountability in the regulatory state, questioning the promises of clarification and 'purity' of accountability relations. Indeed, the case study presented in this chapter suggests that the regulatory state has resulted in a decline of political accountability for former state monopolies, accompanied by the establishment of multiple new types of accountability arrangements (Scott 2000; Lodge and Stirton 2010). These mechanisms may function according to their purpose under business-as-usual conditions, yet we consider crisis situations as a 'litmus test' for the effectiveness of accountability mechanisms in the regulatory state. This leads us to draw upon two literatures that look at similar phenomena from different perspectives, namely the literature on accountability relations (Bovens 2007) and the literature on blame-avoidance behavior (Hood 2011).

In empirical terms, the chapter first maps changes in accountability relations in the wake of the reform of the German federal railways in the mid-1990s. The chapter then uses the case of the Berlin public transport crisis of 2009 to illustrate how these multiple accountability relationships and blame avoidance incentives play out 'when things go wrong'. Finally, the relationship of accountability and blame avoidance as explanatory approaches is discussed.

Accountability in the regulatory state: role clarification, blame avoidance and blind spots

In this section, we first tease out key characteristics of accountability in the regulatory state, as opposed to accountability in the ideal-typical welfare state, which is characterized by the direct provision of public services by public sector organizations (Majone 1997; Scott 2000; Lodge and Stirton 2010). Then we move on to briefly sketch what is arguably the dominant analytical framework for mapping accountability mechanisms and their contribution to ensuring democratic governance (Bovens 2007). We contrast this approach with a blame-avoidance perspective that suggests that a given institutional architecture of public service delivery may also serve the purpose of minimizing blame directed to executive politicians in the case of policy failures (Weaver 1986; Hood 2011). The 'accountability lens' allows us to map the multiplication of accountability relationships in the regulatory state, which are characterized by a typical constellation of 'many eyes' and 'many hands'.

In contrast, the 'blame avoidance lens' allows us to study these institutional arrangements from the perspective of those held to account for their actions, both before and during crisis situations. Accountability and blame avoidance are characterized by complex relationships, which may either resemble a 'cat-and-mouse game between accountability-seekers and blame-avoiders' or may have a positive-sum relationship in which blame avoidance contributes to generating more rather than less accountability (Hood 2014: 605). More specifically, the blame avoidance perspective guides our attention to how institutional arrangements allow political actors and service providers to engage in effective blame avoidance in times of crisis, and to assess the effects thereof on holding the 'right one' accountable. Before turning to these perspectives, a brief overview of service delivery models of the positive and the regulatory state is in order (see also Table 16.1).

The transition from the positive to the regulatory state (Majone 1997) entailed a transformation of state-owned corporations in sectors such as railways, telecommunications and energy supply into multiple, functionally differentiated organizations. This involved the privatization of service delivery functions, as well as the liberalization of markets by breaking up former state monopolies, and hence allowing private companies to compete with the incumbent service provider (Lodge and Wegrich 2012). The rise of independent regulatory agencies is closely associated with this development, whose function is to safeguard the functioning of market mechanisms in liberalized sectors (Gilardi 2008). For instance, privatization and liberalization in the railway sector was followed by the regulation of safety issues, as well as the regulation of infrastructure access (Lodge 2002). Whereas safety regulation aims at preventing harmful business practices, the regulation of infrastructure has the objective to create the conditions for a properly functioning market through ensuring equal access to infrastructure between the incumbent and new service providers (Döhler 2011). Finally, the regulatory state also entails a stronger formalization of relationship between all actors within a given sector, which also implies a supposedly clear delineation of responsibilities ('Who is in charge of what?') (Lodge and Stirton 2010).

In comparison to the classical welfare state, the ideal-typical regulatory state is characterized by 'extended accountability' (Scott 2000) due to a multiplication of organizations being held to account, a multiplication of organizations calling to account, and a multiplication of the underlying values of accountability relations. According to a well-known definition, accountability is 'a relationship between an actor and a forum, in which the actor has an obligation to explain and to justify his or her conduct, the forum can pose questions and pass judgement, and the actor may face consequences' (Bovens 2007: 450). In that sense, accountability is a specific type of social relationship that might also be described by the notion of 'answerability' (Willems and Van Dooren 2011).

First, there is generally no single actor who single-handedly delivers public services in modern government. This has been labeled as the 'problem of many hands' (Thompson 1980): Who should be held to account, given the large number of actors involved in public service delivery? In a setting characterized by the provision of public services by functionally differentiated private and public organizations, the traditional notion of a hierarchical chain of delegation (and a reverse chain of accountability) between principals and agents loses its relevance to pinpoint clear responsibilities (Willems and Van Dooren 2011). This does not mean that accountability in the regulatory state evaporates, but rather that accountability is the result of a system of checks and balances (and hence inevitable tensions and conflicts) between functionally specialized actors (Scott 2000). However, such a system is likely to become dysfunctional if it is dominated or 'captured' by a particularly powerful firm. In the regulatory state, the incumbent service provider tends to be a strong candidate for capturing the regulatory institutions of a given sector.

Second, accountability in the regulatory state in particular is characterized by a multitude of accountability fora that each focus on different dimensions or dominant aspects of behavior (e.g. financial, procedural, legal). This phenomenon has been labeled 'the problem of many eyes' (Bovens 2007), emphasizing the redundancy of accountability relations. Again, such a system is characterized by a constant balancing of different criteria for assessing the delivery of public services. Here, the difficulty lies in assessing just how much redundancy is enough (Scott 2000). In other words, a balance needs to be struck between 'accountability overload' (Willems and Van Dooren 2011), on the one hand, and the potential risk of 'underlap' (Koop and Lodge 2014), in which a particular aspect of service delivery falls 'between the cracks' of the different accountors' spheres of responsibility. However, the assessment of the seriousness of such 'accountability deficits' or blind spots, which are inherent to any institutional design, ultimately is within the eye of the beholder (Mulgan 2014).

We contrast the 'accountability lens' with an alternative view that considers the design of regulatory regimes as being driven by the desire to minimize accountability in the presence of a widespread 'negativity bias' (Weaver 1986), more specifically the individual accountability of elected politicians for omissions in public service delivery (Hood 2011). This perspective underlines the importance of assigning blame or finding a scapegoat when holding actors accountable for crises or policy fiascos (Brändström and Kuipers 2003). That said, blame avoidance might also take place before a crisis event occurs, namely by way of 'institutional design'. Christopher Hood uses the term 'agency strategies' to describe stratagems 'to craft organograms that maximize the opportunities for blame-shifting, buck-passing, and risk transfer to others who can be placed in the front line of blame when things go wrong' (Hood 2011: 67). Two such strategies are particularly relevant for this chapter: the delegation of responsibility to other organizations that are meant to serve as 'lightning rods', such as executive or regulatory agencies, and the design of 'complex collaborative structures that are composed of several organizations or institutions, such that would-be-blamers cannot easily identify which one of a group of organizations is responsible for any given blame event' (Hood 2011: 81). Delegation strategies offer opportunities to deflect blame (and hence avoid being held accountable) to others, whereas partnership strategies are likely to result in buck-passing behavior and the near impossibility to pin down any single actor as responsible for omissions and failures.

To be sure, it might be debatable whether institutional design is *primarily* driven to avoid blame, and in consequence make accountability relations opaque. At the very least, this proposition is hard to prove empirically, despite its attractiveness as a parsimonious explanation for institutional design. However, the proposition has some validity in terms of the effects of institutional design on the attribution of credit and blame (Mortensen 2013). What can be safely assumed is that the institutional design of the regulatory state, which was meant to deliver accountability though a clear allocation of functional responsibilities, may well have unintended side effects that undermine this very objective by offering opportunities for the deployment of blame avoidance strategies. The blame avoidance perspective emphasizes that, after all, it might not be so easy to find a straightforward answer to the question 'Who is responsible?' in the case of a policy failure, despite a formal framework allocating clear responsibilities. The study of crisis situations seems to be well-suited to find out how formal mechanisms of accountability work in practice (Reichersdorfer *et al.* 2013), and whether they open up possibilities for blame avoidance behavior.

Table 16.1 summarizes and compares key characteristics of the ideal-typical positive and regulatory state models. Two points are noteworthy here. First, these are ideal types, hence the empirical reality may look rather different in several respects. As will be elaborated upon below, the railway policy in Germany remained somewhat undecided regarding the degree of 'marketization' aspired. The consequence of this hybridity has been a blurring of the lines of accountability in relation to railway services. Second, we suggest that each ideal type has distinct blind spots that make it vulnerable to particular types of failure, either in terms of biased decision-making (e.g. lack of incentives for user-friendliness in state-owned enterprises) or accountability (e.g. problem of many hands in the regulatory state). This resonates with the observation that all types of accountability relations have distinct deficits (Mulgan 2014). Also, some of the blind spots are more likely to become visible under business-as-usual conditions, whereas others will prevail when a crisis hits, resulting in distinct patterns of attribution of responsibility and blame avoidance.

The railway reform: purification of accountability?

The establishment of the Deutsche Bahn AG (DB) as a (state-owned) stock company in 1994 was the result of a decade-long process characterized by the search for a broad cross-party consensus that was required to achieve the constitutional change the reform entailed. While the details of the reform design were shaped during the final stages of the legislative process when key actors bargained over compromises, the broad direction of the reform was already agreed upon when a federal expert commission tasked with the development of a blueprint for reform was established in 1989. Since the mid-1980s, political support emerged for the introduction of more competition in the railway sector and the commercialization or privatization of the railway provider.

This consensus between the governing coalition in the *Bundestag* of the Christian Democrats and Liberals, on the one hand, and the Social Democrats in opposition, on the other hand,

Table 16.1 Blind spots of accountability and control in two ideal-type institutional models

	Positive state	Regulatory state
Key principles of institutional design with regard to accountability and control	• ministerial responsibility • democratic chain of delegation • integration of roles within same organization • example: safety regulation integrated into corporate structure of federal railways	• specification of roles • institutional separation • checks and balances, redundancy • example: creation of regulatory agencies for safety and infrastructure
Key control mechanisms	• hierarchy through political discretion over state owned enterprises • example: political intervention in operational details of federal railways; tariffs decided by politicians	• competition between service providers, supplemented by regulatory policies and enforcement • example: franchising of regional passenger transportation
Blind spots of institutional model	• lack of incentives for efficient policy choices • trade-off between economic and welfare concerns • example: debt problems of federal railways	• forum drift, lack of attention • regulatory capture by incumbent service provider • example: lenient supervision of incumbent service provider
Blind spots in times of crisis	• executive politicians over-accountable, bureaucracy under-accountable • low credibility of buck passing from executive politicians to service provider • hard delegation more likely to deflect blame from politicians, but blame boomerang to politicians in any case?	• many hands: difficulties to pin down responsibility • multiplication of blame games and blame diffusion

developed against the background of increasingly salient problems of the *Bundesbahn* (federal railways) as a railway operator directly managed by the government under the supervision of the transport ministry. The *Bundesbahn* was a state-owned company regulated by law. Any attempt to grant the federal railways more commercial autonomy was limited by the constitutional provision stipulating that the railway service had to be run as a federal administration (Art. 87 Basic Law). The company had to comply with budgetary rules and legislation governing public services (Lehmkuhl 1996: 72), including civil service laws. Moreover, the governing structures of the federal railways, in a characteristic German fashion, did not only entail direct control by the responsible ministry of transport, and more indirectly parliament, but also gave the state governments and the unions and industry a strong voice in the Administrative Council of the company.

Moreover, the legal framework, the *Bundesbahngesetz*, defined two contrasting governing principles that became increasingly difficult to align. According to the federal railway law, the federal railways should, on the one hand, be managed as an enterprise according to commercial principles, allowing a financing of its business activities by its own revenues. On the other hand, the railway provider was obliged to fulfill its 'public service obligations' (Lehmkuhl 1996: 72). As one observer stated, the state-owned enterprise was a 'foreign object' within the state but also in the economic sphere, which resulted in unclearly defined accountability relations that made it virtually impossible to hold anyone to account (Holst 1997: 87).

The limitations of this governance model became increasingly obvious from the 1970s. Two linked problems put the reform firmly on the political agenda. On the one hand, the railways lost shares of overall transport to road traffic, both in the area of passenger and freight transport. On the other hand, the federal railways were accumulating a rising debt, which was a burden for the federal budget and displayed the unsustainability of the existing railway regime. This development was a result of the spread of car ownership among Germans after the Second World War, but it was accompanied by a decline of the railways as a competitive means of transportation. The policy approach to support the railways at that time was to insulate them from competition, in particular in long-distance passenger services but also in freight transport. And while critics pointed at the privileged position of road transport when it comes to public investment and political support – claiming that the internalization of the real costs of road traffic would give the railways a competitive advantage – it became increasingly obvious that the shielding of the federal railways from competitive forces had problematic effects. In the mid-1980s, when the calls for reform became louder, the internal market reforms of the EC contributed to the development of a consensus towards liberalization of the market and commercialization, if not privatization, of the provider.

In short, when the government expert commission tasked with developing the reform blueprint started its work in 1989, the core ideas of the railway reform also implied a substantial overhaul of the sector's accountability model. The main pillars of the reform proposal were the regionalization of rail passenger transport to the state (*Länder*) level and a constitutional change in order to reorganize the federal railways. The transport minister then opted for an enterprise under private law as the preferred model for organizing the future railway provider. These institutional choices imply a 'hard' delegation of responsibility for regional railway transport to the states, although the actual services may still be provided by the publicly owned company. Moreover, the corporate status of the post-reform company implies a very limited role for the owner, the German state, in running the railway services (see below).

The reform was finally enacted in 1994, when the new stock company DB was created from the merger of the companies *Deutsche Bundesbahn* and *Deutsche Reichsbahn* (the former GDR railways). The new constitutional provision still stipulated that the majority of shares of the new company should remain under state ownership. A holding structure was developed that would allow for a vertical separation of operation and infrastructure within the company – which remains a contested issue until today. Moreover, the commercial service operation was separated from the supervisory and regulatory aspects, whereas the accumulated debt was transferred to a newly created fund.

While the details of the new railway regime will be presented in the following section, this section has highlighted the attempt to simplify – if not purify – accountability relations as an important corollary of the reform. While not necessarily couched in the language of accountability, the de-hybridization of the character of the railway operator, the preference for a private law model and the delegation of regulatory tasks to a new safety regulator are all indications of the influence of the regulatory state model on the reform. Although the reform process might have been dominated by domain-specific ideas and actors (Lodge 2002), the reform clearly has the mark of a regulatory state type of reform. However, unsolved conflicts with regard to the degree of privatization and competition resulted in a continuing state of hybridity.

Many eyes, many hands: the regulatory regime for railway services in Germany

In the following, we provide a brief overview of the regulatory regime for railway services in Germany. To recap, the rationale of the railway reform was to separate political, commercial and regulatory concerns in order to prevent political interference in commercial decisions, hence creating conditions for more efficient and competitive railway services (Benz 1997).

The DB was created in 1994 as a stock company, the so-called first stage of the railway reform. In 1999, the second stage of the reform was implemented, which involved the creation of five stock companies organized under a holding company. These are in charge of the railway network, regional passenger transport, long-distance passenger transport, railway stations and freight transport. As of today, several other stock companies are also part of DB AG, such as DB Schenker Logistics, which provides transportation and logistics services on a worldwide basis. In 2006, the government coalition agreed upon a partial flotation of transport services, though with a clear majority of shares remaining within public ownership for railway infrastructure. That said, there were no plans for abandoning public ownership, which must also be seen against the background of the constitutional guarantee of federal majority ownership of railways infrastructure (Lodge 2002). The flotation was planned for late October 2008, but it was canceled a few weeks earlier by the government against the background of the financial crisis.

The railway reform resulted in a formally much more autonomous railway provider. In spite of full public ownership, the federal government may only influence corporate decisions via its representatives in the supervisory board (as defined by corporate governance legislation applying to stock companies in general), as well as through regulating railway services by law. The federal government appoints three members to the supervisory board, whereas the remaining members are representatives of business, banking and employees. The supervisory board gives strategic guidance to the management board, which alone is in charge of taking operational decisions. Moreover, the management board has to report to the supervisory board on various issues, and the latter may also require the adjustment of corporate practices (Legel 2008).

As a result of the railway reform, the Federal Ministry of Transport has been weakened in the sense that it has much less direct levers of influence over the provision of railway services compared to the status quo ante (Legel 2008). Before the reform, the ministry had wide-ranging powers as regards pricing, budgeting and personnel, among others. The reform has clearly changed the (formal) levers of influence available to the ministry, which have become more indirect, for example through the granting of infrastructure subsidies.

The railway reform has resulted in a multiplication of organizations within the railway sector, each performing distinct functions, and a modification of the functions of existing institutions. The Federal Railway Authority (*Eisenbahn-Bundesamt*) was created in 1994 as a direct consequence of the formal privatization of the national railways. It is a higher federal authority under the sponsorship of the Federal Ministry of Transport, that is, the minister may instruct the agency on both general and operational matters. In terms of scope, the agency is in charge of regulating all railway undertakings under federal ownership, as well as those undertakings operating rolling stock or infrastructure, with the exception of regional railways. However, several state governments have delegated this function to the federal regulator.

The Federal Railway Authority is in charge of a broad range of safety matters (Benz 1997). Among others, it grants operating licenses to railway undertakings, issues safety certificates to railway undertakings (as part of the national transposition of EU legislation), enforces passenger rights and authorizes the construction of railway-related facilities (for example, railway stations, bridges, tunnels). Moreover, the agency authorizes rolling stock and railway infrastructure and has far-reaching powers in overseeing railway undertakings' compliance with various safety regulations (Benz 1997). Finally, the agency is also in charge of granting federal subsidies for infrastructure investments, which are part of the federal responsibility for infrastructure development (Lodge 2002). Moreover, it scrutinizes ex post whether the subsidies have been deployed correctly. However, this policy seems to create incentives for asset sweating: the federal railway undertakings have to cover the costs for the maintenance of railway infrastructure, whereas the federal government subsidizes investments or the replacement of obsolete infrastructure. As a consequence, there are few incentives to devote substantial resources into the maintenance of railway infrastructure (Mitusch 2015).

In addition to safety regulation, the transition from the positive to the regulatory state also entails the creation of a level playing field for all competitors, in particular with regard to access to infrastructure, such as railway lines and train stations. This type of 'regulation for competition' (Döhler 2011: 524) was delegated to the Federal Network Agency for Electricity, Gas, Telecommunications, Post and Railway (*Bundesnetzagentur*) in 2006, marking the transition of a sectoral regulator to a cross-sectoral regulatory agency. This also involved the creation of a so-called Rail Infrastructure Advisory Council, consisting of nine members of parliament and nine representatives of the state governments. The council has an advisory function as regards the agency's duties in the area of regulating access to railway infrastructure, though it also has the right to obtain information from the agency, which has the duty to provide all information that is being requested.

The Federal Network Agency generally operates under the sponsorship of the Ministry of Economic Affairs, yet for railway regulation it is supervised by the Ministry of Transport. However, the actual autonomy of the agency is generally considered as rather substantive, which is underlined by the legal provision that 'general directions' of the ministry to the agency have to be published in the government's official bulletin. The tasks of the agency include the monitoring of compliance with nondiscriminatory access regulations as to the allocation of train paths and the setting of usage charges for infrastructure. The public network providers have to inform the agency about specific types of decisions, and the agency has wide-ranging powers to investigate nondiscriminatory access both ex ante and ex post, and infrastructure providers are obliged to disclose information and support the agency in its investigations. The agency itself is obliged by law to report annually to the federal government on its activities in railway infrastructure access regulation.

Another key element of the railway reform was the delegation of authority regarding the financing and franchising of regional and local passenger transport services to the states (Lodge 2002). However, given the low profitability of these services, the states negotiated the payment of discretionary subsidies for the provision of regional and local transport services. Nevertheless, the regionalization component of the railway reform effectively delegates the responsibility for regional transport to the states, which increasingly use franchising schemes to ensure competition for subsidized services. The services may be provided by the incumbent service provider, or they may be provided by private competitors. As a matter of fact, an increasing proportion of regional railway services is provided by private railway undertakings, as opposed to long-distance passenger transportation, which is still largely dominated by the incumbent.

Finally, as part of its mandate to scrutinize public spending at the federal level, the Federal Court of Audit (*Bundesrechnungshof*) also investigates the infrastructure subsidies to railway undertakings that are administered by the Federal Railway Authority. In this context, the latter has repeatedly reclaimed subsidies paid to subsidiaries of the DB AG that had not been correctly deployed.

It should be obvious by now that the regulatory regime for railways in Germany displays many features of the regulatory state. Most obvious, several regulatory agencies have been created, and there is an increasing share of private competitors, especially in the provision of regional transport services. Also, the federal railways have been transformed into a profit-seeking enterprise with a hands-off relationship with its owner. However, while the provider company was commercialized, it continued to be an integrated company, and hence constitutes an organizational choice that limits the logic of marketization in the sector (given the central and powerful role of DB on the German railway market). Arguably, this hybrid character of the DB is at the core of the crisis episode described in the following section, both in terms of creating favorable conditions for the crisis, as well as in terms of the dynamics of blame attribution that unfolded during the crisis.

The public transport crisis in Berlin: accountability and blame in times of crisis

In this section, we turn to the public transport crisis in Berlin that unfolded since 2009, and involved repeated episodes of service disruption and incidentally complete breakdowns of the service provided by the rapid train operator (the S-Bahn). Since 2009, passengers had to cope with very low service quality, that is, lower frequencies, shorter and overcrowded cars, closure of some lines and so on. Early in 2009, 3,000 train runs were canceled and 5,000 delayed as a result of insufficient preparation for cold weather conditions. In May 2009, a train derailed because of a broken wheel, though luckily nobody was injured. This incident triggered intensified inspections and control by the safety regulator. The regulator identified cuts in maintenance activities by the S-Bahn as the main problem. Subsequently, the safety regulator repeatedly imposed measures to improve the safety of the rolling stock and also the S-Bahn's maintenance activities: wheels had to be replaced, trains had to be taken out of service and maintenance cycles shortened. In September 2009, this development culminated in an almost complete breakdown of the service for three weeks when the majority of the trains had to be taken out of service immediately because the safety regulator detected a defective brake. As a consequence of these repeated incidents, the safety regulator only extended the operation permit of the S-Bahn for one year, instead of the usual 15 years.

While the imminent crisis situation peaked in late summer 2009, and the situation subsequently improved, the following two years saw repeated incidents of reduced services, closure of lines and individual disruptions. Even the reduced timetable could not be delivered in summer 2010 and winter 2010/2011. The line 85 only returned to service after four years of complete closure in June 2013. Lower frequencies, overcrowded trains and unpredictable cancellation of trains became the new standard of the S-Bahn. It was only in August 2014 that the S-Bahn's CEO announced the end of the crisis.

The case is more than a colorful incident of a local public transport problem, since it is tightly interwoven with the politics of accountability in the German railway regime, with the DB as the key actor – and many would say the main culprit of the crisis. The S-Bahn GmbH (that is, limited company) operating the rapid train service is one of the two major commuter and local train services in the Berlin metropolitan region. It is a 100 percent subsidiary of DB (since 1995). It provides the service in the Berlin region on the basis of a purchaser-provider contract with the regional transport authority (VBB). The VBB coordinates the various local transport services in the region on behalf of the two *Länder* governments, Berlin and Brandenburg, which are the major stakeholders of the authority. Such contractual arrangements are common practice in Germany since the regionalization of the local passenger train service, which was a key element of the *Bahnreform* explored above.

The crisis episodes evolved within the framework of the contract running from 2003 to 2017. The contract, negotiated without public involvement or competition, granted the S-Bahn annual subsidies, which, for instance, amounted to €236 million in 2010, but was very limited concerning the specification of service quality or sanctions for cases of contract violation (capped at 5 percent of annual subsidies). Under the leadership of chairman Mehdorn, DB followed an aggressive strategy of cost-cutting and market expansion in order to prepare the company for the flotation that was still on the agenda in the early to mid-2000s. This strategy involved steep increases of profit targets for the S-Bahn Berlin, which amounted to €125.1 million for 2010, up from €9 million in 2005. To match these profit targets, the S-Bahn deployed a variant of the classic strategy of private monopolists with limited incentives to invest in the infrastructure (i.e. asset sweating) – personnel was reduced, maintenance facilities closed, costs were cut for material and maintenance cycles extended. The service disruptions between 2009 and 2013 can be seen as a lagged effect of cost-cutting measures introduced since the mid-2000s.

In terms of accountability, the federal government as the single shareholder of DB did not interfere with that strategy – which is partly an indicator of the managerial discretion of the DB leadership and partly due to shared interests between DB management and the federal government in light of the planned flotation. The Berlin government and the regional transport authority lacked the means to sanction the S-Bahn or influence its cost-cutting strategy under the conditions set by the service contract. Only at the peak of the crisis, when both the Berlin government, and in particular the responsible minister (called 'Senator' in the City State of Berlin), and DB were at the receiving end of a media firestorm, the Berlin government was in a position to renegotiate the contract. Using the threat of an early termination of the contract and the competitive tendering of the S-Bahn service as bargaining chips, the contract was amended to allow for scaled reductions of subsidies (down to zero) in cases of contract breach (i.e. reduced or low-quality services). During the crisis itself, the Berlin government reduced its subsidies to the S-Bahn, which, in addition, had to pay (limited) penalties and indemnified its customers through various compensation schemes.

In short, the accountability arrangement did not facilitate pre-crisis intervention and control, not least because there were two different accountability relations involved, namely the one between DB and federal government, and the one between the S-Bahn and the Berlin government/VBB. And while the latter accountability arrangement was toothless, the former was not engaged with local/regional issues. In other words, the multiplication of accountability relations – in combination with poor contract design – 'allowed' the DB management to pursue a questionable strategy of profit maximizing and asset sweating.

When it comes to the post-crisis accountability dynamics, similar effects of multiplication of accountability relations occurred. Our analysis of the media coverage of the crisis shows that the public blame for the service disruptions targeted the S-Bahn management, but also included the Berlin government (in particular, the responsible senator) and the DB management as owners of the S-Bahn. The media quickly identified the cost-cutting strategy of DB as the major cause of the crisis, and accused the Berlin government for long periods of inactivity and poor handling of both the crisis and the governance of the public transport sector. The federal government did only play a minor role in the media coverage, and was (explicitly) not seeking to get substantially involved. This indicates that the regionalization component of the reform indeed works as a blame-avoidance mechanism for the federal level.

However, while the blame towards the Berlin Senator had an effect and triggered various measures of crisis management and the recalibration of the contract with the S-Bahn, the DB could deflect blame effectively – at least concerning any personal responsibility of the leadership or substantial strategy adjustments. The DB management actively pursued blame-shifting strategies by using the S-Bahn management as a lightning rod – a report commissioned by a law firm squarely put the blame on the S-Bahn management, which was dismissed at the height of the crisis. And while the aggressive cost-cutting strategy could not be continued in light of the crisis and the looming competitive tendering of the S-Bahn service (which then was realized for parts of the rapid train network, with the S-Bahn being the most promising competitor), the DB management could evade any serious accountability measures.

Overall, the situation is characterized by diffused accountability that makes a clear-cut allocation of blame, and thus responsibility for 'doing something' problematic. The DB used the S-Bahn as a lightning rod to deflect blame for its cost-cutting strategy. The relation of the federal government with DB is not obvious to the wider public, and the former has no interest to put the DB into the spot of blame, since about €500 million are annually transferred to the federal budget from the DB profit. The Berlin government is formally responsible for its contractual relation with the S-Bahn and the lack of oversight, but has no influence on the DB business strategy. Since DB is a major employer in Berlin, and the relocation of the DB headquarters was a credible threat by the DB management earlier, the prime minister is said to be reluctant to follow a 'tough' approach towards the S-Bahn.

Discussion: accountability and blame in the regulatory state

Having presented the empirical case – the railway reform and the crisis episode from Berlin – we now turn to a discussion of the theoretical implications of our findings. First, the episode illustrated the multiplication of accountability relationships, which resulted from the railways reform, as well as the vulnerabilities of the new arrangements. In particular, the newly established administrative accountability to the safety regulator has proven to work effectively under the crisis. Also, in contrast to earlier observations of a rather lenient oversight of DB (Lodge 2002), the safety regulator pursued a stringent enforcement approach and showed no signs of being captured by the incumbent service provider. However, the case also exemplified a key weakness of the regulatory state, namely its dependence on the provision of (correct) information by different parts of the regulatory system (Scott 2000). This is exemplified by alleged 'communication problems' between the S-Bahn and the safety regulator over inspection intervals, but also by the demands for publication of the service contract of the S-Bahn by opposition politicians in Berlin.

Second, the episode illustrated different and partly contradicting dynamics of account-holding and blame avoidance. According to Hood (2011), this relationship relates to questions whether defensive strategies of presentational management have contributed to a sharpening of the policy debate and whether policy and operational responsibilities have been clarified (see also Kuipers and 't Hart 2014 on 'crisis induced accountability'). The crisis (and the blame games that surrounded it) sparked a controversial political debate about the future institutional architecture of the rapid train system in Berlin. Eventually, the Senat started a tender for parts of the S-Bahn services. In terms of clarification of policy and operational responsibilities, the crisis resulted in a renegotiation of the service contract with the S-Bahn, which now specifies service levels in much more detail. Also, both the previous and the current contract are now publicly accessible. This suggests that blame avoidance behavior has indeed contributed to a clarification of formal responsibilities.

Third, the crisis episode also illustrates important limitations of blame avoidance behavior. The delegation component of the reform – a 'tied hands' approach towards the operational management of DB, and the delegation of responsibility for regional transportation to the states – was effective in terms of deflecting blame from the federal government. However, although the crisis was primarily caused by the asset-sweating strategy of DB, much of the political blame was directed to the senator in charge of transportation. This suggests that major policy failures will almost inevitably be blamed on executive politicians, no matter how formal responsibility is allocated (Horn 1995). Indeed, dissatisfaction with the delegatee may well 'fire back' onto the delegator (Mortensen 2013). Citizens and the media are unlikely to accept excessive blame-shedding by politicians to the bureaucracy (or to the providers of public services, for that matter) (Mulgan 2014).

That said, our reading of the crisis is that the complex institutional arrangements of the rapid train services (and the institutional structure that resulted from the railway reform more generally) indeed dampened the blame firestorm towards the federal government and the DB management, despite the continuing strong influence of the DB management on its subsidiaries. The delegation of responsibility for local passenger transportation went hand in hand with the attribution of responsibility to the Berlin government for the crisis. However, the complex arrangements obviously have limited the level of blame directed to the latter, despite high overall levels of blame during the crisis.

Conclusion

The case study illustrates that the accountability relations that resulted from the railway reform in the 1990s were ineffective with respect to uncovering the role of the DB in causing the crisis. The multiplication of accountability relations actually created a gap in accountability, that is, DB could impose a cost-cutting strategy, but avoid responsibility for its negative effects (see above). However, the accountability regime was also effective in two respects, namely concerning the role of the safety regulator, which effectively intervened, and also concerning the role of the Berlin government, which had to correct its lenient approach to supervision and contract relations.

Also, the crisis episode shows that a reform that aimed at clarifying and separating commercial, political and regulatory issues, and hence delivering better accountability in the sense of the narrow definition of the term, has only partially fulfilled this objective. The objective of maximizing profits to make the partial flotation of the DB a success was pursued to the detriment of other legitimate concerns such as passenger safety and the provision of services in line with contractual agreements. The institutional arrangements in place before the crisis were insufficient to ensure that the interests of the state governments in healthy infrastructure and rolling stock were taken into account. That said, the state governments obviously could not perform their role as accountability fora vis-à-vis the S-Bahn very well, as the sanctions that could be imposed on the company were largely toothless, which became obvious when the contract was eventually publicized.

The S-Bahn case exhibits many peculiarities, in particular as regards the multilevel nature of the regulatory regime as a consequence of the regionalization component of the railways reform, as well as regards the specific infrastructural conditions, given that only the trains owned and operated by the S-Bahn can be used to provide services on the rail network. The regional governments are thus faced with a kind of 'double monopoly', and hence face a powerful incumbent they cannot easily get rid of without compromising the delivery of railway services altogether. Hence, getting formal accountability relationships right might be an important step to take, but is possibly only one element in ensuring effective regulatory governance for railways.

Acknowledgements

We would like to thank Marian Döhler, Martin Lodge, Per Lægreid and Tom Christensen for their helpful comments on earlier versions of this chapter.

References

Benz, A. (1997) Privatisierung und Regulierung der Bahn. In K. König and A. Benz (eds), *Privatisierung und staatliche Regulierung. Bahn, Post und Telekommunikation, Rundfunk*. Baden-Baden: Nomos, pp. 162–99.

Bovens, M. (2007) Analysing and assessing accountability: a conceptual framework. *European Law Journal*, 13(4): 447–68.

Brändström, A. and Kuipers, S. (2003) From 'normal incidents' to political crises: understanding the selective politicization of policy failures. *Government and Opposition*, 38(3): 279–305.

Döhler, M. (2011) Regulation. In M. Bevir (ed.), *The Sage Handbook of Governance*. London: Sage, pp. 518–34.

Gilardi, F. (2008) *Delegation in the Regulatory State: Independent Regulatory Agencies in Western Europe*. Cheltenham: Edward Elgar.

Holst, A. (1997) Privatisierung und Regulierung im Bereich Bahn. In K. König and A. Benz (eds), *Privatisierung und staatliche Regulierung. Bahn, Post und Telekommunikation, Rundfunk*. Baden-Baden: Nomos, pp. 83–92.

Hood, C. (2011) *The Blame Game: Spin, Bureaucracy, and Self-Preservation in Government*. Princeton, NJ: Princeton University Press.

Hood, C. (2014) Accountability and blame-avoidance. In M. Bovens, R. E. Goodin and T. Schillemans (eds), *The Oxford Handbook of Public Accountability*. Oxford: Oxford University Press, pp. 603–16.

Horn, M. J. (1995) *The Political Economy of Public Administration: Institutional Choice in the Public Sector*. Cambridge: Cambridge University Press.

Koop, C. and Lodge, M. (2014) Exploring the co-ordination of economic regulation. *Journal of European Public Policy*, 21(9): 1311–29.

Kuipers, S. and 't Hart, P. (2014) Accounting for crises. In M. Bovens, R. E. Goodin and T. Schillemans (eds), *The Oxford Handbook of Public Accountability*. Oxford: Oxford University Press, pp. 589–602.

Legel, A. (2008) *Veränderung der Steuerungsmechanismen bei der Privatisierung von öffentlichen Unternehmen: am Beispiel der Deutschen Bahn*. Berlin: WVB.

Lehmkuhl, D. (1996) Privatizing to keep it public? The reorganization of the German railways. In A. Benz and K. H. Goetz (eds), *A New German Public Sector? Reform, Adaption and Stability*. Aldershot: Dartmouth, pp. 71–92.

Lodge, M. (2002) The wrong type of regulation? Regulatory failure and the railways in Britain and Germany. *Journal of Public Policy*, 22(3): 271–97.

Lodge, M. and Stirton, L. (2010) Accountability in the regulatory state. In R. Baldwin, M. Cave and M. Lodge (eds), *The Oxford Handbook of Regulation*. Oxford: Oxford University Press, pp. 349–70.

Lodge, M. and Wegrich, K. (2012) *Managing Regulation: Regulatory Analysis, Politics and Policy*. Basingstoke: Palgrave Macmillan.

Majone, G. (1997) From the positive to the regulatory state: causes and consequences of changes in the mode of governance. *Journal of Public Policy*, 17: 139–67.

Mitusch, K. (2015) *Infrastrukturfinanzierung im Eisenbahnsektor*. Available at: www.forschungsinformations system.de/servlet/is/299303/?clsId0=276639 (accessed 6 October 2015).

Mortensen, P. B. (2013) Public sector reform and blame avoidance effects. *Journal of Public Policy*, 33(2): 229–53.

Mulgan, R. (2014) Accountability deficits. In M. Bovens, R. E. Goodin and T. Schillemans (eds), *The Oxford Handbook of Public Accountability*. Oxford: Oxford University Press, pp. 545–59.

Reichersdorfer, J., Christensen, T. and Vrangbæk, K. (2013) Accountability of immigration administration: comparing crises in Norway, Denmark and Germany. *International Review of Administrative Sciences*, 79(2): 271–91.

Scott, C. (2000) Accountability in the regulatory state. *Journal of Law and Society*, 27: 38–60.

Thompson, D. F. (1980) Moral responsibility of public officials: the problem of many hands. *American Political Science Review*, 74(4): 905–16.

Weaver, R. K. (1986) The politics of blame avoidance. *Journal of Public Policy*, 6(4): 371–98.

Willems, T. and Van Dooren, W. (2011) Lost in diffusion? How collaborative arrangements lead to an accountability paradox. *International Review of Administrative Sciences*, 77(3): 505–30.

PART IV

Accountability, administrative reforms and multilevel governance

17

PRINCIPLES MEET PRACTICALITIES

Challenges of accountability reform in the British civil service

Thomas Elston

Introduction

How should public servants be held to account for the delivery of government programs? Are politicians to be responsible for all aspects of public service provision, no matter their level of direct personal involvement? Or should unelected civil servants 'take the wrap' when things go wrong on the front line? These are complex questions that can be answered in a variety of ways, reflecting different value positions, cultures and administrative traditions. What is striking, therefore, about the organizational and management reforms undertaken by many governments since the 1980s is their demonstration of a growing belief that officials should indeed be more directly accountable for the delivery of public services. How this is achieved, of course, varies between countries, but the idea that bureaucratic performance should be subject to greater scrutiny, with civil servants facing meaningful consequences for success or failure, has found widespread favor.

In the British civil service, such reforms are often discussed in terms of the 'accountable management' principle (Brown and Steel 1979; Gray and Jenkins 1986, 1993; Humphrey *et al.* 1993). This involves delegating downwards within the organizational hierarchy both the authority and the accountability for making decisions, in the hope of enabling and incentivizing better performance. In other words, individual accountability is accompanied by personal empowerment. The idea originated in the automotive industry in the 1920s, was suggested for government in the late 1960s, and was pursued in a series of reforms after 1980 (Flynn *et al.* 1988). To date, scholars have debated the merits and risks of adopting accountable management in government (Gray and Jenkins 1993; Humphrey *et al.* 1993), explored the challenges of designing civil service institutions to meet its requirements (Brown and Steel 1979; Flynn *et al.* 1988; Gray *et al.* 1991), and scrutinized cases where the logic fell down in practice, generally because of political maneuvering and blame games (Barker 1998; Harlow 1999; Polidano 1999). Building on this work, and prompted by the time that has lapsed since the major accountable management reforms began, the current chapter asks a further question: Once established, how easy is it to sustain this joint delegation of authority and accountability in government?

Empirically, the focus is on the most significant of the accountable management reforms pursued in Britain: the creation of some 130 semiautonomous public service agencies during the 'Next Steps' agencification program of 1988–1997 (Gains 2003; James 2003; Elston 2013a, 2014). Drawing on interviews with more than 50 civil servants in the justice policy sector, the chapter considers what forces preserved or undermined accountable management in the long run, and whether practicalities are an inevitable constraint on principles when designing civil service accountability regimes.

The first section defines accountable management more fully, identifies its major challenges of organizational design, and considers how the arm's-length agency model might overcome these. The second section is empirical, charting the gradual decline of agencies in the UK through de-specialization, re-centralization and the re-emergence of hierarchical (rather than contract-like) control by ministries. The third and fourth sections consider what political and administrative factors prompted this weakening in the architecture of accountable management, and what lessons can be learnt more generally about efforts to rebalance political and bureaucratic accountability for public services.

Accountable management and agencification

Accountable management

Accountable management involves 'the delegation to managers of the responsibility for specific resources and the accountability for their use in the pursuit of designated objectives' (Gray and Jenkins 1986: 181). This implies two key assumptions about how organizations should be run. The first is that practical (not strategic) decisions are best made at lower levels of the hierarchy by those with fullest knowledge of the issues at hand, the immediate consequences of alternative courses of action, and the trade-offs between them. The second is that, as a matter of principle and incentive for good performance, the individuals who make these decisions should be those held accountable for whether or not they are proven effective. In part, this reflects a line of reasoning in Western philosophy dating back to Aristotle, who considered voluntariness a precondition for holding an agent responsible for a given action and its consequences (Cooper 2013), yet it contravenes the traditional view that ministers should be responsible for all activities within their ministry, no matter their direct personal involvement.

Each of these assumptions appears logical, but neither is straightforward. Decentralization may well improve the quality of individual decisions (Lindblom 1965), but centralization is often better for overall coordination (Downs 1966). Likewise, although many would agree that it is both nonsensical and counterproductive to blame an individual for an outcome outside of their control, deciding whether ignorance or non-involvement is excusable or a sign of incompetence remains a matter of judgment. Furthermore, as Gray and Jenkins (1986: 182) note, to adopt accountable management in government is to relocate some 'responsibility, answerability (and culpability) away from ministers towards officials'. In democracies, where the legitimacy of state-funded and/or coercive activity depends upon its patronage by elected representatives of the citizenry, it is unclear at what point empowering unelected officials undermines this basic standard.

Alongside these questions of principle, there are also many practical concerns about the feasibility of accountable management in government – and it is these issues of implementation that are the focus hereafter. Four main challenges for organizational design are: objective-setting, delegation, audit and accountability. Each is discussed below.

1 *Objective-setting.* First, if managers are to be responsible for using resources to achieve objectives, as accountable management requires, those objectives must first be agreed. Unfortunately, goals are notoriously difficult to specify in government (see Rainey and Jung 2015), where the measure of profitability is unavailable, the definition of public value often contested or transient, and due process, equality and democracy as important as – but possibly at odds with – substantive policy outcomes. As Wildavsky (1987: 215) remarked: 'To know whether objectives are being achieved, one must first know what they are supposed to be. Yet, the assumption that objectives are known, clear, and consistent is at variance with all experience'. This makes the first step toward accountable management deceptively complex.

2 *Delegation.* Once objectives are set, managers should have sufficient authority to act as they see fit in pursuit of those objectives. Unlike traditional large-scale bureaucracies, where flexibility and personal culpability are sacrificed for tight financial control from the center, such delegation should result in 'unified responsibility for activities and resources' (Gray and Jenkins 1986: 182). But in what areas should decision-making be delegated, and to what extent (Verhoest *et al.* 2004)? How much coordination and control should be sacrificed in favor of delegation? And how willing are politicians to cede authority to subordinates if they should remain answerable – in law or by convention – to legislatures and citizens for decisions that affect public sector performance (Brown and Steel 1979: 305)? There are no easy answers to these questions, making delegation a particularly challenging requirement of accountable management.

3 *Audit.* If objectives have been set and some delegation of authority agreed, accountable management next requires that ministers monitor the performance of officials to determine whether objectives have been met. The issue to overcome here is the information asymmetry between the principal and the agent, and the consequent risk of opportunism (Williamson 1985). Experts have long puzzled over how best to monitor administrative activities performed at arm's length (van Thiel and Yesilkagit 2011). No one solution has proven infallible, and dilemmas and trade-offs are common.

4 *Accountability.* Finally, once performance is determined, agents should be held accountable for their role in producing the observed outcome. A popular definition of accountability is of 'a relationship between an actor and a forum, in which the actor has an obligation to explain and to justify his or her conduct, the forum can pose questions and pass judgement, and the actor may face consequences' (Bovens 2007: 450). Hence, 'the allocation of praise and blame, reward and sanction . . . [are] the hallmarks of accountability in action' (Gray and Jenkins 1993: 55). Practical difficulties here include determining the extent to which specific decisions are responsible for an outcome, and precisely who made those decisions in the first place. There is also the issue of facilitating reward or sanction, which is complicated by the traditional emphasis on equality and meritocracy in public employment to prevent corruption and nepotism (Brown and Steel 1979: 299). Finally, incentives for politicians to claim credit for high performance and deflect blame for mistakes might interfere with the fair allocation of rewards and sanctions (Hood 2011).

Together, these practical challenges – objective-setting, delegation, audit and accountability – create a sizable barrier to realizing the principle of accountable management in government. This is evident from the doctrine's long-drawn-out implementation in the British case, discussed below. Yet, in the late twentieth century, a public management reform emerged that appeared to answer all four challenges simultaneously. This was 'agencification'.

Agencification

The splitting up of large, multipurpose bureaucracies into smaller, task-specific agencies – so-called 'agencification' – was a major trend in many OECD countries and some developing states during the 1980s and 1990s (Thatcher and Sweet 2002; Pollitt *et al.* 2004). Often, arm's-length public agencies were already part of the administrative landscape (Thynne and Wettenhall 2004; Flinders 2008), but this period saw considerable growth in their number and policy reach, as well as emerging consensus on how they should be run. As Pollitt *et al.* (2004: 42) explain:

> The ideal-type model for modern agencies is: where an organization has been clearly and probably formally separated from any other public organization; where it has some degree of discretion over internal rule setting (e.g. over personnel, finance and other arrangements); and where it is subjected to some sort of contractual or quasi-contractual arrangements including reporting of its performance.

In practice, these three characteristics are continua rather than absolutes. Agencies can be more or less detached, can have greater or lesser autonomy in different areas, and can be overseen with stronger or weaker contractual regimes. Hence, Pollitt *et al.*'s so-called 'tripod model' of structural disaggregation, autonomization and contractualization is useful primarily as a framework for comparing the strength of agencification between different countries and over time.

Conceived along these three dimensions, how might agencification overcome the practical challenges of accountable management? First, the teasing apart of different tasks and their allocation to separate authorities can occur along both vertical and horizontal channels, separating functions between superior and subordinate actors or between neighboring actors at the same hierarchical level (Roness 2007). This achieves role purification – that is, a reduction in the operational remit of each individual organization (Christensen and Lægreid 2006: 12). By so lessening the number of objectives that an agency has to meet, the potential for the goal conflict and complexity that traditionally hampered objective-setting in multipurpose public organizations is reduced. Additionally, role purification benefits the audit and accountability requirements of accountable management; for if an agency is responsible for administering but not designing policy, or delivers only one kind of service rather than a whole range, it should be easier to pinpoint the location and cause of poor performance, and then determine culpability. Finally, vertical disaggregation of superior and subordinate parties into clearly separate organizations should reduce political interference by '[insulating] a particular activity from the full force of ministerial and parliamentary control' (Brown and Steel 1979: 309).

The second element of Pollitt *et al.*'s ideal type is autonomization, which reduces constraints on decision-making by local managers. Autonomy is a complex idea with multiple dimensions (Verhoest *et al.* 2004), but accountable management refers specifically to *managerial* autonomy, which relates to decisions over finance, personnel and other operational matters. As with structural disaggregation, the benefits of autonomization are multiple. Enhanced local discretion should lessen central regulations and reduce the number of 'process' (rather than 'output') targets that agencies have to meet, again decreasing goal complexity. For the delegation requirement, autonomization should unify responsibility for resources and activities, enabling and incentivizing more responsive decision-making. And for audit and accountability, autonomization should simplify the monitoring and adjudication process by confining to a single organization the main determinants of performance. No longer will auditors have to weigh the influence of multiple authorities on the focal outcome, since all responsibility for marshaling resources to achieve a particular output rests within a single chain of command. Moreover, autonomization might

Principles meet practicalities

Table 17.1 Implementing accountable management doctrine through agencification reforms

		Four requirements of accountable management			
		Objectives	Discretion	Audit	Accountability
Three dimensions of agencification	Structural disaggregation	Reduced goal complexity – single, not multiple, tasks	Organizational insulation of officials from ministers	Pinpoint culpability	Pinpoint culpability
	Autonomization	Reduced goal complexity – outputs, not processes	Unified responsibility for activities and resources	Pinpoint culpability	Pinpoint culpability Enable reward and sanction
	Contractualism	Explicit statement of goals	Explicit statement of authorities	Standards against which to evaluate	Formalized process of review, praise and/or censure

relax central employment policies, making it easier to implement rewards or sanctions for individual staff.

The final element of the ideal-type agency is ex post control by the setting and measuring of performance targets – contractualism. Generally, such agreements between ministries and agencies are 'soft' contracts, for which there is no adjudication in law (see Binderkrantz and Christensen 2009). Therefore, in terms of objective-setting and delegation, the main benefit of contractualism is to promote credible commitments between principal and agent by explicitly and publicly recording agreed resources, objectives and freedoms. As for audit, quasi-contracts should determine the basis for performance evaluation and provide a governance document against which responsibility for decisions can be traced. Finally, for the accountability requirement, contractualism imposes a cycle of contract setting, execution, review and amendment, and thus institutionalizes the explanation-judgement-consequences process of accountability defined by Bovens (2007), above.

Table 17.1 summarizes this series of conjectures about how the structural disaggregation, autonomization and contractualization achieved by agencification might overcome the four main practical challenges of accountable management. But how optimistic are these hypotheses? Do they account for the complexities of public service delivery in a highly political context? And how sustainable are the solutions in the longer term, given the myriad other pressures on the structure and processes of government? The next section seeks answers to these questions.

Implementing accountable management in the UK

The road to agencification

The initial recommendation for accountable management in British government came in the 1968 Fulton Report on the civil service. Initially, some progress was made with the advent of large 'super-ministries' in the early 1970s, which contained internal delegation 'to accountable units of management' (Prime Minister and Minister for the Civil Service 1970: 6). A few independent public service agencies also emerged with formal autonomy from ministers, although these were mostly confined to activities of low political salience (Massey and Pyper 2005: 85). Latterly, the need for objective-setting and audit was also progressed through attempts at output budgeting and management by objectives (Brown and Steel 1979: Chapter 12). But it was not until the 1980s that more systematic reforms began.

The Financial Management Initiative was launched by the Thatcher government in 1982. It required that government departments develop internal frameworks in which managers understood their objectives, could measure performance against them, had clear responsibility for using resources effectively, and had the information (especially on costs) necessary for exercising those responsibilities (Prime Minister and Minister for the Civil Service 1982: 5). Performance indicators proliferated (Goldsworthy 1991; Greer and Carter 1995), and management information systems developed (National Audit Office 1986). Efforts were also made to implement performance-related pay for top officials (Keraudren 1994), partly fulfilling the consequences aspect of accountability. But merit pay proved difficult to deliver, as did meaningful decentralization. According to Goldsworthy (1991: 5), 'operational managers claimed that in many areas they still lacked the freedom to manage that they needed to improve the delivery of services'.

Thus, of the four practical requirements of accountable management, delegation and accountability proved most troublesome. Treasury cost controls and union reluctance to forego centralized pay bargaining explain some difficulties with performance-related pay (Kessler 1993). But more fundamental was the challenge of correlating individual managers' performance to policy outcomes. As Keraudren (1994: 26–7) explains, 'The various guidelines issued by the government on the award of bonuses and discretionary increments between 1982 and 1988 bore witness to the difficult task of identifying measurable and useful individual performances and linking a given result to an individual effort'.

As for delegation, Brown and Steel (1979: 302–5) identify several factors hindering decentralization, including the need for permanent secretaries (the most senior civil servants) to demonstrate the legality of their departmental expenditure to parliament, and the potential for MPs to question ministers over the smallest details of policy implementation. Indeed, perhaps the greatest barrier to accountable management was the behavioral changes it required of politicians:

> The principle of accountable management implies that a minister will normally decline to intervene in a matter where a civil servant was acting within his [sic.] delegated authority. It is almost impossible to imagine ministers accepting this degree of self-restraint; it is even less likely that MPs would allow them to get away with it, particularly when things went wrong.
>
> (Brown and Steel 1979: 305)

Consequently, if accountable management were finally to be realized in the British civil service, greater separation between ministers and officials, and a radical rethink of their respective accountabilities to parliament, seemed necessary.

Accountable management 2.0: the Next Steps program

Following the limited success of the Financial Management Initiative, the Thatcher government launched the Next Steps agencification program in 1988. A report argued that officials were still subject to central regulations and lacked personal responsibility for organizational outcomes

(Efficiency Unit 1988). Ministers and their advisers were overloaded with political work and more focused on policy and parliament than efficient administration. Consequently, the report recommended that executive agencies be created as organizations focused on implementation. Following the tripod model, these would be headed by chief executives with authority over management and operations and direct responsibility to ministers in separate policy departments. Relationships would be governed by quasi-contractual framework documents, and annual targets set for efficiency and effectiveness.

The Next Steps program ran from 1988 to 1997, during which time 60 percent of the civil service – some 285,000 officials – were removed to 138 agencies across a wide range of activity (James 2003). Although the reforms initially attracted great attention, considered by some to fracture the historic Westminster-Whitehall model of government (Campbell and Wilson 1995), little is known about developments after 1997. Accordingly, the remainder of this section reports upon recent research into the contemporary use of agencies in British government.[1] It follows the three dimensions of Pollitt et al.'s ideal type, describing for each the high-level trends across government and then changes within the justice policy sector specifically.

Background on the justice sector

The justice sector encompasses prisons, probation, courts, tribunals and 'public guardianship' (the legal protection of vulnerable adults). Until the 2000s, some functions were administered locally, while others were spread across several government departments – principally, the Home Office and the Lord Chancellor's Department (Gibson 2008; Elston 2013b). In 2003, the Lord Chancellor's Department became the Department for Constitutional Affairs, which then merged with parts of the Home Office in 2007 to create the Ministry of Justice (hereinafter MoJ). This now oversees the majority of the sector, employs some 90,000 staff (including in various arm's-length bodies), and has an annual budget exceeding £8.7 billion (2012 figures). Despite these extensive structural and policy changes, the agency model continues to be heavily used. This makes for an insightful case on the development of agencies and the doctrine of accountable management since the late 1980s.

1. Structural disaggregation

In line with Pollitt et al.'s model, structural disaggregation along both horizontal and vertical planes was at the core of the Next Steps proposition. Agencies were to have 'a recognizable coherence' to their tasks, rather than being 'an agglomeration of activities' (Jenkins and Gold 2011: 22), and would perform 'executive functions of government, as distinct from policy advice' (Hansard, 18 February 1988), which remained 'firmly the responsibility of the department' (Jenkins and Gold 2011: 14). On this basis, Next Steps effected major changes to the structure of government. Yet, since 1997, the attained horizontal and vertical disaggregation have gradually receded. As Figure 17.1 illustrates, by 2010, the number of separate agencies had declined to 84. This was the result of two principal movements. First, the merger of agencies performing related activities occurred 49 times between 1997 and 2010 (Elston 2013a). Second, de-agencification also occurred 49 times, with agencies being reabsorbed back into departments. This was more common in the devolved administrations of Scotland, Wales and Northern Ireland (16 times) and in the Ministry of Defence (24 times) than elsewhere in government (nine times), where less formal modes of reintegration occurred. Specifically, although some agencies had been granted policymaking responsibilities from the outset, contrary to the official Next Steps position (Trosa 1994; Hogwood et al. 2001), this intensified during the 2000s, with many gaining substantial or even lead responsibility for policy development (Elston 2013a). In the main, the effect was not to devolve further responsibilities to semiautonomous agencies, but to reunify policy and operations within core departments, albeit while retaining the formal agency classification (Elston 2013b).

How do these cross-governmental trends match in the justice sector specifically? Horizontal de-specialization was again significant. HM Prison Service, established in 1993, absorbed the National Probation Service in 2008 to create the much larger National Offender Management Service. The Court Service of 1995 morphed into HM Courts Service in 2005 with the addition of the lower-tier magistrates courts, and the Employment Tribunals Service and Appeals Service agencies were merged to create the Tribunals Service in 2006. These were then further merged to form HM Courts and Tribunals Service in 2011 (see Figure 17.2). Overall, then, the major justice agencies of the 2010s are much larger and more multipurpose than those created during Next Steps. As one official in HM Courts and Tribunals Service observed, 'we are in multiple businesses, you know?'

As for vertical specialization, there has been considerable toing and froing of responsibilities, as summarized by the black and gray ribbons in Figure 17.2. From the outset, HM Prison Service departed from the Next Steps norm by having its chief executive as 'principal policy advisor' to ministers (HMPS 1993: 6). This made the original agency relatively 'self-sufficient' (interview). In the mid-2000s, the agency lost many of these responsibilities to the Home Office, only to see them partially restored in 2008. The MoJ now performs strategic work, while the agency does 'operational policy' (interview). As for the Court Service, in 1995 this had a pure delivery remit, with policymaking centralized in the then Lord Chancellor's Department. A decade later, its replacement Department for Constitutional Affairs devolved policy responsibilities to its three agencies – HM Courts Service, the Tribunals Service, and the Public Guardianship Office. So extensive was this rethink of the Next Steps idea that some agencies undertook policy tasks that were entirely unrelated to their core operational remit (interview). However, after the creation of the MoJ in 2007, these responsibilities gradually returned to the department, leaving once more implementation-focused agencies by 2011.

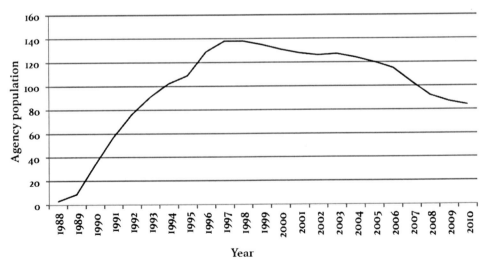

Figure 17.1 UK agency population, 1988–2010
Source: Elston (2013a).[2]

Principles meet practicalities

Altogether, then, both the cross-governmental picture and the justice case study describe considerable re-aggregation after 1997, along both the horizontal and vertical planes. The result is a loss of the role purity that should have benefited accountable management by simplifying the process of objective-setting.

2. Autonomization

Increased management autonomy is the second element of Pollitt *et al.*'s ideal type and is again essential to accountable management doctrine, which sees authority and accountability as

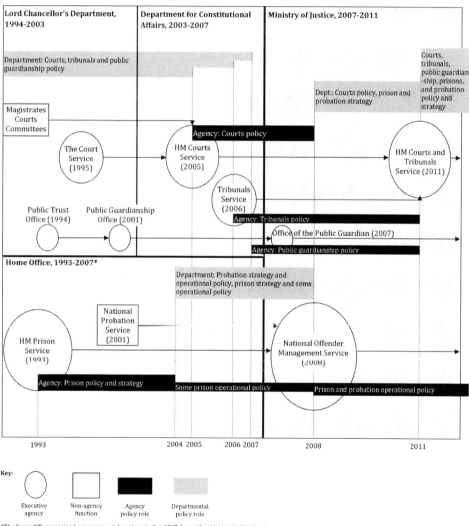

Figure 17.2 Distribution of policymaking responsibilities between justice ministries and agencies, 1993–2011

Source: Derived from documents and interviews.

necessarily intertwined. As the original Next Steps report urged: 'Once the policy objectives and budgets . . . are set, the management of the agency should then have as much independence as possible in deciding how those objectives are met' (Efficiency Unit 1988: 9). Reportedly, Treasury concern for maintaining financial control in such a delegated system delayed the original proposals (Hennessy 1990: 620–1), and, as the reforms progressed, officials still complained of much top-down interference (Efficiency Unit 1991; Trosa 1994). Yet, after further efforts to decentralize in the mid-1990s, opinion changed. With the arrival of the new Labour government in 1997, concern grew that agencies actually had too much autonomy (Office of Public Services Reform 2002), whereupon efforts were made to reign in their independence (Schick 2002; Gains 2003).

De-autonomization was thus frequently described by interviewees in the justice sector. As one senior official reflected:

> The true agency that the Prison Service was had a whole load of things which it managed directly – like estates, procurement – and all of those things are now being delivered as a shared service from the Department.

Similarly, in the field of public guardianship:

> At the time of the [Public Guardianship Office] being set up, it was much more at arm's-length – could determine its own terms and conditions, all those kinds of things. And over time, [we] have become more and more part of the 'parent department'. So that 'purer' Next Steps separation of the executive agency – that's narrowed and narrowed and narrowed.

As for HM Courts and Tribunals Service, one official described how this draining of agency autonomy but retention of separate agency governance structures created new accountability challenges:

> Shared services . . . cause some real tensions for us as an agency, in terms of [the chief executive], as Accounting Officer, a good number of his essential services are not under his direct remit . . . So, for example, ICT is provided by the core Ministry . . . . Estates is part of an overall estates function . . . . Procurement – we don't have our own procurement department . . . . So it gets into some interesting tensions . . . . For instance, if there's a legionella outbreak in a court, and the Health and Safety Executive want to hold somebody to account, is that the agency chief executive who's responsible, or is that the Head of Estates in MoJ who's responsible? . . . If the roof blows off a court, and we can't deliver services . . . and [MPs] jump up and down and want to know why the services have been disrupted, who do they ask for? Do they ask for the head of the agency . . . or the head of the roof-fixing department in MoJ . . . ?

This illustrates the distance traveled since the early Next Steps reforms. Their *raison d'être* had been to align responsibility for resources with responsibility for activities, so that culpability was clearer; and yet, as this official describes, by destroying that single chain of command through the department-wide sharing of functions such as ICT, estates and procurement, latter-day de-autonomization actually confuses accountability for public service failure.

3. Contractualization

Finally, quasi-contractual relations between department and agency is the third characteristic of Pollitt *et al.*'s ideal type. This was realized in Next Steps not only by the putative separation of policy and operations, as if between purchaser and provider, but also through departments creating a framework document, 'tailored to the job to be done, which specifies policies, objectives, the results required, and the resources available' (Efficiency Unit 1988: 10). Monitoring these quasi-contracts would be ministerial advisory boards, designated sponsorship units in departments, or some such other arrangement (Efficiency Unit 1991).

Targets, performance data and framework documents proliferated during the early years of agencification, and became emblematic of the Next Steps idea. But little is known of how contractualism developed thereafter. The 2002 government review into agencies found a 'confused mixture of arrangements', with many departments having no ministerial advisory board or senior-level sponsor of agencies (Office of Public Services Reform 2002: 26). By 2010, many framework documents were out of date, and others were missing altogether (Elston 2013a). In the justice sector specifically, interviewees dismissed their significance, describing them as 'a bit of process' and as making 'no difference whatsoever'.

In addition, the agency sponsorship unit for both the National Offender Management Service and HM Courts and Tribunals Service ended in 2010, after a departmental-wide efficiency review found staff to be uncertain about 'what value . . . we add through sponsoring our executive agencies' (unpublished document). Formal target-setting also ceased at this time. Thus, as one official explained:

> Instead of having an army beavering away on analyzing performance data, and, as often seemed to be the case, looking to provide elephant traps . . . accountability for [agency] performance goes direct to the [MoJ] Board. [There are regular] sessions on performance, and actually all of [the agency's performance data are available to the MoJ board]. There is a degree of trust that [the chief executive] will . . . expose the weaknesses as well as the strengths . . . . If you can accept that, if you can carry that off convincingly, you don't need armies of people. [And the agency already has] an army of people, as you might imagine, so the idea that the Ministry should also have an army of people –.

Therefore, despite the continuing use of the agency classification, contemporary governance within the MoJ has reverted back to a largely hierarchical model, rather than one based on contractual principles. Most chief executives report directly to the departmental management board, the agency's performance figures are accepted without independent challenge from elsewhere in the ministry, and any questioning of the chief executive comes collegiately during department-wide board meetings. Consequently, despite the initial significance of contractualism to the Next Steps model, today this can scarcely be found.

Discussion: political and administrative barriers to accountable management

The empirical account above indicates that executive agencies have proven difficult to sustain in Britain in the long run. On each of the three measures of structural disaggregation, autonomization and contractualization, agencification today is significantly weaker than intended a quarter of a century ago. Given that the reform was also meant to overcome previous entrenched barriers to accountable management, the unavoidable conclusion is that, yet again, this doctrine has proven largely unworkable in the governmental context. But the reasons for this failure are both old and new. Whereas political reluctance to delegate to officials was widely recognized before Next Steps (Brown and Steel 1979), the administrative costs of implementing full-blown accountable management were less apparent in the earlier, less comprehensive efforts of the 1970s and 1980s.

Political barriers

Following the Aristotelian contention that to be deemed responsible for an action, an individual should have acted voluntarily rather than under compulsion (Cooper 2013), the accountable management principle requires that officials have delegated *authority* alongside delegated *accountability*. Officials cannot be accountable for an action foisted on them by a superordinate, just as ministers cannot be blamed for unpredictable administrative blunders lower down in the organizational hierarchy. Yet, despite the greater separation of politicians and officials attempted through Next Steps, ministerial reluctance to forego control over policy implementation still remained an obstacle. Concern grew that agencies '[had] become disconnected from the increasingly well-defined aims of their ministers' (Office of Public Services Reform 2002: 3), and efforts were made to curb manager independence (Schick 2002; Gains 2003). In the justice sector specifically, as early as 1997, a review of HM Prison Service called for 'greater awareness of, and sensitivity to, the nature and demands of ministerial responsibility' (HMPS 1997: 7). Today, the prisons agency has a recognized political and media salience, to the extent that, as one official described, 'When things go wrong in our bit of the world, it is the end of the world' (interview). As a result:

> ministers just cannot comfortably sit at an arm's length . . . . This idea that, somehow, the business of prison or probation can be at arm's length from ministers I just think is always a very challenging political thing to expect of [the minister]. We operate very close to policy and ministers.
>
> *(interview)*

The same is true of court and tribunal administration:

> What I think we have all learnt, and politicians certainly have learnt, is: you can't transfer away risk of cock-ups from ministers . . . So ministers are recognizing that they are always gonna get the absolute [>*] kicked out of them when stupid things happen, and so are not prepared, actually, to release power to the agency and say, you know: 'Fly free my pretties, try not to do anything stupid while you're out there 'cause they'll tell me off'.
>
> *(interview)*

Thus, notwithstanding the major changes in government attempted during the New Public Management era, the level of 'self-restraint' required of ministers in delegating tasks to officials remains as unimaginable today as when Brown and Steel wrote of it nearly four decades ago.

Administrative barriers

Alongside these political impediments, three administrative problems also explain the gradual weakening of agencification as a basis for accountable management. These are increased organizational overheads, reduced coordination of related policy areas, and unrealistic policy-making.

Beginning with efficiency, the additional management costs of operating a structurally disaggregated system compared with a unitary bureaucracy have gradually been recognized since the heyday of new public management. For example, explaining the major de-agencification trend in the defense sector during the mid-2000s, an official cited the increased 'overheads' of a 'very decentralized structure', and described how 'some of the very small agencies just no longer seem to be of a sufficient size to justify . . . some of the requirements that go with agency status, such as the requirement to produce agency accounts' (House of Commons Defence Committee 2006: Question 52). Cost saving also motivated the de-autonomization reported above, with the sharing of common ICT, procurement and estates services between agencies favored for bringing greater economies of scale, despite the detrimental effect on the single chain of command. Efficiency even figured in the rationale for returning from contract-based to hierarchical control of agencies, the abandoned sponsorship function in MoJ being found to involve simply 'managing ourselves' (unpublished document). As one official remarked, 'one of the core principles is that we only do things once. We can't afford to duplicate things'.

Inter-organizational coordination is a second administrative imperative prompting structural reaggregation and undermining the accountable management logic. The Labour government elected in 1997 argued that agencification had fragmented Whitehall, with interrelated policy tasks divided between a multitude of separate organizations. It urged 'all agencies to consider . . . whether there is scope for improving performance by cooperation with bodies beyond the agency boundary' (Minister for the Cabinet Office 1999: v–vi). There was no immediate flurry of mergers, but over time many were effected to improve coordination between interdependent policy areas (Elston 2013a). In the justice sector, the union of HM Prison Service and the National Probation Service in 2008 aimed to promote 'joined-up justice' by smoothing the transition of offenders from custody to community supervision (Senior *et al.* 2008: 70–1). Similarly, the reunification of policy and delivery responsibilities in the Department for Constitutional Affairs was also motivated by a desire to enhance coordination. As one interviewee explained, 'in many circumstances, it doesn't really matter much whether [policy advice comes from] the agency or whether it's in the core department as long it's only being done once and as long as it isn't being done competitively'. Similarly, the permanent secretary at the time described the need to ensure 'both the policy and operational advice comes from the same source' (Constitutional Affairs Committee 2006: 1), implying that their separation led to conflicting rather than coordinated advice to ministers. Overall, then, while role purification brings added focus to an organization, it also risks parochialism that does not accommodate overlapping and interdependent areas of government.

Finally, the need for policymaking to be informed by on-the-ground operational experience further accelerated the demise of the agency model. A review by the Labour government in 2002 found that, since agencification, 'the gulf between policy and delivery is considered by most to have widened' (Office of Public Services Reform 2002: 5). Many interviewees spoke of how policy ideas had been 'throw[n] . . . over the fence' at the agencies, whereupon 'all the weaknesses and problems on deliverability began to emerge'. Accordingly, the decentralization of policy teams in the mid-2000s was intended to ensure that '[policy] proposals are evidence-based and deliverable' (Civil Service Capability Reviews 2006: 6). Although this undermined the role clarity and principal-agent logic intended by Next Steps and required by accountable management, '[T]he practical realities of life – even simply who knows what about what – mean that you ask people to do things on the basis of who they are and what they know, not necessarily where the organizational boundary is' (interview). Thereafter, when policymaking returned from the agencies to the core MoJ after 2007 (see Figure 17.2), this was to facilitate staff cutbacks in agencies and exempt the judicial members of the courts agency board from having any responsibility for government policy (interviews), rather than to re-establish the unworkable role purification that Next Steps had once sought. Indeed, extensive collaboration between department and agency now means that, in practice, the formal organizational boundary is all but overridden (see Elston 2016), with the requirements of accountable management sacrificed in favor of a more integrated justice policy sector.

Conclusion

In conclusion, this chapter has examined the accountable management principle as a basis for reforming the British civil service. It might have charted a very different course, unraveling and critiquing the basic assumptions that underpin this approach to democratic control. As noted at the outset, these assumptions are neither straightforward nor uncontested, despite their superficial appeal. But instead of focusing on matters of principle, the concern has been with practicalities – the important question of how to deliver this accountability logic in the complex, highly politicized institutions of the British state.

As has been shown, implementation can frustrate accountability ideals, and not just because of political resistance. Organizations are dynamic systems, where small changes might have far-reaching consequences for efficiency and effectiveness. In the case of Next Steps, the agency architecture established to meet the practical demands of accountable management not only encountered ministerial opposition, as happened with prior attempts at delegation in government, but also a series of administrative pathologies. Though beneficial for objective setting, delegation, audit and accountability, the structural disaggregation, autonomization and contractualism as practiced in the justice sector also increased operating costs, reduced coordination and made for policy initiatives that were undeliverable on the front line. Therefore, irrespective of normative arguments for or against the idea that ministerial accountability should be circumscribed and should not extend to every minutiae of their policy portfolio, the side effects of adopting accountability management as an alternative make this difficult to sustain in practice.

In other words, as important as principles are, public accountability regimes cannot be derived from beliefs and ideals alone, in isolation from the political-administrative systems that they seek to modify. Accountability mechanisms incur direct and indirect costs. As with any other policy intervention, therefore, alternative solutions must be weighed carefully against one another not only for the values that they extoll and the behaviors they encourage, but also for the demands they place upon organization and management. How much should society pay for its systems of public accountability? Are pressures to save money during the so-called 'age of austerity' leading to undesirable compromises? When, if ever, should the quality of public services – their coordination, efficiency or effectiveness – be sacrificed to improve accountability? These are important questions, too easily set aside in more doctrinaire discussions of political and bureaucratic accountability. Principles are important, but so are practicalities.

Notes

1   For details of this research project, including methodology, see Elston (2013b).
2   Thomas Elston, *Public Policy and Administration*, 28(1): 73. Copyright (c) 2012 by the author. Reprinted by Permission of SAGE Publications, Ltd.

References

Barker, A. (1998) Political responsibility for UK prison security: ministers escape again. *Public Administration*, 76(1): 1–23.

Binderkrantz, A. S. and Christensen, J. G. (2009) Governing Dutch agencies by contract: from negotiated freedom to the shadow of hierarchy. *Journal of Public Policy*, 29(1): 55–78.

Bovens, M. (2007) Analysing and assessing accountability: a conceptual framework. *European Law Journal*, 13(4): 447–68.

Brown, R. G. S. and Steel, D. R. (1979) *The Administrative Process in Britain*. London: Methuen & Co.

Campbell, C. and Wilson, G. K. (1995) *The End of Whitehall: Death of a Paradigm?* Cambridge, MA: Blackwell.

Christensen, T. and Lægreid, P. (2006) Agencification and regulatory reforms. In T. Christensen and P. Lægreid (eds), *Autonomy and Regulation: Coping with Agencies in the Modern State*. Cheltenham: Edward Elgar, pp. 8–49.

Civil Service Capability Reviews (2006) *Capability Review of the Department for Constitutional Affairs*. London: Cabinet Office.

Constitutional Affairs Committee (2006) *Oral Evidence, Tuesday 17th October*. London: The Stationery Office.

Cooper, J. M. (2013) Aristotelian responsibility. In B. Inwood (ed.), *Oxford Studies in Ancient Philosophy, Volume 45*. Oxford: Oxford University Press.

Downs, A. (1966) *Inside Bureaucracy*. Boston, MA: Little, Brown.

Efficiency Unit (1988) *Improving Management in Government: The Next Steps*. London: The Stationery Office.

Efficiency Unit (1991) *Making the Most of Next Steps*. London: The Stationery Office.

Elston, T. (2013a) Developments in UK executive agencies: re-examining the 'disaggregation-reaggregation' thesis. *Public Policy and Administration*, 28(1): 66–89.

Elston, T. (2013b) *Reinterpreting Agencies in UK Central Government: On Meaning, Motive and Policymaking*. PhD thesis, University of Nottingham.

Elston, T. (2014) Not so 'arm's length': reinterpreting agencies in UK central government. *Public Administration*, 92(2): 458–76.

Elston, T. (2016) Conflict between explicit and tacit public service bargains in UK executive agencies. *Governance*. DOI: 10.1111/gove.12191.

Flinders, M. (2008) *Delegated Governance and the British State*. Oxford: Oxford University Press.

Flynn, A., Gray, A., Jenkins, B., Rutherford, B. A. and Plowden, W. (1988) Accountable management in British central government: some reflections on the official record. *Financial Accountability and Management*, 4(3): 169–89.

Gains, F. (2003) Surveying the landscape of modernisation: executive agencies under New Labour. *Public Policy and Administration*, 18(2): 4–20.

Gibson, B. (2008) *The New Ministry of Justice: An Introduction*. Hook: Waterside Press.

Goldsworthy, D. (1991) *Setting Up Next Steps*. London: The Stationery Office.

Gray, A. and Jenkins, B. (1986) Accountable management in British central government: some reflections on the financial management initiative. *Financial Accountability and Management*, 2(3): 171–86.

Gray, A. and Jenkins, B. (1993) Codes of accountability in the new public sector. *Accounting, Auditing and Accountability Journal*, 6(3): 52–67.

Gray, A., Jenkins, B., Flynn, A. and Rutherford, B. (1991) The management of change in Whitehall: the experience of the FMI. *Public Administration*, 69(1): 41–59.

Greer, P. and Carter, N. (1995) Next steps and performance measurement. In B. J. O'Toole and G. Jordan (eds), *Next Steps: Improving Management in Government?* Aldershot: Dartmouth, pp. 86–96.

Harlow, C. (1999) Accountability, New Public Management, and the problems of the Child Support Agency. *Journal of Law and Society*, 26(2): 150–74.

Hennessy, P. (1990) *Whitehall*. London: Fontana Press.

HM Prison Service (HMPS) (1993) *Framework Document*. London: HMPS.

HM Prison Service (HMPS) (1997) *Prison Service Review*. London: HMPS.

Hogwood, B. W., Judge, D. and McVicar, M. (2001) Agencies, ministers and civil servants in Britain. In B. G. Peters and J. Pierre (eds), *Politicians, Bureaucrats and Administrative Reform*. London: Routledge, pp. 35–44.

Hood, C. (2011) *The Blame Game*. Oxford: Princeton University Press.

House of Commons Defence Committee (2006) *Ministry of Defence Annual Report and Accounts 2004–05: Sixth Report of Session 2005–06* (HC 822). London: The Stationery Office.

Humphrey, C., Miller, P. and Scapens, R. W. (1993) Accountability and accountable management in the UK public sector. *Accounting, Auditing and Accountability Journal*, 6(3): 7–29.

James, O. (2003) *The Executive Agency Revolution in Whitehall*. Basingstoke: Palgrave Macmillan.

Jenkins, K. and Gold, J. (2011) *Unfinished Business: Where Next for Executive Agencies?* London: Institute for Government.

Keraudren, P. (1994) The introduction of performance related pay in the British civil service (1982–88): a cultural perspective. *International Review of Administrative Sciences*, 60(1): 23–36.

Kessler, I. A. N. (1993) Pay determination in the British civil service since 1979. *Public Administration*, 71(3): 323–40.

Lindblom, C. E. (1965) *The Intelligence of Democracy*. New York: Free Press.

Massey, A. and Pyper, R. (2005) *Public Management and Modernisation in Britain*. Basingstoke: Palgrave Macmillan.

Minister for the Cabinet Office (1999) *Next Steps Report 1998* (Cm 4273). London: The Stationery Office.

National Audit Office (1986) *The Financial Management Initiative* (HC 588). London: The Stationery Office.

Office of Public Services Reform (2002) *Better Government Services: Executive Agencies in the 21st Century*. London: Cabinet Office.

Polidano, C. (1999) The bureaucrat who fell under a bus: ministerial responsibility, executive agencies and the Derek Lewis affair in Britain. *Governance*, 12(2): 201–29.

Pollitt, C., Talbot, C., Caulfield, J. and Smullen, A. (2004) *Agencies: How Governments Do Things Through Semi-Autonomous Organizations*. Basingstoke: Palgrave Macmillan.

Prime Minister and Minister for the Civil Service (1970) *The Reorganisation of Central Government* (Cmnd. 4506). London: The Stationery Office.

Prime Minister and Minister for the Civil Service (1982) *Efficiency and Effectiveness in the Civil Service* (Cmnd. 8616). London: The Stationery Office.

Rainey, H. G. and Jung, C. S. (2015) A conceptual framework for analysis of goal ambiguity in public organizations. *Journal of Public Administration Research and Theory*, 25(1): 71–99.

Roness, P. G. (2007) Types of state organizations: arguments, doctrines and changes beyond New Public Management. In T. Christensen and P. Lægreid (eds), *Transcending New Public Management*. Surrey: Ashgate, pp. 65–88.

Schick, A. (2002) Agencies in search of principles. In OECD, *Distributed Public Governance: Agencies, Authorities and Other Government Bodies*. Paris, OECD, pp. 33–52.

Senior, P., Crowther-Dowey, C. and Long, M. (2008) *Understanding Modernisation in Criminal Justice*. Buckingham: Open University Press.

Thatcher, M. and Sweet, A. S. (2002) Theory and practice of delegation to non-majoritarian institutions. *West European Politics*, 25(1): 1–22.

Thynne, I. and Wettenhall, R. (2004) Public management and organizational autonomy: the continuing relevance of significant earlier knowledge. *International Review of Administrative Sciences*, 70(4): 609–21.

Trosa, S. (1994) *Next Steps: Moving On*. London: Office of Public Service and Science.

van Thiel, S. and Yesilkagit, K. (2011) Good neighbours or distant friends? Trust between Dutch ministries and their executive agencies. *Public Management Review*, 13(6): 783–802.

Verhoest, K., Peters, B. G., Bouckaert, G. and Verschuere, B. (2004) The study of organisational autonomy: a conceptual review. *Public Administration and Development*, 24(2): 101–18.

Wildavsky, A. (1987) *Speaking Truth to Power*. New Brunswick, NJ: Transaction.

Williamson, O. E. (1985) *The Economic Institutions of Capitalism*. New York: Free Press.

18
MULTIPLE ACCOUNTABILITIES IN PUBLIC-PRIVATE PARTNERSHIPS (PPPS)

How to unravel the accountability paradox?

Tom Willems and Wouter Van Dooren

Introduction

Both in the academic literature and popular press, more horizontal and hybrid forms of governance such as public-private partnerships (PPPs) are mostly associated with democratic deficits due to a shortfall of traditional accountability arrangements (Flinders 2010; Skelcher 2010; Reeves 2013). This association is not self-evident. The spectrum of accountability instruments increases when public responsibilities and tasks are shared between public and private actors. When private accountability to shareholders and investors supplements public accountability to office holders and parliaments, one would expect more accountability. Flyvbjerg et al. (2003), for instance, propose to involve private equity into large infrastructure projects in order to strengthen accountability and to avoid cost overruns.

Yet, in spite of a large and increasing spectrum of accountability instruments, there is still the feeling that there is something wrong with the democratic accountability of PPPs. The objective of this chapter is to unravel this accountability paradox (Willems and Van Dooren 2011). *Why does the accountability abundance not lead to higher perceptions of accountability?* We use the case study of school infrastructure in Flanders to illustrate the often complex and 'messy' reality of how accountability works in practice, and how difficult it is to assess multiple accountabilities in a nuanced manner. The overall impact of hybrid governance on accountability seems more puzzling and ambiguous than often presumed in the literature (see also Christensen and Lægreid 2011).

In the first section, the conceptual framework on accountability is explained. The second section deals with the notion of PPPs as examples of hybrid governance. The third section ties both concepts together and addresses the main problems and questions. After describing the methodology, the fifth section explains the main empirical findings. Finally, we end with five lessons that may help to unravel the accountability paradox found in the Flemish PPP projects.

Accountability

Accountability is defined and interpreted in many different ways. It is used as 'a synonym for many loosely defined political desiderata such as good governance, transparency, equity, democracy, efficiency, responsiveness, responsibility and integrity' (Bovens 2010: 946). This is unfortunate because this conceptual impreciseness has been an obstacle towards empirical progress. The risk of conceptual stretching due to its vague and amorphous nature is captured by many scholars in often very illustrative ways. Accountability is described as a magic concept (Pollitt and Hupe 2011), a cultural keyword (Dubnick 2014), chameleon-like (Sinclair 1995), a golden concept (Bovens *et al.* 2008), ever-expanding (Mulgan 2003), and so on. Flinders (2014) even described it as the über-concept of the twenty-first century.

We understand accountability as a social relationship that involves an obligation to explain and justify one's actions or behavior and can be divided into three distinct phases: information, debate and sanctions (see Bovens 2010). Despite the fact that this definition gives a good insight into its basic functioning, accountability in practice is more complex than the definition suggests (see also Christensen and Lægreid 2011). Many scholars tried to capture the diversity of accountability by formulating rich classifications (e.g. Mulgan 2003; Hodge and Coghill 2007; Bovens *et al.* 2008).

The main processes of accountability take place in *accountability forums*. A forum is a virtual place of debate that is populated by both account-givers who provide information and account-holders who can issue sanctions. We distinguish *five accountability forums*: the political, judicial, administrative, public and market forums (Willems and Van Dooren 2012). These are the different arenas in which instruments of accountability are played out. Account-givers and account-holders typically belong to a specific forum: administrative agencies and cabinet ministers, for instance, to the administrative forum or media players to the public forum. However, willingly or not, account-givers are regularly drawn to other forums: for instance, when an agency has to answer to court for violating legislation or when the media challenges a minister. We do not include a separate forum of professional accountability, because in our view professionals are mainly active within the administrative forum. Administrations, for instance, often support professional associations. Moreover, professional standards are increasingly important in bureaucracies that are expertise-driven.

Since public-private collaboration is increasingly strong, we include the market as a relevant forum where public account-givers have to answer for their actions. PPPs have to provide information to private investors and shareholders who debate and assess this information and can pass sanctions by disinvesting in PPPs. Ratings of public bonds are another example of market accountability. Governments pass information on the robustness of their financial capacity; investors, together with rating agencies, debate this information and ultimately pass sanctions by lowering ratings and disinvesting in the country's public debt.

Accountability has *three distinct meta-functions*, or reasons why governments are being called to account (Aucoin and Heintzman 2000; Behn 2001; Bovens *et al.* 2008). First, governments are held accountable for rules and procedures to prevent unfairness or abuse of power – 'constitutional function'. Second, citizens (or elected representatives) want to have the final say because the ultimate authority and ownership of the state rests with the citizens – 'democratic function'. These two dimensions are concerned with *how government functions*. Third, citizens also care *what government actually accomplishes*. They want to hold governments accountable for their results – 'performance function'. Some authors talk about a shift from procedure to performance accountability due to the growing importance of the last function (Lodge 2004; Fimreite and Lægreid 2009; Poulsen 2009).

Accountability is a key concept for understanding democratic governance (Mulgan 2003). Although accountability and democracy are closely related, it is important to make a distinction between the two concepts. On the one hand, the previous section shows that the democratic control by citizens and their representatives is merely one of the three functions of accountability. There is thus more to accountability than democracy. On the other hand, there is also more to democracy than accountability. Both concepts are intertwined, but have to be treated separately. Philp (2009: 48) wrote that many scholars who are studying accountability are actually dealing with the more substantial problem of legitimacy. Making governments more accountable is seen as increasing their legitimacy. We believe that to be true; accountability is indeed a crucial gateway to democratic legitimacy (Sørensen and Torfing 2005). There are other gateways, such as transparency or citizen participation, but accountability has become one with increasing relevance in our 'distrustful times' (Power 1999; O'Neill 2002; Flinders 2012). Accountability is thus worth studying to gain a better understanding of the current state of our democracies.

Public-private partnerships (PPPs)

Public-private partnerships (PPPs) mean many different things to different people. Hodge and Greve (2013) identify no less than five different variations on the theme: (1) institutional cooperation for joint production and risk sharing; (2) long-term (LT) infrastructure contracts that emphasize tight specification of outputs in long-term legal contracts; (3) public policy networks in which loose stakeholder relationships are emphasized; (4) civil society and community development; (5) urban renewal and downtown economic development. The most visible form of recent PPPs are the long-term infrastructure contract partnerships, most of the time organized around a design, build, finance, maintain model (DBFM). PPPs are thus, in this chapter, understood as long-term public infrastructure projects that are mainly privately financed and operated.

The relevance of studying PPPs extends beyond the field of infrastructure. PPPs are part of what Donahue and Zeckhauser (2012: 4) call collaborative governance: 'carefully structured arrangements that interweave public and private capabilities on terms of *shared discretion*' (original emphasis). Many other researchers have identified similar trends: collaborative public management (Agranoff and McGuire 2003), new public governance (Osborne 2010), interactive governance (Torfing *et al.* 2012), network governance (Koppenjan and Klijn 2004), hybrid organizations (Christensen and Lægreid 2011), and so on. They all stress the following features: it is more *private* governance – the number and scope of non-state or private actors in governance arrangements grows; it is more *horizontal* governance – different partners are supposed to work together in a network context, instead of like subordinates in a top-down structure; it is more *complex* governance – the large number and variety of actors who dynamically interact at different levels decentres and complicates the governance process; it is governance driven by *common objectives or goals* – the interdependency forces the public and private actors to work together to find joint and negotiated solutions that deal with grand societal challenges.

PPPs thus have a relevance beyond the world of infrastructure projects and contracts. They are exemplary of how modern public governance functions nowadays: in collaboration with many private actors, in a more horizontal (network) structure and with a high level of complexity. By focusing on the specific example of PPPs, it becomes possible to study democratic accountability in a more 'hands-on' manner and contribute to a more fine-grained understanding of the current state of democratic governance. In addition, PPPs are an intriguing example to study in terms of accountability, as we will explain in the next section.

What's the puzzle?

Most authors are rather negative about the impact of PPPs on democratic accountability. Three main reasons are mentioned. First, the traditional notion of ministerial responsibility is challenged by involving private actors in executing public tasks (Flinders 2001; Hodge 2009). The minister loses direct control and parliament loses oversight and influence. 'The shift towards greater private sector involvement in public service delivery weakens the thread of accountability between citizens, parliament and those responsible for service delivery (the executive)' (Reeves 2013: 78). Second, there is also a tension between the public demands for openness and the private desire for commercial confidentiality of information (Siemiatycki 2007). 'Excessive secrecy undermined the ability of legislators, auditors, and advocacy groups to challenge the terms of contracts or monitor performance of private operators', as claimed by Roberts (2010: 127). Flinders (2010: 120–1) more broadly argues that there is a 'splintered logic' in the sense that the values and principles on which PPPs are based and promoted are at odds with those traditionally found within the political and public sphere. Third, in addition to the problematic secrecy of the PPP contracts, members of parliament and citizens often lack the resources and expertise needed to scrutinize these specialized and technical legal documents. The complexity and technicality of both the PPP projects and contracts impedes a broad political and public debate and leads to depoliticization (Willems and Van Dooren 2016).

This 'democratic deficit' interpretation due to a shortfall in accountability arrangements is quite dominant in both the academic literature and the popular press (Hodge *et al.* 2010), but it does not quite tell the whole story. Other authors in fact suggested that PPPs could improve accountability for performance. For instance, Grimsey and Lewis (2007: 158) explicitly argue that PPPs offer an opportunity to expand the level of public interest protection due to improved 'value for money' testing, performance indicators, risk analyses and shifting, and so on. Flyvbjerg *et al.* (2003) do not consider PPPs as miracle solutions in terms of accountability, but they also point to their accountability potential.

In previous research, we described these ambiguous and contradictory tendencies as an 'accountability paradox' in the case of Flemish PPP projects (Willems and Van Dooren 2011). The use of PPPs has led to an often well-intended proliferation of control and accountability tools. Although many of them have a strong focus on accountability for performance, some fulfill an outspoken constitutional or democratic function such as the extensive annual progress reports of the Court of Audit in the Flemish Parliament. Yet, and therein lies the paradox, well-informed observers of Flemish PPP policy still perceive accountability in PPPs as rather problematic. More accountability does not seem an easy recipe for success. Some respondents then pointed towards the theoretical advantages of PPPs in terms of accountability, but claimed that some of them (up to now) failed to materialize in practice. The case of Flemish school infrastructure offers an opportunity to study this accountability paradox more in detail.

Qualitative approach: a critical case study of school infrastructure in Flanders

A qualitative research method based on a detailed case study is chosen for. By using a combination of extended document and media analyses with in-depth interviews of key players, we attempt to capture the complexity and multiplicity of how accountability works in practice. It is our aim to present a governance story that presents a nuanced interpretation of the many accountability processes that take place (see also Bevir and Rhodes 2006). Case selection is therefore crucial. School infrastructure in Flanders is considered as a *critical case to study*, which is of strategic importance to the general problem (Flyvbjerg 2006). In order to keep a clean comparative design, a case was needed where infrastructure projects are built following a PPP design alongside traditional direct public provision. The PPP variant and its public counterfactual coexist in the same public-policy context: both are under the supervision of the same minister, involve the same public administration actors, are scrutinized by the same members of parliament (MPs). Our case fits these criteria. Schools have been provided by the PPP organization 'Schools of Tomorrow', as well as through the traditional contracting by the Agency for Infrastructure in Education (AGIOn). Both the PPP and AGIOn operate in the same accountability context.

Flanders urgently needed new school infrastructure. As of December 2013, the investment needs were estimated at €4.5 billion. In 2004, the Flemish government therefore decided to follow a two-track policy to address this high demand. *A first track* was a catch-up PPP program with a total investment value of €1.5 billion. The new schools are being designed, built, financed and maintained (DBFM) by a private partner. This DBFM company makes the school buildings (currently 167 projects) available to the organizing authorities and school boards and takes care of the maintenance for 30 years. In turn, school boards pay a performance-related availability fee for the contract period and afterwards the buildings' ownership is transferred to the schools free of charge. In 2009, AGIOn and PMV (investment company of Flemish government) founded 'School Invest'. They each have 50 percent stake in its capital. In 2010, the DBFM company 'Schools of Tomorrow' was established, which is responsible for the execution of the program. Insurer AG Real Estate and banking group BNP Paribas Fortis make up the private partners who hold a majority share of 75 percent, while the public partner 'School Invest' has 25 percent share. *A second track* is the regular subsidy system through the public agency AGIOn, which is responsible for subsidizing the purchase, construction and renovation of school buildings with an annual budget of ca. €200 million. AGIOn is a public agency under ministerial hierarchy, with some operational decision-making authority delegated to the agency head. This direct ministerial control is crucial for the research design in order to compare it with the PPP program.

Out of the accountability paradox

Thus far, we argued that PPPs have more opportunities for accountability: PPPs are held to account on more forums of accountability. Yet, the perceived levels of accountability are generally assessed to be lower. How come this abundance of accountability does not lead to high levels of perceived accountability? In this section, we provide some answers, illustrated with the case of school infrastructure in Flanders. We first demonstrate that PPP are subjected to a wider range of accountability mechanisms compared to traditional procurement through AGIOn (1), and further explain how accountability also has some impact (2). Next, we discuss why accountability is perceived to be problematic by many (3), and how this coincides with a forum shift (4). Finally, we ask whether we have too much accountability (5).

Actual and external accountability

The claim that there are multiple accountabilities is not new (e.g. see Romzek and Dubnick 1987). Nevertheless, it remains crucial to verify if this presupposed multiplicity is actually present. It is not enough to know that there are many diverse formal accountability processes that, in theory, could take place. They have to manifest themselves in practice. A previous article on the Flemish school infrastructure case (Willems 2014) made two distinct arguments on its democratic accountability.

First, the many different accountability mechanisms at play were mapped in both the DBFM project and the direct public provision through AGIOn. Accountability is in both variants definitely *multifaceted*. Although this is a relevant finding, it does not tell us a lot about the interconnectedness of all those accountability mechanisms. Second, the importance of the actual and external nature of accountability was underlined. Although the public agency AGIOn faces some relevant account-holders in principle, accountability processes are mainly *latent* and stay *internal*. The DBFM project 'Schools of Tomorrow' is immediately somewhat suspicious due to its size, financial value and novelty. It gets the political and public attention that trigger *actual* processes of accountability. Those processes are also *external* from the start, meaning that they are followed by some relevant 'outsiders' such as politicians and journalists. This emphasis on the actual and external nature of these accountability processes is crucial in assessing PPPs from a democratic point of view. It is mainly through opening up to the political and public forums, and involving these two forums actively, that they gain democratic legitimacy in the eyes of the citizens and those who represent them (see also Papadopoulos 2010). To sum up, many accountability mechanisms are present both for AGIOn and PPP. For PPPs, the market involvement adds a forum for accountability. The main difference between AGIOn and the PPP, however, is not the bare number of accountability mechanisms. The difference is that the PPP's financial impact and novelty has activated more circuits of accountability.

Impactful accountability

A vital question regarding accountability mechanisms is: Do they matter anyway? Or are they just paper exercises without real impact? When overviewing the many accountability processes in the Flemish DBFM project 'Schools of Tomorrow', active members of parliament (MPs) seem to get some things done. In the previous legislature, a few MPs succeeded in enforcing the Flemish government to extensive and frequent parliamentary reporting. Court of Audit reports were demanded on the topic of PPPs and made visible to a broader audience. The media were informed by the MPs and do report repeatedly on the PPP project. There were even some significant policy changes in the DBFM program after accountability processes in the political and public forums.

The following example illustrates how accountability works in practice. The VSKO (Flemish Secretariat of the Catholic Education Network) calculated that between 73 and 120 percent of the annual operating costs of their schools would be absorbed by the availability fee to be paid to the DBFM company. The whole operation therefore would become unaffordable. The protest mainly came from the subsidized Catholic Education Network. They represent more than 70 percent of the schools in Flanders. They have to finance their school infrastructure for 30 percent with regard to primary schools and 40 percent with regard to secondary schools. The public educational network GO! (public education) is 100 percent financed by the Flemish government. MP Jos De Meyer, who is close to the Catholic Education Network, sounded the alarm. The minister recognized the financial difficulties of the Catholic Education Network and the risk on unequal treatment in comparison with public schools. After a discussion in the parliamentary commission, the minister decided to increase the subsidy by 11.5 percent. The media reported on the initial interpellation of Jos De Meyer, the discussion in the commission and the final decision of the minister to increase the subsidy.

Two respondents emphasized the role played by the MPs and the media to realize this policy change, while one respondent minimized their role and referred to the informal consultation with the educational networks as the main driver. The subsidized Catholic Education Network threatened to drop out of the DBFM program, which would endanger the whole program. Besides, the balance between the public and subsidized educational networks is perceived as something very delicate. It is important to note that the process of accountability starts with bottom-up protest from the Catholic schools network, which is channeled into the political forum through the political representative of the Christian Democratic Party. He acts as a megaphone by informing the media on this complex topic, who in turn inform their readers. MPs supported by their network lead the way in this case; the media follow.

This example shows that active MPs can play a role in fueling a process in which the minister is held to account and, perhaps more important, can have an actual impact by adjusting public policy. Different actors in different forums are actively checking and scrutinizing the same subject, isolated questions or pressures intermingle, gain momentum and are coordinated. A chain of reactions is started that turns internal processes into external ones. Impactful accountability is the end result. When we compare this with the regular subsidy system through AGIOn, there is a remarkable difference. MPs ask questions and the media do report, but the attention is limited and focused on individual schools. The actual operational performance of AGIOn as public agency is no item in the political and public forums, while the PPP is scrutinized. There was very little actual and external accountability with any impact regarding the regular subsidy system through AGIOn.

Accountability proves that accountability is broken

The empirical findings thus demonstrate that more accountability forums and actors are active in the DBFM project 'Schools of Tomorrow', that those forums and actors behave more actively, and even that they get results in terms of accountability. There is more accountability in Flemish PPP school infrastructure than in the regular subsidizing system through the public agency AGIOn. Yet, some important events or incidents, often with great symbolic value, have overshadowed this factual increase of accountability mechanisms and processes and led to a lower perception of accountability.

First, the DBFM framework contract between the Flemish government and the private consortium was kept secret. On 10 June 2010, the financial close between the private partners AG Real Estate and BNP Paribas Fortis and the public partner 'School Invest' (AGIOn and PMV) took place, by the establishment of the DBFM company 'Schools of Tomorrow'. Several MPs demanded closer inspection into the DBFM framework contract of the program. The educational networks also repeatedly demanded closer inspection into this framework contract. The minister and the private partners were very reluctant to meet this demand, because of a clause in the contract about commercial confidentiality. Ultimately, it was decided that MPs, during a period of five days, could look into the contract. The MPs had to accept a confidentiality obligation and could not take notes or copies or consult someone else. This 'ad hoc' settlement falls short of the norm of information release on PPPs in other countries (see Siemiatycki 2007). In addition, the actual 'clients' to the DBFM program – the educational networks and the school boards – still have no access to the DBFM framework contract due to clauses of commercial confidentiality. The media reported several times on this struggle for access. The scrutiny from parliament has mainly uncovered what many now perceive as obscure dealmaking. Paradoxically, accountability mechanisms have demonstrated accountability deficits. A substantial discussion on the contract did not occur.

Second, the requests for release of a preliminary advice of Eurostat (the statistical office of the EU) on the DBFM project 'Schools of Tomorrow' was kept secret. Eurostat had serious doubts about its ESA (European System of Accounts) neutrality of the PPP, due to the high government guarantee. They questioned whether such a large DBFM program (total value of €1.5 billion) with a high government guarantee can be kept off balance and formulated a negative preliminary advice. Since the autumn of 2010, three MPs have been asking to get access to this preliminary advice of Eurostat, given its implications for the general Flemish public budget. The Flemish ministers systematically answered that they would not communicate while the technical discussions with Eurostat are still going on. After more than three and a half years, the MPs still have not received a satisfying answer and explanation to their relevant question. It seems rather evident that such episodes have an impact on the perceptions of accountability and transparency. The media also reported several times on this struggle for access. Again, accountability mechanisms in the political and public forum have uncovered accountability deficits.

These two incidents overshadow the many accountability mechanisms. The damage in terms of accountability and transparency sticks firmly in the minds of the politicians, media, affected stakeholders and the general public. The desire to keep, at crucial moments in the decision-making process, certain vital documents and contracts behind closed doors is probably an important key to solve this accountability paradox. The impact of these mistakes in terms of accountability and transparency is amplified by their resonance in the media.

Accountability deficit or forum shift?

The perception of an accountability deficit also depends on the reach of accountability over the different forums. Opinions differ as to how many forums are to be addressed. Are PPPs accountable to the political forum (Flemish MPs), and the public forum (media and the general public)? Or the direct stakeholders in a PPP project that populate the administrative forum of implementation? In the case of 'Schools of Tomorrow', direct stakeholders are the educational networks and involved school boards. This makes a huge difference.

A respondent in the school infrastructure case points to the particular features of the policy domain 'education', which he describes as very 'politically sensitive' and a 'balancing act' with a very strong tradition of informal consultation with the educational networks. Yet, he claims that this is as democratic as any other policy domain, but the checks and balances do not happen through the Flemish Parliament but through civil society. He implies that the regular subsidy system through AGIOn scores high on accountability to the networks and school boards, and low on accountability to the Flemish Parliament, media and general public. The advent of the DBFM project leads to a forum-shifting: it is more accountable to the parliament, media and general public, but less to the educational networks and school boards. What is preferable in terms of democratic accountability? To paraphrase Mark Bovens, the answer would be: 'it depends' on the criteria used, even on the researcher's own interpretation of what constitutes democratic legitimacy. One respondent described it in the following manner:

> There are indeed few critical questions regarding the regular subsidy system. Just some parliamentary questions on the school in the backyard of the MPs. It remains the domain of the educational networks. DBFM gets a lot more attention, but does this also mean superior control and monitoring?

This observation raises more profound questions on accountability and democracy.

Too much accountability?

Although accountability may be a goal worth pursuing, it also comes with some costs. When does the cost of accountability surpass the benefits? How much accountability is enough (Pollitt 2008)? Many public officials complain already about existing accountability overloads (Bovens *et al.* 2008). Flinders (2011) points to the pathological effects of the 'politics' of accountability.

He claims that too much accountability can be as problematic as too little, and points to the link between increasing levels of accountability and the falling levels of public confidence in politics. Michael Power (1999) wrote more than a decade ago about 'the audit society' and increasingly empty rituals of verification. This audit society is often self-defeating in its proliferation of control and accountability mechanisms that have little pay-off or purpose and whose costs can be huge, as is powerfully illustrated by Anechiaro and Jacobs (1996) in their classic work *The Pursuit of Absolute Integrity*. When authors discuss accountability overloads, they mostly discuss an overload of mechanisms in increasingly more forums. As we argued above, there are good reasons why more mechanisms do not necessarily lead to perceived accountability. So, when does this multiplicity get in the way and become itself a burden?

Regarding the case of Flemish school infrastructure, we argue that more accountability and transparency is needed. In spite of having more and improved accountability processes in the DBFM program 'Schools of Tomorrow' compared to its public provision counterfactual, the intensity of the democratic accountability should also not be exaggerated. Although the DBFM project gets some news coverage, most respondents admit that given its financial scope and societal relevance – cost price €1.5 billion on a total Flemish government budget of ca. €28 billion – one would expect even more public attention. For instance, the media describe the most determining phases of the DBFM project, but their coverage is usually just generalist and informative. The total number of articles on the topic is therefore considerable, but the few extensive and evaluative ones are limited and restricted to the Flemish business papers. Respondents provide several reasons for this moderate news coverage: DBFM is just too technical and complex; there is a preference to focus on specific and more personal stories; and many delays in the project lead to some saturation.

The same goes for the way the project is dealt with in parliament. In two parliamentary commissions, you find a handful of MPs who follow this large PPP project very closely and keep it on the political agenda. They are limited in number, but their focus and engagement are crucial. Arguably, only two or three MPs really scrutinize this DBFM project. The most critical MP also belongs to the ruling majority. In a system that is dominated by political parties, this is quite unusual. He is, however, closely linked to the subsidized free education network, which remains the main provider of education in Flanders, and is consequently the main 'customer' in the DBFM project. This link with the sector is necessary to acquire expertise to be able to perform the control task adequately.

In general, technical and complex policymaking such as PPPs seem to have a tendency to fly beneath the public and political radar, so every opportunity and mechanism to hold them to account seems welcome. Alasdair Roberts (2010) calls privately financed and operated long-term infrastructure projects and contracts (PPPs) one of the most powerful illustrations of the 'logic of discipline': a shift of functions and responsibilities away from elected political actors to specialized 'technocratic' actors. The contemporary policy choice for PPP as mode of governance has become largely apolitical, meaning that it has been argued for as something that is obvious, logical and even inevitable. PPP has been reduced to a neutral management or procurement tool, of which the political character is concealed. Yet, PPPs are about public infrastructure with a high budgetary and social impact, and therefore need political and societal debate and support (Willems and Van Dooren 2016).

Conclusion

Papadopoulos (2013) identifies collaborative governance and cooperative policymaking, of which PPPs are an important example, as one of the main challenges to democratic politics. He says that the influence of democratic politics on political decisions has been weakened in general, but he also points to the various paradoxical and puzzling aspects of some transformations. It is by recognizing these complexities that we contribute to a more fine-grained understanding of the current state of democratic governance. This chapter provides some empirical support for Papadopoulos' main argument. The detailed case study of school infrastructure in Flanders illustrates the often complex nature of how accountability works in practice. The impact of horizontal and hybrid forms of governance such as PPPs on democratic accountability is more ambiguous than often presumed in the literature. This chapter therefore strongly nuances the quite popular negative assessments of accountability arrangements in PPPs based on actual empirical research.

We have identified five lessons that could help to unravel the accountability paradox. First, *actual and external* accountability is crucial from a democratic governance perspective. It is mainly by opening up to public and political forums, and involving those distinct forums actively, that democratic legitimacy is gained. Second, the *impact* of accountability should not be overlooked. Whether accountability processes take place with or without certain consequences makes a huge difference in terms of assessing them. Third, the importance of *certain 'symbols'* in terms of accountability and transparency is not to be underestimated, especially given their large resonance in the mass media. Fourth, it also depends on the chosen account-holder: *to whom* is one being accountable? Again, being accountable to the public and the elected politicians who represent them in the public and political forums is nowadays probably more important in terms of democratic governance. Fifth, whether multiple and redundant accountabilities become a burden rather than a blessing depends on the political *saliency of the subject*. When dealing with complex and technical policy matters such as PPPs – with a high budgetary and societal impact and a tendency to fly beneath the political and public radar – more visible and impactful accountability processes should be welcomed rather than feared.

References

Agranoff, R. and McGuire, M. (2003) *Collaborative Public Management: New Strategies for Local Governments*. Washington, DC: Georgetown University Press.
Anechiaro, F. and Jacobs, J. B. (1996) *The Pursuit of Absolute Integrity: How Corruption Control Makes Government Ineffective*. Chicago, IL: University of Chicago Press.
Aucoin, P. and Heintzman, R. (2000) The dialectics of accountability for performance in public management reform. *International Review of Administrative Sciences*, 66(1): 45–55.
Behn, R. (2001) *Rethinking Democratic Accountability*. Washington, DC: The Brookings Institution.
Bevir, M. and Rhodes, R. A. W. (2006) *Governance Stories*. New York: Routledge.
Bovens, M. (2010) Two concepts of accountability: accountability as a virtue and as a mechanism. *West European Politics*, 33(5): 946–67.
Bovens, M., Schillemans, T. and 't Hart, P. (2008) Does public accountability work? An assessment tool. *Public Administration*, 86(1): 225–42.
Christensen, T. and Lægreid, P. (2011) Complexity and hybrid public administration: theoretical and empirical challenges. *Public Organization Review*, 11(4): 407–23.
Donahue, J. D. and Zeckhauser, R. J. (2012) *Collaborative Governance: Private Roles for Public Goals in Turbulent Times*. Princeton, NJ: Princeton University Press.
Dubnick, M. (2014) Accountability as a cultural keyword. In M. Bovens, R. E. Goodin and T. Schillemans (eds), *Oxford Handbook of Public Accountability*. Oxford: Oxford University Press, pp. 23–38.
Fimreite, A. L. and Lægreid, P. (2009) Reorganizing the welfare state: partnership, networks and accountability. *Public Management Review*, 12(3): 281–97.
Flinders, M. (2001) *The Politics of Accountability in the Modern State*. Aldershot: Ashgate.
Flinders, M. (2010) Splintered logic and political debate. In G. A. Hodge, C. Greve and A. E. Boardman (eds), *International Handbook on Public-Private Partnerships*. Cheltenham: Edward Elgar, pp. 115–31.

Flinders, M. (2011) Daring to be a Daniel: the pathology of politicized accountability in a monitory democracy. *Administration & Society*, 43(5): 595–619.

Flinders, M. (2012) *Defending Politics: Why Democracy Matters in the Twenty-First Century*. Oxford: Oxford University Press.

Flinders, M. (2014) The future and relevance of accountability studies. In M. Bovens, R. E. Goodin and T. Schillemans (eds), *Oxford Handbook of Public Accountability*. Oxford: Oxford University Press, pp. 661–72.

Flyvbjerg, B. (2006) Five misunderstandings about case-study research. *Qualitative Inquiry*, 12(2): 219–45.

Flyvbjerg, B., Bruzelius, N. and Rothengatter, W. (2003) *Megaprojects and Risk: An Anatomy of Ambition*. Cambridge: Cambridge University Press.

Grimsey, D. and Lewis, M. K. (2007) *Public Private Partnerships: The Worldwide Revolution in Infrastructure Provision and Project Finance*. Cheltenham: Edward Elgar.

Hodge, G. (2009) Accountability. In P. O'Hara (ed.), *International Encyclopaedia of Public Policy: Governance in a Global Age* (Vol. 3). Perth: GPERU, pp. 1–17.

Hodge, G. and Coghill, K. (2007) Accountability in the privatized state. *Governance*, 20(4): 675–702.

Hodge, G. and Greve, C. (2013) Introduction: public-private partnership in turbulent times. In C. Greve and G. Hodge (eds), *Rethinking Public-Private Partnerships: Strategies for Turbulent Times*. London: Routledge, pp. 1–32.

Hodge, G. A., Greve, C. and Boardman, A. E. (eds) (2010) *International Handbook on Public-Private Partnerships*. Cheltenham: Edward Elgar.

Koppenjan, J. F. M. and Klijn, E.-H. (2004) *Managing Uncertainties in Networks: A Network Approach to Problem Solving and Decision Making*. London: Routledge.

Lodge, M. (2004) Accountability and transparency in regulation: critiques, doctrines and instruments. In J. Jordana and D. Levi-Faur (eds), *The Politics of Regulation: Institutions and Regulatory Reforms for the Age of Governance*. Cheltenham: Edward Elgar, pp. 124–44.

Mulgan, R. (2003) *Holding Power to Account*. New York: Palgrave.

O'Neill, O. (2002) *A Question of Trust*. Cambridge: Cambridge University Press.

Osborne, S. P. (ed.) (2010) *The New Public Governance? Emerging Perspectives on the Theory and Practice of Public Governance*. London: Routledge.

Papadopoulos, Y. (2010) Accountability and multi-level governance: more accountability, less democracy? *West European Politics*, 33(5): 1030–49.

Papadopoulos, T. (2013) *Democracy in Crisis? Politics, Governance and Policy*. Basingstoke: Palgrave Macmillan.

Philp, M. (2009) Delimiting democratic accountability. *Political Studies*, 57(1): pp. 28–53.

Pollitt, C. (2008) *The Essential Public Manager*. Maidenhead: Open University Press.

Pollitt, C. and Hupe, P. (2011) Talking about government: the role of magic concepts. *Public Management Review*, 13(5): 641–58.

Poulsen, B. (2009) Competing traditions of governance and dilemmas of administrative accountability: the case of Denmark. *Public Administration*, 87(1): 117–31.

Power, M. (1999) *The Audit Society: Rituals of Verification*. Oxford: Oxford University Press.

Reeves, E. (2013) Mind the gap: accountability and value for money in public-private partnerships in Ireland. In C. Greve and G. Hodge (eds), *Rethinking Public-Private Partnerships: Strategies for Turbulent Times*. London: Routledge, pp. 78–97.

Roberts, A. (2010) *The Logic of Discipline: Global Capitalism and the Architecture of Government*. Oxford: Oxford University Press.

Romzek, B. and Dubnick, M. (1987) Accountability in the public sector: lessons from the Challenger tragedy. *Public Administration Review*, 47(3): 227–38.

Siemiatycki, M. (2007) What's the secret? Confidentiality in planning infrastructure using public/private partnerships. *Journal of the American Planning Association*, 73(4): 388–403.

Sinclair, A. (1995) The chameleon of accountability: forms and discourses. *Accounting, Organizations and Society*, 20(2–3): 219–37.

Skelcher, C. (2010) Governing partnerships. In G. A. Hodge, C. Greve and A. E. Boardman (eds), *International Handbook on Public-Private Partnerships*. Cheltenham: Edward Elgar, pp. 292–306.

Sørensen, E. and Torfing, J. (2005) The democratic anchorage of governance networks. *Scandinavian Political Studies*, 28(3): 195–218.

Torfing, J., Peters, G., Pierre, J. and Sörensen, E. (2012) *Interactive Governance: Advancing the Paradigm*. Oxford: Oxford University Press.

Willems, T. (2014) Democratic accountability in public-private partnerships: the curious case of Flemish school infrastructure. *Public Administration*, 92(2): 340–58.

Willems, T. and Van Dooren, W. (2011) Lost in diffusion? How collaborative arrangements lead to an accountability paradox. *International Review of Administrative Sciences*, 77(3): 505–30.

Willems, T. and Van Dooren, W. (2012) Coming to terms with accountability: combining multiple forums and functions. *Public Management Review*, 14(7): 1011–36.

Willems, T. and Van Dooren, W. (2016) (De)politicization dynamics in public-private partnerships: lessons from a comparison between UK and Flemish PPP policy. *Public Management Review*, 18(2): 199–220.

though challenging the account

19
DIGITAL ERA GOVERNANCE REFORM AND ACCOUNTABILITY
The case of Denmark

Niels Ejersbo and Carsten Greve

Introduction

This chapter concerns the evolution of digitalization reforms in the Danish public sector and how there has been a shift in emphasis on accountability for digitalization from most professional and bureaucratic accountability towards political and legal accountability. This topic is important as digitalization is emerging as one of the most vibrant reform areas in the public sector (OECD 2014). Governments have to face the challenge of how to ensure adequate accountability for this reform.

More generally, reforms and modernization of the public sector has been widespread during the past decades. Reform objectives were typically focused on increased efficiency and lower costs, but other objectives such as citizen involvement and reduction of red tape were formulated as well. Reforms had often intended or unintended consequences on accountability. The ability to hold public officials accountable is seen as a cornerstone in a democratic society, and it comes as no surprise that accountability plays an important role in the reforms and changes taking place in the public sector. Reforms can have huge impact on the ability to hold public officials accountable and can have consequences for administration, and for democracy more broadly. Accountability is often studied in terms of 'more or less'. The question has been whether reforms have positive or negative consequences for accountability. Accountability is not a one-dimensional concept (Romzek 2000), and it covers a number of aspects, which makes it difficult to talk about more or less in an absolute sense. In order to capture some of the complexity characterizing the relationship between reform and accountability, we suggest a more dynamic perspective on the relationship between reform and accountability. Or, as Olsen (2013: 449) puts it: 'Rather than assuming equilibrium, a starting point is the fluidity, ambiguities, inconsistencies and tensions of democratic politics and the evolving nature of who is accountable to whom for what under different contingencies and with different implications'.

It is possible that accountability relationships evolve over time and emphasis may change from one aspect of accountability to another. This is not just a matter of better or worse, but how different aspects of accountability are affected during a reform process and how emphasis on the different aspects changes over time.

We pose the following research questions: How can we understand the relationship between public sector reform and accountability? How does accountability change during a reform process for digitalization? We look specifically at digitalization reforms and how forms of accountability have changed during the reform process and how these reforms have influenced accountability. Denmark has, through comprehensive strategies, initiated large changes in how IT and digital solutions are used in the public sector. The policy effort has been concentrated in four successive digital reform strategies that have helped the transformation. The key organizational levels – central government, regions and local government – have worked together in a collaborative way, led by the Ministry of Finance.

We combine the concept of digital era governance (DEG) (Dunleavy et al. 2006; Margetts and Dunleavy 2013) with the concept of the neo-Weberian state (NWS) (Pollitt and Bouckaert 2011) to describe the reform trends in the Danish public sector. By combining DEG and NWS, we can give a more accurate account for administrative reforms that have moved beyond New Public Management (NPM). We draw on the understanding of accountability presented by Bovens (2007), and to categorize the different aspects of accountability we are inspired by Romzek and Dubnick's (1987) four accountability systems: bureaucratic accountability, legal accountability, professional accountability and political accountability. We argue that accountability in relation to digital reforms has changed from professional accountability to bureaucratic accountability and now political accountability with legal accountability issues looming in the horizon.

The chapter uses Denmark as a case of how a country systematically has pursued digitization reforms and built an efficient digital infrastructure that is transforming public service delivery, and how attention on accountability has changed from professional accountability to bureaucratic accountability and moves towards political accountability.

Digitalization reform in the Danish public sector is a relevant case to show how accountability changes during an important reform. OECD points to Denmark as one of the leading countries when it comes to digitization in the public sector (OECD 2013). Digital changes are now at the center of government reform. Digital changes have impact not only inside the public sector, but also directly for citizens.

The chapter is based on analysis of Denmark's digital service strategy documents and other documents describing digitization and reform efforts from 2001 to 2014. The empirical data on the digital strategies were collected as part of a Danish research project on modernizing government during three decades. We have systematically collected strategy reform documents covering major modernization efforts in the Danish public sector from 2001 through 2014. In the following analysis, we focus on digitization reforms and the four digitalization strategies as part of the modernization efforts. The data are supplemented with recent OECD data on uptake of digital era policy reforms and on OECD reports on digitalization.

The chapter is organized as follows: The second section explains the theoretical framework of DEG, NWS and accountability. The third section looks at the evolution of digital infrastructure and digital services in Denmark. The fourth section is the discussion on which accountability forms relate to the digital strategies. The fifth section is the conclusion where the emphasis of accountability is shifting from professional accountability to bureaucratic accountability and political accountability.

Theoretical framework: reform and forms of accountability

The section presents two recent concepts of forms of public management reforms: DEG (Dunleavy et al. 2006; Margetts and Dunleavy 2013) and the NWS (Pollitt and Bouckaert 2011).

Both concepts have been used to characterize modern public sector development after the NPM movement, which is either said to be in decline or facing a 'post-NPM' period (Christensen and Lægreid 2011). The second part of this section discusses different forms of accountability.

Combining digital era governance and the neo-Weberian state

Dunleavy, Margetts and colleagues invented the concept of digital era governance (DEG) as they were characterizing digital era developments as opposed to the NPM trend. Controversially, they argued that 'NPM is dead, long live DEG'. They (Dunleavy *et al.* 2006; Margetts and Dunleavy 2013: 6) described three features in opposition to NPM's disaggregation, competition and incentivization: *reintegration* means that services and processes are being 're-governmentalized'; that new government processes are being created so things only have to be done once instead of several times; that shared service centers are set up to squeeze costs; that radical simplification of services, organizations and policies are aimed for. In short, they argue for a streamlining and centralized service structure again. *Need-based holism* is an attempt to build client-focused services where the user is put at the center of attention. Using digital solutions, governments can respond to users directly in real time. *Digitization* focuses on digital changes and the opportunity to *'completely embrace'* digital solutions in contact with users/citizens (i.e. digitizing interactions with citizens and business). It will make the users/citizens do more of the administration themselves, a sort of do-it-yourself government (from your touchscreen at your choice of digital device). Margetts and Dunleavy (2013) recently described the latest development in Web-based and social media, including big data, peer production, democratization of innovation, crowdsourcing, wikinomics, and network effects and all kinds of platforms for social media, including Facebook and Twitter.

NWS describes a public sector where there is a key governing role of the central government; democracy is the crucial legitimation for public actions; a modern public administration with legality for all; the public manager as a special category and professional public management; a service-oriented approach to citizens and the possibility of coproduction (Pollitt and Bouckaert 2011: 118–19). Pollitt and Bouckaert list 'Weberian' elements as: 'reaffirmation of the role of the state as the main facilitator of solutions to the new problems of globalization, technological change, shifting demographics, and environmental threat'; reaffirmation of representative democracy; reaffirmation of administrative law; preservation of the idea of public service [. . .]', and the 'neo' elements being: shift from internal bureaucratic focus to external orientation towards meeting citizens' needs and wishes; more consultation with citizens; achievement of results (performance management) rather than rule-following; trend towards being a professional manager attentive to citizen/user needs. Added to that could be an emphasis on bigger organizations and loyal implementation of reform initiatives. What we have witnessed in recent years is a renewed emphasis on big-sizing and of larger span-of-controls. Organizations are merging with each other and many public management reforms have created bigger organizational units. There is also a new interest in implementation (Patashnik 2008; Weaver 2010) as reform promises have to be kept and citizens expect to see results from politicians' reform efforts. In Pollitt and Bouckaert's (2011: 119) words: the NWS is 'a vision of a modernized, efficient, citizen-friendly state apparatus'.

Until now, the two concepts of DEG and NWS have been discussed separately. The idea here is to combine them as DEG trends influences and accelerates the development of NWS. Pollitt and Bouckaert (2011: 123) acknowledge the concept of DEG, but they remark that 'However, at this point in time it is not possible to comparatively to apply the DEG model across the broader horizon of public management reform as a whole – it is just too early, and the necessary data has not been assembled'. Margetts and Dunleavy (2013: 2) acknowledge NWS, but remark that:

> A number of other 'post-NPM' shift of ideas have been proposed, including a re-emphasis upon neo-Weberian ideas, or alleged "post-bureaucratic" modes of organization. However, the evidence cited for all these successor ideas is scattered and unconvincing, especially because pervasive patterns of digital changes remain peripheral in all these accounts.

So they are both aware of each other's concepts, but feel that the necessary data and evidence are missing.

Theoretically, we argue that there is some common ground between the two concepts and that the two in combination give a better understanding of public sector reform. We also argue that the digital changes explain the renewed interest in bigger organizations and citizen focus.

- *Both NWS and DEG focus on the shift towards bigger units able to process more information and making governments more efficient.* Pollitt and Bouckaert call it 'the reaffirmation of the role of the state' and 'greater orientation on the achievement of results'. Dunleavy *et al.* call it 'reintegration' and talk about 'creating new government processes to do things once instead of many times'.
- *Both NWS and DEG focus on new ways to provide customized service to citizens, but also involving citizens in providing and making solutions for themselves* (as opposed to NPM, who emphasized purely marketized solutions). Pollitt and Bouckaert call it the shift from internal bureaucratic rule following towards an external orientation towards meeting citizens' needs and wishes. They also mention 'a range of devices for consultation with [. . .] citizens' views'. Dunleavy *et al.* term it 'needs-based holism' and argue that digital developments allow for 'redesign of services from a client perspective'.

Where they differ is that Pollitt and Bouckaert put more emphasis on the role of representative democracy, administrative law, on direct citizen representation, on the professional manager. Dunleavy *et al.* focus more on the opportunities connected to digital changes. Even though they emphasize a distance to the more radical forms of NPMs, they do talk about 'results' and 'professional managers', 'a professional culture of quality and service' (Pollitt and Bouckaert 2011), and 'government business models' and adapting 'private services' delivery processes (Dunleavy *et al.* 2006), so it is not completely removed from NPM's focus on managerialism and markets.

Accountability

The ability to hold public officials accountable is seen as a cornerstone in a democratic society, and it comes as no surprise that accountability plays an important role in the reforms and changes taking place in the public sector. On the one hand, some reforms are aimed at improving accountability and have it as an official objective. Reforms may cause concerns about accountability and spark discussions about less accountability or reduced possibilities in holding officials accountable. Accountability has positive connotations and has become a goal in its own right (Bovens 2007). The focus on accountability and the instruments used to increase accountability also has its critics: 'there are many different forms and styles of accountability, some of which are not as democratic or benign as the term might imply' (Shore and Wright 2004: 103). They also point to the unintended consequences of the different instruments used to hold organizations or people accountable. Critics of accountability emphasize the need to pay close attention to processes and instruments used in connection with accountability – and not just see accountability as a desirable and neutral instrument.

The relationship between an actor and a forum may be understood as a principal-agent relationship (Bovens 2007). In the public sector, this is a relevant approach to understand the relationship between the actor and the forum. However, applying a principal-agent approach does not necessarily say very much about the content of the relationship and the different forms of accountability involved. In their analysis of the Challenger tragedy, Romzek and Dubnick (1987) outline four systems of accountability based on whether the forum is internal or external on the one dimension and the degree of control given to the forum on the other dimension. These accountability systems can be regarded as standards used when assessing the action of the actor. The four accountability systems are useful to describe the accountability issues in the relationship between the forum and the actor. A *bureaucratic accountability* system (internal/high degree of control) is based on 'an organized and legitimate relationship between a superior and a subordinate in which the need to follow "orders" is unquestioned; and a close supervision or a surrogate system of standard operating procedures or clearly stated rules and regulations' (Romzek and Dubnick 1987: 228). Bureaucracy has been established, which means that rules must be followed. It can also include political formulated goals that must be fulfilled. In relation to reform and reorganizations, specifying responsibilities and strengthening executive leadership tied to bureaucratic accountability (Romzek 2000: 24). In a *legal accountability system* (outside/high degree of control), the 'relationship is between two relatively autonomous parties and involves a formal or implied fiduciary (principal/agent) agreement between the public agency and its legal overseer' (Romzek and Dubnick 1987: 229). In this case, the forum has the possibility to apply legal sanctions to the actor or to sanction based on a contractual agreement. This may go beyond court of law and include commission or special entities to scrutinize (Romzek 2000: 25). An example could be the formation of a new legal institution to oversee new digital services. The third system is termed *professional accountability* (internal/low degree of control). This is characterized by 'placement of control over organizational activities in the hands of the employee with the expertise or special skill to get the job done. The key to the professional accountability system, therefore, is deference to expertise within the agency' (Romzek 2000: 229). It is professional norms that are the standard and determine the expectations. The content of reforms will be influenced and judged against professional norms and standards. In relation to digitization reform, the expertise, knowledge and norms of IT experts will set the standard. In a *political accountability* system (external/low degree of control), the key element is responsiveness to key stakeholders. These may include the general public, elected officials, agency clientele or special interest groups. The key elements are openness, freedom of information and responsiveness. This type of accountability systems illustrates the large number of interest and players that can be involved in an accountability relationship. As digitization reforms expand and digitized solutions and services become more widespread, the voice of different stakeholders will become more important. The reaction from the general public or comments from interest groups must be taken into account, and elected officials or civil servants in charge of digitization reforms can face new and changing groups of stakeholders.

Public sector strategies for digital service reform in Denmark

The Danish government has been pursuing an active top-down-driven reform strategy for digitalization for a number of years. The official digital strategies have been formulated since

2001. Digitalization (then known as e-government) has been a part of Danish efforts for modernization of the public sector since the early 1980s. There is a discussion regarding whether the changes are driven by technological innovations only. Our argument here is that the government has been consciously developing a reform strategy for how the Danish public services become digitalized.

Digital government is on top of the reform agenda and it plays an important role in reforms of the public sector. Denmark also shows up on the top of rankings of digital government from OECD and other international organizations. However, in the Danish context, digitalization and e-government must also be understood as a driver or as a means to an end. Digital government has been high on top of the reform agenda for a number of years in Denmark. There were early reports about Denmark as an 'information society' in the 1990s. In the early 2000s, a Digital Task Force was created. The Digital Task Force was a collaboration between central government, regional governments (then, counties), and local governments. The purpose was to make a common digital strategy for all levels of government. The Digital Task Force in-sourced key personnel from the other parts of the public sector, and also worked closely together with the private sector. The focus was to make a coherent and visible strategy for formulating and implementing digital changes in the Danish public sector. In 2011, an Agency for Digitisation was established under the Danish Ministry of Finance as a replacement for the Digital Task Force. In the digital government reforms, the three layers of government are working closely together: central governments, regional government and local governments. Since 2001, there have been four subsequent strategies. It is to these strategies we now turn.

Four digitalization strategies

The first digital strategy was called 'Towards the digital public administration – vision and strategy for the public sector'. The strategy was published in 2001. The strategy had four signposts: (1) The digital public administration must prepare citizens and enterprises for the network society. (2) The public administration must work and communicate digitally. Reports, payments and so on should be digital. (3) The public sector should deliver services that are citizen-centered. (4) The tasks of the public sector should be handled where they are handled best, and not be seen as belonging to any one organization. Digital solutions make it easier and less costly to share information. The four signposts were followed up with eight specific areas of intervention.

The second digital strategy was called 'The public sector's strategy for digital administration 2004–2006'. The strategy was published in 2004. It built on the previous reform. A number of signposts were announced: (1) The public sector should deliver joined-up and citizen-centered services. Services should be designed with citizens in mind. (2) Digital services should create improved service quality and should free resources. Investments in digital infrastructure should pay off. Digital projects should result in better products, faster response time, etc. or simply that fewer resources should go to providing the same quality of services. (3) The public sector should work and communicate digitally. Work processes should be supported digitally. (4) Digital administrative services should be based on a coherent and flexible IT infrastructure. (5) Public managers should lead by example and secure implementation of the organization's vision. For each of the signposts, there were clear targets attached.

The third digital strategy was called 'The strategy for digitization of the public sector 2007–2010: towards better digital service, improved efficiency and stronger collaboration'. The strategy was published in 2007. 'Prioritizing and coordination' were the keywords. There were three strategic signposts: (1) better digital services; (2) improved efficiency and effectiveness; and (3) stronger commitment and collaboration for digital solutions.

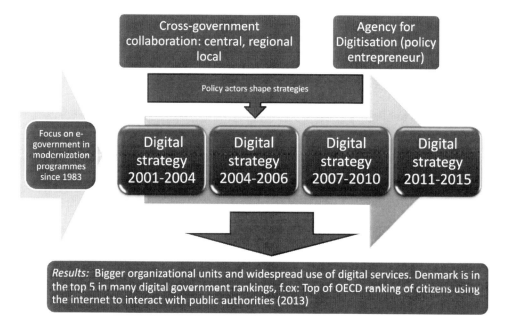

Figure 19.1 Path to digital government in Denmark

The fourth and current digital strategy ran from 2011 to 2015. The strategy was called 'The path to digital welfare'. It was published in 2011. The strategy focused on three items: (1) no more printed forms and letters; (2) new digital welfare; and (3) digital solutions for closer collaborations. The strategy meant that by 1 November 2014, all communication between citizens and the public sector must be digital. The strategy had 12 areas of focus and 60 specific initiatives all together. The government keeps track of how far the implementation of the strategy has gone, and implementation to attention is important in reforms (Patashnik 2008). A new digital strategy has been decided for 2016–2020.

The government has also launched a special initiative called 'The path to digital welfare 2013–2020', which focuses on public services in the welfare state sector for citizens, such as tele-medicine or self-help in exercising after a hospital operation. The initiative has seven areas of focus. The initiative was published in 2013.

At the release of the initiative for digital welfare, the Minister for Economics and the Interior, Margrethe Vestager, remarked:

> As a citizen you will get better services when we are using digital solutions – and at the same time we are getting more freedom to spend the society's money where they do most good [. . .] We shall try out and assess the technological possibilities so we can adopt new solutions continuously and develop our welfare society.
>
> *(press release, 2013)*

The local governments have their own digital strategy in addition to the national strategies. Local Government Denmark has a 'Local Governance Digital Advisory Council'. Local Government Denmark made a 'local government digital strategy in 2010' with 32 specific projects before they entered into the cross public sector strategy mentioned above. Local Government

Denmark is planning a new local government digital strategy for the period 2016–2020. Work on the new strategy has commenced. Local Government Denmark (2015) attributes efficiency savings to introduction of digital services. The areas where local governments have budgeted for efficiency savings in 2016 is digital mail, IT systems and digital self-service solutions.

Denmark has thereby had a consistent and evolving strategy for implementing digital era governance changes in the public sector. The goal is to make sure that 'digital service is good service' to the citizens (Frelle-Petersen and Jensen 2014). The focus on digital government has been stronger in recent years as the utilization of big data is beginning to emerge. Other countries have begun to make specific strategies. The UK government launched the 'Government Digital Inclusion Strategy' in December 2014, building on the government digital strategy from 2013 (Cabinet Office UK 2013, 2014).

There were other actions by the government in relation to digitalization: (1) The government took all the tasks related to payment of welfare checks to citizens in need, and put the operation of these tasks in the hands of a large private company. The government contracted out payment of welfare services to a big data center called UdbetalingDanmark ('Payment Denmark'). It is a part of a pension company called ATP. Danish public organizations are using social media strategies, and Denmark is one of the countries with the most Facebook users. (2) The Agency for Digitisation (2012a) has launched a program model that instructs organizations on how programs should be implemented. The Agency for Digitisation has also issued specific guidelines about what constitutes 'a business case'. (3) In 2012, the Danish government joined the Open Government Partnership. The responsibility for the Danish policy lies within the Agency for Digitisation (2013). The Open Government Partnership action plan was updated in January 2015, and two new areas of interest will be added: 'Open data' and 'Distribution of open government'.

Denmark has showed some clear results for digitization. Denmark ranks at number 2 on providing open access to data in the open index 2014. Denmark is number 1 in an OECD survey on how much citizens are in contact with the public sector via the Internet. Nine out of 10 citizens in Denmark aged 25–34 used the Internet to interact with public authorities (OECD 2013). Denmark is number 1, with 84 percent, in the European Union indicator for 'citizens' use of eGovernment services during the last 12 months'. Denmark ranks at number 2 in 'strategic government capabilities' in the Sustainable Government Indicators report in 2014. Denmark has dropped from number 4 in 2012 to number 16 in 2014 in the United Nations e-government survey on 'world e-government leaders'. Denmark ranks at number 4 in households' access to broadband in OECD's broadband map. Denmark is number 1 in the EU's indicator for 'households with access to the Internet at home', at 90 percent.

Digitalization drives reform efforts

Digitalization is an important tool in other types of reform, such as increased collaboration and coordination among different public sector agencies and actors. The Danish common digital strategy involves central government, regional governments and local governments. Collaboration is also requested in the health sector, where all the different parts of the health delivery system have to work together to ensure a flow for the patients in their treatments. Collaboration is also required in the labor market sector, especially in the effort to find training opportunities and new jobs for unemployed people.

Earlier studies of public management reforms in Denmark showed how reforms were influenced by NPM and how the reform agenda was dominated by NPM items (Hansen 2011; Greve 2012; Ejersbo and Greve 2014). This section has highlighted three ways that the reform efforts have signaled a DEG/NWS profile. First, digitalization has been a top-down effort, effectively pushing through a digital reform agenda from the central policymakers while taking advantage of ongoing technological innovations. Second, digitalization has supported and boosted efforts to make larger organizations and administrative service centers. The result is a Neo-Weberian focus on bigger organizational units. Third, the digitalization possibilities in connecting to citizens in new ways and providing digital-based services supports the neo-Weberian emphasis on a more citizen-centered state where services can be made more efficient by providing them digitally.

A reform movement that covers both DEG and NWS is likely to lead to more complex forms of accountability. The common ground between DEG and NWS emphasize coordination, reintegration and bigger organizations, on the one hand, and citizen focus and service orientation, on the other. The attempt to increase coordination and bigger units will emphasize bureaucratic accountability. It can lead to a push for common solutions and on common rules and procedures. Coordination can be achieved through different mechanisms such as hierarchy and bureaucratic procedures (Peters 1998). This will also make a clear distinction between superior and subordinate. Coordination efforts can also be supported by introducing new technologies or common technological platforms. Citizen focus and service orientation includes providing customized services and getting citizens involved in the provision of services. The latter can give citizens insight and better knowledge of the service provision process, which in turn can give them a platform for asking questions. Digitalization gives citizens, politicians and bureaucrats easy access to information and access to more information. A more citizen-oriented approach triggers a broader set of accountability aspects with specific emphasis on political accountability. On the other hand, 'transparency is *not* something which seems to fit neatly into some of the groupings which we have found are important for other aspects of reform' (Pollitt and Bouckaert 2011: 111, emphasis in the original). This suggests that reforms may trigger an increased emphasis on different forms of accountability, and that it is difficult to formulate clear expectations to the relationship between reform trends and changes in specific aspects of accountability. Nevertheless, we expect that a combination of DEG and NWS will put more emphasis on bureaucratic accountability and political accountability.

Discussion: how accountability changed for digital era governance strategies

This section discusses how forms of accountability have changed during the process of digital era governance reforms. All forms of accountability are, to some extent, present during the described period. Our argument here is that the attention and weight of the form of accountability has changed from professional accountability in the first strategy to bureaucratic accountability in the second and third strategies, and is now moving into a phase of political accountability in the fourth strategy. The legal accountability form looms in the horizon as citizens' legal demands are occurring.

The first development concerns the *professional accountability*. This was very evident when the digital strategies were first introduced. The key issue was to make public managers, employees and citizens aware of the opportunities in digitization of services. A key driver was to create enthusiasm for digital solutions. At that time, there were few mandatory digital services; it was up to organizations and citizens if they wanted to use the new service possibilities available to them. The organization of the digital strategies was trusted to the Digital Task Force. It was situated in the Ministry of Finance, but it was a collaborative project between the regions and the local governments. There was a board for the Digital Task Force where leaders from central government, regional government and local governments had their seats. The public managers were accountable to the board, which was accountable to the political leaders in central government, regional government and local government, but a main agenda item was to get recognition from the digital professionals about the new digital solutions that were being introduced. At the end of this period, the pressure for stepping up the digital strategy and committing public organizations to adopt the digital solutions became stronger. A new organization was needed.

In 2011, the Ministry of Finance formed the Agency for Digitisation as part of a reorganization of the ministry. The main emphasis for accountability changed to *bureaucratic accountability*. The Agency for Digitisation became responsible for formulating and implementing the digital strategy. The Agency for Digitisation got a performance contract with the Ministry of Finance. The Agency for Digitisation became the main bureaucratic organization responsible for digitization in Denmark. In the strategy itself, there was a new emphasis on mandatory solutions. Generally, bureaucratic rules and formal procedures became part of the work with digitization. A target was set for getting people to receive digital post by November 2014, for example. Citizens had to get a specific written permission to opt out of the system. A full campaign effort was made to get Danes to adopt the new digital solutions. Although the Agency for Digitisation used persuasive powers and tried to convince citizens to adopt digital solutions, hard pressure was applied in the end as the government made a decision to shift to digital post by this said date. At the same time, the digital strategy had to produce savings that could be used by the Ministry of Finance. The bureaucratic accountability chain was very evident. Mandatory digital solutions were also introduced inside the public sector. Shared Administrative Service Centers were introduced in late 2008, and the following years standardized IT solutions were implemented in ministries and the majority of state agencies. After some organizational and technical difficulties, the organizational responsibility was transferred to the Ministry of Finance. As the digital strategy, with its mandatory requirements, was rolled out, accountability for the reform became a matter of compliance with bureaucratic requirements (i.e. bureaucratic accountability).

In recent years, politicians have begun to address digital strategy issues. We therefore note a shift in emphasis towards forms of *political accountability*. In 2013, the government, the regional governments and the local governments announced the strategy on 'Digital welfare – new opportunities for the welfare society'. The aim was to innovate services that were close to the citizens. At the same time, the government was aiming for savings through the new digital solutions. The new initiative specifically for 'digital welfare' was aimed for 2013–2020. Ministers were visible at the press conference that launched the report. Politicians have come forward in this period as media debate has started to rise on the new mandatory digital solutions that citizens have to accept. The news media began to report stories on citizens who could not use a computer and could not get access to the public sector. Therefore, political accountability for the digital strategies is starting to attract interest. There are new direct links between politicians and citizens. Politicians at central government level, but also in the regional governments and local governments, now have to answer to citizens about services delivered or supported by digitalization.

Legal accountability is beginning to show itself on the horizon in Denmark. There are debates about how the government can protect the personal data of citizens. There is also a discussion of how citizens can try to complain in order to receive benefits that are supported by digital service delivery systems. A recent scandal in the Danish tax authority concerning a failed IT system has left many homeowners in limbo in terms of setting the right tax for their property. After all public sector organizations stopped sending information about services, financial support, etc., there have been examples with citizens that have missed deadlines and, as a consequence, lost the opportunity to get public support. Now and in the future, it can have severe consequences if citizens don't check their email or digital platforms. Furthermore, issues relating to personal data security and data protection have to be addressed. There is also the question of what governments do with the big data available.

The move from professional accountability to bureaucratic accountability, and now towards political accountability and legal accountability, may also be related to the shifting status of the digital reforms. In the beginning, the digital reforms had an internal focus and were primarily driven by 'idealists' and 'nerdy' people with a technical focus. They slowly increased in importance and scope, and are now very visible and have direct consequences for citizens. Digital public service delivery has, at the same time, moved up on the political agenda. The path from professional accountability to bureaucratic accountability to political accountability may be typical for reforms that are initiated inside the system, whereas reforms started based on a political debate will take a different path.

The move towards the combination of DEG and NWS reforms means that accountability forms are changing as well. Even though it is not possible to show causal relations between reform types and specific changes in accountability relations, it is suggested here that DEG/NWS elements such as reorientation of the service delivery model and customized services to citizens actualize a variety of accountability aspects.

Conclusions: how public sector strategies for a neo-Weberian organization of the public sector and the digital era lead to changing forms of accountability from professional, to bureaucratic, and towards political and legal accountability

Denmark is pursuing a coherent public sector strategy to enhance digital infrastructures and digital services. The digitalization reform has been a top-down reform project from the Danish government. Formulating and implementing digital government has been a priority for consecutive Danish governments. Denmark has pursued four consecutive digital strategies across local, regional and central government level. The digital strategy is also now focused on the welfare services to citizens and how citizens can become coproducers and use digital tools in public service delivery. A new digitalization strategy for the period 2016–2020 was decided in 2016.

Denmark is practicing all of the elements (reintegration, needs-based holism, digital changes) identified by Dunleavy, Margetts and colleagues on digital era governance. There is reintegration as a new digital infrastructure is being built. There is needs-based holism as new digital solutions are made with citizens in mind and are user-friendly ('borger.dk' as an example). There are many digital changes introduced that create a more citizen-oriented public service delivery system. The government focuses on making data available, supporting the big data trend. And government in various ways interact via social media with citizens. The digital era supports neo-Weberian state decisions: the public sector is reintegrating tasks in services in larger organizational units. The public sector has witnessed structural reforms in many policy areas, creating larger units. Reforms on digital changes are driving public sector changes more generally.

There has been a shift in emphasis in the forms of accountability for the digital strategies over a period of 10–15 years. The dominant form of accountability was at first professional. The focus was on getting the digital solutions right and receiving recognition for that among digital peers. That changed to bureaucratic accountability when the Ministry of Finance stepped up its game, and the Agency of Digitisation took overall responsibility for digital era governance policy. The third change in emphasis came with increased focus on political accountability as the digital strategies were rolled out and where citizens and media began asking about how politicians could endorse this. Politicians have begun to address digital changes and to discuss blame and reap rewards if digital strategies are going well. Denmark's increasing international profile in digital era governance strategies make the public managers accountable to the government and the parliament that are again are accountable to the public. The looming issue of accountability concerns legal accountability as more and more services are becoming digitised and start having real consequences for citizens' daily lives. Citizens are beginning to protect themselves and become critical of digital solutions, and disputes may arise in the future of Internet security, personal data protection and other issues.

References

Behn, R. (2001) *Rethinking Democratic Accountability*. Washington, DC: Brookings Institution Press.
Bovens, M. (2007) Analysing and assessing accountability: a conceptual framework. *European Law Review*, 13: 447–68.
Cabinet Office UK (2013) *Government Digital Strategy*. Available at: www.gov.uk/government/publications/government-digital-strategy (acessed 29 July 2016).
Cabinet Office UK (2014) *Government Digital Inclusion Strategy*. December 2014. Available at: www.gov.uk/government/publications/government-digital-inclusion-strategy/government-digital-inclusion-strategy (accessed 29 July 2016).
Christensen, T. and Lægreid, P. (eds) (2011) *The Ashgate Research Companion to New Public Management*. Aldershot: Ashgate.
Danish Agency for Digitisation (2012a) *Cross-Governmental Programme Model*. Available at: www.digst.dk/Servicemenu/English/Policy-and-Strategy/Interministerial-Project-Office/Programme-Model (accessed 29 July 2016).
Danish Agency for Digitisation (2012b) *Basic Data*. Available at: www.digst.dk/Servicemenu/English/Digitisation/Basic-Data (accessed 29 July 2016).
Danish Agency for Digitisation (2013) *Open Innovation Data Strategy*. Available at: www.digst.dk/Servicemenu/English/Policy-and-Strategy/Open-Data-Innovation-Strategy-ODIS (accessed 29 July 2016).
Danish Agency for Digitisation (2015) *OGP handlingsplan udvides* [Open Government Plan Extended]. Press release, 7 January.
Danish Government (2012) *Regeringens 2020-plan. Danmark i arbejde* [The Government's 2020 Plan: Denmark at Work]. Copenhagen: Danish Government.
Danish Government (2013) *Open Government: National Action Plan 2013–2014*. Copenhagen: Ministry of Finance.
Danish Government, Local Government Denmark, Danish Regions (2001) *Towards the Digital Public Administration: Vision and Strategy for the Public Sector*. Copenhagen: Danish Government.
Danish Government, Local Government Denmark, Danish Regions (2004) *The Public Sector's Strategy for Digital Administration 2004–2006*. Copenhagen: Danish Government.
Danish Government, Local Government Denmark, Danish Regions (2007) *The Strategy for Digitalization of the Public Sector 2007–2010: Towards Better Digital Service, Improved Efficiency and Stronger Collaboration*. Copenhagen: Danish Government.
Danish Government, Local Government Denmark, Danish Regions (2011) *The Digital Path to Future Welfare: E-Government Strategy 2011–2015*. Copenhagen: Danish Government.
Danish Government, Local Government Denmark, Danish Regions (2013) *Digital Welfare: New Opportunities for the Welfare Society*. Copenhagen: Danish Government.
Dunleavy, P., Margetts, H., Bastow, S. and Tinkler, J. (2006) *Digital Era Governance: IT Corporations, the State and E-Government*. Oxford: Oxford University Press.
Ejersbo, N. and Greve, C. (2014) *Moderniseringen af den offentlige sektor 3. udgave* [The Modernization of the Public Sector, 3rd edition]. Copenhagen: Akademisk Forlag Business.
Frelle-Petersen, L. and Jensen, S. U. (2014) Digital service er god service [Digital service is good service]. *Administrativ Debat*, 3: 12–15.

Greve, C. (2012) *Reformanalyse* [Reform Analysis]. Copenhagen: DJØFs Forlag,
Hansen, H. F. (2011) NPM in Scandinavia. In T. Christensen and P. Lægreid (eds), *The Ashgate Research Companion to New Public Management*. Aldershot: Ashgate, pp. 113–29.
Local Government Denmark (2015) *De effektive kommuner. Kommunernes effektiviseringsarbejde 2013–2014* [The Efficient Local Governments]. Copenhagen: Local Government Denmark.
Margetts, H. and Dunleavy, P. (2013) The second wave of digital era governance: a quasi-paradigm for government on the Web. *Philosophical Transactions of the Royal Society*, 371: 1–17.
OECD (2013) *Governance at a Glance: Denmark*. Paris: OECD.
OECD (2014) *Recommendations of the Council on Digital Government Strategies*. Paris: OECD.
Olsen, J. P. (2013) The institutional basis of democratic accountability. *West European Politics*, 36(3): 447–73.
Patashnik, E. M. (2008) *Reforms at Risk*. Princeton, NJ: Princeton University Press.
Peters, B. G. (1998) Managing horizontal government: the politics of coordination. *Public Administration*, 76(2): 295–311.
Pollitt, C. and Bouckaert, G. (2011) *Public Management Reform: A Comparative Analysis – New Public Management, Governance, and the Neo-Weberian State* (3rd edition). Oxford: Oxford University Press.
Romzek, B. (2000) Dynamics of public accountability in the era of reform. *International Review of Administrative Sciences*, 66(1): 21–44.
Romzek, B. S. and Dubnick, M. J. (1987) Accountability in the public sector: lessons from the Challenger tragedy. *Public Administration Review*, 47(3): 227–38.
Shore, C. and Wright, S. (2004) Whose accountability? Governmentality and the auditing of universities. *Parallax*, 10. 100–16.
Weaver, R. K. (2010) *But Will It Work? Implementation Analysis to Improve Government Performance*. Washington, DC: Brookings.

20
THE DYNAMICS OF THE EU ACCOUNTABILITY LANDSCAPE

Moving to an ever-denser union

Anchrit Wille

The expansion and proliferation of accountability in the EU system

The landscape of accountability institutions in the EU slowly becomes denser. The shift from national, state-based policymaking to the EU level, and the continuous expansion of the executive sphere in the EU, is accompanied by a growing concern about how to organize democratic accountability in the complex multilevel web of European governance.

This concern has prompted for a gradual expansion of a system of EU-level checks and balances. The EU, while pursuing closer integration, has, through Treaties since the Single European Act 1986, pursued an agenda of strengthening accountability and democratization. Following the Treaty of Lisbon 2007, the role of the directly elected European Parliament and national parliaments was expanded to secure improved accountability within the ordinary legislative process. In parallel with this political aspiration for organizing democratic accountability, there was a marked concern for improved administrative and financial accountability. The establishment of an ombudsman, complaint-handling mechanisms, a whistle-blower protection act, rating agencies, inquiry committees and a host of auditors are indicators of a distinct proliferation of accountability in the EU system. Together, it has produced a list of procedures, mechanisms and forums that have been devised to hold the EU executive to account that has become longer and equally varied. Most of these accountability arrangements follow democratic and administrative reforms.

This chapter explores how the accountability landscape in the EU has evolved over time. It examines the rise of accountability provisions and focuses on the accountability forums that play a role in holding EU executive actors to account. Rather than assuming equilibrium, this chapter takes the fluidity, ambiguities, inconsistencies and the evolving nature of accountability as a starting point (cf. Olsen 2013: 449). Whereas previous work often concentrated on a single institutional arena in isolation, this chapter will explore accountability in the EU from an integrated systemic view that emphasizes linkages across all of the major forums that hold the executive to account. Instead of focusing on one institution, the chapter shows how different accountability forums are related, and how they interact and adapt to one another over time. The aim is an exploration of the web of accountability arrangements that has been woven around the EU executive: What pivotal watchdog institutions, accountability forums and arrangements have come into being for holding the EU executive powers accountable?

To sketch a tentative portrait of the EU accountability landscape, this exploration draws on the insights from existing (case) studies. In addition, annual reports of several EU institutions are used to document the development of oversight and accountability practices. The chapter aims to enhance the understanding of the way in which the EU's institutional accountability framework has evolved and fits within today's presumptions about how power should be controlled and accountability achieved. The picture presented is one of a dynamic, differentiated and complex accountability landscape that provides the groundwork for overseeing the European executive.

The EU accountability landscape: a dynamic institutional order

A central element of good governance is the question of how power is allocated, legitimated, applied and, above all, being subject to checks and balances. As the scale of European legislative and executive power increased, the demand for more accountability increased with it.

What is accountability?

The concept of 'holding to account' obliges officials to disclose information, to explain and justify the exercise of authority, and to submit to sanctions if necessary (Bovens 2007: 450). Three stages are key to an accountability relationship in this definition. First, the provision of information and reporting, and exploring whether accountees have met the standards expected of them. Second, the debate, in which accountees are questioned and required to defend and explain themselves. Third, passing judgment in which actors are sanctioned for falling below the standards expected of them, or rewarded for achieving or exceeding them.

Most accountability sequences do not include all these stages, or not all stages are performed by the same forum. In an accountability landscape, different forums can play a different role in the accountability process. Some institutions specialize on the checking and investigation, and others have the possibility of probing questions, debate and final deliberation (Curtin 2009: 270)

The capacity to hold to account relies, thus, on a combination of structures, mechanisms and procedures that is concerned with ex post oversight. The opportunity for 'holding executive power to account' is essential for democratic systems, and can take different forms – *political, administrative, professional, legal or social* (Bovens 2007: 454–7) – depending on the forum of accountability. These different forums make inquiries about policies that are or have been in effect; they scrutinize past executive actions, and call executive officers to account for their actions. Next to the courts and parliaments there is a wide range of quasi-legal forums of auditors, inspectors, and controllers, supreme audit institutions (SAIs), anticorruption agencies and ombudsoffices that are exercising independent and external political, administrative and financial supervision in modern democracies. Together, these different institutions provide for an accountability *landscape*.

Accountability: an evolving landscape

The accountability landscape should not be treated as a static structure, but rather as dynamic evolving practices (Bovens *et al.* 2010: 192). Building the EU into a polity that appeals to democratic standards of legitimacy implies the institutionalization of a variety of established systems, procedures and mechanisms prescribing who is accountable to whom for what (Olsen 2010: 450). Alongside the allocation of more powers and own financial resources in the EU, and the transfer of functions from national to supranational institutions, the political debate about democracy and legitimacy in the EU grows more intense in the late 1990s, raising questions about the accountability of the EU's executive bodies. The development of the institutional landscape of accountability is, thus, part of a struggle for 'good' government at the EU level and a process of legitimization through accountability (cf. Laffan 2003: 77). It is likely to be a controversial, politicized and dynamic process in which EU actors cope with the tensions between multiple, contested and dynamic conceptions and standards of accountability (Olsen 2010, 2013).

The development of the accountability landscape manifests itself along several rudiments. To start, it becomes evident in a system of delineated *obligations* of the (new) executive bodies to give account to (new) *accountability forums*. These rudiments give institutional shape to the 'Who is accountable to whom?' question. Many of the obligations arise out of constitutions or treaties, or are imposed by laws or rules. The creation of these new obligations and forums leads, in turn, to the rise of *new accountability relationships*, and a process of integration of the information, debating and sanctioning function.

The rise of *accountability practices* follows the rise of these new accountability provisions. Actors bargain with each other over how those in power are held publicly responsible for their decisions and how accountability provisions should be interpreted, and which one of the several procedures for holding to account should be chosen. Existing forums renegotiate their powers and generally try to broaden the scope of their control and of their powers of investigation, debate and sanctioning (Bovens et al. 2010).

Negotiation of a stronger use of new accountability provisions and the emergence of new *accountability networks* (Harlow and Rawlings 2007), together with the maturation of new *standards* for accountable behavior, are signs of an evolving accountability landscape. Modifications in the norms that guide the behavior of institutional actors and a rearrangement of systems of accountability is part of a wider process of institution building both in organizational terms and in terms of establishing and upholding a normative framework.

The literature on accountability generally focuses on accountability as a dyadic relationship. Accountability is handled as a model of one actor accounting to one forum. In practice, accountability in the EU involves a complex cast of actors operating at the European, national and subnational levels, in which accounting takes place in a range of ways to a whole cast of accountability forums (Bovens et al. 2010). This chapter perceives, based on previous work on institutions (Thelen 2004; Mahoney and Thelen 2009; Olsen 2010, 2012), the accountability landscape as an integrated system in which various arenas cohere in important ways, characterized as they are by institutional complementarities.

Moreover, mapping the accountability landscape means that we need to move beyond the static single institutional analysis. It requires embedding institutions into their broader historical and evolutionary context to see how these institutions are adapting to the new international political and administrative context in which they operate. Institutional dynamics occur as forums, constrained by the weight of inherited practice, innovate in pursuit of their goals (Thelen 2012). New expectations become entrenched, and create coordination costs and provide incentives for further changes.

Understanding the dynamics of the evolving accountability landscape

Understanding the dynamics of the changing accountability landscape requires that the evolving and contested nature of the question 'Who is accountable to whom for what and how?' is taken as a point of departure rather than assuming its equilibrium. 'Accountability is part of structuring and restructuring process in less institutionalized contexts and in transformation periods when accountability relationships are shaped and reshaped as part of constituting and reconstituting a political community', writes Olsen (2015: 426). Evolving democratic political orders and institutional landscapes that are in a permanent transformation, such as the EU, are in a continuous search for, and struggle over, what are legitimate accountability regimes.

What institutional forms emerge and how they evolve in the institutional landscape is not only a matter of (re)structuring, but also of substance. Explaining why institutional change takes place and to understand the direction of change is rarely the result of a single dominant process, but rather a combination of sometimes interacting and coevolving processes taking place at different levels, at different speeds, and in different ways (Olsen 2010: 14). Political contestation about what institutions are most likely to secure accountability is one of the dynamics through which accountability regimes evolve. But also ambiguities and 'gaps' that exist by design or that emerge over time between formal institutions are drivers of change. Public sector reforms have been used to introduce new or improve old accountability arrangements and to repair these gaps. Yet, how the relative strengths of these forces of change and public sector reforms map onto the accountability landscape also depends on the existing institutions. The development of an accountability landscape is a continuous adaptive process. As the world around accountability forums changes, their successful operation depends on their active ongoing adaptation on the social, political context in which they are embedded (Héritier 2007; Olsen 2010, 2013).

The remainder of this chapter addresses the emergence of the EU accountability landscape. It first describes the expansion and diversification of accountability in the EU along six rudiments. An exploration of its emerging contours can expose the rudiments of accountability surrounding the new executive powers in the EU. Then, based on this stocktaking, the chapter reflects on the outcomes of this transformation of EU governance.

The emergence of the EU accountability landscape

The mapping of the evolving accountability landscape focuses on six separate rudiments. These are: (a) the emergence of new accountability obligations; (b) the rise of new forums and watchdog institutions; (c) the multiplication of accountability relationships; (d) the maturation of new standards for accountable behavior; (e) the rise of accountability practices; and (f) the emergence of accountability networks.

Accumulation of accountability obligations

A key development underlying the accountability landscape is the accumulation of formal (and informal) responsibilities and obligations of the (new) EU executive bodies to provide information (and justification) on their actions. Not only treaties have become the spearhead for constituting and reforming the accountability obligations in EU governance. The rise of ethical frameworks, whistle-blower acts, transparency initiatives, auditing requirements and performance contracts have all contributed to form the basis of the EU accountability landscape. Together, they have added new rules and procedures on top or instead of the old ones; in many cases, it concerns a sharpening of the provisions about 'who is responsible for what', and expanded stipulations to inform and report to (new) political and administrative forums. A long series of revisions of the Treaties have changed the framework of accountability in which the core EU institutions operate (Curtin 2009; Bovens *et al.* 2010; Wille 2013). These core executive bodies, like the European

Commission and the European Council, have become, in their accountability obligations, more distinctly linked to the democratic arenas. But also the large number of European agencies, established since the mid-1990s (Busuioc 2010; Koop 2011), has been tied to new (often contested) reporting requirements and obligations to other supervisory and accountability forums.

Emerging forums and powers of oversight

What bodies are there for holding the EU executive to account? Owing to the growing complexity of the expanding EU political-administrative system, we witness the expansion and proliferation of formal accountability forums and mechanisms.

One of the pillars in the EU accountability landscape, present from the very start, is embodied by the European Court of Justice (ECJ), materializing *legal accountability*, which is the most unambiguous type of accountability. The ECJ has a responsibility for ensuring that the rules laid down under the Union Treaties are observed, together with the national courts of the member states. The ECJ is not only guaranteeing the respect of Community law, but also ensuring the mutual limitation of the powers of its actors – European institutions, national governments and individuals.

Another pillar in the EU landscape is *political accountability*, which has evolved by the institutional design and development of parliaments both at the European and member state level. Launched in 1952, the Common Assembly of the European Coal and Steel Community, as the EP was then known, amounted to little more, in the words of the English political scientists Scully, Hix and Farrell, than 'a multi-lingual talking shop' (Scully et al. 2012: 671). Having first acquired limited budgetary powers in 1970, the European Parliament has since continued to expand its remit and responsibilities. The Maastricht Treaty (1992) marked the beginning of Parliament's metamorphosis into the role of co-legislator. At the same time, the Parliament also progressively acquired oversight powers over the Commission, establishing and reinforcing political accountability at the supranational level of the EU (Hix and Hoyland 2013; Wille 2013).

Until the late 1980s, it was sufficient to increase the EP's powers to make up the democratic deficit in the EU (Dehousse 1998). But the need for *political accountability* forums at the national level has led to a trend from national parliaments to reinforce their own powers vis-à-vis their own national executives for the performance of the role of representing their national interests at the EU level (Bovens et al. 2010: 194). Strengthening parliamentary scrutiny and participation rights at the domestic level is thus seen as a measure to address the perceived 'democratic deficit' in EU decision-making – the reason for affording the strengthening of their oversight role a prominent place in the Lisbon Treaty.

The importance of improved *financial accountability* faced the EU with a change in the financing of the EU budget as a result of the 1970 and 1975 budget treaties. This created political pressure for the establishment of a stronger external auditing capacity in the EU. The European Court of Auditors (ECA) was established in 1977, but assumed the status of a full institution of the Union in 1993 (Laffan 2003: 764–5). As the EU's external auditor, also called the 'guardians of the EU's finances', it is to carry out the audit of the EU finances and to contribute to improving EU financial management and report on the use of public funds.

In addition, the EU's Anti-Fraud Office (OLAF) was set up on 1 June 1999, and its aim is the fight against fraud, corruption and other irregularities identified in the Community budget (Pujas 2003; Cini 2007: 165). Fraud and irregularities, which became visible in the reports of the newly installed ECA, was then presented as a problem that ought logically to be addressed by the European Community's (EC) own anticorruption agency, and no longer by member states alone.

External *administrative accountability* was further developed by the establishment of the European Ombudsman by the Maastricht Treaty. The first European Ombudsman was appointed by the European Parliament in 1995. Any EU citizen or entity may appeal to the Ombudsman to investigate an EU institution on the grounds of maladministration: administrative irregularities, unfairness, discrimination, abuse of power, failure to reply, refusal of information or unnecessary delay. The independence of, and easy accessibility to, the Ombudsman largely explains the success of this form of 'soft justice', as opposed to the length, cost and formalism of traditional legal action (Magnette 2003). The Ombudsman has no binding powers to compel compliance with his or her rulings, but the overall level of compliance is high.

In short, new forums were enacted that recognized the importance of the oversight function and the capacity for holding the executive to account. But who are they holding to account?

The proliferation of accountability relationships

The substantial growth in the number of executive actors – there are currently 12 executive bodies and 40 agencies operating at the EU level – that need to be held to account, combined with the evolving number of forums that watch over these executive institutions and bodies, provides for a proliferation of accountability relationships. A selection of these accountability relationships between the main accountability actors and the main forums is displayed in Table 20.1.

This collection of accountability relationships is represented in matrix form and it shows what types of accountability have become key in the EU landscape. The accountability relationships are not only qualified in terms of type, but also in terms of vigor – based on an assessment of Curtin (2009: 274). The table indicates that in the web of relationships, legal accountability is fairly crystallized out, and that in the field of political and administrative accountability new relationships are evolving or have the potential to develop further.

Though this chapter will not analyze further the details of these accountability relationships, it is clear that with the empowerment of the EP and national parliaments, and the establishment of the ECA and the European Ombudsman, political and administrative accountability have become more germane in the EU polity and that it is these relationships that have the potential to be built up.

Table 20.1 The accountability matrix: accountability forums in relation to executive actors

Executive actors	EU watchdogs: accountability types and forums				
	Legal	*Political*	*Political*	*Financial*	*Administrative*
	Court of justice	EP	National parliaments	Court of auditors	Ombudsman
European Commission	Strong	Strong	Weak	Medium	Medium
European Council	Medium	Weak	Weak Medium	None	None
Council of Ministers	Strong	Weak	Medium	Medium	Medium
Agencies	Medium	Medium	None	Medium	Medium
Comitology committees	Medium	Medium	None	None	Medium
ECB	Medium	Medium	None	Medium	Medium

Source: Curtin (2009: 274), adapted by author.

Evolving standards: the institutionalization of accountability doctrines

As an unsettled polity, the EU had no shared vision of how accountability was to be organized and legitimized (Olsen 2013). But holding to account means that there must exist a set of criteria for measuring accountable behavior. If there are no standards or expectations, there can be no accountability. The drive for accountability is, therefore, closely linked with the emergence of new standards of accountability, and making intangible normative meanings palpable.

The new watchdog institutions allowed for new practices and ideas to be introduced to EU governance. Once established, these new institutions worked to build on their mandate. It was part of the 'building of institutional identities and winning acceptance for the office' (Olsen 2013: 466). Using the mission statements of the pivotal accountability forums in the Union as an indicator of the main standards they are pursuing (displayed in Table 20.2), we see the crystallization of a normative accountability framework. By spelling out these principles as the main purpose of the institution, the accountability forum contributes to a 'constitutionalization' of this normative framework in the Union. By its reports and assessment of the EU practices in terms of these standards, forums not only helped holding the executive to account. They also acted to enhance the normative framework of accountability in the Union (Cini 2007).

The European Court of Justice (ECJ), for instance, has played, from the start, an indispensible role in the EU's accountability landscape, putting forward the rule of law (Curtin 2009). The Court of Auditors was part of a wider 'advocacy coalition' for improved financial management in the EU (Laffan 2003). The first Ombudsman, Jacob Söderman, has gained a reputation for promoting norms for openness in the EU (Magnette 2003; Erkkilä 2012: 65). The EP fleshed out norms of political accountability and responsibility of the Commission. All institutions acted as advocates for improved accountability in relation to the policies and finances of the Union. The growing salience of these watchdogs can be perceived as part of a wider attempt to expand and solidify the ethical framework of the democratic fabric of the European Union, which consists in subjecting 'all of the Union's institutions to standard sets of rules and procedures, or scrutiny by agents who are dedicated to a single task but responsible for applying it across the entire EU institutional system' (Peterson and Shackleton 2012: 401). Within a very limited time frame, the EU has developed its own legal, political and administrative order (Curtin and Egeberg 2008; Curtin 2009: 203).

Evolving accountability practices

In the accountability landscape, different forums can play a different role in the accountability process. Some of the institutions are specializing in the checking and investigation stage, and others focus on probing questions, debate and final deliberation (Curtin 2009: 270). Particularly, the ECJ and the EP have been able to develop certain 'strong arm tactics' to enable the actor in question to suffer some consequences as a result of having being held to account

Table 20.2 The EU accountability standards (based on mission statements of institutions)

European Court of Justice (ECJ)	European Parliament (EP) and national parliaments	European Court of Auditors (ECA)	European Ombudsman (EO)	European Anti-Fraud Office (OLAF)
Rule of law	Political scrutiny and responsibility	Sound financial management	Principles of good administration	Integrity

Table 20.3 The development of accountability practices in the EU (index)

		2006	2013	2006 = 100%
ECJ	New cases	537	622	116%
	Completed cases	546	719	132%
	Pending cases	731	787	108%
EP	Parliamentary questions	6,075	10,632	175%
ECA	Specific annual reports	23	51	222%
	Special reports	11	24	218%
	Opinions	8	14	175%
Ombudsman	Inquiries opened	267	350	131%
	Inquiries closed	250	461	184%
OLAF	Incoming information	822	1,294	157%
	Cases opened	148	253	171%

(Curtin 2009. 272). To assess the development of accountability practices in the EU, the 'output' of the different accountability forums is taken as a proxy indicator of changes in account-holding activity.

Table 20.3 displays the growth in EU accountability by registering the development in activity in the different institutional domains. The index in this table measures the changes in the output and performance of the different watchdogs. The index is calculated by comparing the performances (or output) of the institutions in the observation period (2013) in relation to those of the reference period (in which the index is given a value of 100 in 2006). Comparing index numbers indicates that the largest relative increase in accountability activity has taken place within the domains of political and administrative accountability (i.e. in parliamentary questioning, the number of ombudsman inquiries opened, and the amount of special reports from the ECA).

The ECJ may have a greater legal authority than the EP, but over the years the EP has also become a much more powerful actor and its oversight function has gained ground steadily during the past decade. One of the most popular and visible methods to ensure executive accountability, posing questions, increased in the 15 years. Several factors have increased a greater incidence of accountability practices. Among them are the growing number of MEPs, the increasing staff resources and the committee structure with 22 committees, but also indications of fraud and mismanagement, and the resignation of the Santer Commission, have had a profound effect on the emphasis that is placed on accountability.

Also, the European Court of Auditors (ECA) has worked to expand its own role. It has no judicial functions and does not impose sanctions on individual officials or institutions. Hence, the basis of its contribution rests on the outcome of its audits as expressed in reports. Accountability is promoted through publication and the dissemination of reports about the practices of financial management in the EU (Laffan 2003). The emergence of accountability practices in the EU has also evolved by the role of the European Ombudsman and OLAF. On the one hand, acting as a Court, the Ombudsman addresses individual complainants and defines and applies 'general principles' to solve the cases submitted to it (and in its interpretation building a doctrine of 'good administration'). On the other hand, acting as a parliamentary organ, and with the strong support of the EP, the Ombudsman uses his powers of inquiry and proposition to suggest wide-ranging reforms of European governance (and in doing so, promoting the principles of transparency, participation and explanation). OLAF, investigating cases of fraud, and assisting EU bodies and national authorities in their fight against fraud has an increasing caseload. Both institutions had a growing number of inquiries opened and closed in the past years. In 2013, OLAF not only opened a high number of investigations; it also issued the highest number of recommendations in the last five years.

An evolving multilevel accountability network

Although single forums are an important locus of accountability, in practice effective and efficient accountability is realized by the cooperation of different forums or watchdogs. When accountability is achieved because a group of autonomous forums work together to achieve it, we are dealing with an accountability network. Harlow and Rawlings (2007: 13) reserve the term 'for a network of agencies specialising in a specific method of accountability'. The search for enhanced accountability in the EU has contributed to the emergence of links and forms of social organization between different forums in the EU accountability landscape. These networks are emerging *horizontally* between the political and administrative forums at the supranational level, and *vertically* between forums cutting across the different levels of governance.

To start, *horizontally*, a dual, or pooled, political and administrative network of accountability emerged. To ensure political accountability, most modern democratic societies need accurate and complete publicly available information as a basis for their political debates and decision-making. Political scrutiny can only be undertaken by parliaments with some effective parallel systems for checking, monitoring and redress. The European Court of Auditors does extensive technical work tracking the use of EU monies across the member states and beyond – as befits an audit body. It leaves, however, the *political* dimension of accountability to the Parliament and the Council (Laffan 2003: 776). Its reports provide the raw material for the process of holding political actors accountable. The results of the Court's work are used by the Commission and the Parliament (and the Council as well as by member states) to monitor financial management of the EU budget. The Auditor's work provides an important basis for the annual discharge procedure whereby the Parliament, basing its decision on the recommendations from the Council, decides whether the Commission has met its responsibility for the execution of the previous year's budget. In addition, the European Ombudsman is helping to oversee and scrutinize executive power in the form of fire alarms (cf. McCubbins and Schwarz 1984). The growing cooperation of the ECA, the EO and the EP can be perceived as part of a wider attempt to enhance the democratic fabric of the Union (Laffan 2003: 775). Effective oversight relies increasingly on mutually supportive networks of accountability partners.

The development and strengthening of accountability arrangements at the supranational level (as OLAF and ECA), the empowerment of the EP and the Ombudsman, were indicative for a shift from the national to the supranational in the European accountability landscape. National accountability structures on their own were insufficient given the development of the EU budget. Adequate political and financial accountability required institutions at the EU level, and this justified the empowerment of the EP and the establishment of a Court of Auditors. However, with the gradual Europeanization of public policymaking, the need for *vertical* multilevel cooperation and coordination became present.

The development of vertical networks promoting accountability in all main areas – political, administrative, judicial – is discernible and displayed in Table 20.4. The primary purpose of these vertical networks is institutional cohesion and the effective functioning of accountability in a multilevel context.

Traditionally, the ECA saw its role in terms of horizontal control and accountability, but in the 1990s it began to highlight the national dimension of financial accountability. In the areas

Table 20.4 An evolving multilevel accountability network

Judicial network	The Court in **cooperation with the courts and tribunals of the member states** ensures a uniform application and interpretation of EU law.
Parliament network	**Conference of European Affairs Committees (COSAC)**: representatives from EP and national parliaments. **Inter-parliamentary EU Information Exchange (IPEX)** facilitating the information flow. **Parliamentary Week** connecting parliamentarians from the EU. The **European Court of Auditors** (ECA) cooperate with the **Supreme Audit Institutions** (SAIs) of the member states, in particular through participation in the **Contact Committee**, a forum for exchange of information on the audit of EU funds.
Ombudsmen network	The European Network of Ombudsmen: the **EO and the national and regional ombudsmen**, and similar bodies of the EU member states.
Anti-fraud network	The OLAF Anti-Fraud Communicators Network (OAFCN): the information and communication link for **the national investigative services**, with which OLAF cooperates in the member states.

of the budget where management is shared, member states cooperate with the Commission in setting up supervisory and control systems – internal control – to ensure that funds are spent properly and in accordance with the rules. Internal control thus has an EU as well as a national dimension. In addition to the work done by the Court, many national audit institutions audit European funds that are managed and spent by national administrations, giving shape to the emergence of a multilevel accountability network.

The vertical, multilevel character of the accountability networks is also observable in *parliamentary* oversight. The Treaty of Lisbon bestowed more powers on both the EP and national parliaments. From 2009, national parliaments and the EP work on a series of proposals for improving inter-parliamentary relations, dialogue and cooperation further. The main objectives of this cooperation between the EP and the national parliaments are: (a) to promote the exchange of information and best practices between the national parliaments of the European Parliament with a view to reinforcing parliamentary control, influence and scrutiny at all levels; and (b) to ensure effective exercise of parliamentary competences in the EU. An example of a joint parliamentary meeting is the 'European Parliamentary Week' (EPW), which brings together parliamentarians from all over the European Union to discuss economic, budgetary and social matters. Moreover, the European Parliament committees regularly invite members of the national parliaments to their meetings to discuss new Commission legislative proposals.

But also, in terms of holding the EU executive to account, we find new initiatives of cooperation. National parliaments want to have a stronger control and influence over EU decision-making. The EP wants to have a better oversight of the functioning of the national systems when it comes to the effective implementation of the EU budget (Cipriani 2010: 47–8) and introduced a multilevel internal control framework of the single audit.

A comparable multilevel accountability network emerged to ensure *legal* accountability. The ECJ is often portrayed as existing in 'splendid isolation' in Luxembourg, given its formal independence enshrined in the Treaties. But the Court is actually surrounded by specialized and often very circumscribed legal communities. The ECJ and lower national courts have developed a mostly cooperative relationship: national courts receive guidance on European

Community (EC) law from the Court, and the ECJ relies on national courts to refer cases and apply EC law (most EU law is applied by national courts). The European Court of Justice (ECJ) has played, from the start, an indispensable role in the EU's accountability landscape putting forward the rule of law (Kelemen and Schmidt 2012). This relationship has been symbiotic, with both the ECJ and lower national courts benefitting. The ECJ's relationship to national courts has been fundamental to its development as a supranational institution.

The accountability landscape in an era of political and administrative reform

It is clear that this accountability landscape is not created in a single 'big bang' nor does it follow a clear and single logic. Individual components were forged at different historical junctures, brought into being by different political actors and coalitions (cf. Thelen 2004: 285).

It clumps different genres or types of accountability together – political, administrative, financial and judicial. The development of these arrangements over the previous decades, occupied with the political task of solving the accountability deficit in the EU, was part of a dynamic, fragmented and often ad hoc reform process, full of inconsistencies and tensions of continuous transformation. Accountability is construed in interaction between actors with different perspectives within a certain institutional playing field, and at the same time these interactions change the nature of the playing field. Each EU enlargement has given the new member states the opportunity to bring in 'their' conception of accountability and to try to integrate some of the founding principles of their national constitutional cultures in the Treaties:

> It is no surprise that strengthened control by Parliament ranked high on the European agenda after the United Kingdom and Denmark joined the EU. Likewise, the establishment of the principle of transparency and of extra-judicial control mechanisms coincided with the membership of Sweden and Finland.
>
> *(Costa et al. 2003: 668)*

Two different broader dynamics of change can be distinguished, profoundly shaping the 'trajectory' of accountability in the EU and forming the contours in this evolving landscape. First, the 'parliamentarization' of the EU, through the empowerment of the EP and the tentative commitments of national parliaments, developed since the Single European Act with the Treaties of Maastricht, Amsterdam, Nice and Lisbon, has resulted in the emergence of mechanisms with the aim to ensure democratic accountability in the EU, both from a supranational and inter-governmental perspective. With the Lisbon Treaty 2007, the debate surrounding the role of national parliaments remains one of securing improved accountability within the ordinary legislative process. After Lisbon, accountability can be pursued either through parliamentary scrutiny of the minister or through the subsidiarity monitoring. This development is part of a broader trajectory in the direction of more democratization and politicization (cf. Olsen 2010; Wille 2013).

A second and related development driving the contours of the accountability landscape is the concern with rationalization and functionality (cf. Olsen 2010: 92). 'The multiplication of accountability mechanisms in the EU is part and parcel of a general trend towards greater control of public authorities and more accountability from decision-making authorities in the Western world over the past 30 years' (Costa *et al.* 2003). New institutions have been established with the task of overseeing and checking governments, and of preventing and sanctioning instances of maladministration, fraud and corruption (Rosanvallon 2008). The growth and the complexity of the EU administration, increased budget resources and the multilevel character of the EU governance systems made the establishment of an effective accountability landscape progressively critical. The diffusion of professional ideas about good governance, enhanced administrative performance and institutional transparency (Erkkilä 2012) elicited the emergence of auditors, ombudsmen and audit bodies. These non-majoritarian 'guardian' type institutions play a major role in democratic governance in all political systems. The key to their legitimacy lies in their independence. These regulatory control mechanisms progressively gained their new position and tasks as they were regarded as being needed by the EU institutional structure. The need for reliable information and procedures increases as parliaments progressed from rubber-stamping to informed institutions (cf. Pelizzo and Stapenhurst 2013: 66). In calling for these new watchdogs to control and assess the EU executive, the EP itself has shown the importance in the EU of these new non-parliamentary control procedures as complementary to the classical parliamentary oversight tools.

Looking back at seven decades of institutional dynamics, political in tandem with administrative reforms have been crucial for instituting the principles of the EU accountability landscape. The cumulative result of these political and administrative reforms is an extensive accountability landscape that covers the behaviors, decisions and actions of both politicians and civil servants operational in the EU.

Moving to an ever-denser accountability landscape

New challenges

The development of a denser accountability landscape generates a number of new challenges to supporting an effective accountability system. To conclude this chapter, I will briefly mention a few of them. First, there is the problem of many hands, many levels and many eyes. Accountability in the EU is not confined to neat single-level interactions. In multilevel governance, as in every complex organization, this relationship includes many executive agents with 'many hands' that have to be coordinated and many principals with 'many eyes' to hold this executive accountable (Bovens 2007). A growth of accountability forums and a multiplication of accountability mechanisms have resulted in cascading levels of accountability, and this sometimes makes the question 'To whom is account to be rendered?' a complicated one. EU institutions are thus accountable in a range of ways to a whole cast of accountability forums. The coexistence of multiple accountability logics may be a safeguard measure, but can easily lead to diffuse systems of accountability in which the separation of powers is not as clearly established as in national constitutional traditions. A lack of coordination and an increased compartmentalization of different forums and modes of accountability implies that the efficiency effects of the multiplication of accountability mechanisms in the landscape can remain indecisive.

A second challenge is the question: Who watches the watchmen? Watchdogs exercise power, and with power comes responsibility. The multiplication of oversight powers therefore leads to a new problem: the growth of a controlling class, which makes the question 'Who watches the watchdogs?' progressively important. Political watchdogs are electoral accountable to citizens, but this is different for the non-majoritarian watchdogs. The question 'To whom are they answerable?' accordingly becomes more significant, depending on the power and autonomy of the watchdogs in question. When they are wrong, what are the means to hold them accountable?

A final challenge concerns the democratic anchorage in the accountability landscape. This largest challenge is perhaps to shape democratic accountability arrangements by means of democratic legitimacy. The growth of accountability forums does not automatically mean more democracy. Administrations may operate in remoteness from political and democratic institutions, and this remoteness from parliaments and voters can be the object of deliberate institutional design (as in the case of agencies) in order to make institutions less sensible and less responsive to short-term political concerns. However, the growth and uncoupling of the accountability of official representative bodies increase the number of actors in the accountability landscape who are involved in the policy process without being democratically authorized ex ante and without being subject to democratic control ex post (Papadopoulos 2007: 476). Depoliticization tendencies limit the possibilities of voters to respond with electoral sanctions. The danger is that the politics of the EU remain the secretive politics of international relations and unable to convert into the relatively open and transparent politics of representative democracy (Curtin 2009; Papadopoulos 2010). In an age where EU governance becomes increasingly salient, but also more contested, it is important that executive power is surrounded by democratic mechanisms through which the governed can give their consent and policymakers can be held accountable.

Conclusion

The European Community was, from the start, set up as a hybrid institutional system based on the intertwining of sometimes-competing logics and objectives. The EU, in the words of Olsen (2010: 81), is 'a conceptual battleground and an institutional building site'. The continuous expansion and fragmentation of the executive sphere in the EU in the past decades, whereby core institutions tend to delegate an increasing proportion of their tasks to bodies that are either under their direct control or granted some form of independence in the decision-making process, have made the governance structure more varied and dense (Flinders 2004; Curtin 2009).

The development of new watchdogs and their strengthened scrutiny in the past decades points to an increased relevance of accountability and control over the EU executive. So far, the EU's complex multilevel network governance structures cutting across decisional levels has a mélange or mixture of overlapping or competing or complementary powers and responsibilities and a diversified set of accountability relationships that lead to a mixture of accountability mechanisms operating at European, national and subnational levels (cf. Bovens *et al.* 2010; Papadopoulos 2010). This mixed order of multiple horizontal and vertical accountability regimes, arrangements and practices at distinct levels in the EU demonstrates an ever-denser institutional landscape.

References

Bovens, M. (2007) Analysing and assessing accountability: a conceptual framework. *European Law Journal*, 13(4): 447–68.

Bovens, M., Curtin, D. and 't Hart, P. (eds) (2010) *The Real World of EU Accountability: What Deficit?* Oxford: Oxford University Press.

Busuioc, E. M. (2010) *The Accountability of European Agencies: Legal Provisions and Ongoing Practices*. Delft: Uitgeverij Eburon.

Cini, M. (2007) *From Integration to Integrity: Administrative Ethics and Reform in the European Commission*. Manchester: Manchester University Press.

Cipriani, G. (2010) *The EU Budget: Responsibility Without Accountability?* Brussels: CEPS Paperbacks.

Costa, O., Jabko, N., Lequesne, C. and Magnette, P. (2003) Introduction: diffuse control mechanisms in the European Union – towards a new democracy? *Journal of European Public Policy*, 10(5): 666–76.

Curtin, D. (2009) *Executive Power of the European Union: Laws, Practices and the Living Constitution*. Oxford: Oxford University Press.

Curtin, D. and Egeberg, M. (2008) Tradition and innovation: Europe's accumulated executive order. *West European Politics*, 31(4): 639–61.

Dehousse, R. (1998) European institutional architecture after Amsterdam: parliamentary system or regulatory structure? *Common Market Law Review*, 35(3): 595–627.

Erkkilä, T. (2012) *Government Transparency: Impacts and Unintended Consequences*. Basingstoke: Palgrave Macmillan.

Flinders, M. (2004) Distributed public governance in the European Union. *Journal of European Public Policy*, 11(3): 520–44.

Harlow, C. and Rawlings, R. (2007) Promoting accountability in multilevel governance: a network approach. *European Law Journal*, 13(4): 542–62.

Héritier, A. (2007) *Explaining Institutional Change in Europe*. Oxford: Oxford University Press.

Hix, S. and Høyland, B. (2013) Empowerment of the European Parliament. *Annual Review of Political Science*, 16: 171–89.

Kelemen, R. D. and Schmidt, S. K. (2012) Introduction: the European Court of Justice and legal integration – perpetual momentum? *Journal of European Public Policy*, 19(1): 1–7.

Koop, C. (2011) Explaining the accountability of independent agencies: the importance of political salience. *Journal of Public Policy*, 31(2): 209–34.

Laffan, B. (2003) Auditing and accountability in the European Union. *Journal of European Public Policy*, 10(5): 762–77.

Magnette, P. (2003) Between parliamentary control and the rule of law: the political role of the Ombudsman in the European Union. *Journal of European Public Policy*, 10(5): 677–94.

Mahoney, J. & Thelen, K. (eds) (2009) *Explaining Institutional Change: Ambiguity, Agency, and Power*. Cambridge: Cambridge University Press.

McCubbins, M. D. and Schwartz, T. (1984) Congressional oversight overlooked: police patrols versus fire alarms. *American Journal of Political Science*, 28(1): 165–79.

Olsen, J. P. (2010) *Governing Through Institution Building: Institutional Theory and Recent European Experiments in Democratic Organization*. Oxford: Oxford University Press.

Olsen, J. P. (2013) The institutional basis of democratic accountability. *West European Politics*, 36(3): 447–73.

Olsen, J. P. (2015) Democratic order, autonomy, and accountability. *Governance*, 28(4): 425–40.

Papadopoulos, Y. (2007) Problems of democratic accountability in network and multilevel governance. *European Law Journal*, 13(4): 469–86.

Papadopoulos, Y. (2010) Accountability and multilevel governance: more accountability, less democracy? *West European Politics*, 33(5): 1030–49.

Pelizzo, R. and Stapenhurst, F. (2013) *Government Accountability and Legislative Oversight*. New York: Routledge.

Peterson, J. and Shackleton, M. (2012) *The Institutions of the European Union*. Oxford: Oxford University Press.

Pujas, V. (2003) The European Anti-Fraud Office (OLAF): a European policy to fight against economic and financial fraud? *Journal of European Public Policy*, 10(5): 778–97.

Rosanvallon, P. (2008) *Counter-Democracy: Politics in an Age of Distrust*. Cambridge: Cambridge University Press.

Scully, R., Hix, S. and Farrell, D. M. (2012) National or European parliamentarians? Evidence from a new survey of the members of the European Parliament. *JCMS: Journal of Common Market Studies*, 50(4): 670–83.

Thelen, K. (2004) *How Institutions Evolve: The Political Economy of Skills in Germany, Britain, the United States and Japan*. Cambridge: Cambridge University Press.

Thelen, K. (2012) Varieties of capitalism: trajectories of liberalization and the new politics of social solidarity. *Annual Review of Political Science*, 15: 137–59.

Wille, A. (2013) *The Normalization of the European Commission: Politics and Bureaucracy in the EU Executive*. Oxford: Oxford University Press.

INDEX

accountability 1, 3, 255–6
   actual 66–8, 259–60
   ad hoc forums 182
accountable management 240–1
   accountability 241
   administrative barriers 250–2
   audit 241
   delegation 241
   justice sector 245–9
   next steps program
   objective-setting 241
   political barriers 250
   UK 243–5
administrative 3, 62
   agency theory 46–7
   austerity 208, 211–13
   blame 231–4
   civil society 108
   cognitive legitimacy 135
   constitution perspective on 6, 210
   content of 3, 17
   contract 108
   criteria for assessing 209–10
   deficit 209, 262
   democratic 258
   democratic-optimistic interpretation of 22
   democratic order 15–17
   democratic perspective on 6, 24–6, 210
   dependent variable 31–2
   diagonal 1
   dilemma 7, 181–2
   dimensions 105
   direction 110–11
   doctrines 286
   dynamics 75–8
   external 259–60
   formal 66–8

formal impossibility of hierarchical 5
governance reform 267
horizontal 1
hybrid welfare administrative systems 61–2
impactful 260–1
independent variable 32
institution-centred approach to 15, 21–3, 25
institutional routines 20–1
internal security crises 182
learning perspective on 6, 210
legal 3, 62
legitimacy 34–8, 134–5
managerial 3–4, 62
market 4, 108–9
mechanism 2–3
moral legitimacy 134
multilevel network 288–90
multiple 255
normative basis 109–10
overload 5, 15, 209
paradox 7, 255, 259–63
performance 7, 32–4, 146, 150–1, 156–7
performance management 120–1
political 3
political transformation 23–4
practices 286–8
pragmatic legitimacy 134
professional 3, 63
regimes 15
reform 239
regulatory state 224–6
restructuring process 21–3
settled situations 5
social 3
social services 90
societal 94–5
societal security 167–8

Index

task perspective on 6
transparency 167–8
trust-based 107
unsettled situations 5, 194, 196–9
vertical 1
virtue 2–3
welfare state reforms 1, 45
administrative reforms 194
agencification 242–3
agency theory 4–5, 18, 25, 46–7, 52
   motivation 47–8
   welfare 51–3
Askim, J. 73
austerity 208
   constitutional perspective 214–16
   democratic perspective 213–14, 216
   learning perspective 215, 217–18

Behn, R. 205
blame games 189–90
Bovens, M. 9–10, 27–8, 73, 116, 131, 159, 205, 221
Busuioc, E.M. 178, 292
Byrkjeflot, H. 57, 117
choice 123–4, 126, 130
choice overload 94
Christensen, T. 9–10, 43, 57, 73, 89, 144, 192, 205
collaborative governance 90, 94, 100
coping strategy 91, 101
coproduction 94–5, 98
cultural-institutional perspective 63–4, 69–70, 79, 86–8, 143, 149–50
   accountability change 79

digital era reform 267, 269–70
   Denmark 271–5
   public sector strategies 271–4
Dubnick, M. 10, 28, 74, 132, 205

Ejersbo, N. 278
Elston, T. 253
Emerson, K. 91, 94
EU accountability landscape 280–2
   accountability obligations 283–4
   dynamic institutional order 281
   evolving landscape 281–2
   oversight 284

Fimreite, A.L. 89, 192
Flinders, M. 28, 43, 206, 264–5
forum shift 262

Gailmard, S. 57
governance 49–50
   incentives 50
   monitoring 50
   preferences 49

   procedures 50
   relationship management 49
   selection 49
Gray, A. 253
Greve, C. 265, 278

Halachmi, A. 10, 221
Hansen, H.F. 221
healthcare 55, 105, 119
   accountability concepts 106–9
   Denmark 111–15, 126–7
   England 124–6
   dimensions of accountability 111–12
   Germany 127–9
   hospital performance management 119
   Norway 111–15
Hodge, G. 265
Hood, C. 28, 178–9

immigration 54–5, 133
   Denmark 138–40
   Germany 140–2
   Norway 136–8
   systems 133–4
incentive 127
inquiry committees 180
   Germany 186–9
   Norway 183–6
internal security crises 180

Jann, W. 43, 160
Jantz, B. 10, 73, 89
Jenkins, B. 253

Koppell, J. 29

Lægreid, P. 9–10, 29, 43, 89, 117, 144, 160, 192, 205–6
Larsen, F. 73
layering 1
learning 119, 126–7, 129–30
legitimacy 35–6, 119, 121–2, 128–30
   cognitive 39–40
   input 35–6
   normative 39–40
   output 35–6
   performance 38–40
   pragmatic 39–40
liberal-constitutional democracy 18
Lodge, M. 178–9, 235

March, J.G. 10, 29, 73, 206
Mulgan, R. 10, 73, 206

neo-Weberian state 269–70
new leisure class 98
New Public Management 1, 23

Olsen, J.P. 10–11, 29, 44, 57, 73, 206, 293
open structure 18

performance management 119–24
   learning model 122, 130
   steering and control perspective 122, 130
   legitimacy perspective 123–4, 130
   personalized services 90, 93
performance paradox 7
Pollitt, C. 11, 44, 132, 160
post-New Public Management 1
public–private partnership 255, 257
public sector reforms 76–8
   accountability dynamics 76–8
public transport crisis 223, 231–3

railway reform 226–8
   regulatory regime in Germany 229–31
reform strategies 77–8
   compliance-based systems 77
   contrived randomness 78
   integrity-oriented approach 78
   managerial 77
reform trajectories 80–1
   Germany 82–3, 85–6
   Norway 80–1, 83–5
regulatory reform 223
   positive state 227
   regulatory state 227
Romzek, B. 11, 74, 117–18, 160–1
Rubecksen, K. 161

sanction 120–3, 129–31
Scharpf, F. 44
Schillemans, T. 11, 29, 58, 205, 207
school infrastructure 258–9
social innovation 90, 92–5
social microfinance 98
social services 90
   effects of choice 93
   personalized 93

societal security 165–6
   flood defense 168, 174–5
   food safety 168, 174–5
   intelligence 168, 172–3, 175
steering 121–3, 128–31
stewardship theory 46–7, 52
   motivation 47–8
   welfare 51–3
structural-instrumental perspective 63–4, 69–70, 78–9, 86–8, 143, 150
   accountability change 78–9
   forms of specialization and coordination 169

task-specific perspective 148–9
terrorist attack in Norway 200–1
Tonurist, P. 103–4
transparency 120–1, 167–8

unsettled situations 194
   characteristics 196–7
   crises 198–200
   reform 197–8

value for money 123–6
Van Dooren, W. 207, 266
Vrangbæk, K. 116–18, 132

Wegrich, K. 235
welfare administrative systems 64–6
   Denmark 64–6
   Norway 64–6
welfare reforms 146, 151–3
   Denmark 151–3
   Germany 151–3
   Norway 151–3, 200
welfare state transitions 91–2
'wicked' problems 2, 61, 133, 166, 177, 194–6, 199, 201, 203
Wille, A. 293
Willems, T. 207, 266